D1616902

Professional Psychology in Transition

Meeting Today's Challenges

Herbert Dörken

and Associates

Foreword by Senator Daniel K. Inouye

Professional Psychology in Transition

Jossey-Bass Publishers

San Francisco • London • 1986

PROFESSIONAL PSYCHOLOGY IN TRANSITION
Meeting Today's Challenges
by Herbert Dörken and Associates

Copyright © 1986 by: Jossey-Bass Inc., Publishers
433 California Street
San Francisco, California 94104

&

Jossey-Bass Limited
28 Banner Street
London EC1Y 8QE

Library of Congress Cataloging-in-Publication Data

Dörken, Herbert.
   Professional psychology in transition.

   (The Jossey-Bass social and behavioral science series)
   Includes bibliographies and index.
   1. Psychology—Practice—United States.   2. Insurance,
Mental health—United States.   3. Mental health services
—United States.   I. Title.   II. Series.
BF75.D67   1986   616.89′0232   85-45900
ISBN 0-87589-678-2 (alk. paper)

Manufactured in the United States of America

JACKET DESIGN BY WILLI BAUM

FIRST EDITION

Code 8609

The Jossey-Bass
Social and Behavioral Science Series

Foreword

For more than a decade, I have worked with my colleagues in the United States Congress and with the elected leadership of the American Psychological Association to ensure that our nation's psychologists are deemed autonomous providers under each of our federal health care programs. During these efforts I have become convinced that members of the psychological profession possess a tremendous wealth of clinical and scientific expertise that can be of significant benefit to society. For example, in my judgment, we are now entering the era of prevention, and it has been our nation's psychologists, our behavioral scientists, who have led the way. Similarly, from a public policy frame of reference, it is becoming increasingly evident that the behavioral aspects of health care must be considered paramount, especially in those programs that are developed for our nation's senior citizens, a group that will soon constitute more than 20 percent of our population.

Yet, during the past decade I have become all too aware that very few of our nation's politicians really appreciate the intensive training and clinical expertise of members of the psychological profession. Often, even the most basic information is simply not understood—for example, what is the scope of the various state psychology practice acts? And, are psychologists authorized to practice within the walls of a hospital? Further, it has been painfully evident that individual psychologists do not spend enough time with the elected officials who represent them to impress upon them, in a personal and firsthand fashion, the importance of their clinicians, scientists, and educators.

From my own background research, I have come to the conclusion that part of the reason for this political and public policy vacuum is the simple fact that even our nation's psychologists do not have ready access to accurate and definitive information about their profession's accomplishments. They do not possess the information necessary to establish a long-term and sustained legislative strategy.

In my judgment, this book by Dörken and Associates, a sequel to their earlier publication *The Professional Psychologist Today,* will go a long way toward fostering and encouraging this all-important public dialogue. The authors are well-known psychologists, and they have a long and distinguished track record in working to establish viable health care policies on both the local and national level. Their collective views should be of considerable interest, not only to today's practicing psychologists but also to generations of future practitioners who have been, and who will continue to be, influenced by their thinking. I might also note that much of what is compiled in this farsighted document is of direct consequence to all of our nation's health care providers who are not physicians—our psychiatric nurses, clinical social workers, optometrists, and podiatrists, to mention just a few.

The first part of *Professional Psychology in Transition* provides a dramatic description of the virtual explosion of psychological expertise—in terms of both the number of practitioners and the range of services offered—that has occurred throughout our nation during the past decade. For example, the number of licensed psychologists has more than doubled to approximately 45,000. Various chapters under this section highlight the extent to which both private and public sector insurance companies currently provide coverage for psychological services. Even a casual review of the material provided clearly indicates that today a significant proportion of our nation has direct access to a wide range of services provided by these practitioners. The data presented will undoubtedly be useful in challenging a number of popular misconceptions (or myths) about our nation's mental health practitioners and the roles that the various professional disciplines play.

I found it especially interesting to note that the Department of Defense ascertained through the CHAMPUS program that approximately 97 percent of the inpatient mental health services that psychiatrists have traditionally billed for also fall legally within the scope of practice authorized for psychologists.

Similarly, the chapters that address the coverage of psychological services by the various federal statutes suggest that although monumental progress has been made (for example, within the federal criminal code), considerably more must still be done. Having been compelled during the closing hours of the 1st Session of the 99th Congress (1985) to withdraw an amendment that would have provided greater access to psychological services under the Rural Health Clinic provisions of Medicare and Medicaid, I am painfully aware of the need to educate my colleagues on Capitol Hill if we are to ensure that the most modern and state-of-the-art mental health expertise is to be made readily available under Medicare and Medicaid.

Part Two provides the reader with intriguing glimpses into the evolving nature of professional psychology and raises a number of fundamental questions regarding the appropriate scope, or definition, of its eventual practice. During my efforts in the Congress on behalf of the profession, I have, on countless occasions, had to address the issue of whether psychologists could be considered to be "practicing medicine without a medical license." Why, for example, have the various training institutions not developed clearly identifiable *comprehensive* (which would include the provision of inpatient care) psychological services centers? Why is it that psychologists' own perceptions of themselves appear to be the primary factor limiting their scope of practice? I have no doubt that someday we will see the formal sanctioning of psychologists prescribing various psychotropic medications, but I fear that development is still far in the distant future. I say this even though there is a real and pressing need for this expertise today, especially in our nation's nursing homes. What roles should traditional educational institutions play in this ongoing development? A number of steps are being taken by the various state licensing boards to ensure that only high-quality, state-of-the-art, and demonstrably appropriate psychological expertise will be provided to beneficiaries. Yet, is this really enough? Is this the correct approach?

The authors raise a wide range of issues that should ultimately result in organized psychology collectively tightening up its thinking and being able to clearly define its societal mission. How else, for example, can society decide what roles the various types of psychologists should play within our present and future health delivery system? Who should (and who will) ultimately define psychology's destiny? What limitations, if any, should society impose? What are the gaps in psychology's knowledge base, or in its professional practice, and how can they be most effectively addressed? This section of the book provides considerable food for thought for those directly involved in the profession's educational endeavors. It directly questions what their underlying goals and basic assumptions should be.

I have no doubt that faculty and students reviewing this section will find much to ponder; unfortunately, there are no easy solutions. From my own vantage point, the increasing importance of true interdisciplinary collaboration becomes ever clearer. In fact, psychology may very well find that to maximize its own contributions, it must rely on others; especially if it wishes to obtain direct access to facilities such as nursing homes and those patients who are suffering from terminal illnesses.

The final part of the book describes in considerable detail various strategies (including legislative) that professional psychologists may decide to pursue to ensure a viable market for their services. Again, it is quite important for the reader to realize that psychology is a growing and dynamic profession. I have no doubt that even today many health professionals (including undoubtedly some psychologists) still consider psychological services a synonym for verbal psychotherapy, and long-term psychotherapy at that. Yet, in my judgment, the future for our nation's psychologists lies instead with their growing generic *health care* expertise. This would, of course, include providing psychotherapy where appropriate, but it is not limited to this particular clinical modality.

A number of the authors stress the significance of the ever-escalating cost of health care and how political responses to this phenomenon are leading to very aggressive efforts to install objective measures of accountability. In their judgment, and in mine, in the long run health care cost containment may have a greater impact on our nation's health delivery system, including our very definition of quality care, than any of us can predict at this point in time. Not only are dramatic changes occurring in the organizational nature of the system, including, for example, providing greater support for health maintenance organizations (HMOs) and other prepaid approaches, but the traditional relationships between hospitals and individual private practitioners are also being seriously reevaluated. It would not be unreasonable to predict that the health delivery system of tomorrow will be drastically different from the one we know today. These are the challenges presented to readers of this book. And I fully expect that the documentation presented in this outstanding publication will be of considerable assistance to those psychologists who become willing to personally enter into the political and public policy process in order to help shape the destiny of their own profession.

Washington, D.C.   Daniel K. Inouye
March 1986   *United States Senator*

Preface

Professional psychology is changing, must change: the marketplace has changed, health care is becoming industrialized, and competition is on the doorstep. Market considerations are coming to the fore. Is there a public demand for psychological services? Do professional psychologists have a product to deliver? Do they have specific treatments for specific disorders? Are these treatments effective? Are they cost-effective, considering the alternatives? How widely can clinical psychologists distribute or deliver their services? Will they contract on scale? At volume discounted rates? Will the quality and effectiveness be sustained? For the dramatically growing numbers of clinical psychologists, these are the tough questions ahead, ones that cannot all be answered on an individual basis. Nor are they only being posed by psychologists. Such questions will increasingly be directed by clients, employers, third parties, corporations, and legislators, not only to clinical psychologists, but to all mental health and other health professionals.

These fundamental outcome-related questions, with their underlying public expectancy that rehabilitation can be accomplished on a cost-effective basis, are coming to the fore. Implicit in such mounting public expectancy is the assumption that competition, inter- and intraprofessional, will intensify. Such expectations have major implications for two of the cornerstones of practice: how clinical psychologists are trained and what new knowledge gained from psychological research can be applied to improve or expand practice. These are not distant horizons. They are performance demands and issues facing clinical psychology today—issues of concern not only to practitioners but to those in training as well.

Professional Psychology in Transition documents professional psychology's dramatic growth, its progressive recognition under federal law, growing third-party reimbursement, and the diversity of patients treated. New perspectives on practice are presented in terms of both professional preparation and professional orientation. The issue of ensuring competency by legislating standards is also explored, and recent research into general health care that suggests new opportunities for practice and for further research is evaluated. The future of professional psychology lies in competitive strategies that hold not simply the potential for survival or the promise of new opportunity but the assurance of success. Economically viable models of actual practice organizations and the opening of new practice markets through legislation are both systematically described. Cost is seen as a major force behind changes now underway, changes perhaps not yet apparent to many practitioners or those responsible for the preparation of future practitioners, but changes that are revolutionizing health care nevertheless. The impact of these changes on clinical psychology is discussed as are new directions for practice, with their inherent hazards and opportunities.

The contributing authors are all well known through their publications or presentations at professional meetings, and all have made major contributions to the advancement of psychology as a health profession. With one exception, all have held positions in the governance of the American Psychological Association or have been senior officers of the association. Through their involvement at the cutting edge of progress, the authors convey how clinical psychology must change to sustain and advance its involvement in health care delivery. All chapters were written expressly for this volume and draw on each author's major expertise.

Professional Psychology in Transition builds on *The Professional Psychologist Today* of a decade ago (Dörken and Associates, 1976), which gave an account of the founding of the practitioner profession of clinical psychology. Much of what was written in the 1976 volume is pertinent today, yet the new themes of 1986 are both more complex and more dramatic. This book and its predecessor complement each other. Taken together, they demonstrate that professional psychology has come of age.

The 1976 projections of professional psychology's human resources have now been substantially surpassed, as shown in a tally of psychologists licensed for independent practice as of mid-1985. Rather than describe professional standards, as the earlier book did, this work focuses on issues of training and orientation: the general validity of the practitioner-scholar model, psychology's growing contribution to aspects of general health care, the increasing connection between psychological care and medical care, competency assurance, enforcement, and the behavioral specifics of unacceptable practice. The 1976 book offered an encyclopedic account of how clinical psychology gained its program and statutory recognition. We now report further positive gains at the federal level and illustrate how markets have been dramatically changed by a decade of systematic advocacy at the state level. These expanding markets in particular illustrate the long-range effectiveness of implementing a systematic "how-to" strategy. An understanding of the forms of health insurance, which the 1976 volume provided, helped set the stage for growth in third-party reimbursement reported by psychologists and empirically illustrated by carrier with interstate comparisons in this new book. The changing patterns in utilization of the mental health professions carries significance for today and the future. While the chapters on peer review and professional autonomy of 1976 are not repeated, the theme of an independent health profession runs throughout the 1986 text. The issues facing professional psychology a decade ago have been partly resolved, and partly expanded, only to be joined by others. We now provide detail on some 20,000 patients of clinical psychologists and appreciate more fully the psychological aspects of general health care, the source of referrals, the extent to which these patients are under concurrent medical care, and some distinctions between patients seen in fee-for-service and salaried practice.

What has happened—the growth of the profession; what is happening—new perspectives on practice; and what can happen—strategies for competition—these themes form the three parts of this book. (The thirteen individual chapters are briefly described in the introductions to their respective parts.)

The dramatic increase in the number of licensed psychologists is fundamental evidence of professional growth. Part One also provides for the first time large sample data on the diversity of patients seen by clinicians. It also documents the growth in third-party reimbursement to psychologists, their proportionately growing share of outpatient mental health services and, with each session of Congress, their increasing recognition under federal law.

Part Two seeks to provide an optimal perspective for practice. Training must be brought into closer synchrony with the realities of practice, and the emphasis in orientation should favor a role as practitioner rather than as technician. Though public protection is the central purpose of licensing, the day-to-day realities of this principle are seen in the behavioral specifics of unacceptable practice. This part concludes with a literature review of the breadth of horizons and of professional opportunity in general health care as distinct from mental health services.

Part Three addresses several strategies that will enable professional psychology to remain competitive. Though the most obvious is enhanced recognition under state law, psychology's legislative program in all but a few states is fledgling at best. With cost driving systemic health care reform, the time for alternatives to an independent, office-based practice has come. Several operational alternatives are described, rounding out the theme of this book: how to grow, enhance practice, compete, and succeed.

Professional Psychology in Transition has been written with practicing psychologists most in mind, but it should also be useful to all psychologists concerned with the future of our profession. Psychology students in graduate schools and training programs should also benefit from discussions of the forces that will influence their careers and their profession. In addition, the information contained in this volume should help other health professionals, legislators, policy makers, and planners—anyone who has the responsibility of regulating and improving the delivery of vital health services to the public in the most effective and efficient ways—to recognize the contributions professional psychology can make.

Davis, California   Herbert Dörken
March 1986

Contents

The Authors

Herbert Dörken has been involved in an ongoing mix of applied research, resource development, public administration, advocacy, and legislative consultation for some thirty-five years. He received his M.Sc. degree (1947) from McGill University in psychology and his Ph.D. degree (1951) from the University of Montreal in clinical psychology.

After leaving Canada's Department of National Health and Welfare as consultant psychologist, he developed and later directed Minnesota's statewide network of community mental health centers from 1959 until 1962. He was then in succession deputy director, chief of psychology, and chief of research for the California Department of Mental Hygiene from 1962 to 1973. He then transferred to the University of California at San Francisco, where he was adjunct professor and research psychologist until his retirement in 1982. Now scientific director of the Biodyne Institute and co-principal investigator (with Cummings) of a five-year psychological offset study of the Medicaid population of Oahu, he was a registered lobbyist for the California State Psychological Association from 1982 to 1984, has been a health plan advocate since 1983 for the California Psychological Health Plan and a consultant and advocate for Treatment Centers of America since 1984, and became a legislative consultant for the Hawaii Psychological Association in 1984.

In 1979, Dörken received the first Distinguished Professional Contributions Award for Applied Psychology as a Professional

Practice from the American Psychological Association following similar awards from the California (1973) and Illinois (1977) Psychological Associations. He is author of twenty-five draft bills enacted into law and some 100 journal articles. While chair of the American Psychological Association Committee on Health Insurance, he authored, together with associates, *The Professional Psychologist Today: New Developments in Law, Health Insurance, and Health Practice* published in 1976.

Bruce E. Bennett is a clinical psychologist with a private practice in Northbrook, Illinois. He received his B.S. degree (1966) from Ohio State University and his M.S. degree (1968) and Ph.D. degree in clinical psychology (1971) from the Illinois Institute of Technology. Bennett is a past president of the Illinois Psychological Association and currently serves as executive officer and health service consultant to the association. He has served on the American Psychological Association's Committee on Health Insurance, Committee on Professional Practice (chair, 1981), Board of Professional Affairs (chair, 1984), Policy and Planning Board, and the Council of Representatives. In addition, Bennett is the chair of the Association for the Advancement of Psychology and has served as the head of its Special Projects Committee. Bennett currently chairs the Board of Professional Affairs Task Force on Marketing and Promotion of Psychological Services, which deals with all aspects of current and future markets for clinical psychologists.

Lewis G. Carpenter, Jr., president of Carpenter Ranches, received his M.A. degree (1943) in psychology from Stanford University and his Ph.D. degree (1950) in clinical psychology from the University of California at Berkeley. He has worked for many years in psychiatric hospitals, primarily with psychotic adults and, since 1967, has represented the California State Psychological Association as legislative advocate at the state capital in Sacramento.

Nicholas A. Cummings is president and clinical director of the American Biodyne Centers, Inc., and the Biodyne Institute. He is also president of the National Academies of Practice, is a former president of the American Psychological Association, and was chief psychologist for Kaiser-Permanente in San Francisco for twenty-five years. He established all four campuses of the California School of Professional Psychology. Cummings received his A.B. degree (1948) from the University of California at Berkeley in psychology, his M.A. degree (1954) from Claremont Graduate School in psychology, and his Ph.D. degree (1958) from Adelphi University in clinical psychology.

Patrick H. DeLeon is executive assistant to U.S. Senator Daniel K. Inouye. He received his B.A. degree (1964) from Amherst College, his M.S. and Ph.D. degrees (1966 and 1969) in clinical psychology from Purdue University, his M.P.H. degree (1973) from the University of Hawaii, and his J.D. degree (1980) from Catholic University. His prime interests have been public service and the interface between psychology and the law. In 1984 he received an award from the American Psychological Association for Distinguished Early Career Contributions to Psychology in the Public Interest, and in 1985 he was awarded the Harold M. Hildreth Award from Division 18 (Public Service). He is the recipient of the Division 38 (Health Psychology) 1980 Award to a Younger Member for Contributions to Health Psychology and the 1984 Association for the Advancement of Psychology National Achievement Award to a distinguished psychologist. He has served on the American Psychological Association Council of Representatives, is past chair of the Board of Professional Affairs, and past president of Division 41 (Psychology and the Law). He is a diplomat in clinical and forensic psychology, a charter member of the National Academies of Practice, and associate editor of the *American Psychologist.*

Ronald E. Fox is professor and founding dean of the School of Professional Psychology at Wright State University. In addition, he is president of University Psychological Services Association, a faculty-owned, professional corporation. He holds the A.B. degree (1954) in English, the M.A. degree (1961) in psychology, and the Ph.D. degree (1962) in clinical psychology, all from the University of North Carolina at Chapel Hill. Fox, a member of the board of directors of the American Psychological Association since 1982, became its recording secretary in 1986. His current interests center on patterns of practice for training professional psychologists.

Alan G. Kraut is deputy executive officer for national policy studies at the American Psychological Association, where he has also served as administrative officer for special programs in scientific psychology, administrative officer for scientific affairs, and director of national policy studies. He received his B.S. degree (1973) from the University of Connecticut and his M.A. degree (1975) and Ph.D. degree (1977) in psychology from Syracuse University. From 1977 to 1980, he was assistant professor of psychology at Virginia Polytechnic Institute and State University. In his current position, Kraut bears responsibility for directing government relations and lobbying activities for the American Psychological Association.

David A. Rodgers is staff member and head of the section of psychology at the Cleveland Clinic Foundation in Cleveland, Ohio. He is currently a member of the American Psychological Association's task force on the structure of the association and formerly served on the blue ribbon commission to review the structure of the association. In addition, he has been a member of the association's Policy and Planning Board and Council of Representatives, and he has served on other psychology boards and committees in which he has been concerned with the structure and definition of psychology. He received his B.S. degree (1948) from the University of Oklahoma in chemical engineering and his Ph.D. degree (1953) from the University of Chicago in psychology.

Joy Stapp served as the administrative officer for human resources research with the American Psychological Association from 1978 to 1985. In this role, she was responsible for establishing the human resources research office, which is in charge of designing, conducting, and analyzing surveys of psychology's national labor force and training system. She has authored numerous articles on psychology's human resources and has been an invited participant and discussant at workshops, symposia, and conventions. She has also served as the American Psychological

Association's elected representative to the Scientific Manpower Commission since 1981, where she has just completed a two-year term as its president (1984-1985).

Stapp received her B.A. degree (1970) in mathematics and psychology from the University of Texas at Austin, her M.A. degree (1971) in psychology from the University of California at Santa Barbara, and her Ph.D. degree (1975) in social psychology from the University of Texas at Austin and has previously taught at the University of California at Berkeley, the University of California at Los Angeles, and Georgetown University. She is currently working as a behavioral science consultant near Washington, D.C.

George C. Stone is professor of medical psychology at the University of California at San Francisco, where he is also director of graduate academic programs in social and behavioral science of the Department of Psychiatry. He was senior author of *Health Psychology: A Handbook* (1979), the first editor of the journal *Health Psychology* from 1980 to 1984, and was elected president of the Division of Health Psychology of the American Psychological Association, to serve in 1985-1986. He received his A.B. degree (1948) in psychology, his M.A. degree (1951) in psychology, and his Ph.D. degree (1954) in experimental psychology, all from the University of California at Berkeley.

Gary R. VandenBos is the deputy executive officer for communications with the American Psychological Association, and he previously served as the director of the association's Office of National Policy Studies. He is a clinical psychologist active in private practice, formerly served as a director of a community mental health center, and was the research coordinator for the Michigan State Psychotherapy Research Project with Schizophrenics. From 1982 to 1984, he was a visiting professor of clinical psychology at the University of Bergen in Norway. He is the coauthor of *Psychotherapy with Schizophrenics: The Treatment of Choice* (1981), the editor of *Psychotherapy: Research, Practice, Policy* (1980), and the coeditor of *Psychology and National Health Insurance* (1979). He received his B.S. degree (1967) in psychology and statistics and his M.A. degree (1969) in personality psychology from Michigan State University and his Ph.D. degree (1973) in clinical psychology from the University of Detroit.

Arthur N. Wiens is professor of medical psychology and director of clinical training and medical psychology outpatient services at the Oregon Health Sciences University. He has served as president of the American Association of State Psychology Boards and on the board of directors of the Professional Examination Service and of the Council for the National Register of Health Service Providers in Psychology. He received his B.A. degree (1948) and his M.A. degree (1952), both in psychology, from the University of Kansas and his Ph.D. degree (1956) in clinical psychology from the University of Portland.

Jack G. Wiggins is president of the Psychological Development Center, Inc., and managing partner of Ohio Computest. He is currently insurance chairman of the Division of Psychotherapy as well as of the Division of Independent Practice of the American Psychological Association. He has been active in the adoption of several state and federal laws affecting the practice of psychology and the business of insurance. He received his B.A. degree (1948) in psychology from the University of Oklahoma, his M.A. degree (1951) in psychology from Southern Methodist University, and his Ph.D. degree (1952) in clinical psychology from Purdue University.

Professional
Psychology
in Transition

Meeting Today's
Challenges

Part One

Trends in the
Profession

The chapters in Part One seek to capture the growth of clinical psychology, not simply its numbers but its growing recognition under the law and by third parties and the range of patients served. As documented in Chapter One, between 1974 and 1985 the number of licensed psychologists more than doubled, and there is an expanding reservoir from which future practitioners may develop. Clinical psychology as a practice profession is now substantially larger than its major competitor, psychiatry.

Chapter Two reports a survey of 20,000 patients of psychologists. Whereas psychologists compete with psychiatrists but complement the nonpsychiatric physician, we find, not surprisingly, that they receive more referrals from the latter than from the former. Notable also is that 24 percent of these 20,000 patients were under concurrent medical care, reflecting the fact that medicine and clinical psychology do collaborate regularly in patient care. The proportion of clinical psychologists who are in full-time fee-for-service practice has continued to accelerate.

Third-party reimbursement between 1977 and 1980, the subject of Chapter Three, showed a major growth in the extent of reimbursement to psychologists but no change of consequence in the proportional distribution among the carriers. Because reimbursement has become an increasing and significant proportion of practitioner income, shifts in the marketplace that jeopardize or augment this dependent relationship to a third party

1

alter the stability of the independent practitioner. The data presented in Chapter Four, however, on the CHAMPUS, the largest single health plan in the country, reflect the increasing penetration of clinical psychologists into outpatient mental health services. Indeed, in about a third of the major CHAMPUS states, psychologists are providing more such service than psychiatrists. Inpatient services are another matter. In either setting, however, very few of the services provided by psychiatrists are services that only a physician can provide. The potential for a further shift in service delivery between the professions is there.

Meanwhile, as Chapter Five demonstrates, the increasing recognition of the profession by Congress is encouraging the growth of clinical psychology. Now specified as a health profession for training support, clinical psychology was accorded parity throughout the recent reformation of the federal Criminal Code. Such developments, when added to legislation formerly in place, such as the Rehabilitation Act, Federal Employee Health Benefits Act, and workers' compensation for federal employees, place psychology in a sound position not only to accomplish further legislative objectives but to continue to influence the development of our nation's health care and social policies.

Herbert Dörken
Joy Stapp
Gary R. VandenBos

1

Licensed Psychologists:
A Decade of Major Growth

If psychology is to be a major force in health care, then in addition to its research and teaching contributions, it must have a substantial practitioner base. There were indications in the early seventies that the proportion of psychologists engaged in practice was beginning to escalate and also that the number of licensed psychologists had begun to increase apace. Concurrently, in 1974, Congress enacted watershed legislation recognizing the practice of psychology (see Chapter Five), and by that time twenty states (beginning in 1968) had enacted freedom-of-choice laws recognizing psychological services under health insurance, including four of the five states with the largest numbers of licensed psychologists. The *National Register* survey yielded the first unduplicated count of psychologists licensed/certified among the states in December 1976, and the growth began to look impressive. All subsequent studies have indicated a continuing growth, while the national review of mid-1985, to be reported here, affirms that the growth has indeed been dramatic.

Among the early indications that the number of psychologists licensed/certified for independent practice was growing apace were Dörken (1976) and Dörken and Whiting (1976). An attempt to achieve a fifty-state count in 1974 (Dörken) was thwarted because three states (Missouri, South Dakota, Vermont) did not yet have licensing laws, two (Iowa, Pennsylvania) had enacted laws too recently to have developed directory information, and one (Hawaii) refused to provide directory information. For the forty-five remaining jurisdictions (forty-four states and the District of Columbia), actual directories were reviewed to eliminate out-of-state residents. The unduplicated count totaled 18,058 (based on state directories issued between January 1973 and February 1975), yielding a ratio of 0.959 psychologists per 10,000 population. Projecting on this basis for the other three states where statutory recognition had been gained brought the count to 19,508. Projected nationally, it would have been 20,126. The ratio per 10,000 population, incidentally, ranged from a low of 0.316 (Alabama) to a high of 2.083 (Massachusetts), while the range in number of licensees was from 26 (Nevada) to 3,192 (New York).

The *National Register* count of 25,510 (December 1976), reduced by 243 for those out of the country or with "inadequate address," was 25,267. This was equivalent to a 25.3 percent growth in two years. Using survey research of ten states, Dörken and Webb (1981) later found a growth of 26.8 percent from 1976 to 1979.

The 1985 Survey

Every informal indication was that the burgeoning growth of licensed/certified psychologists had continued. It seemed time to attempt to obtain another unduplicated national count. Judy E. Hall, executive secretary for the New York State Board for Psychology, kindly supplied a directory for all state boards. With the exception of Alaska (no phone number given), all boards were contacted by phone. The author (Dörken) identified himself and said he was doing research on licensed psychologists nationally and would appreciate knowing the number of psychologists currently licensed at the independent practice level and resident in the state. The date of the directory or listing was also sought.

The range in response from the state boards was almost more interesting than the data on the licensees. Although no attempt was made to survey U.S. possessions and territories, it was learned incidentally that there were 768 licensed psychologists in Puerto Rico as of August 1985. Several states had at hand the exact number by county, state, out-of-state, and foreign. Several others had it also but would release it only on written request and with the purpose stated. The majority knew the number currently licensed but not the number who were state residents. Several offered to count the out-of-state addresses for a return phone call; several offered to call back with the information and did; several offered, if the caller would wait, to count on the spot; and several offered to send their directory, no charge. Nine states sent a directory on payment of a nominal charge (range $2 to $18), while three others stated the number of current or active licensees and offered a printout (not purchased) at a cost exceeding $60 ($92 for Rhode Island).

The phone calls were made from mid-July through August, and the contact person in several states was away on vacation, requiring a call back two or three weeks later. In some states it was necessary to thread the bureaucracy with as many as five or six calls to reach the right party, some annoyed by the bother, some cordially relaying the information at hand. Only two states asked to be informed of their state resident count. The District of Columbia was distinctive among the jurisdictions contacted, most of which had been both cordial and informative to the extent feasible for them. The first call to the D.C. office was greeted with "You gotta be kidding," then laughter, and then the person hung up. A second attempt the next day produced an even less satisfactory response! Faith Tanney kindly generated the "best estimate" figure through the District of Columbia Psychological Association.

The unduplicated count for the fifty states was obtained:

- by actual count from directories, fifteen states;
- by phone discussion with agency staff, twenty-four states; and
- by letter from the state board, four states.

For seven states the number currently licensed was available, but the number out of state had to be estimated (Florida, Iowa, Massachusetts, New Jersey, Rhode Island, Utah, Virginia) and was derived by considering the proportion of out-of-state licensees in neighboring states. For these seven states a ratio of 15 percent was set for the first two, 20 percent for the next three, and 7.5 percent and 10 percent for the final two.

The end product is a national unduplicated count of psychologists licensed/certified for independent practice as of mid-1985 of 45,536. There were some exceptions to the June, July, or

August rosters. Four states update their directories toward the end of each year, and thus their information is about a half year out of date. Arkansas had expected a new directory in July, but by the end of August it was still not available. Averaging the growth in each of these five states separately over the eight years and projecting a half year's growth onto four and a year's growth onto Arkansas would yield a projected total of 45,683 (of the 147 augmentation, 120 derived from Texas). The directories of six states were produced in the spring of 1985, but no attempt was made to project the additional quarterly growth. Thus, the eight and a half years from the *National Register* survey of December 1976 to the present mid-1985 survey saw an 80.8 percent growth nationally, or an increase of 9.5 percent a year (the average, but accelerating, increase in licensees per year was 2,402). At this rate (45,683 × 1.095) there will be over 50,000 licensed psychologists by 1986. Over the eleven years between Dörken's 1974 and 1985 surveys, during which the unduplicated number of licensees increased from 20,126 to 45,683, the growth had been 127 percent. For detailed findings by state, see Table 1-1.

Out-of-State Psychologists

The number of psychologists who are licensed in one jurisdiction but live in (or give their address as in) another can be very substantial, amounting to about 25 percent of the licensees in eight states (Arizona, Hawaii, Idaho, Kentucky, New Hampshire, North Carolina, North Dakota, West Virginia) and about 20 percent in another seven (Alabama, Arkansas, Connecticut, Indiana, Kansas, South Carolina, Wisconsin). However, this proportion is less than 10 percent in six states (Colorado, Louisiana, Maryland, Oklahoma, South Dakota, Texas).

In some states, the out-of-state count is minimal, reflecting psychologists who have recently moved out of the area but still retain their licensure. One state with few active out-of-state licensees attributed its low count to a mandatory continuing education requirement. In some states, practicing across the border is quite common. By far the greatest overlap in any jurisdiction occurs in the District of Columbia. Dörken (1976), by directory count, found

73 D.C.-licensed and D.C.-resident psychologists in 1974 and 291 D.C.-licensed but resident in D.C., Maryland, or Virginia. Two years later the *National Register* survey (Mills, Wellner, and VandenBos, 1979) yielded a count of 403, suggesting that some duplication had not been eliminated. Then, in 1979, Dörken and Webb (1981), in cooperation with the *National Register,* derived a count of 759 D.C. licensees with addresses in the District or in Maryland or Virginia. In August 1985 the District of Columbia Psychological Association supplied a "best estimate" of 450 psychologists licensed and resident in the District, among about 860 currently active D.C. licensees. Thus, close to half the D.C. licensees do not live in the District, a nonresident proportion far higher than for any state (although the proportion reached levels just over 25 percent for West Virginia and Kentucky).

Freedom-of-Choice Laws

There are now only eleven states without freedom-of-choice (FOC) laws. These states have 8.3 percent of the U.S. population and 5.3 percent of the licensed psychologists and the same proportion of American Psychological Association (APA) members. Table 1-1 lists the FOC states in order of passage and the other states alphabetically. For each state, the table shows the 1984 U.S. census estimate, the number of APA members, the number of licensees reported in the 1976 *National Register* survey, the number of licensees found in the 1985 survey of licensed psychologists, the percentage increase between the 1976 and 1985 surveys, the number of 1985 licensed psychologists per 10,000 population, and selected details of the FOC law. The first five FOC laws were enacted in 1968 and 1969. From 1970 to 1974, fourteen more states passed such legislation, and another fourteen did so over the next five years. Since 1979 seven more states have enacted FOC laws. Overall, in four of these jurisdictions, health care service plans such as Blue Shield are not covered. Seven of these laws have provisions for policies or plans written or issued for delivery from outside the state, and in three states psychologists are also explicitly included under worker's compensation. Six states have enacted revisions of their FOC

Table 1-1. Licensed Psychologists by State (With and Without Freedom-of-Choice Laws), 1985.

No.	State	FOC Law Enacted	4/84 Census (in 1,000s)	1985 APA Members	No. Lic. Psy. 12/76[a]	No. Lic. Psy. 1985	Register Date	Percentage Increase	No. Lic. Psy. per 10,000 pop.	Explanatory Notes[b]
1	N.J.	'68 + 12/73	7,490	2,284	880	1,305c	8/85	48	1.74	B OS
2	Mich.	6/68	9,019	2,019	529	1,083	8/85	105	1.20	(B)—1981
3	Utah	3/69 + '75	1,655	312	136	311	6/85	129	1.88	B OS
4	N.Y.	6/69	17,697	7,861	3,463	5,412	7/85	56	3.06	(M) B OS
5	Calif.	'69 + '74 + 9/80	25,521	8,072	3,213	6,626	5/85	106	2.60	(M) B WC—9/77 OS-9/81
6	Mont.	3/71	824	141	74	124	8/85	68	1.50	M WC
7	Okla.	6/71	3,366	494	159	321	7/85	102	0.95	B
8	Colo.	7/71	3,196	993	318	726	8/85	128	2.27	M
9	Wash.	'71	4,332	957	276	854	7/85	209	1.97	(B) 12/74
10	Md.	7/72	4,322	1,777	553	1,390	7/85	151	3.22	M B OS
11	Va.	9/73	5,595	1,478	491	574c	7/85	17	1.03	M B
12	Mass.	12/73	5,771	2,886	1,520	2,999c	6/85	93	5.20	M B OS
13	Ohio	1/74	10,728	2,123	1,803	2,643	7/85	47	2.46	M (B) 5/74 WC—5/80
14	Tenn.	2/74	4,705	813	427	653	12/84	53	1.39	(M) B
15	Kans.	3/74	2,438	570	247	347	11/84	40	1.42	(M) B
16	Nebr.	4/74	1,603	273	157	224	12/84	43	1.40	B
17	Miss.	7/74	2,601	240	103	192	6/85	86	0.74	B
	FEHBA	7/74	—	—	—	—	—	—	—	F B WC—9/74
18	Hawaii	'74c + 4/84	1,037	253	82	190	7/85	132	1.83	B OS
19	La.	'74 + 7/75	4,477	476	172	336	8/85	95	0.75	(M) B
20	Ark.	3/75	2,338	215	162	183	7/84	13	0.78	M B
21	Minn.	5/75	4,157	1,036	697	1,010	7/85	45	2.43	M B
22	Oreg.	5/75	2,664	607	209	442	8/85	111	1.66	M B
23	Conn.	6/75	3,144	1,187	402	743	4/85	85	2.36	M B
24	Maine	6/75	1,151	253	156	227	7/85	46	1.36	M B
25	N.H.	1/76	967	256	91	198	7/85	118	2.05	M B
26	D.C.	1/76 + 12/81	619	880	403	450c	8/85	12	7.27	B
27	Ill.	12/76	11,494	2,633	1,122	2,002	6/85	78	1.74	(M) B
28	Tex.	5/77	16,079	2,660	1,039	1,998	12/84	92	1.24	B
29	N.C.	6/77	6,128	1,122	297	895	7/85	201	1.46	B

No.	State											OS
30	N.Mex.	9/77	1,422	283	89	8/85	201	126	1.41		B	
31	W.Va.	'77	1,967	199	109	4/85	229	110	1.16	M	B	
32	Pa.	4/78	11,900	3,205	2,132	3/85	3,412	60	2.87		B	
33	Nev.	7/79	910	170	51	8/85	110	116	1.21			
34	Ga.	3/80	5,792	1,016	314	6/85	666	112	1.15	(M)	B	
35	Mo.	12/80	4,981	928	222	8/85	1,040	368	2.09	(M)	B	
36	Ala.	4/82	3,973	467	157	2/85	279	78	0.70		B	
37	Fla.	6/82	10,879	1,938	614	7/85	1,146c	87	1.05	(M)	B	
38	Ariz.	9/83	3,020	835	318	7/85	737	132	2.44		B	
39	Wyo.	3/85	523	114	51	7/85	88	73	1.68		B	
40	Ind.	3/85	5,413	865	530	6/85	757	43	1.40		B	
	Total FOC	—	215,898	54,891	23,768		43,123	81.4	2.00		—	
			91.7% of	94.7% of	94.1% of		94.7% of					
	National		235,561	57,961	25,267		45,536					

States Without Freedom-of-Choice Laws

	State									
	Alaska	500	107	30	8/85	69	130	1.38		
	Del.	609	141	58	7/85	82	41	1.35		
	Idaho	999	105	70	8/85	55	-21	0.55		
	Iowa	2,902	436	136	7/85	332c	144	1.14		
	Ky.	3,727	390	313	6/85	288	-8	0.77		
	N.Dak.	687	104	49	6/85	70	43	1.02		
	R.I.	956	232	121	4/85	165c	36	1.73		
	S.C.	3,294	352	160	8/85	241	51	0.73		
	S.Dak.	703	94	25	8/85	115	360	1.64		
	Vt.	528	172	58	7/85	201	247	3.81		
	Wis.	4,758	937	479	7/85	795	66	1.67		
	Total non-FOC	19,663	3,070	1,499		2,413	61	1.23		

aUnduplicated, state resident, licensed/certified for independent practice as of 12/76 per National Register Report #2, 3/4/77.

bUnless otherwise specified, statute applies only to disability (health) insurance policies recognized under the Insurance Code. M, mental health coverage mandatory; (M), must be provided if requested by the insured group; psychologists recognized for reimbursement; B, specified language providing for coverage of Blue Shield contracts; (B), included by negotiation; OS, specific language requiring recognition of psychological services for state residents under policies issued out of state; WC, specific language providing for coverage under worker's compensation plans; (WC), negotiated inclusion in state fund; F, P.L. 93-363 applies to all federal employee health plans and P.L. 93-416 applies to federal work injuries compensation.

cEstimated, see text.

laws, usually to cover Blue Shield plans or to resolve problems concerning out-of-state issuers.

As the U.S. Supreme Court determined in June 1985 (84-325 and 84-356) that the Employee Retirement Income Security Act (ERISA) did not preempt state laws mandating minimum mental health benefits, the introduction of legislation mandating mental health benefits in all group health insurance can be expected in a number of states in 1986. It may be through such a vehicle that several states will acquire an FOC law.

As noted previously (Dörken, 1976, 1983), the ratio of licensed psychologists to population, while increasing over the years, has consistently averaged higher in FOC than in non-FOC states. In 1975 the number of licensed psychologists per 10,000 population was 1.13 for the twenty-three states then with FOC laws, 0.96 for all forty-five jurisdictions with licensing. The average was 1.22 for the thirty-seven FOC states in 1982, 0.87 for the non-FOC states (1.18 average for all states). By 1985 the ratio for FOC states had risen to 2.00, while for non-FOC states it was 1.23 (average for all states, 1.93).

Not unexpectedly, FOC states, on average, had more licensed psychologists (1,078) than non-FOC states (219). Numbers alone are not the full explanation, however, since states with but 88 or 110 licensees (Wyoming and Nevada) had enacted such law, while states with 795 and 332 licensees (Wisconsin and Iowa) had not. Given that there are relatively few states without such direct recognition law and that such recognition brings distinct professional advantages, the time may be at hand for psychology's national association (APA) to assist its affiliated state associations in bringing such legislation to passage. Targeting the three or four states each year with the best likelihood for passage should make it possible to see such law across all states by, say, 1988, twenty years after the enactment of the first such law in New Jersey.

Growth Rate

Over the past two decades, the expanding practice opportunities have seen an increase in the number of clinical psychologists being trained, a postgraduate shift from other specialties into clinical practice, and a progressive increase in the numbers of psychologists involved in health care delivery. This growth from 1974 to 1979 was described by Dörken and Webb (1981). Of the licensees responding to a ten-state survey in 1980, 80.5 percent were health service providers (11.1 percent salaried, 69.4 percent in fee-for-service practice some of the time).

The growth in numbers of licensed psychologists over the past decade is clearly impressive, but of course, the U.S. population has also been increasing. Table 1-2 shows the increase relative to population between 1974 and 1985, using 1976 data for the six states without licensing or a licensee count in 1974. From every perspective the District of Columbia is an anomaly, with its 642 percent growth, which is explained by the many government agencies in the nation's capital that have attracted many psychologists who are involved in health issues and who also sustain some practice. Idaho, at the other end of the spectrum, was the only state to show a loss in ratio (15 percent). Nationally, relative to population, the unduplicated number of licensed psychologists has slightly more than doubled over this time span (103 percent increase). Growth has been less than 50 percent in five states (Delaware, Idaho, Illinois, Utah, Wyoming) and over 200 percent in five states plus the District of Columbia—only consulting psychologists counted at both times. States with growth between 100 and 200 percent numbered twenty-three.

Casual review of the growth of licensed psychologists by census region does not reveal any apparent trends, nor did the Sunbelt appear to be a major growth factor (only 58 percent, 82 percent, and 72 percent in Arizona, California, and Texas). Small states are apparently not penalized (see Alaska at 119 percent; Montana, 150 percent; New Hampshire, 163 percent; and Nevada, 157 percent). Thus, it is neither size nor sunshine but, we suspect, the degree of recognition accorded the profession in any particular state (put otherwise, the practice and employment opportunities) that accounts for the extent of growth.

U.S. resident membership in the American Psychological Association has also shown continued growth. It was 35,690 in 1974, 40,590 in 1976, 54,352 in 1983, and 57,961 in 1985, a 62 percent growth over these eleven years. Not all licensed psychologists are

Table 1-2. Number of Licensed Psychologists (Unduplicated) Relative to Population, by State, 1974 and 1985.

State	No. Licensed/Certified Psychologists 1974	1985	No. per 10,000 Population 1974	1985	Percentage Increase
Ala.	112	279	0.32	0.70	119
Alaska	21	69	0.63	1.38	119
Ariz.	318	737	1.54	2.44	58
Ark.	62	183	0.30	0.78	160
Calif.	2,953	6,626	1.43	2.60	82
Colo.	253	726	1.02	2.27	123
Conn.	293	743	0.95	2.36	148
Del.	57	82	0.99	1.35	36
D.C.	73	450a	0.98	7.27	642
Fla.	396	1,146a	0.52	1.05	102
Ga.	196	666	0.41	1.15	180
Hawaii	N.A.	190	0.93b	1.83	97
Idaho	50	55	0.65	0.55	-15
Ill.	1,414	2,002	1.26	1.74	38
Ind.	350	757	0.66	1.40	112
Iowa	N.A.	332	0.47b	1.14	142
Kans.	199	347	0.87	1.42	63
Ky.	107	288	0.32	0.77	141
La.	161	336	0.43	0.75	74
Maine	74	227	0.72	1.36	89
Md.	420	1,390	1.03	3.22	213
Mass.	1,212	2,999a	2.08	5.20	150
Mich.	405	1,083	0.45	1.20	167
Minn.	215	1,010	0.55	2.43	342
Miss.	91	192	0.40	0.74	85
Mo.	0	1,040	0.46b	2.09	354
Mont.	43	124	0.60	1.50	150
Nebr.	124	224	0.80	1.40	75
Nev.	26	110	0.47	1.21	157
N.H.	62	198	0.78	2.05	163
N.J.	732	1,305a	0.99	1.74	76
N.Mex.	62	201	0.56	1.41	152
N.Y.	3,192	5,412	1.75	3.06	75
N.C.	283	895	0.54	1.46	170
N.Dak.	40	70	0.62	1.02	65
Ohio	1,342	2,643	1.25	2.46	97
Okla.	119	321	0.45	0.95	111
Oreg.	169	442	0.76	1.66	118
Pa.	N.A.	3,412	1.80b	2.87	59
R.I.	110	165a	1.13	1.73	53
S.C.	129	241	0.47	0.73	55
S.Dak.	0	115	0.36b	1.64	356
Tenn.	224	653	0.54	1.39	157
Tex.	845	1,998	0.72	1.24	72
Utah	157	311	1.36	1.88	38
Vt.	0	201	1.22b	3.81	212
Va.	172	574a	0.36	1.03	186
Wash.	241	854	0.70	1.97	181
W.Va.	84	229	0.47	1.16	147
Wis.	424	795	0.93	1.67	80
Wyo.	46	88	1.30	1.68	29
Total	18,058	45,536	0.96	1.93	103
Projected Total	20,126	45,683	—	1.94	—

Note: The total numbers of psychologists per 10,000 population were calculated using the total population for the United States as a whole, and, for this reason, these figures will not coincide with an average calculated from the data for the fifty states.
aNumber currently licensed for independent practice known, number out of state estimated to derive number (unduplicated) of state-resident licensed psychologists.
bNumber per 10,000 population in 1976; no licensees or number not available in 1974.

APA members, although the 1978 survey of a random sample of
APA members (VandenBos, Stapp, and Kilburg, 1981) found that 84
percent of doctoral-level health service providers were licensed.
Consistently, 86 percent of the respondent licensees in the 1980 ten-
state survey who were health service providers were also APA
members (only 57 percent belonged to their state psychological
association). Given that at least 14 percent of licensed psychologists
are not APA members and that 16 percent of the APA-member
doctoral-level health service providers (HSPs) are not licensed
psychologists (to say nothing of the non-HSP members, who would
be far less likely to be licensed), the two groups fail to overlap by
not less than 30 percent.

From a state-by-state perspective, we see in Table 1-1 that
generally there are more APA members than licensees in the
individual states (to be expected, given the larger national total,
57,961 versus 45,683). However, the situation is reversed in seven
states. In four of these states (Pennsylvania, Missouri, West
Virginia, Vermont) master's-level psychologists may be fully
licensed, a fact that may in part account for this situation. The
differentials in Massachusetts, Ohio (school psychologists not
included), and South Dakota do not seem to have a common
explanation. Given that only 57 percent of licensees in the 1980
survey belonged to their state psychological association, the overlap
between licensing and membership appears even less complete than
at the national level.

Thus, the universe of U.S. psychologists is larger than any
of these groupings (licensing, national-level membership, state-
level membership) and larger still to the extent that some
psychologists are neither licensed nor APA members. Add to this the
incomplete overlap with state, or even local, psychological
associations, and the basic question is before us: How large is the
universe of U.S. psychologists?

The 1983 APA Census

This section examines the characteristics of licensed
psychologists using data collected for the 1983 Census of
Psychological Personnel (Stapp, Tucker, and VandenBos, 1985).

Conducted by the American Psychological Association, this was the first attempt in over a decade to describe the *universe* of psychological personnel in the United States, including licensed and nonlicensed personnel, APA members and nonmembers, practitioners, researchers, educators, and so forth. Identified was a universe of 102,101 individuals, 78.4 percent of whom completed and returned a questionnaire that assessed degree level, degree field and current major field, licensure/certification, age, sex, ethnicity, employment status, employment settings, and involvement in research activities, educational activities, and provision or administration of health/mental health services. With APA membership at 54,352 in 1983, the census identified another 47,749 persons with some level of involvement in psychology. A sizable number are probably school psychologists, generally credentialed in states under criteria and a process separate from licensing. Many, if not the majority, belong to separate organizations of school psychologists. There are also a sizable number of persons with master's degrees or some graduate study in psychology who are not school psychologists; some are continuing their graduate study and some are otherwise employed. Stapp (1983) estimated that one-third to one-half of those with master's degrees in psychology find employment in psychology in the year following graduation (84,000 master's degrees in psychology were awarded from 1973 to 1983).

The six-figure standing of the 1983 census is certainly impressive of itself, and it also sheds further perspective on the near-future resources of psychology. To the extent that nonlicensees in this census have ambitions for future practice in health care, then, following the "tip of the iceberg" theme advanced by Dörken and Whiting (1976), the licensed psychologists of today may well be but the tip of a *Titanic*-sized iceberg!

The census results are described in detail in Stapp, Tucker, and VandenBos (1985). For our purposes here, we have examined the subset of respondents to the census who indicated that they held a doctoral degree and were licensed/certified for the independent practice of psychology ($N = 32,982$). Their demographic characteristics are of interest. The median age of these respondents was 42, less than the median age of the respondents to the 1977 and 1980 Dörken and Webb surveys at 45.9 and 43.2 respectively. On the average, then, the practitioners of psychology have become progressively younger. The explanation is found in Table 1-3, which shows that many respondents received their doctorates relatively recently. When these data were collected, in 1983, only 2.5 percent of the respondents had received their doctorates before 1950, another 11.5 percent from 1950 to 1959, and somewhat over a fifth (21.4 percent) between 1960 and 1969. More than half (51.7 percent) had obtained their doctorates between 1970 and 1979. Of course, because Table 1-3 is based on respondents holding doctorates, it underestimates the total population of licensed psychologists. In fact, since 1972 the annual doctorate production in psychology has averaged about 3,000 per year; to be precise, 32,744 doctorates have been awarded between 1973 and 1983. This reflects the tremendous growth that has occurred since the midsixties, from 954 doctorates awarded in 1965 to more than three times that number (2,883) awarded in 1976 and even higher numbers every year since then.

Almost 70 percent of these licensed doctoral respondents were male (69.5 percent). However, this proportion will decrease, as the percentage of women awarded doctorates has increased progressively from 19.8 percent in 1965 to 47.5 percent in 1983. As for ethnicity, there are very few minorities among licensed doctoral

**Table 1-3. Year of Highest Degree Among
Licensed Doctoral Respondents, 1983.**

Year of Highest Degree	N	Percentage
Before 1940	258	0.8
1940–1944	185	0.6
1945–1949	358	1.1
1950–1954	1,641	5.0
1955–1959	2,154	6.5
1960–1964	2,549	7.7
1965–1969	4,507	13.7
1970–1974	7,833	23.7
1975–1979	9,244	28.0
1980 or after	4,176	12.7
Not specified	77	0.2
Total	32,982	100.0

psychologists: 1.6 percent black, 1.3 percent of Hispanic origin, 0.9 percent Asian, and 0.2 percent American Indian. The absolute number of minority doctorates awarded each year over the past decade, however, has been increasing.

Table 1-4 shows the degree field and current major field of the licensed doctoral respondents to the 1983 census. It is obvious that there has been some quite substantial postdoctoral shifting, as reported earlier by Dörken and Webb (1979, 1981). The current major field was clinical psychology for 63 percent of these psychologists, whereas this had been the degree field for only 48.2 percent, in effect a 14.8 percent "gain," representing almost 4,900 psychologists. By contrast, there were declines of 5.9 percent and 4.7 percent in counseling and educational psychology, respectively. Of note is that the proportion currently in industrial/organizational psychology had more than doubled from those with that degree field. Other shifts by field and field clusters are reported in Table 1-4.

Over 96 percent of the licensed doctoral respondents indicated that they were currently employed, the remainder being retired, seeking employment, and so forth. About one-third (32.9 percent) reported independent practice as their primary employment setting. Most of these individuals (26.7 percent of the respondents) reported individual private practice; fewer reported group psychological practice (4.4 percent) or medical/psychological group practice (1.8 percent). Hospitals were the primary settings for 11.8 percent of the respondents and clinics for 9.6 percent. Combined, this health care cluster includes over half (54.3 percent) of the respondents, 58 percent if medical schools are included. Of special interest was the finding that 25 percent of those working in hospitals were employed in general hospitals, reflecting psychology's increased involvement in "physical" health care services. Other frequently reported settings included universities (14.7 percent); business, government, and other settings (9.5 percent); colleges, schools, and other educational settings (9.9 percent); counseling centers and other human service settings (6.6 percent); with 1.3 percent unspecified.

In addition to their primary employment, 61.4 percent of the employed respondents reported a secondary employment setting

Table 1-4. Degree Field and Current Major Field Among
Licensed Doctoral Respondents, 1983
(N = 32,982).

Field	Frequency as Degree Field	Frequency as Current Field	Change
Clinical	48.2%	63.0%	+14.8%
Industrial/ Organizational	2.0	4.2	+2.2
Community	0.3	1.2	} +1.0
Psychometric	0.4	0.5	
Counseling	18.0	12.1	–5.9
{ Social	2.3	0.8	
{ Personality	1.4	0.4	–3.8
{ Developmental	3.2	1.9	
{ Educational	7.3	2.7	–4.8
{ School	4.9	4.7	
{ Experimental	4.0	1.0	
{ Physiological	0.9	0.3	–4.4
{ General	1.6	0.8	
Other[a]	5.5	6.4	+0.9

[a]Includes all degree fields that did not exceed 0.5% in either degree or current major field: cognitive, comparative, engineering, qualitative, psycholinguistics, psychopharmacology, and systems, plus other fields in psychology, others not in psychology, and fields not specified.

and 22.7 percent reported a tertiary setting. For those with secondary employment, 45.0 percent were in independent practice, 14.6 percent in business, government, and commerce (mostly self-employment or consulting firms), and 9.7 percent in university settings. Those with tertiary employment were also most frequently employed in these settings.

In what activities were these psychologists engaged? Of the employed respondents, 88.3 percent were involved in provision or administration of health/mental health services, 69.0 percent in education, and 44.4 percent in research. Added, these three clusters alone would exceed 200 percent, underscoring that diversity is a key characteristic of psychologists. The large majority of psychologists are involved in more than one activity. For example, three of four doctoral psychologists who are involved in health/mental health services are also involved in research or education or both. Stapp, Tucker, and VandenBos (1985) summarized it well: "Psychology is a pluralistic science and profession that is addressing an extremely wide set of national concerns through a diversity of activities, conducted in a host of settings with a range of populations."

References

Dörken, H. "Laws, Regulations, and Psychological Practice." In H. Dörken and Associates, *The Professional Psychologist Today: New Developments in Law, Health Insurance, and Health Practice*. San Francisco: Jossey-Bass, 1976.

Dörken, H. "Health Insurance and Third Party Reimbursement." In B. Sales (ed.), *The Professional Psychologist's Handbook*. New York: Plenum, 1983.

Dörken, H., and Webb, J. T. "Licensed Psychologists in Health Care: A Survey of Their Practices." In C. Kiesler, N. Cummings, and G. R. VandenBos (eds.), *Psychology and National Health Insurance: A Sourcebook*. Washington, D.C.: American Psychological Association, 1979.

Dörken, H., and Webb, J. T. "Licensed Psychologists on the Increase: 1974-1979." *American Psychologist*, 1981, *36*, 1419-1426.

Dörken, H., and Whiting, F. "Psychologists as Health Service Providers." In H. Dörken and Associates, *The Professional Psychologist Today: New Developments in Law, Health Insurance, and Health Practice*. San Francisco: Jossey-Bass, 1976.

Mills, D., Wellner, A., and VandenBos, G. R. "The National Register Survey: The First Comprehensive Study of All Licensed/Certified Psychologists." In C. Kiesler, N. Cummings, and G. R. VandenBos (eds.), *Psychology and National Health Insurance*. Washington, D.C.: American Psychological Association, 1979.

Stapp, J. *Summary Report of 1982-83 Survey of Graduate Departments of Psychology*. Washington, D.C.: American Psychological Association, 1983.

Stapp, J., Tucker, A., and VandenBos, G. R. "Census of Psychological Personnel: 1983." *American Psychologist*, 1985, *40*, 1317–1351.

VandenBos, G. R., Stapp, J., and Kilburg, R. "Health Service Providers in Psychology: Results of the 1978 APA Human Resources Survey." *American Psychologist*, 1981, *36*, 1395–1418.

2

Herbert Dörken
Gary R. VandenBos

Characteristics of 20,000 Patients and Their Psychologists

In 1977 Dörken and Webb (1979) surveyed all licensed psychologists in ten "states" (Alabama, California, District of Columbia, Florida, Illinois, New York, Ohio, Rhode Island, South Carolina, and Texas) regarding their fee-for-service activities. These states, at that time, included about 47 percent of all licensed psychologists in the country and about 46 percent of the national population. California and New York contained 54 percent of the licensed psychologists and 54 percent of the respondents. In fact, the rank order of the number of respondents and the number of licensees by state was the same for all ten states, indicating some balance in representation. At the time the original 1977 survey was undertaken, these were the ten states for which the Civilian Health and Medical Program of the Uniformed Services (CHAMPUS) had been reporting mental health service-utilization data (see Chapter Four); data for all states are now available.

In 1980, with the assistance of James T. Webb (Dörken and Webb, 1981), the psychologists in these ten states were again surveyed, using an extensive computer-scan-scored questionnaire (with support provided by the National Institute of Mental Health).

Acquisition of the data for this chapter was made possible by Grant MH-26852 from the Mental Health Development Branch, National Institute of Mental Health.

Findings from that survey on third-party reimbursement for psychological services are reported in Chapter Three; aspects of hospital practice were reported elsewhere (Dörken, Webb, and Zaro, 1982).

In addition to obtaining demographic data about the psychologists themselves (to be reported later in this chapter) and some further indication of the rapid growth of licensed psychologists as health or mental health practitioners (see Chapter One), a major objective of the second survey was to learn something about the patients of these psychologists—their demographic characteristics, the source and purpose of their referral, their history of mental and physical health disorder, medication, concurrent medical care, treatment plan, and types of services being rendered.

To avoid the bias of high-frequency-visit patients (or more dramatic cases), we did not seek information on the last case seen (or on "a" case or a "typical" case). Rather, we asked respondents to supply data on their "three most recent *new* cases." Thus, our objective was a representative (albeit small) sample of patients who had just begun to receive health care from these licensees.

A total of 8,762 (57.1 percent) of the 15,334 licensees responded with usable returns. (Another 353 returns could not be tallied by the computer.) Considering the complexity and length of the survey questionnaire, this level of response was particularly gratifying. Of the respondents, 6,078 (69.4 percent) were in fee-for-service (FFS) health practice some portion of their time, and an additional 972 (11.1 percent) provided patient care services only on a salaried basis. The remaining 19.5 percent of licensed psychologists responding were not health service providers, either FFS or salaried.

From this respondent pool of 7,050 health service provider psychologists (6,078 and 972), there should have been data on 21,150 patients if each health service provider had submitted information on three patients. In actuality, we received information on treatment parameters for 20,072 patients (95 percent complete return) and on the demographic characteristics of 19,908 patients (94 percent complete return). Barton and others (1980) have suggested that when the interest throughout the population is similar, as it is among licensed psychologists, it is probable that those who respond are representative of the target population.

It has been reported earlier that the number of hours of services provided by psychologists in fee-for-service practice shows a bimodal distribution, some providing only a few hours a week and others practicing full time (Dörken and Webb, 1979). Does the kind of patients seen differ with the extent to which a psychologist is in FFS practice? To answer this question, we aggregated responses separately for respondent health service providers who were salaried only; those who were in very part-time practice (VPT-FFS), defined as one to ten hours a week; those in part-time practice (PT-FFS), defined as eleven to nineteen hours a week; and those in full-time practice, defined as twenty or more hours a week (FT-FFS 20). The survey instructions were explicit that practice time be recorded separately from time spent in teaching, research, administration, agency consultation, or other nonhealth services. Data were also aggregated within the FT-FFS 20 group of psychologists for those who were in practice thirty-one or more hours a week, on the average (FT-FFS 31), to learn whether discernible qualitative differences in practice go with such concentration on practice.

The existence of psychologists, or "clinical psychologists," in private practice in consequential numbers is a quite recent phenomenon (Dörken, 1977; see also Chapter One). Just what are these numbers? Of the 1980 licensed psychologist respondents, 34.3 percent were in full-time practice on an FT-FFS 20 basis, 18.4 percent on an FT-FFS 31 basis (leaving 15.9 percent in the twenty-to-thirty-hour range). Of the licensed psychologists in health care (80.5 percent of the respondents), the proportion in full-time private practice was 42.6 percent and the proportion in full-time private practice on an FT-FFS 31 basis 22.9 percent. In their 1981 report, VandenBos, Stapp, and Kilburg had found that of health service providers in psychology almost 19 percent were engaged primarily in private practice. Restricting the survey to licensed psychologists who were also health service providers, as here, resulted in a practice proportion more than double this size. In effect, then, by 1980, full-time private practice was well on the way to becoming *the* form of professional service delivery for psychologists engaged in health care. Now, what about their patients?

Patient Characteristics

Table 2-1 presents data on the demographics of the patients seen by the five categories of psychologists (that is, salaried and four increasing ranges of FFS involvement). The big differences are consistently between salaried psychologists and all categories of FFS. Salaried health service providers (HSPs) report higher percentages of male patients, single patients, younger patients, inner-city residents, patients who are students, and patients of low income than FFS providers. This pattern suggests that a sizable portion are working in organized care settings serving a somewhat higher proportion of adolescents (and slightly more likely to be located either in inner-city areas or in rural areas).

Of course, there were substantial differences among the three patients reported by some psychologists. However, when aggregated by the five categories of psychologists, the first-, second-, and third-reported patients were so similar that they were averaged in Tables 2-1 through 2-3 for ease of presentation.

While 89 percent of the cases of FFS practitioners were Caucasian, we see that in salaried settings about 25 percent of the cases were minorities, indicating that agencies and institutions are more likely to serve minorities than private practitioners.

The age of the patients of FFS psychologists is somewhat younger than might be expected, at a median age of 29 to 30 years and an interquartile range of 18–20 to 36–38 years, but the age ranges of patients of salaried psychologists were even lower. Thus, in the main, the psychologists were older than their patients, even though the median age of FFS psychologists was only 43 years (interquartile range 36.2 to 53.3), reflecting the relative youth of this health profession.

Only about 12 percent of the cases of FFS psychologists were inner-city or rural residents, but that level doubled for salaried psychologists. The impression is that salaried HSP psychologists are somewhat more likely to work in inner-city facilities (where private practices tend not to be located) or in rural areas (where most service delivery is occurring through community mental health centers, family and child guidance centers, and other organized care

Table 2-1. Patient Demographic Characteristics by Category of Provider.

Characteristic	FT-FFS 31	FT-FFS 20	PT-FFS	VPT-FFS	HSP salaried
			Provider Category		
N [a]	4,632	8,627	2,744	5,802	2,735
Sex					
Percentage male	49	45	44	47	58
Marital status					
Single	42%	43%	46%	48%	59%
Married	41	40	38	36	26
Sep./Div.	16	16	15	14	14
Widowed	1	1	1	1	1
Race					
White	90%	90%	88%	88%	75%
Black	5	5	7	7	17
Chicano	3	3	3	3	6
Other	2	2	2	1	2
Age (years)					
Quartile 1	17	22	21	18	15
Median	39	30	30	29	26
Quartile 2	36	37	37	37	35
Residence					
Urban	46%	47%	49%	44%	46%
Inner city	5	5	4	5	12
Suburban	43	42	42	43	29
Rural	7	6	6	9	12
Occupational status					
Professional	31%	32%	27%	24%	10%
White-collar	16	16	17	15	7
Blue-collar [b]	11	11	11	11	11
Homemaker	10	9	9	8	6
Student	23	23	24	29	39
Unemployed	6	6	5	6	13
Retired	1	1	1	1	2
Disabled	3	3	4	5	10
Income					
$0	4%	3%	4%	3%	8%
<10,000	12	11	14	16	35
10,000–14,999	12	13	14	15	19
15,000–19,999	15	16	17	17	14
20,000–34,999	34	33	32	34	18
35,000+	24	23	20	16	6
Percentage of charges paid by third party					
0	34%	36%	39%	42%	32%
1–40	11	11	9	6	2
41–80	37	35	33	25	10
81+	17	16	18	18	9
Salary, no fee	1	1	2	9	46

[a]The sum of all cases reported by all providers in each category. Thus, for FT-FFS 20, 8,627 is the sum of 2,888 + 2,877 + 2,862—the first, second, and third cases reported, respectively. The sum for all cases, all provider categories was 19,908.

[b]Farm/seasonal <1%.

systems rather than FFS practices). Among the VPT-FFS providers, there is a slight elevation in the percentage of providers located in rural settings, compared with the other FFS categories, a finding that we suspect reflects persons at academic locations in rural areas providing a very few FFS hours (and this possibility is supported by an elevation in the percentage of students they see).

A sharp contrast between salaried and FFS psychologists was evident in the occupational class of their cases. Only about 17 percent of the cases of salaried psychologists were either professional or white-collar, in contrast to almost half the cases of FT-FFSs. The salaried psychologists served a proportion of unemployed (13 percent) about twice that of their FFS colleagues; likewise, at 10 percent, of people who are disabled. But students, at 39 percent, were the largest occupational category seen by salaried HSPs, compared with 23 percent for FT-FFSs.

Not surprisingly, salaried psychologists saw a higher percentage of patients who do not personally and directly control their own economic destiny (children, students, unemployed, and so forth). From this fact, the differential income levels of the patients seen by FFS and salaried psychologists could be predicted. About 60 percent of the patients seen by salaried psychologists had incomes under $15,000 (or no income at all), in contrast to about 30 percent of the patients seen by FFS psychologists. Over half the cases of FFS psychologists had incomes of $20,000 or higher, while only one-fourth of the cases of salaried psychologists did.

Some 46 percent of the cases of salaried-only psychologists were seen on a salary (or "no fee") basis, although for almost 20 percent of their patients a third party did cover 41 percent or more of the "fee" (presumably paid to the organized care setting). However, almost no patients of FFS providers were seen on a "no fee" basis (except for those in VPT-FFS practice, where the proportion was 9 percent of those seen), whereas slightly over half of all FFS patients had 41 percent or more of their charges paid by third parties. However, the data also illustrate that mental health services are not well covered by most insurance plans. On the average, one of every three patients was paying for his or her psychological health care completely out of his or her own personal funds (only 17 percent of FFS psychologists had 81 percent or more of the costs of this care reimbursed).

Practice Aspects of Cases Seen

An active practice is based on many factors, most of them qualitative and not accessible by direct survey, such as competence and community reputation. Referral sources are more tangible. We begin to see some differences that are progressive according to the extent that one is involved in fee-for-service practice.

Former patients were the primary source of one-fourth of the patients seen by FT-FFSs, one-fifth for PT-FFSs, and one-seventh for VPT-FFSs (and only one-twentieth for salaried psychologists). The same trend, though not as distinctive, was found for physician referrals—accounting for one-sixth of referrals to FT-FFS 31 down to one-ninth for VPT-FFSs. Interestingly, referrals from physicians to FFS psychologists, with the exception of VPT-FFSs (who were like salaried psychologists in that respect), always equaled or exceeded the combined referrals from psychiatrists and social workers. Tyron (1983) also found a greater proportion of referrals from physicians than psychiatrists. Psychologists and physicians, of course, often enjoy a complementary role in patient care, whereas even though psychologists certainly collaborate with the other two mental health professions, a two-way perception of the other as competitor often exists as well.

As might be expected, psychologists in salaried positions received more referrals from schools, community or government agencies, and court systems (and, as noted above, decidedly fewer referrals from former patients) than FFS psychologists. These "public systems" accounted for 30 percent of referrals to salaried psychologists, compared with fewer than 16 percent of referrals to FFS providers. In addition, salaried psychologists were somewhat less likely to receive referrals from other psychologists than their FFS colleagues. Further detail is provided in Table 2-2.

The purpose of the referral in the majority of cases (somewhat over half for salaried psychologists, about three-fourths among FFS psychologists) was treatment. Referral for evaluation

Table 2-2. Referral Source, Purpose, and Treatment Plan by Category of Provider (N = 20,072).

Characteristic of Case	Provider Category				
	FT-FFS 31	FT-FFS 20	PT-FFS	VPT-FFS	HSP salaried
N^a	4,643	8,696	2,778	5,880	2,718
Referral source					
Self	15%	16%	20%	24%	24%
Former patient	23	24	20	15	6
Psychologist	11	14	16	15	7
Physician	17	15	13	11	14
Psychiatrist	9	8	7	8	9
Social worker	5	5	6	5	7
School, agency, court	15	14	14	19	30
Business, industry	1	1	1	1	1
Clergy	2	2	2	2	1
Purpose of referral					
Treatment	76	78	77	70	55
Evaluation	18	16	17	21	32
Consultation	4	4	4	5	8
Crisis intervention	2	2	2	3	5
Frequency of visits planned					
Daily	1	1	0	1	4
Several/week	14	13	10	5	11
Weekly	61	64	66	61	43
Biweekly	5	5	4	5	4
Monthly	0	0	0	1	1
Intermittent	5	5	5	6	13
Not again	13	12	14	20	23
Current plan/disposition					
Retain in treatment	74	74	72	61	56
Continue evaluation	10	10	10	9	14
Refer out	4	3	3	5	9
Case closed	8	9	12	20	14
Service not required	3	3	3	5	6

[a]The sum of all cases reported by all providers in each category. Thus, for FT-FFS 20, 8,696 is the sum of 2,914 + 2,896 + 2,886—the first, second, and third cases reported, respectively. The sum for all cases, all provider categories was 20,072.

accounted for one-third of the cases of salaried psychologists and one-sixth of the cases seen by FFSs (with the exception of VPT-FFSs, where it was one-fifth). Referrals for consultation and crisis intervention combined accounted for fewer than 7 percent of all referrals to FFSs (but 13 percent for salaried providers).

The majority of practitioners planned to see their patients weekly. This was over 60 percent of FFSs but only 43 percent for salaried providers. For a small proportion of cases, the plan was to see the patient several times a week. The latter proportion ranged from 5 percent for VPT-FFSs to 14 percent for the FT-FFS 31 category. FT-FFSs did not expect to see one-eighth of their cases again, and this proportion rose to one-fifth for VPT-FFSs (and almost one-fourth for salaried HSPs).

In a parallel manner, the majority of providers expected their new patients to remain in treatment for a while (range, 56 to 74 percent). Only 3 percent of FT-FFSs felt their services were not required, while 12 percent of FT-FFSs had closed their cases or referred them to another practitioner (although 25 percent of the cases of VPT-FFSs were closed or transferred). Stated otherwise, the more time psychologists spent in FFS practice, the less likely were their new cases to be reported as closed or as not requiring service (25 percent decreasing to 11 percent).

Thus, we see some distinct differences in referral patterns between salaried and FFS psychologists—not only in their referral sources but in the purpose of the referral and in their plans for service or disposition. Of course, the impending industrialization of health care (see Chapters Twelve and Thirteen) can be expected to change the patterns of referral seen here, probably dramatically, particularly where outreach and advertising are used and in settings having multidisciplinary professional partners and in practices based on network contracting. Moreover, the increasing market saturation by health conglomerates and other organized systems will progressively "soak up" the patient population able to make an open choice of provider.

History of Medical Care and Disability

Much rhetoric passes between psychologists and psychiatrists over the ultimate importance of mind or body (an artificial dualism in search of straw men—or women), which is about as useful as a debate over whether length or width contributes more to a surface-area measurement. Generally, psychologists are not as impressed with the medical competence of psychiatrists as psychiatrists themselves are (or, at least, as psychiatrists claim in policy debates).

Medical problems can, however, create or masquerade as psychological problems (see Hall and others, 1978; Taylor, 1982, for a cogent description of alerting cues). This is something that psychologists acknowledge. When an evaluation of such a potential is warranted, it appears that most psychologists are of the belief that the evaluation will be more thorough and more reliable when conducted by a physician who is still an active medical practitioner, such as a general-practice physician.

It is well known, of course, that many physical health complaints are somatizations of psychological concerns. And physical ailments can be aggravated by psychological problems, including high-risk life-styles. It has been estimated that 60 percent of visits to medical practitioners are for concerns that are mainly psychological or behavioral (Kelly, 1975). Even with physical conditions that are secondary to psychological distress, psychologists do not typically see the psychiatrist as most competent to deal with such concurrent medical conditions.

These interprofessional rivalries are more often manifested at the interorganization level (for example, in policy debates at the state or federal level) or within organizational structures (such as hospital hierarchies) than between individual practitioners personally concerned for patient care. The ultimate issue is "market monopoly" versus "consumer choice" (or, stated otherwise, control of "turf," or the economics of mental health care). The rivalry between clinical psychology and psychiatry is over power, control, and economic resources.

In policy debates, psychiatrists argue that patients will be harmed because psychologists *might* fail to diagnose or evaluate potentially fatal medical conditions. Yet, even though for years psychologists have carried professional liability insurance, no case has yet to be judged against a psychologist for failure to provide for needed medical intervention or collaboration with medical practitioners.

Because of this all too frequent controversy, it was of particular interest to learn something of the physical health problems of the patients seen by psychologists. The survey therefore sought data on these matters, as well as the patients' history of medical/mental health care and their history of medication use. Those data are given in Table 2-3.

There was no evidence of physical problems or illness in somewhat more than half the new cases seen by respondents. Accordingly, no medical consultation was sought in almost 30 percent of the cases. However, just over one-fifth of the FFS psychologists' patients were concurrently under medical care, in more than one-tenth of cases the FFS had received a report from the patient's physician, and in about 7 percent of cases he or she had obtained or planned to obtain medical consultation. In general, the majority of patients, like the majority of the general population, are healthy.

Among salaried psychologists, somewhat more (28 percent) of their patients were under concurrent medical care, and somewhat more of these psychologists (17 percent) had received a report from the patient's physician. This may simply have been inherent in their salaried situation—as noted earlier, a higher percentage of patients seen by psychologists in salaried settings are disabled individuals.

However, what these data show, and show quite clearly, is that psychologists provide services to a good many patients who are receiving, have received, or will receive medical attention. This finding argues strongly that psychologists do not practice in isolation and that psychologists are cognizant of the need for medical care when it is appropriate for their patients. Hofrichter (1980), surveying a random sample of Pennsylvania psychologists, reached the same conclusion. The large majority (72 percent) of psychologists in that survey reported using medical consultants. Further detail on the same survey is provided by Bascue and Zlotowski (1980).

Overall, about 30 percent of the patients reported on had received prior psychotherapy (whether from the same or different therapists is unknown). Almost one-fifth of patients seen by

Table 2-3. History of Medical Care and Disability Among Patients by Category of Provider.

Aspect of History	Provider Category				
	FT-FFS 31 (N = 4,643)	FT-FFS 20 (N = 8,696)	PT-FFS (N = 2,778)	VPT-FFS (N = 5,880)	HSP salaried (N = 2,718)
Physical problems[a]					
No evidence of illness	56%	58%	60%	55%	49%
Under physician's care	22	20	21	20	28
Have physician's report	12	11	10	10	17
Have scheduled consultation with physician	7	7	7	6	8
No physician consultation being sought	29	31	30	29	24
History of[a]					
Alcohol abuse	9	9	8	8	15
Drug abuse	8	8	7	7	12
Prior psychotherapy	30	32	31	29	27
Prior organic treatment	5	5	4	6	11
Hospitalization for mental disorder	6	6	7	8	18
Legal system involved	14	12	12	12	17
Physical disability	13	13	13	13	19
Clients receiving in past month[a]					
Minor tranquilizer	10	10	9	8	9
Major tranquilizer	3	2	3	4	13
Antidepressant	6	5	4	4	6
Other prescription	6	6	8	7	11
No medications known	63	64	63	57	43

[a]Items do not add to 100% because all that applied were marked.

salaried psychologists had a history of hospitalization for mental disorder, 11 percent having received prior "organic" treatment (electroshock, psychoactive medication), while about one-fifth had a known physical disorder, disability, or illness. A history of alcohol abuse or drug abuse was more common among patients of salaried psychologists also. These proportions, particularly for prior hospitalization, were much lower among FFS patients, indicating a difference in the population served by these psychologists. It seems clear that these respondents were aware, in general, of the medical condition of their patients and the extent of prior treatment for various disorders. With the exception of prior psychotherapy, these indexes were all somewhat higher for salaried psychologists. That 30 percent of the patients of FFS psychologists had received prior psychotherapy may be indicative that some are benefiting from intermittent psychotherapy throughout the life cycle (Cummings and VandenBos, 1979).

Somewhat over 60 percent of the patients of FFS psychologists had not received any medication within the past month, although this was true for only 43 percent of the cases of salaried psychologists. About 24 percent of the cases of all FFS psychologists had received either minor or major tranquilizers, antidepressants, or other medication within the past month. Since items in this subsection never added to as much as 100 percent, it appears that patients were unlikely to be on more than one type of medication at a time. Again, the psychologists were generally well aware of the medication situation of their patients, and, obviously, this medication was concurrent with their psychological care in most cases. Moreover, the information provided was on the three most recent new cases seen prior to completing the survey. The proportion with medication unknown could be expected to decrease further with subsequent visits.

Demographic Characteristics of Psychologists

Relatively few licensed psychologists have only salaried professional work (see Table 2-4)—only 11 percent of all licensed psychologists who responded to our survey; 14 percent of those who were providing health services. This is consistent with the findings of VandenBos and Stapp (1983). For those in fee-for-service practice, the distribution of hours engaged in such FFS practice is bimodal. Forty-nine percent of FFS respondents are engaged in fee-for-service practice on a full-time (twenty or more hours) basis and 35 percent on a very-part-time (one to ten hours) basis. Only 16 percent of FFS respondents are in the ten-to-nineteen-hour range. This distribution suggests that psychologists either see themselves as fully "in private practice" or else see their FFS practice as only an incidental aspect of professional life (perhaps to round out a university or other salary).

Licensed psychologists are predominantly male, although there is some variation in relation to the extent of FFS practice. Seventy-five percent of those in FT-FFS 31 practice are male but only 65 percent of those in salaried positions. Nonetheless, there has been a quite significant gain in the number of female psychologists over the past decade (Stapp, Fulcher, and Wicherski, 1984). Minority representation among licensed psychologists has remained relatively stable during the past ten years, as reflected by the fact that only 4 percent of the present respondents were not Caucasian.

If there is any doubt that psychology is still a relatively young profession, look at its practitioners. Twenty-five percent of the respondents were under thirty-six years of age (thirty-eight years for those in full-time practice). Fully 75 percent of licensed psychologists have not even reached their midfifties, and the median age of respondents was in the low forties (for FT-FFS 31, forty-five years of age). This is a stable and consistent finding (see VandenBos, Stapp, and Kilburg, 1981; VandenBos and Stapp, 1983).

With the exception of salaried psychologists, 91 percent of licensed psychologists held their doctorate by 1980. With the adoption of a doctoral standard for independent practice licensure in all but four states (and the gradual phase-out of those "grandparented" with lesser degrees), the nondoctoral practitioner is well on the way to becoming another disappearing, though vocal, minority (Stapp, Tucker, and VandenBos, 1985). The progressively increasing surplus of fully trained practitioners will bring added resistance to the use of lesser-credentialed personnel.

Table 2-4. Demographic Characteristics of Licensed Psychologists as Health Service Providers by Category of Provider (N = 7,050).

Characteristic	Provider Category				
	FT-FFS 31	FT-FFS 20	PT-FFS	VPT-FFS	HSP salaried
N (Percentage of sample)	1,610 (22.8)	3,001 (42.6)	950 (13.5)	2,127 (30.2)	972 (13.8)
Sex					
Percentage male	75	70	67	70	65
Race					
White	96%	97%	96%	96%	95%
Black	1	1	2	2	1
Other	3	2	2	2	4
Age (years)					
Quartile 1	37	37	35	35	35
Median	45	44	42	41	43
Quartile 3	54	54	52	51	53
Education					
Hold doctorate	92%	92%	92%	90%	84%
Received highest degree in state	57	57	56	51	44
Received highest degree out of state	41	41	42	48	54
Received highest degree outside U.S.	2	2	2	1	2
Professional affiliations					
Member, APA	90%	89%	88%	84%	81%
Member, state psychol. assn.	71	67	56	49	47
Member, local psychol. assn.	62	58	48	45	37
In Nat'l Register	67	63	57	44	37
None of the above	3	3	4	6	9

	92	91	85	72	47
Carry malpractice insurance	92	91	85	72	47
Specialization					
Clinical/health/rehab					
Currently	90%	89%	83%	76%	73%
Trained as	65	64	60	54	60
Counseling/developmental					
Currently	7	7	9	13	12
Trained as	16	20	18	20	18
Practice setting					
Solo practice	64%	65%	61%	54%	13%
Informal group	20	19	14	10	3
Formal group	13	12	8	5	9
Community center	2	3	13	21	52
Inpatient health facility	1	2	5	10	23
Area population					
<50,000	8%	8%	9%	16%	18%
50,000–749,000	33	33	32	37	39
750,000+	59	59	58	46	43
Third-party coverage					
Percentage of patients with no insurance	4	3	6	17	19
Percentage of respondents reporting that >40% of charges paid by third-party	51	51	51	42	19
Percentage of pts. without public assistance	41	43	45	53	48
Percentage of respondents reporting that >70% of pts. receive no publ. assist.	10	8	13	12	14

Having a practice tends to reduce one's mobility. With greater involvement in practice it is somewhat less likely that one's final degree was awarded outside the state of current practice. By contrast, we see that the majority of salaried psychologists received their final degrees out of state. Few licensed psychologists (in contrast to psychiatrists) are foreign-trained—under 2 percent.

Within professional association membership, a hierarchy exists from national to state to local association membership, and within each level of membership there is a greater tendency to belong the more extensive one's practice. There is a gap between national (APA) and state psychological association membership, almost 20 percent for FT-FFS 31 and increasing to 35 percent for VPT-FFS. Thus, extent of membership, which perhaps reflects one's professional identity and professional needs, is found to be related to the extent of involvement in practice, suggesting that involvement in practice does bring with it some greater appreciation of professional values. However, the fact that only 59 percent of FFSs belong to their state psychological association is indicative of the extent to which psychologists have failed, as yet, to understand the necessity for political representation at the state level to expand the conditions of practice (see Chapter Ten). Although only 37 percent of respondents in salaried positions were listed in the *National Register,* this contrasts to 67 percent of those in FT-FFS 31 practice reflecting a recognition that register listing facilitates third-party reimbursement.

The large majority of respondents report that they carry professional liability insurance. However, only 47 percent of respondents in salaried positions report carrying such individual professional liability policies. The few individuals in full-time FFS practice without this coverage might well ask themselves whether it is a real economy to be "self-insured," as they are surely liable and are risking all their assets (unless their liability is limited to the assets of their professional corporation).

With the growing involvement of psychologists in health care, a higher proportion (some 83.5 percent of FFSs) now identify themselves as clinical, health, or rehabilitation psychologists than were trained in these specialties. This postdoctoral shift in "field of present identification" is quite substantial (also see VandenBos,

Stapp, and Kilburg, 1981). Thus, it appears that the realities of the marketplace, including third-party reimbursement, bring about some practitioner reorientation.

When one thinks of FFS practice, the tendency is to think of solo practitioners, and this is certainly the modal style, exceeding 60 percent for all FFS providers except VPT-FFSs. But by 1980 over 30 percent of FT-FFSs were engaged in group practice on a formal or informal basis (and 22 percent of PT-FFSs but only 15 percent of VPT-FFSs). This suggests that a number of serious practitioners have come to realize the inherent business advantages of group practice (see Chapter Eleven). The salaried psychologists were predominantly employed at community mental health centers or inpatient health facilities. With the rise of competitive and alternative organized systems, it appears that opportunities will now be expanding for formal group practice and salaried or contract positions in the private sector.

The majority of the practitioners provided their services in communities with a population of three-fourths million or greater, with the exception of VPT-FFSs and salaried psychologists. About one-sixth of those in the latter two categories were situated in locales with under 50,000 population, compared with only one-twelfth of FT-FFSs. The very large majority of full-time practitioners are drawn to the big city.

A major issue for FFS practitioners (more so than for most salaried psychologists) is access to third-party reimbursement. Leaving aside the VPT-FFSs, psychologists in FFS reported that fewer than 4 percent of their patients were without any health insurance coverage. In fact, a slight majority claimed that over 40 percent of their charges were paid by third-parties. The reverse was true for public assistance coverage; only about 10 percent claimed that 40 percent or more of their clients were carried by public programs, while over 40 percent of respondents held that none of their patients had public assistance support. Stated otherwise, it appears that many psychologists in active practice, if not the majority, are not involved as practitioners with such federal and state government programs as Medicaid, vocational rehabilitation, or social welfare.

Services Rendered by Licensed HSPs

The survey sought information on eleven procedures, and Table 2-5 shows, first, the proportion of practitioners who used each procedure to any extent and, then, the proportion of hours allocated to each.

As expected, nearly all psychologists in any FFS category provided individual psychotherapy, but only 86 percent of salaried health care provider psychologists did. Family therapy was the next most common procedure, substantially more common than group therapy and rendered by about 80 percent of psychologists, but with a clear gradation according to extent of FFS practice from 85 to 65 percent. The next most common procedure used to any extent by these practitioners was assessment, used by 84 percent of salaried psychologists but only 73 percent of FFS psychologists. In other words, 27 percent of FFS psychologists did no assessment.

Hypnosis, though long established, was used by fewer than one-third of the psychologists, while biofeedback, presaged as the hottest new development (with some research data to support its effectiveness for certain health problems), was used by fewer than 15 percent. It was even less commonly used than play therapy! About two-thirds of psychologists provided some clinical consultation, over half engaged some of the time in crisis intervention, and about one-quarter provided some forensic services. In general, the extent to which diversified services are provided varies directly with the extent of time in FFS practice.

In examining the proportion of hours devoted to these procedures, we see that only one, individual psychotherapy, involves a substantial proportion of available hours, about 38 percent for FFSs, only 27 percent for salaried psychologists. Not surprisingly, the less one is in practice, the greater the proportion of time in assessment, 21 percent for salaried psychologists. Clinical consultation is the only other function that engages at least 10 percent of service delivery time. The other eight procedures are, in general, used to a rather incidental degree.

Finally, let us look at the types of presenting disabilities of the patients served by these licensed psychologists. Virtually all psychologists saw patients with emotional, mental, or behavioral disorders, and this accounted for about 66 percent of the time of FFS psychologists, less for salaried psychologists. Both in the proportion of psychologists serving some patients and in the proportion of hours rendered, more service was provided to substance abusers (drug/alcohol) than to the developmentally disabled/retarded. But substance abuse accounted for less than 12 percent of psychologists' time and mental retardation/developmental disability for only slightly over 9 percent. Moving from the more traditional mental health services to health care, we see that only about 16 percent of service time was directed to the psychological aspects of illness, disease, accident, or injury—these areas of as yet underdeveloped service potential are vastly greater than the mental health area.

Discussion

In her survey of a sample of psychologists listed in the *National Register of Health Service Providers in Psychology* who were engaged exclusively in private practice, Tyron (1983) found that a substantial majority (69 percent) reported that their practices had increased over the past five years. She went on to speculate whether a saturation in the private-practice market might not be ahead (see Part Three). She also noted that newer practices were being located in the Sunbelt areas, where practitioners charged higher fees, a trend that can only aggravate the "cost crunch" in health care.

Taube, Burns, and Kessler (1984) have reported on the 1980 National Medical Care Utilization and Expenditure Survey (NMCUES), a household sample. Of the population sampled, 715 (4 percent) had seen a psychiatrist or psychologist or otherwise had a "mental health" visit during the year; 180 had received over half their care from an office-based psychiatrist and 169 from an office-based psychologist. Taube and associates note the major growth within both professions, although the growth of psychologists in organized settings was threefold between 1968 and 1978. Psychologists and psychiatrists each accounted for one-third of the ambulatory mental health visits. Such comparability is striking, considering that, because of differences in insurance recognition,

Table 2-5. Services Rendered and Conditions Treated by Licensed Psychologists in Health Care by Category of Provider.

Service or Condition	Provider Category				
	FT-FFS 31 (N = 1,610)	FT-FFS 20 (N = 3,001)	PT-FFS (N = 950)	VPT-FFS (N = 2,127)	HSP salaried (N = 972)
Percentage providing some:					
Individual psychotherapy	98	98	97	92	86
Crisis intervention	60	56	55	50	64
Group therapy	52	46	42	40	49
Family therapy	85	84	79	65	59
Play therapy	37	36	31	19	21
Behavior therapy	39	37	38	36	40
Biofeedback	18	15	10	10	10
Hypnosis	37	34	30	18	14
Assessment	76	73	73	72	84
Clinical consultation	70	67	68	66	79
Forensic consultation	39	33	22	20	26
Percentage of Total Hours per Week Spent in:					
Individual psychotherapy	44	45	36	30	27
Crisis intervention	5	5	5	7	8
Group therapy	6	4	6	7	7

Family therapy	9	10	9	9	8
Play therapy	3	4	3	3	3
Behavior therapy	5	5	5	7	6
Biofeedback	2	2	1	1	1
Hypnosis	4	4	4	3	0
Assessment	12	12	17	18	21
Clinical consultation	6	7	10	12	13
Forensic consultation	3	3	3	3	4

Percentage Serving Some Clients Having Primarily:

Illness/disease	63	58	48	39	46
Injury/accident	52	46	36	26	29
Alcohol/drug abuse	74	66	55	47	58
Mental retardation/dev. disabil.	52	48	43	41	49
Mental/behavioral disorders	99	99	99	96	94

Percentage of Total Hours per Week Spent with:

Illness/disease	9	9	10	10	10
Injury/accident	6	6	6	6	6
Alcohol/drug abuse	10	10	11	13	14
Mental retardation/dev. disabil.	7	7	9	11	13
Mental/behavioral disorders	68	68	64	61	57

psychiatrists' patients paid an annual average of $113 out of pocket, compared with $216 for psychologists.

The Taube, Burns, and Kessler article differs from the present report in most respects and comparisons are difficult. About 60 percent of the NMCUES patients were female, a somewhat higher proportion than in the present study, where psychologists' patients appeared even younger and, perhaps as a consequence, had lower incomes. The objectives of the two studies were, of course, different: to study mental health care within total health care in a representative sample of the U.S. household population (the 4 percent utilization rate should be noted) and to obtain data on psychologists and their patients. Both studies present new, if not really comparable, information. Notable in the present study is the extent to which psychologists are providing services to patients who are or have been under medical care and the extent to which psychology has become a practice-oriented profession.

References

Barton, J., and others. "Characteristics of Respondents and Non-Respondents to a Mailed Questionnaire." *American Journal of Public Health*, 1980, *70*, 823–825.

Bascue, L., and Zlotowski, M. "Psychologists' Practices Related to Medication." *Journal of Clinical Psychology*, 1980, *36*, 821–825.

Cummings, N. A., and VandenBos, G. R. "The General Practice of Psychology." *Professional Psychology*, 1979, *10*, 430–440.

Dörken, H. "The Practicing Psychologist: A Growing Force in Private Sector Health Care Delivery." *Professional Psychology*, 1977, *8*, 269–274.

Dörken, H., and Webb, J. T. "Licensed Psychologists in Health Care: A Survey of Their Practices." In C. Kiesler, N. Cummings, and G. R. VandenBos (eds.), *Psychology and National Health Insurance: A Sourcebook*. Washington, D.C.: American Psychological Association, 1979.

Dörken, H., and Webb, J. T. "Licensed Psychologists on the Increase: 1974–1979." *American Psychologist*, 1981, *36*, 1419–1426.

Dörken, H., Webb, J. T., and Zaro, J. S. "Hospital Practice of Psychology Resurveyed: 1980." *Professional Psychology*, 1982, *13*, 814–830.

Hall, R., and others. "Physical Illness Presenting as Psychiatric Disease." *Archives of General Psychiatry*, 1978, *35*, 1315–1320.

Hofrichter, D. "Psychologists and Medical Issues." *Pennsylvania Psychologist*, Jan.–Feb. 1980, p. 5.

Kelly, A. Testimony representing the American Medical Association before the Subcommittee on Health, House Committee on Ways and Means, November 1975.

Stapp, J., Fulcher, R., and Wicherski, M. "The Employment of 1981 and 1982 Doctorate Recipients in Psychology." *American Psychologist*, 1984, *39*, 1408–1423.

Stapp, J., Tucker, A., and VandenBos, G. R. "Census of Psychological Personnel: 1983." *American Psychologist*, 1985, *40*, 1317–1351.

Taube, C. A., Burns, B., and Kessler, L. "Patients of Psychiatrists and Psychologists in Office-Based Practice: 1980." *American Psychologist*, 1984, *39*, 1435–1447.

Taylor, R. *Mind or Body: Distinguishing Psychological from Organic.* New York: McGraw-Hill, 1982.

Tyron, G. "Full Time Private Practice in the United States: Results of a National Survey." *Professional Psychology*, 1983, *14*, 685–696.

VandenBos, G. R., and Stapp, J. "Service Providers in Psychology: Results of the 1982 APA Human Resources Survey." *American Psychologist*, 1983, *38*, 1330–1352.

VandenBos, G. R., Stapp, J., and Kilburg, R. "Health Service Providers in Psychology: Results of the 1978 APA Human Resources Survey." *American Psychologist*, 1981, *36*, 1395–1418.

Herbert Dörken
Jack G. Wiggins

3

Trends in Third-Party Reimbursement: How Carriers Differ

Recent Developments in State and Federal Law

Since a mid-1977 survey reporting on 1976 third-party reimbursement experience (Dörken and Webb, 1980), ten additional states (New Mexico, Pennsylvania, Nevada, Georgia, Missouri, Alabama, Florida, Arizona, Wyoming, and Indiana, in that order) have passed direct recognition legislation, bringing to thirty-nine plus the District of Columbia the number of states where the public is assured access to a licensed psychologist for covered benefits under group health insurance plans. West Virginia's mandatory mental health law, having the same freedom of choice (FOC) effect, is included in the tally; and late in 1981 the District of Columbia approved new legislation, supplanting prior law with major loopholes, to assure direct recognition of psychological services in all group disability insurance. In Hawaii recognition was based on agreement under that state's Prepaid Health Care Act (Chapter 393, Hawaii Revised statutes [H.R.S.], 1974), which is a universal coverage law (all employed persons and dependents must be covered)—the only state law of its kind in the country. However, separate FOC legislation was enacted in 1984. Thus, the principle of patient FOC of psychologist practitioner now extends by law to

This survey was made possible by grant MH-26852 from the National Institute of Mental Health to the senior author.

44

about 92 percent of the national population. The chronology of this progress is detailed in Chapter One, including the fact that the recognition is incomplete in the District of Columbia, Colorado, Montana, and Nevada inasmuch as Blue Shield (health care service) plans are not covered. In eight states the recognition extends to policies written out of state and in four to worker's compensation also (Montana, California, Ohio, Hawaii). It extends to federal employees as well under P.L. 93-416.

The intervening years since the 1977 survey, however, have brought no new federal law with major positive effect on third-party reimbursement to psychologists (but see Chapter Five). To the contrary, the Employee Retirement Income Security Act (ERISA, P.L. 93-406), which had been widely interpreted to preempt state insurance laws relative to employee welfare benefit plans, led to a progressive undercutting of state FOC laws, particularly among the increasing number of major employers that elected to become self-insureds. This was clarified in the 8-0 Supreme Court decisions Nos. 84-325 and 84-356, handed down on June 3, 1985, in *Metropolitan Life Insurance Co.* v. *Massachusetts* and *Travelers Insurance Co.* v. *Massachusetts*. These decisions upheld the Massachusetts law mandating minimum mental health benefits in all health insurance applying to state residents unless employers were strictly self-insured. These minimum benefit laws were also held to be independent of the collective bargaining process and therefore not preempted by the National Labor Relations Act either. State statutes mandating particular types of providers were seen as a law "which regulates insurance" and thereby are not preempted either. "Parties to a collective bargaining agreement providing for health insurance are forced to make a choice: either they must purchase the mandated benefit, decide not to provide health coverage at all, or decide to become self-insured, assuming they are in a financial position to make that choice."

Law is one thing, compliance another. The progression of IPA-type (individual practice association) health maintenance organizations, recognized under P.L. 93-222, the Health Mainte-nance Act, as physician fee-for-service practice entities, rarely, if ever, have psychologists as members. Some do not even refer to psychologists, despite state FOC laws. In states where the law is clear, this impasse will have to be resolved in the courts.

Practitioner Growth

Growth in the number of psychologist practitioners per se has been a major factor in forcing improved third-party reimbursement. A ten-state survey of licensed psychologists in the late spring of 1980 (Dörken and Webb, 1981), based on directories of 1979, found an unduplicated total of 15,334 psychologists, a 42.2 percent increase over 1974 (or 8.4 percent a year). From 1976 to 1979 the number of licensed psychologists grew at an annual rate approaching 9 percent (26.8 percent total—Dörken and Webb, 1981), so that by 1985 those survey findings were understated by the growth of the intervening six years. According to the data of the *National Register of Health Service Providers in Psychology*, December 1976, the growth between that time and mid-1985 was 106.2 percent in California, 67.2 percent in New York, 78.4 percent in Illinois, and 60 percent in Pennsylvania—almost 78 percent among these four states averaged. The licensees of these four states made up 39.3 percent of the national total in December 1976. Projecting nationally the total of licensed psychologists, eight and one-quarter years later (in March, 1985) had reached 45,369 (17,830 ÷ .393). Note that by actual tally, conducted in August 1985, the total count was 45,683 (Chapter One), illustrating the representativeness of the ten-state sample.

As detailed in Table 3-1, 8,762 (57.1 percent) of the known licensees returned usable responses to the 1980 survey. This was a 49.4 percent increase in respondents over 1977. Of these respondents, 6,659 (76 percent) were health service providers (HSPs), of whom 6,078 (69.4 percent) were engaged in some fee-for-service (FFS) practice, in contrast to 59.6 percent three years prior. Stated otherwise, 91 percent of HSPs are FFSs. The overall higher response rate, coupled with an increase in the proportion of psychologists who are FFS, resulted in a 74 percent increase in the number of FFS respondents. Returning to the national picture, all indications are that the proportion of licensed psychologists engaged in health care today is at least as large as in 1980. If so, then there are about 34,480

Table 3-1. Licensed Psychologists and Fee-for-Service
Respondents in Ten States, 1977 and 1980.

Finding	1977	1980	Three-Year Percentage Increase
No. licensed psychologists	12,095	15,334	26.8
No. respondents	5,865	8,762	49.4
Respondents as percentage of licensees	48.5	57.1	—
No. in fee-for-service (FFS) practice	3,494	6,078	74.0
FFSs as percentage of respondents	59.6	69.4	—

licensed HSP psychologists and about 31,500 involved in FFS
practice. The growth in the number of psychologist practitioners
has been dramatic over the past decade. Indeed, Taube, Kessler, and
Feuerberg (1984), reporting on the 1980 National Medical Care
Utilization and Expenditure Survey of ambulatory mental health
care, found that 23.5 percent of the 9.6 million people receiving
such care were seen primarily by office-based psychologists, 24.5
percent by office-based psychiatrists, 17.2 percent by physicians, and
11.6 percent by social workers, while "11.9 percent were seen in
organized settings"—fewer than one-eighth of persons seen for *all*
ambulatory mental health care. Thus, the account of third-party
reimbursement reported here presents detail on an aspect of care
that those authors found to represent nearly one-fourth of all
ambulatory mental health care in 1980.

This account of third-party reimbursement is based on the
reported experience of FFS psychologists in the ten states surveyed
in 1979. The demographic and other characteristics of these
practitioners and their patients are described in Chapter Two. It
suffices to note here that the number of licensed psychologists had
increased from 12,153 to 15,334 between July 1976 and July 1979.
Further detail is presented in Table 3-2. Again, it appears that
FOC legislation may be a factor in increasing the ratio of licensed
psychologists to population, since the states with no or limited FOC

Table 3-2. Ratio of Licensed Psychologists to Population by State, 1979.

Variable	State								Total, 10 States
	N.Y.	D.C. area	S.C./ Ala./R.I.	Fla.	Ohio	Ill.	Tex.	Calif.	
No. licensed psychologists	3,956	759	506	648	2,260	1,686	1,158	4,361	15,334
Population (in millions), July 1979	17,648	10,001	7,620	8,860	10,731	11,229	13,380	22,694	101,224
No. psychologists/10,000 pop.	2.24	0.76[a]	0.66	0.73	2.11	1.50	0.87	1.92	1.51
Date of FOC law	1969	Some[b]	None[c]	1982[c]	1974	1976	1977	1969/74	—

[a]1.57 for D.C. only.
[b]Federal employees in 1974, individual policies in 1976, full FOC in 1982.
[c]Alabama's and Florida's laws, passed in 1982, postdated the survey.

law had the lowest ratios (the District of Columbia, because of
federal law and its federal employees, is a special exception), while
the two states whose laws were passed around the time of our first
survey (Illinois, Texas) had an intermediate level and those whose
laws preceded the first survey had the highest ratios (see also
Dörken and Webb, 1980).

Reimbursement Experience

The reimbursement experience of 1979 tended to follow the
pattern of 1976, with a similar proportion of visits by carrier. Thus,
the increase in billings is more quantitative than due to a major
shift in billing patterns. The proportion of visits billed to
commercial carriers did increase from 42.5 to 46.1 percent; however,
this may be a consequence of requesting more diverse information
(on seven major carriers instead of five) rather than a greater
concentration by practitioners on billing to commercial carriers. It
should also be noted that the report on the prior survey was based
on full-time practitioners, not all FFS psychologists as detailed here
in Table 3-3. This table provides detail, by carrier, on the number
of billing psychologists, the number of visits billed, the average
number of visits per billing psychologist, the proportion of visits
billed to a particular carrier of all visits billed, and the proportion
of FFSs reporting satisfactory claims experience.

The increase in the volume of billed visits reported (from .6
to 1.6 million) was not due simply to an increase in the number of
FFS psychologists, although this certainly was a factor, but also to
an increase in the level of billing by psychologists, from an average
of 166 to 270 visits billed by each practitioner—a 63 percent increase
in volume in three years. The increase in visits billed to Blue
Shield/Cross (Blues) essentially followed this pattern, while the
extent of billing to the CHAMPUS grew at a slower rate (36 percent)
and that to the rapidly growing individual practice associations
(IPAs, a type of HMO) stayed constant although the number of
practitioners billing an IPA roughly doubled. The net result is that
all IPAs accounted for fewer than 2 percent of all visits billed by
psychologists, reflecting their medical proprietary interests.

Table 3-3. Third-Party Billing and Reimbursement Experience by
Carrier, Fee-for-Service Psychologists in Ten States, 1976 and 1979.

Carrier	No. psychologists billing	No. visits (in 1,000s)	Avg. no. vists per billing psychologist	Percentage of total visits	Percentage paid regularly/ often
	1976 (N = 3,494)				
Medicare	355	8.7	25	1.5	42
Medicaid	670	44.4	66	7.7	62
Social welfare, voc. rehab.	952	60.4	63	10.4	84
CHAMPUS	1,066	52.8	50	9.1	82
Worker's compensation	364	9.3	26	1.6	79
Blue Shield/Cross	1,839	142.3	77	24.6	68
FMC/IPAs	240	14.6	61	2.5	85
Aetna	1,408	51.8	37	9.0	87
Travelers	1,055	39.6	38	6.8	85
Metropolitan	1,025	43.5	42	7.5	84
Prudential	1,184	48.3	41	8.4	91
Equitable					
Connecticut General					
Occidental	526	15.3	29	2.6	90
All other health insurers	643	47.4	74	8.2	85
Total	3,494	578.4	166	99.9	—
	1979 (N = 6,078)				
Medicare	813	34.2	42	2.1	45
Medicaid	1,041	107.5	103	6.6	59
Social welfare,	1,057	79.0	75	4.8	69
voc. rehab.	1,100	65.1	59	4.0	94
CHAMPUS	1,660	113.6	68	6.9	75
Worker's compensation	757	30.2	40	1.8	81
Blue Shield/Cross	3,410	420.7	123	25.7	73
FMC/IPAs	474	29.3	62	1.8	85
Aetna	2,473	113.7	46	6.9	89
Travelers	2,029	79.2	39	4.8	88
Metropolitan	1,878	89.0	47	5.4	88
Prudential	2,360	113.6	48	6.9	91
Equitable	1,603	56.7	35	3.5	92
Connecticut General	1,423	55.6	39	3.4	90
Occidental	872	24.4	28	1.5	91
All other health insurers	2,957	224.6	76	13.7	86
Total	6,078	1,636.4	270	99.8	—

As before, it is apparent that the variation among practition-ers in carriers billed must be very substantial, even though some FFS psychologists gave no or an incomplete account of their billings. For example, only 56 percent of FFS psychologists reported any billing to the Blues in 1979, the highest proportion to any carrier. And if the average visits by carrier per billing psychologist were totaled, they would reach 930, rather than the average of 270 for all FFSs. This shows that individual practitioners concentrate their billings among different groups of carriers, no doubt reflecting the type of coverage widely available in a state rather than simply the extent of practice.

When viewed state by state, the data show some notable interstate differences (Table 3-4). We see that the proportion of visits billed to Medicaid was highest in New York (except New York City), Ohio, and California, where psychologists were recognized under the state Medicaid plan. In South Carolina, Alabama, and Florida, where there was no FOC law, psychologists were more dependent on recognition under federal law—hence the higher proportion of billings in these states to vocational rehabilitation, the CHAMPUS, and worker's compensation (P.L. 93-416, FECA), while, conversely, their billings to the Blues were at the lowest levels among the states. In Ohio Metropolitan has a bigger share of the market than Prudential because of its major accounts in the steel industry; the result is evident in Table 3-4. The Foundations for Medical Care (FMC) began their IPAs in California, and Occidental Life is headquartered in that state. Thus, it is not surprising that billings to these third parties, though a small proportion of all billings, were highest there. The dependency of D.C. psychologists on the Federal Employee Health Benefit Plan is apparent from their relatively high proportion of billing to the Blues and Aetna, particularly the Blues, perhaps because of their first dollar coverage.

As a percentage of all respondents, FFSs are highest in New York (80 percent), lowest in Ohio (54 percent). The volume of billing by psychologists also varies among the states, though not in the same order, being highest in the District of Columbia and least in South Carolina/Alabama, a range of 440 to 122 visits billed per FFS, on the average, by state. The value to practitioners of third-

Table 3-4. Percentage of Visits per Carrier and Value of Visits by State, Fee-for-Service Psychologists, 1979.

Carrier	State								Total, 10 States[a]	
	N.Y.	D.C. area	S.C./Ala.	Fla.	Ohio	Ill.	Tex.	Calif.	FFS	FT-FFS 20[b]
Medicare	1.2	0.4	2.5	2.3	1.4	0.7	1.7	3.4	2.1	1.8
Medicaid	8.4	1.9	1.2	0.7	7.3	0.7	1.0	9.5	6.6	6.1
Soc. welfare	1.9	0.5	5.7	3.8	5.3	1.7	1.6	8.8	4.8	4.3
Voc. rehab.	1.9	1.3	22.6	14.5	8.7	8.2	6.0	1.4	4.0	3.8
CHAMPUS	1.7	7.1	25.6	17.7	1.7	2.3	11.0	9.4	6.9	7.4
Worker's comp.	0.8	0.6	4.1	4.4	1.1	1.7	3.8	2.1	1.8	2.0
FMC/IPAs	0.5	0.1	2.7	0.3	0.2	1.4	1.1	3.8	1.8	2.0
Blue Shield/Cross	17.9	54.6	12.7	10.2	40.4	34.5	24.0	19.3	25.7	25.4
Aetna	8.4	9.3	4.1	8.2	6.7	7.2	9.0	5.4	6.9	7.2
Travelers	7.0	3.5	2.1	5.2	3.6	6.2	6.5	4.4	4.8	5.0
Metropolitan	9.0	1.3	2.8	4.3	7.5	4.2	6.9	3.3	5.4	5.3
Prudential	10.4	4.9	2.6	5.3	3.2	10.0	7.6	6.4	6.9	7.2
Equitable	5.6	2.3	1.9	2.9	2.0	3.7	2.9	3.2	3.5	3.6
Conn. General	4.7	3.0	0.9	5.7	2.3	2.3	3.6	3.2	3.4	3.6
Occidental	0.3	0.4	0.4	0.9	0.6	0.9	1.4	3.9	1.5	1.6
All other health insurers	20.2	8.7	8.2	13.6	8.1	14.4	12.0	12.4	13.7	13.6
Total visits billed (in 1,000s)	369.4	138.7	18.1	53.8	192.2	115.3	112.9	615.3	1,636.4	1,287.5
No. FFSs	1,743	315	149	257	695	597	483	1,791	6,078	3,001
FFSs as percentage of respondents	80.0	70.3	69.6	68.9	54.0	61.6	69.6	70.8	69.4	34.3
Avg. visits billed/FFS	212	440	122	209	276	193	234	343	270	429
Median fee ($)	39.90	44.95	40.23	45.46	40.33	40.06	49.64	45.29	40.47	45.11
Avg. value/FFS ($)	8,456	19,778	4,908	9,501	11,131	7,732	11,616	15,534	10,927	19,352

[a]Rhode Island is included in 10-state totals but is not listed separately since the 47 FFS respondents were <1% of all FFS.
[b]Psychologists in full-time FFS practice, defined as 20 or more hours a week.

party reimbursement is a function of three factors: the extent to which they are engaged in FFS practice, the number of such visits billed to a third party, and the fee charged. In 1979 the median "hourly" psychotherapy fee charged by FFS practitioners ranged from a low of $39.90 in New York (perhaps because that state had the highest proportion of FFSs) to a high of $49.64 in Texas, a difference of almost $10, or 25 percent. As a consequence of these variations, the average value of visits billed by FFS practitioners differed substantially among states, ranging from nearly $20,000 in the District of Columbia to less than $5,000 in South Carolina/ Alabama. Incidentally, although practicing psychologists deliver a range of services, the single most predominant procedure by far (81 percent of all outpatient procedures under the CHAMPUS) is the psychotherapy hour. Consequently, the fee for this procedure was used as the benchmark for projecting revenue from all visits.

When those in full-time FFS practice (defined as twenty or more hours weekly, designated FT-FFS 20) are compared with those in practice some of the time (FFS) for the ten states combined, it is apparent that the average value of third-party billings is almost twice as high for the former ($19,352 in contrast to $10,927). The FT-FFS 20 group made up slightly more than a third (34.3 percent) of all respondents. Notable, however, is the high similarity between all FFSs and the subgroup in full-time practice in terms of the proportion of visits they bill to a particular carrier. This detail, also shown in Table 3-4, suggests that, on the average, the difference in billings between a full-time and a some-time practice is one of extent rather than kind. A difference of 0.5 percent was found in only three programs: fewer billings by FT-FFSs to Medicaid and social welfare, more to CHAMPUS.

The claims experience of psychologists varies substantially by type of carrier and by state, as shown in Table 3-5, but not between full-time and some-time practice. This suggests that there is a substantial consistency by carrier in the handling of psychologists' claims and that the variance is due to state law or, in the case of some federal programs, to different fiscal intermediaries. When the claims experience of those in very part-time practice (VPT, ten or fewer hours weekly), part-time practice (PT, eleven to

Table 3-5. Practitioner Claim Experience by State and Carrier: Percentage of Fee-for-Service Psychologists Reporting Their Claims as Paid Regularly or Often, 1979.

Carrier	State								Total, 10 States	FT-FFS 20
	N.Y.	D.C. area	S.C./Ala.	Fla.	Ohio	Ill.	Tex.	Calif.		
Medicare	58	a	a	a	a	a	a	49	45	41
Medicaid	75	a	a	a	59	a	a	58	59	57
Soc. welfare	79	a	a	a	62	a	a	70	69	69
Voc. rehab.	98	a	a	94	94	94	97	88	94	93
CHAMPUS	77	75	a	66	59	a	62	82	75	74
Worker's comp.	a	a	a	a	a	a	a	87	81	80
FMC/IPAs	a	a	a	a	a	a	a	86	85	85
Blue Shield/Cross	75	86	a	41	74	76	65	76	73	72
Aetna	93	87	a	80	84	91	86	91	89	89
Travelers	95	a	a	a	83	85	86	88	88	88
Metropolitan	93	a	a	a	76	82	88	91	88	89
Prudential	96	88	a	a	85	87	87	92	91	91
Equitable	97	a	a	a	83	95	89	93	92	92
Conn. General	93	a	a	a	78	a	86	92	90	89
Occidental	a	a	a	a	a	a	a	92	91	90
All other insurers	94	89	a	a	83	82	77	88	86	86

Note: Rhode Island, one of the 10 CHAMPUS reporting states before 1980 and one of the survey states, had only 47 FFS respondents and was therefore not separately tabulated but was included in the total.

aN = <100 practitioners for regularly/often paid plus often/regularly questioned.

nineteen hours weekly), and full-time practice (FT, whether defined as twenty or more hours weekly or as thirty-one or more hours weekly) was compared for all major carriers, no variation of consequence among these categories of practitioners was found. With some minor exceptions, such as Metropolitan and Connecticut General in Ohio, FFS psychologists reported that their claims were regularly or often paid (as distinct from being often or regularly questioned) at a quite consistently high level by the commercial carriers. With the exception of the District of Columbia, no doubt because of the federal employees' plan, claims satisfaction with the Blues was always at a lower level, and it dropped appreciably in Florida, where there was no FOC law at the time. The positive claims experience with vocational rehabilitation (though accounting for only 4 percent of all visits billed) for these state-federal programs was generally the best in any state, undoubtedly because authorization is required before services can be rendered and billed to the state agency administering this program.

The federal CHAMPUS program, probably because it uses five different fiscal intermediaries for these ten states, showed a range in satisfactory claims experience from 82 percent in California (Blue Shield of California) to 59 percent in Ohio (Mutual of Omaha). Overall, claims experience was worst with Medicare, while Medicaid was the second least satisfactory. Some beneficiaries of all three of these government programs may have outside coverage. Employed dependents of active-duty military personnel having private insurance coverage must coordinate benefits—that is, use the CHAMPUS to back up what is missing in their other coverage. Of course, "Medigap" insurance is widely available to assure coverage that is more comprehensive than that available under Part B of Medicare. Similarly, Medicaid eligibles may have some other health-plan coverage through a family member. States are beginning to mandate coordination of benefits by law. In Hawaii, for example, the recovery through coordination came to $4.7 million in fiscal year 1982, derived from a Medicaid population of 87,903, or 8.5 percent of the state's population.

In a state with an FOC law and a policy providing for some outpatient mental health services, psychological services would be recognized for these "Medigap" Medicare patients. This "double coverage" would have the effect of somewhat decreasing utilization under the CHAMPUS and Medicaid, since it would show these services not as allocated to the federal program but to the particular third party. Nonetheless, it illustrates the tie-in that can occur operationally between federal and state laws for the user.

Turning to the value of the visits billed, as reported in Table 3-6, we see not only an increase in such visits from 1976 to 1979 but an increase with increasing extent of practice, as would be expected. The median therapy fee (derived from the usual fee of each respondent for a psychotherapy hour) also rose over these three years, though only 15 percent, and it was higher according to extent of practice, being $39.92 for VPTs in 1979 and $45.26 for FT-FFS 31. There is not only an appreciable increase in third-party billing relative to gross professional income over the three years, from 17.9 to 29.1 percent, but a quite dramatic climb in the proportion of income to be derived from third parties as FFS practice increases. For those in VPT practice, third-party billings accounted for only 9 percent of gross income, whereas for those in FT practice at the higher level (thirty-one or more hours weekly), such billings accounted for just over half of gross income.

To give some indication of the income potential of a major third party to psychologist practitioners, in Table 3-7 we show the visits billed and their value by extent of FFS practice for Medicaid, CHAMPUS, the Blues, Aetna, Prudential, and "all other insurers," these being the six carriers with the largest volume of visits billed by all FFS psychologists. Note that the proportion of visits billed to these six major carriers is consistently about two-thirds of all billings, regardless of the extent of practice, another indication that practice varies more by extent than by kind, at least so far as third parties are concerned.

When we look at the value of visits billed to major carriers by extent of practice, Table 3-7 shows that VPT-FFS + PT-FFS + FT-FFS 20 always somewhat exceeds all FFS. This artifact is due in part to rounding and in part to the increasing median fee by level of practice. In any event, it is clear that even for ten states the financial significance of these carriers to practitioners is very substantial. For example, the CHAMPUS, at $4.6 million, when

Table 3-6. Number and Dollar Value of Therapy Visits and Annual Value of Visits Billed to Third Parties Relative to Total Professional Income, 1976 and 1979.

Variable	1976 All FFS	1979 All FFS	1979 VPT-FFS (1–10 hrs/wk)	1979 PT-FFS (11–19 hrs/wk)	1979 FT-FFS (20+ hrs/wk)	1979 FT-FFS (31+ hrs/wk)
No. of respondents	3,494	6,078	2,126	951	3,001	1,610
Total no. of visits per year (in 1,000s)	578.4	1,638.4	154.3	173.4	1,287.5	858.9
Avg. no. of visits per year per psychologist	166	270	73	182	429	533
Median therapy fee	$35.11	$40.47	$39.92	$40.23	$45.11	$45.26
Total value of visits per psychologist	$5,828	$10,927	$2,914	$7,322	$19,352	$24,124
Median gross professional income	$32,595	$37,535	$32,487	$37,168	$46,052	$47,153
Third-party billings as a percentage of gross professional income	17.9	29.1	9.0	19.7	42.0	51.2

Table 3-7. Value of Visits Billed to Third Parties by Extent of Practice and by Carrier, 1979.

Practitioner Category	Carrier						Subtotal	Total Visits	Subtotal as Percentage of Total
	Medicaid	CHAMPUS	Blue Shield/Cross	Aetna	Prudential	All other insurers			
All FFS (N = 6,078)									
No. billing	1,041	1,160	3,410	2,473	2,360	2,957			67
No. visits (in 1,000s)	107.5	113.6	420.7	113.7	113.6	224.6	1,093.7	1,636.4	
Avg. visits/psy.	103	98	123	46	48	76		270	
Median fee								$40.47	
Value (in millions)	$4.4	$4.6	$17.0	$4.6	$4.6	$9.1			
VPT-FFS (N = 2,126)									
No. billing	252	283	874	441	358	709			65
No. visits (in 1,000s)	15.9	5.4	41.4	8.3	7.9	21.0	99.9	154.3	
Avg. visits/psy.	63	19	47	19	22	30		73	
Median fee								$39.92	
Value (in millions)	$0.6	$0.2	$1.7	$0.3	$0.3	$0.8			
PT-FFS (N = 951)									
No. billing	120	232	548	374	375	467			69
No. visits (in 1,000s)	12.1	8.0	50.6	11.1	11.4	25.9	119.1	173.4	
Avg. visits/psy.	101	34	92	30	30	55		182	
Median fee								$40.23	
Value (in millions)	$0.5	$0.3	$2.0	$0.4	$0.5	$1.0			
FT-FFS 20 (N = 3,001)									
No. billing	623	1,150	2,020	1,673	1,643	1,812			67
No. visits (in 1,000s)	78.4	95.0	327.5	92.7	92.7	175.2	861.5	1,287.5	
Avg. visits/psy.	126	83	162	55	56	97		429	
Median fee								$45.11	
Value (in millions)	$3.5	$4.3	$14.8	$4.2	$4.2	$7.9			
FT-FFS 31 (N = 1,610)									
No. billing	343	690	1,127	955	938	986			66
No. visits (in 1,000s)	52.1	61.4	215.7	63.4	61.3	110.3	564.2	858.9	
Avg. visits/psy.	152	89	191	66	65	112		533	
Median fee								$45.26	
Value (in millions)	$2.4	$2.8	$9.8	$2.9	$2.8	$5.0			

projected nationally represents a value of $9.7 million (4.6 ÷ .474) to psychologist practitioners, and this is underreported to the extent that respondents did not fully report their billing to this (or any other) program. If nonrespondents had billed to the same extent as respondents, then the program value would have been $17 million (9.7 ÷ .571). In fact, CHAMPUS paid $13.9 million to psychologists in 1980 ($17.2 million in 1981) for all mental health procedure visits (see Chapter Four). Thus, there was a very great economic benefit to the profession in gaining clear statutory recognition under this federal program—and in sustaining it. Dependents of military personnel plus retired military personnel and their dependents number about 6.2 million. The economic value of Medicaid, at $4.4 million, despite inclusion that ranges among the ten states from severely restricted to quite limited—all with varying utilization controls—is nonetheless substantial and indicative of what would be accessible with full recognition under all state laws. A small proportion of Medicaid beneficiaries also have other third-party coverage. In states with FOC laws but without Medicaid recognition for psychologists, these beneficiaries do, to this extent, have access to psychological services.

The Blues, at $17 million among respondents of these ten states, $35.9 million nationally, $62.8 million among all licensees (projected as in the CHAMPUS above), also make it very apparent that the contest for parity recognition of psychologists in health service plans across the country holds major fiscal incentives both for psychologists and for those who would restrict or exclude their practice.

The dollar value of direct consumer access in a state and equality of coverage between physical and mental disorder is very significant both in the aggregate and for individual practitioners. The umbrella of "all other insurers" contained an economic value of $9.1 million in the ten survey states ($19.2 and $33.6 million, projected as above), and this could be augmented with loophole-proof FOC laws including a statutory interlock among all FOC states, such as S.B. 693, Chapter 588 (1981). This law deems that psychologists providing services in California to patients covered by insurance issued in another FOC state shall have their services recognized. It is also probable that more systematic acquisition of provider status with a broader range of carriers would produce a further increase.

Not included in this billing among states to individual carriers is the extent of billing for psychological services through intermediaries. Among FFS psychologists we see in Table 3-8 that billing through/by another practitioner is more common in states without FOC legislation (South Carolina, Alabama, and Florida) and is done for 9–10 percent of psychologists there; overall, about 4 percent of psychologist practitioners use this method regardless of the extent to which they are involved in private practice. Similarly, as also detailed in Table 3-8, some psychologists without an established FT-FFS practice are more likely to bill through a facility (about 13 percent versus 7 percent). The extent of billing by those few who arrange/allow for this external billing resource is substantial, amounting to an average of $5,585 (138 × $40.47) for those FFSs who bill through another practitioner, $8,863 (219 × $40.47) for those who bill through a facility. Incidentally, it is probably illegal for facilities to employ psychologists on salary and then bill for their services (Dörken, 1979a; Attorney General of California, 1979).

Another consideration among FFS practitioners is the extent to which their patients have third-party health care coverage, private or public. This information is in Table 3-9. With the exception of South Carolina/Alabama and Florida, states without FOC laws, relatively few FFSs indicated that all their patients had some private health insurance coverage for their services. In other states, with the exception of the District of Columbia (probably because of the federal employees), somewhat over 40 percent of FFSs reported that 41 percent or more of their patients had private health insurance coverage.

As for public assistance, the large majority (63 percent) of D.C. psychologists had no patients with such coverage, whereas it was more common in Ohio and California, where psychologists are recognized under their state Medicaid plan. Again apart from Ohio and California, fewer than 10 percent of FFSs in a state reported that 41 percent of more of their patients had public assistance coverage. When full-time practitioners are contrasted to all FFSs, there is

Table 3-8. Extent of Intermediary Billing for Fee-for-Service Practitioners by State and by Extent of Practice, 1979.

Type of Intermediary Billing	State								Practitioner Category				
	N.Y.	D.C. area	S.C./ Ala.	Fla.	Ohio	Ill.	Tex.	Calif.	FFS-VPT	FFS-PT	FFS-FT 20	FFS-FT 31	All FFS
Under other practitioner													
Percentage of respondents	1	3	10	9	3	6	6	3	3	5	4	4	4
Avg. no. visits each	96	111	97	128	163	134	131	176	84	144	167	168	138
Under health facility													
Percentage of respondents	11	15	12	8	11	9	10	10	13	14	8	7	11
Avg. no. visits each	171	208	257	166	180	177	232	243	220	209	197	192	219

Table 3-9. Extent to Which Patients of Fee-for-Service Psychologists Have Third-Party Coverage and Extent of Practice, 1979.

Type of Coverage	State								Total, 10 States	FT-FFS 20
	N.Y.	D.C. area	S.C./Ala.	Fla.	Ohio	Ill.	Tex.	Calif.		
Private insurance										
Percentage of respondents reporting that no pts. have ins.	6	3	17	12	8	10	9	7	8	3
Percentage of respondents reporting that 41+% of pts. have ins.	44	77	19	20	53	43	48	42	45	53
Public assistance										
Percentage of respondents reporting that no pts. have publ. assist.	58	63	30	35	27	50	42	26	41	39
Percentage of respondents reporting that 41+% of pts. have publ. assist.	6	3	9	9	15	8	7	15	10	8

little difference in the proportion of clients with public assistance but a larger proportion who have private insurance.

Discussion

Although 11 percent of the population has Medicare coverage, only 2.1 percent of billings were to that program, and they produced the least favorable claims experience; indeed, 87 percent of reporting psychologists billed no visits to Medicare (see Table 3-3). Since psychologists are recognized under this federal health insurance program only for assessment on medical referral, these findings reflect the statutory restrictions. Experience under state Medicaid programs, where psychological services can be included at state option but are often restricted, yielded the second least favorable experience. Although Medicaid accounted for 6.6 percent of all billings, only one-sixth of psychologists reported billing visits to these federally matched state programs. Substantial variation in level of psychological services (see Table 3-4) is related to the extent to which psychologists are recognized in the state plan under Title XIX of the Social Security Act. Even with recognition, Medicaid services are often highly regulated by utilization controls, depressed rates, referral or prior authorization conditions, low dollar limits, and so on. Nonetheless, despite a maximum fee of $27.80 in 1981 and a limit of two visits a month, California psychologists were paid $11.9 million from this program in that year. The 2,249 psychologists who provided MediCal (Medicaid) services earned an average of $5,288. Again, this illustrates the value for practitioners of being recognized in *all* potential practice markets. Not all practitioners will be involved in each market, but practice options and specialization potential are broadened.

Experience with commercial carriers (the insurance industry) was highly favorable: 86 to 92 percent of the respondents having experience with a particular carrier reported that they were regularly or often paid by that carrier. These carriers accounted for 46.1 percent of all visits billed. By contrast, Blue Cross/Blue Shield accounted for but 25.7 percent of visits billed, and only 73 percent of the psychologists reporting claims experience with the Blues found it to be favorable. Three years earlier 24.6 percent of psychologists' billed visits were billed to the Blues, 68 percent having favorable claims experience. Thus, little if any net progress has occurred over these three years with this carrier. It was the preeminent single insurer, however, and the lowest proportion of fee-for-service psychologists, 24 percent, reported no billings to the Blues (plus 20 percent who provided no information).

Of the 154.3 million persons in 1979 under age sixty-five with physicians' expense coverage under private programs, 59 percent had regular group health insurance, while 41 percent had Blue Cross, Blue Shield, or a medical society plan (*Sourcebook of Health Insurance Data,* n.d.). Within the ten survey states, 41,434 million, or 54 percent, had such coverage from insurance companies, while 35,646 million, or 46 percent, subscribed to the Blues. The proportions with commercial and with Blues coverage are closer to parity among the survey states than nationally. Thus, the much lower proportion of billings to the Blues relative to population covered is consistent with the claims experiences reported for 1976, as is the less satisfactory reimbursement experience. Again, it appears that some selective reduction in reimbursement of psychologist practitioners by Blue Shield plans and limitation of psychological services to Blue Shield members have occurred.

The federal CHAMPUS program, accounting for 6.9 percent of all billings, was lower proportionately than in 1976 (9.1 percent) and showed a somewhat less favorable claims experience. Vocational rehabilitation, when split out from social welfare, though only 4 percent of all billings, yielded claims experience that was highly favorable, no doubt owing to its prior authorization procedures and recognition under federal law (P.L. 93-112).

Worker's compensation continued to account for few claims (1.8 percent); indeed, only 12 percent of these FFS psychologists reported any such billings in 1979. The reason is likely that, of the survey states, psychologists are recognized only under worker's compensation by statute in California and under the state compensation fund in Ohio by negotiation (see also Dörken, 1979b). Coverage under worker's compensation has expanded in recent years, and health/rehabilitation benefits are substantial, not to mention the need for disability evaluation. The dollar volume of premiums for this casualty insurance is increasing to a greater extent than that for health insurance. It is a mystery, then, why psychologists have not pursued recognition under state labor laws with the same vigor given to being amended into insurance codes. Perhaps it is a reflection of their business naiveté.

Of the benefits paid nationally in 1979, $29.3 and $20.0 billion came from Medicare and Medicaid, respectively, with $29.6 and $27.7 billion from the insurance industry and the Blues and medical society plans, plus $3.3 billion of hospital and medical benefits under worker's compensation (*Sourcebook of Health Insurance Data*, n.d.). It is again obvious that, relative to dollar volume of benefits paid, psychologists experience very minimal participation under the Social Security programs of Medicare and Medicaid.

As noted before, it is likely that there has been a substantial underreporting of third-party coverage for psychological services, not simply because of failure to report but also in part because some practitioners serve patients with health care coverage but nonetheless refuse to take assignment or to bill, holding that their contract is with the patient and therefore it is up to the patient to bill to recover the costs.

It may well be, however, that third-party reimbursement is generally unlikely to exceed 50 percent of practitioner income, inasmuch as most health policies/programs today have a modest (increasingly less so) deductible or "spend down" requirement that the patient must pay, plus a copayment requirement of 20 to 50 percent. Some other policies will pay only up to a low maximum fee, substantially less than the prevailing rate. Hence, even with favorable collection, it appears that the optimal level of third-party reimbursement generally will not exceed 50 percent of a practitioner's fee-for-service gross income, except in a specifically focused and carefully managed practice. Indeed, for the FT-FFS 31 group it was 51.2 percent (see Table 3-6).

Another factor in third-party reimbursement, and one that is likely to exert an increasing effect, is competition. We have reported on the dramatic increase of licensed psychologists in recent years (Chapter One), and surely psychologists will begin to compete with one another for patients. But as Frank (1981b) has noted, a considerable amount of psychotherapy is provided by general practitioners (which is widely reimbursable, in contrast to counseling services of some nondoctoral providers). Moreover, the country is experiencing a growing oversupply of physicians. Thus, not only psychologists but general practitioners may be viewed as substitutes in demand for psychiatrists' services—that is, psychiatrists are faced with increasing competition. Indeed, Frank reports that in states that have adopted FOC psychologist laws, psychiatrists' fees are lower, all other factors held constant—between 8.3 and 9.5 percent lower than in states that have not adopted such legislation. Conversely, increases in psychologists' fees would raise the demand for psychiatrists' services. Thus, as psychologists' fees increase, there will be some cause for consumers to move toward psychiatrists (see Chapter Twelve).

McGuire and Montgomery (1981), following study both of laws mandating mental health coverage and of FOC laws recognizing psychological service in group health insurance, have found that the former is associated with growth in the numbers of both psychologist health service providers and psychiatrists. However, passage of a mandate has a substantially greater near-term effect on the growth of psychologists than of psychiatrists, 51 percent versus 19 percent. The supply of psychologists is thus more responsive to a mandate, probably because it is more common for psychiatric services to be covered under health insurance even in the absence of a mandate. An FOC law for psychologists, it was noted, does not solely affect that profession but was found to have a positive effect on the demand for psychiatrists' services, presumably by creating a more positive environment for mental health services.

The increasing supply of mental health practitioners, coupled with a growing governmental and public concern over rising health care costs, is very likely to see external forces directed to practitioners to achieve price relief via competition. Illustrative was the adoption in conference by the California legislature, in June 1982, of A.B. 3480, Chapter 329. It enabled third parties to contract in the private sector on alternative rates with hospitals and with practitioners, even to limit the choice of provider to those on contract. There will be increasing pressure to be a "preferred" or "exclusive" provider—that is, by contract to agree on rate. Meanwhile, to control spiraling Medicaid costs, the state will negotiate rates with hospitals for Medicaid beneficiaries, eliminating access to the hospitals that are least cost-efficient. Both public- and private-sector third parties will be well aware of rate changes as they occur. It may become progressively less feasible to "opt out of" any contracting or price competition and still have a full-time practice.

Another perspective on third-party coverage was provided through the three most recent new cases seen (Chapter Two). Here we note only that of 20,000 reported cases, in only 51 percent did a third party cover 41 percent or more of the professional charges of these psychologists.

Psychological services are not recognized or are seriously limited for a substantial proportion of the population. How substantial? The 27.5 million Medicare enrollees, the monthly average of 8.5 million Medicaid beneficiaries (*Sourcebook of Health Insurance Data,* n.d.), the 26.6 million with no insurance coverage (Kasper and others, n.d.), the 35.6 million with hospital insurance but no major medical coverage (since psychological services are usually part of supplemental rather than basic benefits), and the 3.6 million (27.6 × .129) having major medical coverage but not residing in a state with direct recognition for psychological services add up to 101.8 million (with unknown overlap), or, in 1977–1978 (when these data were largely drawn), to 47.4 percent (101.8 ÷ 214.6) of the national population. If we assume that only 20 percent of those with health-plan coverage in FOC states are employed by self-insured corporations that exercise the ERISA preemption to avoid payment to psychologists, then another 39.2 million can be added to the non-psychologist-covered rolls. Allowing that some Medicare and some Medicaid beneficiaries do obtain some psychological services, it appears, broadly stated, that only about 40 percent of the population has health-plan coverage for direct access to psychologists. This underscores the fact that the private practice of psychology, if it is to flourish, must draw its income from a broader array of third parties. Such market expansion will become possible only as federal laws (such as those regulating Medicare, Medicaid, ERISA, and HMOs) and state laws (such as those regulating worker's compensation, health care in correctional facilities, hospital practice, and professional corporations) are amended to recognize the practice of psychology—not simply for mental health services but for health care.

References

Attorney General of California. Opinion No. 79-410, June 14, 1979.

Dörken, H. "Hospital Practice: Fees, Not Salaries." *Clinical Psychologist*, 1979a, *33*, 24.

Dörken, H. "Worker's Compensation: Opening Up a Major Market for Professional Practice." *Professional Psychology*, 1979b, *10*, 834-840.

Dörken, H., and Webb, J. T. "The Hospital Practice of Psychology: An Interstate Comparison." *Professional Psychology*, 1979, *10*, 619-630.

Dörken, H., and Webb, J. T. "1976 Third-Party Reimbursement Experience: An Interstate Comparison by Insurance Carrier." *American Psychologist*, 1980, *35*, 355-363.

Dörken, H., and Webb, J. T. "Licensed Psychologists on the Increase: 1974-1979." *American Psychologist*, 1981, *36*, 1419-1426.

Frank, R. G. " 'Freedom of Choice' Laws: Are They a Nuisance?" Preliminary draft mimeo, University of Pittsburgh, 1981a.

Frank, R. G. "Pricing and Location of Physician Services in Mental Health." Preliminary draft mimeo, University of Pittsburgh, 1981b.

Kasper, J., and others. "Who Are the Uninsured?" Unpublished report of 1979 survey, National Center for Health Services Research, U.S. Department of Health and Human Services, n.d.

McGuire, T., and Montgomery, J. "Mandated Mental Health Benefits in Private Health Insurance Policies: A Legal and Economic Analysis." Working paper CHS-40, mimeo, Center for Health Studies, Institution for Social and Policy Studies, Yale University, 1981.

Sourcebook of Health Insurance Data, 1980-1981. Washington, D.C.: Health Insurance Institute, n.d.

Taube, G., Kessler, L., and Feuerberg, M. *Utilization and Expenditures for Ambulatory Mental Health Care During 1980.* Data Report No. 5, DHHS Pub. No. (PHS) 84-20000, National Center for Health Statistics, U.S. Public Health Service. Washington, D.C.: U.S. Government Printing Office, 1984.

4

Herbert Dörken

The Expanding Role of Clinical Psychology in Mental Health Services: The CHAMPUS Experience

Few health plans maintain extensive data on the utilization of mental health services, particularly large-scale plans where the volume of data lends some confidence to the kinds of service delivered, by whom, at what cost, and for how long. Moreover, the data available under the Civilian Health and Medical Program of the Uniformed Services (CHAMPUS) for fiscal years 1980 and 1981, the focus of this report, can be compared with earlier data, such as those of 1975 (Dörken, 1977), for indication of any consequential trends. The findings from a data base of this volume should also enable managers to plan more effectively and assist the administration in setting its policy for government-sponsored health care.

This chapter would not have been possible without the data and technical comments supplied by OCHAMPUS staff. The author is particularly appreciative of the assistance of Alex Rodriguez, OCHAMPUS medical director, and Richard Barnett, chief of the statistics branch. The review comments of Patrick DeLeon, executive assistant to Senator Daniel Inouye, and of Gary VandenBos, deputy executive officer of the American Psychological Association, were also very helpful.

It must be understood that although this report is based on data from the CHAMPUS program, the views expressed are those of the author and are independent of those of OCHAMPUS or its representatives or beneficiaries.

CHAMPUS is the largest health plan in the country, covering an estimated 6.52 million eligibles in fiscal year 1982, and it is funded through the annual Department of Defense Appropriations Act.

From the perspective of clinical psychology, this program has special significance. It was among the first (1970) to formally recognize clinical psychologists as independent direct-access practitioners. The initial military directive has since been superseded by recognition in statute and one that is unusually explicit: "None of the funds . . . in this Act . . . shall be available for . . . any service . . . which is not medically or psychologically necessary to diagnose and treat a mental or physical illness, injury, or bodily malfunction as diagnosed by a physician, dentist, or a clinical psychologist, as appropriate" (sec. 844, P.L. 95-111, 1977). Further statutory specifics on CHAMPUS are provided in DeLeon, VandenBos, and Kraut (1984). The beneficiaries, then, have been free to choose a psychologist, psychiatrist, or other recognized provider for more than a decade. Consequently, how they would exercise their choice is no longer speculative. The data to be presented are witness to the fact and can be contrasted to the choices made when there are access barriers such as a required medical referral, or when only a few visits are allowed, or when there is a low dollar ceiling on benefits. No such restrictions have applied to psychological services in this plan since 1970. Chapter Three, on third-party reimbursement, shows the CHAMPUS in relation to other third-party payers from the psychologist practitioner's perspective (10.4 percent of all third-party income).

As a military-related benefit, the CHAMPUS is a largely government-paid health plan. It is not health insurance. There is no prepaid premium and no indemnification of health care costs from such revenue. With its minimal deductibles and only a moderate copayment requirement, it is without any serious financial barriers to mental health care such as are often found in group health insurance or, more particularly, in health care service plans under a medical egis.

In 1973 to 1975, the data were available only for ten reporting states. However, in 1976 several major contracts were made with different (third-party) claims-processing intermediaries. Problems in data reporting occurred. Then in 1977 the federal government changed its fiscal year, resulting in a one-time fifteen-month year. Broad and general reliable data did not become available again until 1980. By then, however, the data were not simply for ten states, as in reports for 1973, 1974, and 1975, but for all fifty states plus the District of Columbia. Some data comparison between these years can be found in Dörken (1979). In many states the claims volume was minimal. Indeed, in thirty-two states the volume of visits was less than 1 percent of the national total. By contrast, almost one-quarter of CHAMPUS providers were in California in 1981, with about another 7 percent each in Florida and Texas and 5 percent in Virginia, these four states accounting for 44 percent of all the program providers.

Since active-duty military personnel, the large majority male, receive their health care within the military services and are therefore not part of the CHAMPUS until they retire, a larger proportion of this population is female than is typically found in employee group health insurance. Specifically, of those beneficiaries who used mental health services, half were spouses, 22 percent sons, 16 percent daughters, and 12 percent retirees.

The cost or price figures to be reported are the total cost—that is, the government cost plus the copayment. Services necessary to meet the modest deductible are "lost"/not included. In both 1980 and 1981, owing to a lag in billing, processing, and payment, the data were only 95 percent complete (92 percent for professional outpatient services in FY 1980, 94 percent in FY 1981). The data are reported on this basis without conversion to a 100 percent level.

There are more facts and more detail to be derived from these aggregate data on mental health services utilization than is practical to report here. The analysis to follow, however, will focus on provider visits, procedures, and cost, some interprofession and interstate variance, and program volume. After noting some of the health-plan requirements and other circumstances specific to the CHAMPUS, the significance of the findings is discussed.

Utilization

Based on an eligible population of 6.52 million in 1982 and 85,277 outpatient users in 1981 (all visits), the utilization rate was

1.3 percent. There were 15,791 inpatient users in 1981, or 0.24 percent of the eligibles. Combined, the 87,586 unduplicated mental health users were 1.34 percent of those eligible for CHAMPUS care (1.41 percent corrected to 100 percent). This is somewhat lower than the 1.53 percent level of national utilization found in 1975 and is well under the levels reported for employed populations, at generally between 2 and 5 percent (Wells and others, 1982), the almost unlimited benefit here notwithstanding.

If one contrasts the eighties with 1975 (Table 4-1), it is apparent that psychiatry has exercised its preeminence over inpatient services, with a corresponding lesser involvement of attending physicians. This may reflect the concern within organized psychiatry in recent years to more clearly establish its practice and presence in general hospitals. Also apparent in Table 4-1 is the minor, though slightly growing, role of psychologists in inpatient services. In outpatient care the shift in delivery between professions was quite different. Though still the dominant provider group, psychiatry saw a tenth of its market shift to psychologists and social workers in about five years. Indeed, in six of the nineteen states each having more than 1 percent of the visits nationally, the total number of visits to psychologists in 1981 exceeded the outpatient visits to psychiatrists (Arizona, California, Colorado, Hawaii, Texas, and Washington). Visits to social workers exceeded those to psychiatrists in California, Colorado, and Texas. In part this shift may be due not simply to consumer choice but to the changing availability of providers with the growth in numbers of psychologists and social workers nationally and to accessibility, that is, somewhat better distribution of these professionals geographically and, of course, their growing statutory and thereby public recognition among the states.

It must be emphasized that the numbers of visits shown in Table 4-1 for 1975 are for ten states, the only data available at the time, while for the later years the reporting covers all fifty states. In- and outpatient visits for these same ten states in 1981 numbered 128,729 and 545,034, respectively, an overall total of 673,763. This represents a 28.5 percent *decrease* in the number of visits over this six-year period in the face of 3.2 percent increase in the number of

Table 4.1. Mental Health Services Delivered by Profession, In- and Outpatient, Fiscal Years 1975, 1980, and 1981.

Site	Year	No. Visits	Percentage of Visits by Profession				
			M.D.s	Psychiatrists	Psychologists	Social Workers	Other
Inpatient	1975[a]	257,200	20.4	69.7	1.2	1.1	7.6
	1980	279,660	10.9	82.6	2.6	1.1	2.9
	1981	283,999	9.6	81.7	3.3	1.3	4.1
Outpatient	1975[a]	684,599	6.7	48.8	21.4	8.3	14.8
	1980	926,500	5.0	39.7	28.0	18.6	8.6
	1981	981,567	5.7	36.2	29.0	20.0	9.0

[a]Ten-state data.

beneficiaries. In 1981, 81 percent of the visits were outpatient, compared with 73 percent in 1975. In part the 28.5 percent reduction in total visits in these ten states is attributable to an 8 percent decrease in the proportion of beneficiaries nationally who were mental health users, from 15.3 to 14.1 per thousand. Another major factor was the initiation of peer review, which had a utilization control effect, plus the adoption of higher standards/controls over residential treatment centers, curtailing some of the long-duration stays. The result is that inpatient visits dropped to but half (50.05 percent) of their 1975 level, while there was also a 20 percent decrease in outpatient visits. Since inpatient visits carry associated hospital costs, they assume particular significance in the overall allocation of CHAMPUS mental health dollars. This 50 percent drop represents a cost forgone of almost $6 million for these visits (128,471 × $46.69/visit), not to mention a hospital cost forgone of over $60 million (22,507 admissions ÷ 2 × $5,562/adm.). Dramatic as this reduction was because of the cost of hospital services, inpatient psychiatric care nonetheless represented 78.2 percent of total government costs for mental health services in 1981.

Procedures. There is a lot of rhetoric about treatment armamentariums, but when services are grouped by type of treatment approach, as in Tables 4-2 and 4-3, it is apparent that about 80 percent of all outpatient visits are for one-on-one individual psychotherapy. The psychotherapy "hour" is by far the dominant procedure for all professions, although about one-eighth of individual outpatient psychotherapy with psychiatrists was brief therapy, quite likely a mixture of brief support and medication review. On an inpatient basis, however, the brief forms of psychotherapy were almost as common as "hourly" therapy for psychiatrists, perhaps reflecting the economic efficiency of their hospital practice.

The other procedures, although they may be emphasized by some individual practitioners, are, in the aggregate, a minor aspect of total services rendered. Nonetheless, some emphasis on particular procedures, or lack of them, by profession is of interest. Group therapy accounted for a tenth of the visits to "others," probably to mental health clinics. As measured by the absolute volume of visits, psychologists and social workers each supplied two to three times

Table 12. Outpatient Mental Health Visits, All States, by Profession and Procedure, Fiscal Years 1980 and 1981.

Procedure	Attending M.D.		Psychiatrist		Psychologist		Social worker		Other[a]	
	1980	1981	1980	1981	1980	1981	1980	1981	1980	1981
Brief psychotherapy (<31 min.)										
No. visits	7,414	7,704	45,489	44,977	6,347	5,229	382	639	5,985	7,587
Percentage by prof.	15.9	13.7	12.3	12.7	2.4	1.8	0.2	0.3	7.5	8.6
All other individual psychotherapy										
No. visits	31,312	37,268	285,823	264,221	214,102	227,620	146,727	161,567	56,544	57,880
Percentage by prof.	67.0	66.4	77.6	74.4	82.3	79.9	84.9	82.2	71.3	65.5
Group psychotherapy										
No. visits	3,926	3,825	17,509	16,467	8,173	8,063	2,959	7,393	9,407	9,004
Percentage by prof.	8.4	6.8	4.8	4.6	3.1	2.8	1.7	3.8	11.9	10.2
Family psychotherapy										
No. visits	1,933	2,344	6,884	7,075	16,980	22,751	12,523	17,078	2,971	3,158
Percentage by prof.	4.1	4.2	1.9	2.0	6.5	8.0	7.2	8.7	3.4	3.6
Evaluation										
No. visits	251	445	3,242	4,060	512	927	3,774	6,279	796	587
Percentage by prof.	0.5	0.8	0.9	1.1	0.2	0.3	2.2	3.2	1.0	0.7
Testing										
No. visits	644	800	3,816	3,765	5,600	12,612	897	588	1,905	2,335
Percentage by prof.	1.4	1.4	1.0	1.0	2.2	4.4	0.5	0.3	2.4	2.6
Supervision										
No. visits	266	161	495	332	241	—	—	—	177	—
Percentage by prof.	0.6	0.3	0.1	0.1	0.1	—	—	—	0.2	—
Medical only										
No. visits	205	408	1,598	1,920	—	—	—	—	401	362
Percentage by prof.	0.4	0.7	0.4	0.5	—	—	—	—	0.5	0.4
All procedures[b]										
No. visits	46,706	56,164	368,463	355,543	260,115	285,014	172,790	196,469	79,426	88,377
Percentage by prof.	98.3	94.3	99.0	96.4	96.8	97.3	96.7	98.5	98.2	91.6

Total visits, all procedures, all professions, all states, 1980, 926,500; 1981, 981,567.

[a] Physician specialists other than psychiatrist or attending physician; mental health clinics; emergency room visits; marriage, family, child counselors; pastoral counselors; occupational therapists; "those not otherwise classified."
[b] All procedures with <10 visits, all professions, excluded. Psychoanalysis, psychodrama, narcosynthesis, phone consultation, biofeedback, environmental intervention also excluded. No procedure code for behavior therapy.

Table 4-3. Inpatient Mental Health Visits, All States, by Profession and Procedure, Fiscal Years 1980 and 1981.

Procedure	Attending M.D.		Psychiatrist		Psychologist		Social worker		Other[a]	
	1980	1981	1980	1981	1980	1981	1980	1981	1980	1981
Brief psychotherapy (<31 min.)										
No. visits	15,147	12,594	95,481	89,523	1,205	1,670	436	117	2,594	4,392
Percentage by prof.	49.8	46.1	41.4	38.6	16.6	18.0	14.3	3.3	32.3	37.6
All other individual psychotherapy										
No. visits	7,546	8,891	104,188	102,352	3,471	4,277	1,529	2,543	2,128	3,630
Percentage by prof.	24.8	32.5	45.1	44.1	47.8	46.2	50.1	66.3	26.5	31.0
Group psychotherapy										
No. visits	2,253	631	10,486	12,574	307	592	278	365	1,037	1,356
Percentage by prof.	7.4	2.3	4.5	5.4	4.2	6.4	9.1	9.5	12.9	11.6
Family psychotherapy										
No. visits	295	233	1,339	1,882	258	347	447	501	—	136
Percentage by prof.	1.0	0.9	0.6	0.8	3.6	3.7	14.6	13.1	—	1.2
Evaluation										
No. visits	212	413	1,960	4,134	—	52	214	28	—	451
Percentage by prof.	0.7	1.5	0.8	1.8	—	0.6	7.0	0.7	—	3.9
Testing										
No. visits	918	442	4,275	3,337	1,748	2,211	117	119	112	426
Percentage by prof.	3.0	1.6	1.9	1.4	24.1	23.9	3.8	3.1	1.4	3.7
Supervision										
No. visits	220	251	3,367	2,269	—	65	—	2	—	100
Percentage by prof.	0.7	0.9	1.5	1.0	—	0.7	—	0.1	—	0.9
Medical only										
No. visits	3,561	3,392	7,590	5,448	—	—	—	21	1,543	1,013
Percentage by prof.	11.7	12.4	3.3	2.3	—	—	—	0.5	19.2	8.7
All procedures[b]										
No. visits	30,410	27,349	230,902	231,886	7,264	9,264	3,053	3,834	8,031	11,666
Percentage by prof.	99.1	98.2	99.1	95.4	96.3	99.5	98.9	96.6	92.3	98.6

Total visits, all procedures, all professions, all states, 1980, 279,660; 1981, 283,999

[a]See note a, Table 4-2.

as much outpatient family therapy as psychiatrists. Psychologists generally think of testing as their province, but Table 4-2 shows that it is a small province indeed (only 4.4 percent of all psychologist visits in 1981) and one that is shared by others. However, on an inpatient basis testing accounts for about one quarter of all psychologist visits, many probably for diagnostic assessment on medical referral. Of course, fewer than 10 percent of inpatient visits were supplied by all nonphysicians in either year.

Certain procedures, detailed in Table 4-4, can be provided only by physicians. The key point to note here is that although attending physicians and psychiatrists may have a medical perspective (and certainly the training), they billed for procedures exclusive to them by licensure in only about 1 out of 200 of their outpatient visits. Thus, despite the considerable emphasis politically and interprofessionally on the essential and pivotal role of psychiatry and medicine in the treatment of mental disorders, it appears that, for over 99 percent of outpatient visits to psychiatrists, those services were within the scope of practice of some nonphysician providers. That is, the extent of overlap between, say, psychiatrists and psychologists in services actually rendered is the overwhelming fact, not the type of services that one provides that the other does not. In 1981, 96.4 percent of psychiatrist visits were for brief psychotherapy, other individual psychotherapy, group therapy, and family therapy, all clearly within the clinical psychologist's competence. Add testing to that and the overlap is 97.5 percent, without tally of the capacity of psychologists for evaluation or supervision.

It has been argued that outpatient services attend to many with problems in living or adjustment but that when patients are hospitalized, they are "sick" and require close medical/psychiatric care. The data, however, show that only about 3 percent of psychiatrist visits for inpatient care in mental disorder involved procedures that could be provided only by a licensed physician. This is at such variance with what might be expected given the dominant role of psychiatry in inpatient services that it bears a closer look.

Table 4-4 lists these procedures together with the number of visits for each to attending physicians and psychiatrists in 1981.

Table 4-4. Use of Medical Procedures: Outpatient and Inpatient Visits to Attending Physicians and Psychiatrists in All States and In Four Major States, Fiscal Year 1981.

Code	Procedure	50 states + D.C.		Calif.		Fla.		Tex.		Va.	
		Att. M.D.	Psych.	Att. M.D.	Psych.	Att. M.D.	Psych.	Att. M.D.	Psych.	Att. M.D.	Psych.
Outpatient											
90862	Chemother. mgt.	344	1,501	0	0	0	0	0	0	14	759
90821, 92836, 93838	Convulsive therapy	89	449	11	51	51	19	1	92	0	0
90829	Insulin shock sub coma	19	33	0	8	0	0	0	0	0	0
90872	Subconvulsive EST	8	20	0	0	0	0	0	0	6	8
90898	Daily hosp. care, att. M.D.	27	3	0	0	0	0	0	0	0	0
	Total medical visits	487	2,006	11	59	51	19	1	92	20	767
	Medical visits as percentage of all visits	0.9	0.6	0.1	0.1	0.5	0.1	0.0	0.5	3.4	0.9
Inpatient											
90862	Chemother. mgt.	3,024	3,279	0	0	0	0	0	0	19	857
90821, 92836, 92838	Convulsive therapy	310	1,812	27	213	133	174	105	474	0	0
90829	Insulin shock sub coma	7	10	1	0	0	0	0	0	0	0
90872	Subconvulsive EST	49	58	0	0	0	0	0	0	0	0
90898	Daily hosp. care, att. M.D.	2	289	0	0	0	9	0	0	0	0
92835	Insulin shock ther.	0	14	0	0	0	0	0	0	0	0
	Total medical visits	3,392	5,462	28	213	133	183	105	474	19	857
	Medical visits as percentage of all visits	12.4	2.4	0.6	0.6	2.4	0.9	5.9	2.2	4.1	1.3

Note: Psychiatric procedure visits in the four states shown here were 58.9% of all outpatient and 61.2% of all inpatient visits in all 51 states.

Chemotherapy management constituted 75 percent of all these billed outpatient medical procedures by psychiatrists and 60 percent of the inpatient medical procedures but only 0.4 percent and 1.4 percent of their total visits. The second group of medical procedures in rank, convulsive therapy, accounted for only about 0.8 percent of all inpatient visits to psychiatrists. Even among attending physicians, total medical procedures accounted for only one in eight inpatient visits.

It is not credible, of course, that there would have been no use of psychoactive drugs by psychiatrists or attending physicians in three major CHAMPUS states in 1981—California, Florida, and Texas. Rather, when used, prescription and drug management were apparently adjuncts to some other billed procedure. Brief psychotherapy is a likely possibility. In any event, Table 4-4 indicates that shock and drugs, as sole treatments billed, are not the mainstay of psychiatric care.

Reimbursement procedures require that when psychotherapy is being provided, services in connection with chemotherapy management are to be included in the allowable charge for psychotherapy (CHAMPUS, 1985). Chemotherapy management is payable only as an independent procedure. It is unfortunate that there is no procedure distinction between psychotherapy with and without psychoactive medication, because it would be valuable to know the extent to which drugs are an adjunct to mental health care. Perhaps the appropriate definition of *medical psychotherapy* is "psychotherapy with drugs."

Returning to the predominant use of one-on-one individual "hourly" psychotherapy, we find that there are two procedures, 90805 (psychotherapy, verbal, fifty minutes) and 92803 (psychotherapy, adult or child, forty-five to fifty minutes, office), which nationally accounted for three-quarters and two-thirds of psychiatrist outpatient visits in 1980 and 1981, respectively, and about four-fifths of the visits to psychologists (but see under "Discussion").

Fees. Psychotherapy is a time- and labor-intensive endeavor. In a fee-for-service system there are four ways, singly or in combination, to increase income: work more hours, charge more per visit, see more than one person at a time, charging for each, or

Table 4-5. Payment for Psychotherapy by Procedure, Duration o⌐

| | | Dura- | Attending Physician | | | | | |
| | | tion | No. visits | | Avg. paid ($) | | $/min. | |
Code	Procedure	(min.)	1980	1981	1980	1981	1980	1981
Inpatient								
90805	Psychotherapy, verbal	50	2,814	1,998	52.81	58.00	1.06	1.16
6		25	4,218	2,724	28.51	28.86	1.14	1.15
7		15	963	586	23.34	24.33	1.56	1.62
90854	Psychotherapy, inpatient	45–50	1,377	1,091	52.84	57.66	1.06	1.15
5		20–30	4,710	3,519	26.39	28.91	1.06	1.16
6		<20	330	783	16.85	23.77	1.12	1.52
92804	Psychotherapy, hospital	45–50	2,374	5,166	48.95	67.77	0.98	1.36
7		25	3,956	4,196	29.04	36.87	1.16	1.47
12		15	881	674	21.28	23.02	1.42	1.53
Outpatient								
90805	Psychotherapy, verbal	50	13,505	10,428	46.66	50.33	0.93	1.01
6		25	2,277	2,012	28.92	30.58	1.16	1.22
7		15	569	415	17.13	19.62	1.14	1.31
92803	Psychotherapy, office	45–50	14,417	23,478	49.73	58.42	0.99	1.17
6		25	2,655	3,568	29.42	34.31	1.18	1.37
11		15	747	765	18.05	22.16	1.20	1.48
92831	Family therapy	45–50	517	875	53.97	57.64	1.08	1.15
90810	Psychotherapy, group	90	1,139	490	26.24	27.19	0.29	0.30
92817	Group therapy, office	90	865	988	23.70	28.48	0.26	0.32

Notes: Divisor was 50, 25, and 15 minutes in each set, except group therapy (see minutes in Tir⌐ column).

— fewer than 100 visits and thus no entry.

Social work visits were largely reported under different procedural numbers with differe⌐ time frames in these years.

reduce the time of the session but not reduce the charge proportionally. There are limits, however, on the hours a practitioner is willing to do this work and the number of patients available to many practitioners. The economics of one's clientele or the third party also set some limit on fees, while formation of therapy groups is usually possible only in a large practice (and makes the practice larger). The more subtle effect is the relation between time and fee. What the CHAMPUS data show is that "time is money, but less time is more money!" The trend from the fifty-minute to a forty-five-minute "hour" is, of course, already a 10 percent gain.

Session, and Profession, All States, Fiscal Years 1980 and 1981.

Psychiatrist						Psychologist					
No. visits		Avg. paid ($)		$/min.		No. visits		Avg. paid ($)		$/min.	
1980	1981	1980	1981	1980	1981	1980	1981	1980	1981	1980	1981
42,831	41,035	52.75	57.06	1.05	1.14	1,119	1,329	42.39	50.85	0.85	1.02
49,147	44,086	31.77	32.81	1.27	1.31	771	1,167	26.09	28.62	1.04	1.14
11,898	10,021	20.01	25.21	1.33	1.68	—	—	—	—	—	—
8,739	14,768	53.58	57.54	1.07	1.15	309	366	55.05	54.40	1.10	1.04
7,379	12,987	28.81	35.65	1.15	1.43	—	161	—	—	—	—
1,918	1,457	21.78	21.95	1.45	1.46	—	—	—	—	—	—
46,473	41,355	62.24	69.42	1.24	1.39	1,866	2,005	56.91	67.92	1.14	1.36
22,417	18,929	33.89	39.03	1.36	1.56	285	249	32.29	38.40	1.29	1.54
2,080	1,467	23.14	26.36	1.54	1.76	—	—	—	—	—	—
163,688	141,785	50.82	54.36	1.02	1.09	82,059	89,739	47.51	53.01	0.95	1.06
22,854	22,469	29.86	31.66	1.19	1.27	2,749	3,272	27.59	30.44	1.10	1.22
3,890	3,119	17.95	20.68	1.20	1.38	145	171	20.21	19.74	1.35	1.32
111,079	97,375	57.58	63.70	1.15	1.27	129,562	133,634	55.75	62.54	1.11	1.25
13,450	11,614	33.58	38.17	1.34	1.53	3,214	1,563	35.98	35.34	1.44	1.41
1,747	1,451	20.98	23.45	1.40	1.56	130	102	18.28	23.97	1.22	1.60
2,424	3,150	68.40	80.47	1.37	1.61	10,539	17,043	65.55	79.11	1.31	1.58
5,515	5,099	25.83	29.01	0.29	0.32	2,353	2,746	25.55	27.96	0.28	0.31
2,131	1,682	26.38	30.16	0.29	0.34	3,239	2,419	25.82	26.54	0.29	0.29

There are four sets of psychotherapy procedures which are time-based, billed in triads from fifty to fifteen minutes, and whose utilization is sufficient to study the relation of cost to time. One triad is commonly used in both outpatient and inpatient settings. Table 4-5 displays these procedure triads (and also family and group therapy), showing the number of visits in all states, the average amount paid per visit, and the amount paid per minute.

Among the three outpatient and two inpatient triads, it is generally clear that the cost per minute varied inversely with the time involved. Stated otherwise, as the length of therapy visits decreased, the cost per minute of professional time rose. This has previously been alluded to (Dörken, 1977, p. 709). A differential rate by time is one clear way to increase income within the same time frame. There was one exception each for attending physicians

(90806) and psychologists (92811, an infrequently used procedure by the latter profession). Among psychiatrists the progressive rise was clear throughout.

Looking down the 1981 psychiatrist column showing dollars per minute for the five triads, the per-minute gains from "hourly" to quarter-hour visits were 47, 27, 27, 27, and 23 percent, respectively. Psychologists did not have sufficient brief inpatient visits to make the same calculation but among the outpatient triads posted 25 and 28 percent gains. The major difference was that only a small proportion of psychologist visits were for brief psychotherapy. For psychiatrists the number of "half hour" inpatient visits coded as 90806 was the greatest in its triad and the number coded as 90855 was substantial; these procedures showed gains of 15 and 24 percent, respectively.

Family therapy is a procedure gaining increasing widespread attention for its effectiveness. It was rendered most frequently by psychologists. On a per-minute basis its reimbursement was almost 50 percent higher than for individual hourly outpatient psychotherapy for both psychiatrists and psychologists in 1981. For group therapy the per-minute rate was at the 30¢ level, give or take a few pennies. For a traditional group of eight, that would convert to $2.40 per minute of professional time, double the individual hourly psychotherapy return and some 50 percent higher than the return in family therapy. Even for a group of six, or $1.80, there is a clear, albeit largely unheeded, economic incentive. In summary, psychiatrists appear to have discovered the economic advantage of short therapy sessions, particularly for inpatient services, while psychologists are becoming active in family therapy. The economic leverage of group therapy has yet to be widely pursued.

Quite apart from these considerations, the matter of which profession is paid more, either on the average or by procedure, has become a delicate issue clouded by various views of usual and customary charges, provider efficiency, or use of alternative (discounted) rates. Regardless, there was sufficient utilization to make a psychology/psychiatry comparison for fourteen procedures in 1981. The psychologists' average cost was *less* in but one instance (92811, but based on only 102 visits). A correct picture of interprofessional differences in fees is obtained only by comparing rates for the same procedures—or, better still, for total management of comparable cases, but the latter data are not available.

Visits. Interdisciplinary care, the treatment team, is often touted as the optimum for patient care. Rhetoric clearly exceeds fact, for the typical and, it is assumed, preferred mode of practice is solo. This is clearly the case for psychiatrists in both outpatient and inpatient care, since they were the sole providers for about three-quarters of the patients they saw in 1981. The same was true of psychologists in outpatient care. For inpatient services psychologists more often than not practiced jointly with psychiatrists (in 1981, 35.4 percent compared with 29.4 percent), probably because their hospital privileges required it. For 23 percent of the beneficiaries seen by psychologists and 30 percent by social workers as inpatients, it was as part of a combination of three or more therapists, the treatment team.

Another perspective on how the different professions serve CHAMPUS beneficiaries is given by comparing the proportion of visits by profession by age range of the patient. In outpatient services, about 25 percent of psychologists' and 22 percent of social workers' visits were for those aged five to fourteen years. Psychiatry delivered about 15 percent of its services to this age group. The proportions were fairly evenly matched over the ages from fifteen to thirty-four; twenty to twenty-four was a period of lower involvement, only about 7 percent of any profession's visits. Psychiatrists provided almost 50 percent of their outpatient services to those aged thirty-five to sixty-four, while only a third of psychologists' or social workers' visits were for this age group. Age variations were not so evident for inpatient services, although over 40 percent of psychologists' visits were for adolescents (age fifteen to nineteen) and about one-third of psychiatrists' visits. Again, the period twenty to twenty-four years of age was one of lesser use of mental health services than in earlier or later years.

To what extent do the services provided by the several professions differ according to specific diagnosis? CHAMPUS visits are tabulated by twenty three-digit diagnostic codes (International Classification of Diseases, adapted for use in the USA, 9th edition), and six of these diagnoses accounted for almost 95 percent of all outpatient visits among all states. One-half of all visits carried a neurosis diagnosis, about 20 percent were for transient situational disturbances, close to 10 percent were behavior disorders of childhood, somewhat more than 5 percent each were viewed as personality disorders or schizophrenias, and the affective psychoses accounted for 3 to 4 percent of visits.

In the distribution of outpatient visits by diagnosis among the four states with the highest concentration of visits, interstate variation is apparent. Between years, the proportion of visits by diagnosis by state was quite consistent except for Texas, where it appears that behavior disorders of childhood were more emphasized in 1980 and transient situational disturbances in 1981. It is very unlikely that the patient population changed so abruptly in a year; rather, a different diagnosis probably became preferred by the providers. Psychiatry preempted the field most clearly in Virginia, accounting for about 70 to 80 percent of visits for personality disorder, transient situational disturbance, and behavior disorders of childhood. Otherwise, for persons considered to have a personality disorder, the major providers were psychologists in some 40 to 50 percent of the visits, followed by social workers, at about 25 to 30 percent of the visits in California, Florida, and Texas. Essentially the same distribution obtained for the behavior disorders of childhood. Both these professions were also the major providers in these three states for persons with a transient situational disturbance. The extent of services provided by psychologists to neurotics was comparable to that provided by psychiatrists in Texas, but less in Florida and more in California. Psychiatry was clearly the major provider for the schizophrenias and affective psychoses; nonetheless, in California, psychologists delivered about one-quarter of the services for the former, social workers for the latter. Thus, except in Virginia and, of course, for inpatient services, where psychiatry essentially holds a monopoly, there are distinct differences among the professions in the diagnoses more commonly served.

On an outpatient basis, it is clear for all professions and all six of the most frequent diagnoses that all but 1 or 2 percent of patients are seen within sixty visits. It is worth noting, nonetheless, that the visits to patients beyond sixty in a year could be estimated at 13 percent of all outpatient visits in 1980, 11.5 percent in 1981.

Among attending physicians in 1981, depending on the diagnosis, some 24 to 33 percent of their patients were seen for one visit only. The pattern for "all other professions" was similar for the schizophrenias, affective psychoses, and neuroses. Depending on the diagnosis, psychiatrists saw some 12 to 15 percent of patients only once, psychologists some 7 to 11 percent. In general, psychiatrists, psychologists, and social workers saw about 90 percent of their patients within twenty-four visits.

Turning to inpatient visits and recalling that about 24 percent of such psychologist visits were for testing, we have an explanation for the quite high proportion of patients seen only once by this profession. Indeed, psychologists see only about one-quarter of their inpatients for more than eight visits. The attending physician had a similar one-visit pattern. By contrast, some 10 percent of inpatients seen by psychiatrists had more than sixty visits, whether their diagnosis was schizophrenia, transient situational disturbance, or childhood behavior disorder. In sharp contrast to outpatient services, the visits beyond sixty per patient accounted for 42 to 43 percent of all inpatient visits in 1980 and 1981.

Some might say that only psychiatrists and, to some degree, other physicians are capable of caring for the inpatient. The capability, however, may be due more to lack of access by the nonphysican provider than to lack of ability or training, particularly when the patient's condition is essentially behavioral rather than medical.

The frequency distribution of visits by diagnosis or profession contains no obvious break. The gradation of visit frequency is such that the curve depicting number of beneficiaries plotted against number of visits has a much higher concentration of low counts for outpatient visits and more frequent extended use of inpatient services, up to 109 or more visits in a year. The lack of any obvious break in the frequency distribution of visits does mean, however, that cutting points for peer or utilization review have to be based on some arbitrary standard or program limit.

Crude estimates of the cost of care per patient can be obtained by dividing the total visits by the number of beneficiaries and multiplying the average number of visits thus derived by the average cost per visit. This calculation, summarized in Table 4-6, tells us something about the cost of professional services. For inpatient services, the average amount paid per hospital admission was added in. The average number of visits per beneficiary is stable between the years, at around eighteen visits for inpatients and under twelve for outpatients. Given that hospitalized beneficiaries had an average of 1.4 to 1.5 admissions a year, there were about twelve visits per hospitalization, on average. Although the number of visits was comparable between years, the cost per visit and per hospital admission rose. Together these increases resulted in a cost per beneficiary being hospitalized that was approximately fourteen times the cost per beneficiary cared for as an outpatient in either year.

In-patient services, though serving fewer beneficiaries and providing fewer professional visits (see Table 4-6), accounted for 78.2 percent of CHAMPUS expenditures for mental health services in 1981. It is not surprising, then, that Congress has recently placed

Table 4-6. Average Cost and Extent of Visits, All Psychiatric Procedures, All Practitioners, All States, Fiscal Years 1980 and 1981.

	Inpatient		Outpatient	
	1980	1981	1980	1981
Total no. visits	279,660	283,999	927,500	981,567
Unduplicated no. beneficiaries	15,352	15,791	79,375	85,277
Avg. no. visits per beneficiary	18.2	18.0	11.7	11.5
Avg. amt. paid per visit	$42.05[a]	$46.89[a]	$46.77	$51.51
Avg. cost for all visits per beneficiary	$765.31	$844.02	$547.21	$592.37
Avg. amt. paid per hosp. admission	$4,682.14	$5,562.00	—	—
Avg. no. admissions per beneficiary	1.5	1.4	—	—
Avg. hosp. cost per beneficiary	$7,023.21	$7,786.80	—	—
Avg. cost of care per beneficiary	$7,788.52	$8.630.82	$547.21	$592.37

[a]Average paid-for hospital services per patient day, 1980 and 1981, $150.24 and $179.15.

a sixty-day limit on inpatient hospital care. It would also seem rational to consider partial hospitalization (not a current benefit) or other alternatives to acute psychiatric hospitalization. Not only the amount but the proportion of costs expended for inpatient care has been rising, from 74.6 percent in 1979 to 78.7 percent in 1982—another good reason for seriously considering that, by policy, hospitalization for mental disorder should be the last alternative used.

All controlled studies have shown that there are alternatives to hospitalization, more effective and never more costly in the aggregate (Kiesler, 1982). The proponents of community mental health services, as well, hold that much. hospitalization is unnecessary and that most care could be provided, without the hazards of institutionalization and in many instances more effectively, on an outpatient basis. If one thinks only in terms of limits on cost and service, it should be obvious that, with a fourteen-to-one margin in cost, a lot of outpatient services or alternative care could be provided in lieu of hospitalization.

Leaving cost aside for the moment, it is instructive to derive the total hospital days (697,717) by multiplying the number of admissions (22,507) by the average duration of stay (31.0 days) in 1981. When these total days are divided into the total number of inpatient visits (283,990), we find that there was an average of 0.4 visits a day in 1981, the same as in 1980—less than one professional visit in every two days. This suggests that some of the inpatient service is less than intensive treatment. Is it cost-efficient? Was the extent of hospitalization necessary? CHAMPUS policy allows for up to five inpatient sessions per week, except where medical review finds that the patient's condition warrants "crisis intervention."

In 1975 there was an evident inverse relationship between age and duration of hospital stay, and the ratio of professional visits to days hospitalized was age-related. Thus, children (aged one to fourteen) had one visit for each 4.1 days hospitalized, adolescents (fifteen to nineteen) one for 2.4 days, and adults one for 1.2 days. It was speculated whether the differentials were due to clinical need or provider interest (Dörken, 1980). In 1981 the age contrast, though less sharp, was clearly bimodal. Persons in the age groups one through four years, five through nine, ten through fourteen, fifteen through nineteen, twenty through twenty-four, twenty-five through thirty-four, thirty-five through forty-four, forty-five through fifty-four, and fifty-five through sixty-four received, on average, one professional inpatient visit, respectively, for every 3.46, 2.99, 2.84, 2.80, 2.30, 2.10, 2.07, 2.54, and 2.73 days of hospitalization. Again, children apparently receive less intensive treatment, while the mid-aged adult (twenty-five to forty-four) is the "preferred" patient. Nor was the extent of youth admissions negligible. In 1981 patients aged nineteen or younger accounted for 32 percent of all admissions, adolescents (fifteen through nineteen) 22.3 percent.

It should be noted that CHAMPUS inpatient data includes care both in acute hospital settings and in residential treatment centers (RTCs), where care is generally less intensive. Some in OCHAMPUS believe that much of the inpatient care for adolescents was actually being structured as RTC care. This may help to explain why Congress in 1983 imposed a sixty-day cap per year on psychiatric inpatient (but not RTC) care.

Earnings. Then there is the question of what professions earn from the CHAMPUS program, in the aggregate, and by provider. With the increased number of visits in 1981 over 1980 and an increase in the amount paid per visit, it is clear that the sums paid to each profession increased between these two years. Totaled up, they represent "big bucks," as displayed in Table 4-7. The sharp income advantage to the profession of psychiatry in inpatient services is obvious. In round numbers, this $10 million advantage to psychiatry from one program in one year is some explanation for the degree to which organized psychiatry is resisting the acquisition of hospital medical staff privileges by psychologists across the country.

The uncertain extent to which providers may have been duplicated in 1981 leaves the validity of the average amount earned per practitioner by profession somewhat in doubt. Surprisingly, the income per participating provider on the whole, whether psychiatrist, psychologist, or social worker, was quite similar. The earnings of the average attending physician were quite modest, less than $500 each year, on the average. But for participating psychiatrists, psychologists, and social workers, the average came to a not incidental sum, over $3,500 each in 1980.

Table 4-7. Value to Profession and Provider of CHAMPUS Visits, Outpatient and Inpatient, Fiscal Years 1980 and 1981.

Profession		No. Visits		Avg. Cost per Visit		Value to Profession			No. Providers	Value per Provider
		Outpatient	Inpatient	Outpatient	Inpatient	Outpatient	Inpatient	Total		
Attending	1980	46,706	30,410	$42.34	$34.57	$1,977,532	$1,051,274	$3,028,806	6,424	$471
Physician	1981	56,164	27,349	49.53	42.91	2,781,803	1,173,545	3,955,348	9,026	438
Psychiatrist	1980	368,463	230,902	48.69	43.12	17,940,463	9,956,494	27,896,957	7,763	3,594
	1981	355,543	231,886	52.74	47.53	18,751,338	11,021,542	29,772,880	12,305	2,420
Psychologist	1980	260,115	7,264	52.08	49.78	13,546,789	361,602	13,908,391	3,969	3,504
	1981	285,014	9,264	58.47	54.49	16,664,769	504,795	17,169,564	7,856	2,186
Social worker	1980	172,790	3,053	38.64	32.00	6,676,606	97,696	6,774,302	1,910	3,547
	1981	196,469	3,834	42.02	33.78	8,255,627	129,513	8,385,140	3,845	2,181

Table 4-8. Visits and Proportion by Profession in Five

State	Year	Attending Physician		Psychiatrist	
		No. visits	Provider percentage	No. visits	Provider percentage
Outpatient					
California	1980	9,142	2.9	88,905	28.0
	1981	15,108	4.7	76,515	23.6
Colorado	1980	2,424	6.4	11,441	30.0
	1981	1,953	5.3	9,642	26.4
Florida	1980	7,489	13.2	21,496	37.8
	1981	9,315	15.1	20,827	33.9
Texas	1980	3,846	6.0	17,393	27.3
	1981	2,130	2.8	17,857	23.9
Virginia	1980	a	a	80,853	80.5
	1981	582	0.5	88,921	75.4
All states	1980	46,706	5.0	368,463	39.7
	1981	56,164	5.7	355,543	36.2
Inpatient					
California	1980	1,472	3.1	42,208	89.3
	1981	4,340	9.4	37,126	80.2
Colorado	1980	5,227	36.9	7,267	51.3
	1981	5,164	35.4	7,049	48.3
Florida	1980	6,263	18.1	27,165	78.7
	1981	5,586	18.9	21,873	73.8
Texas	1980	4,842	15.6	22,845	73.8
	1981	1,794	6.2	21,892	76.0
Virginia	1980	260	0.4	61,304	99.3
	1981	467	0.7	67,458	97.7
All states	1980	30,410	10.9	230,902	82.6
	1981	27,349	9.6	231,886	81.7

[a]Fewer than 100 visits.

[b]Includes all psychiatric procedure visits, including those for nonpsychiatric diagnostic codes, b excludes nonpsychiatric procedures for psychiatric diagnostic codes. Including the latter would increase the outpatient visits 20.6% in 1980, 24.5% in 1981, and the inpatient visits 10.7% in 1980, 8.9% in 1981.

Interstate variation. Finally, there was some notable variation among states in the degree to which the several professions served CHAMPUS beneficiaries. In part this may be due to practitioner supply and in part, for nonphysician providers, the extent to which they are recognized by law in their state, generating some climate of public acceptance. In any event, this variation among states is illustrated in Table 4-8, showing the number and proportion of visits by profession for the five states with the largest

States and in All States, Fiscal Years 1980 and 1981.

Psychologist		Social Worker		Other		Total	National
No. visits	Provider percentage	No. visits	Provider percentage	No. visits	Provider percentage	Visits	Percentage
126,185	39.7	88,101	27.7	5,440	1.7	317,778	34.3
128,446	39.7	95,078	29.4	8,535	2.6	323,688	33.0
11,180	29.4	9,911	26.0	3,133	8.2	38,089	4.1
10,753	29.4	10,424	28.5	3,758	10.3	36,530	3.7
13,945	24.5	11,858	20.8	2,116	3.7	56,904	6.1
14,727	23.9	12,362	20.1	4,265	6.9	61,496	6.3
21,392	33.6	15,500	24.3	5,603	8.8	63,742	6.9
25,616	34.2	22,131	29.6	7,062	9.4	74,844	7.6
8,773	8.7	1,396	1.4	9,311	9.3	100,390	10.8
16,009	13.6	4,603	3.9	7,793	6.6	117,908	12.0
260,115	28.0	172,790	18.6	79,344	8.6	927,500[b]	—
285,014	29.0	196,469	20.0	88,308	9.0	981,567[b]	—
2,812	5.9	271	0.6	522	1.1	47,285	16.9
3,270	7.1	409	0.9	1,143	2.5	46,209	16.3
786	5.6	605	4.3	275	1.9	14,160	5.1
1,385	9.5	547	3.7	453	3.1	14,598	5.1
332	1.0	186	0.5	575	1.7	34,521	12.3
220	0.7	446	1.5	1,497	5.1	29,622	10.4
987	3.2	816	2.6	1,462	4.7	30,952	11.1
1,096	3.8	1,150	4.0	2,891	10.0	28,824	10.1
142	0.2	a	a	a	a	61,731	22.1
793	1.1	130	0.2	188	0.3	69,036	24.3
7,264	2.6	3,053	1.1	8,031	2.9	279,660[b]	—
9,264	3.3	3,834	1.3	11,666	4.1	283,999[b]	—

volume of services—over 62 percent of all outpatient services, about two-thirds of all inpatient services.

Attending physicians were rarely involved in outpatient services in Virginia, but they delivered about 14 percent of such services in Florida. For all states they provided 5.7 percent of outpatient mental health visits in 1981 (9.6 percent inpatient). In 1975 it was 5.1 percent. This proportion was reviewed by the government in 1978 and reported as 4.3 percent over a three-month period, somewhat underreported (U.S. General Accounting Office, 1980). Whether general physicians have had training in the treatment of mental disorder comparable to that of mental health specialists is another matter.

Psychiatrists were the major providers overall, delivering more than three-quarters of outpatient services in Virginia but fewer outpatient services than psychologists in California and Texas. The level of outpatient services by psychologists was highest in California, almost 40 percent. Nationally, psychologists provided over one-quarter of outpatient mental health services, social workers about one-fifth.

While one-sixth of the inpatient visits overall were delivered in California, almost one-quarter were delivered in Virginia, where psychiatry had a nearly complete monopoly.

Attending physicians provided more than one-third of the inpatient services in Colorado, while psychiatry held a virtual monopoly over such services in Virginia (and the adjacent District of Columbia). Nationally, other professions, with few exceptions, in contrast to their roles in outpatient services, were an incidental factor in providing inpatient services. Only in California and Colorado did psychologists consistently deliver over 5 percent of these services and only in Colorado did social workers consistently deliver over 3 percent of them.

Referring back to Table 4-4, we note that although the use of strictly medical procedures was uncommon, there was some definite interstate variation. Virginia alone accounted for almost half and one-quarter of all the chemotherapy management visits to psychiatrists nationally on an out- and inpatient basis, respectively. Texas psychiatrists, however, accounted for 17 and 26 percent of the total convulsive therapy out- and inpatient visits, respectively. In California, Florida, and Texas not one visit was paid for chemotherapy management.

Unfortunately, reliable data on the number of CHAMPUS beneficiaries per state are not available. Such data would enable calculation of utilization and cost variations by state. Even so, there appears to be evidence of significant provider-driven regional/local variations in mental health services utilization.

Reimbursement Conditions

Mental health benefits under the CHAMPUS are comprehensive, but they do require some financial participation by the user and also have a catchment-area condition.

To benefit from the use of health services in the community, individuals must pay for the first $50 of outpatient costs; families have a $100 deductible. For outpatient services, dependents of active-duty personnel must pay 20 percent of subsequent costs, while retired personnel and their dependents have a 25 percent copayment requirement. For hospital costs, the dependents of active-duty personnel must pay the greater of $5.50 a day (FY 1981; $6.30 in FY 1982) or $25 per admission, while for the others it is again 25 percent of all costs. In all cases, the patient is responsible for all noncovered services and any disallowed charges that may result from the care provided. In addition, persons eligible for CHAMPUS benefits who live within forty miles of a military hospital are required to obtain their inpatient nonemergency health care there unless they have been issued a Certificate of Non-Availability (CNA). Outpatient mental health services are seldom available in military treatment facilities, and so it is not surprising that in both fiscal years 17 percent of CHAMPUS dollars were spent for mental health care.

Discussion

CHAMPUS maintained an extensive—too extensive—procedure code list in 1981. Billing and reporting could be simplified by consolidating a number of like procedures and eliminating others that are not used. A more concise list of procedures that accurately reflected actual practice would also simplify analysis of the mental health service utilization data and make the reports more meaningful for professionals, planners, and the administration alike.

Since there were more visits to psychiatrists in 1981 than any other provider group, it is instructive to look at their billed outpatient procedures. Of the twenty procedure codes for family therapy, three were not used, only six had more than 100 visits, and only two had more than 1,000. For psychotherapy not specified as brief, there were nineteen procedure codes, seven of them not used (including two for psychoanalysis), while the following six accounted for 99.6 percent of all billings:

90802	Individual psychotherapy, 45–50 min.	4,774 visits
90805	Psychotherapy, verbal, 50 min.	141,785 visits
90844	Individual psychotherapy, 45–50 min.	23,841 visits
90854	Psychotherapy, inpatient care, 45–50 min.	2,163 visits
92803	Psychotherapy, adult or child, 45–50 min., office	97,375 visits
92804	Psychotherapy, adult or child, 45–50 min., hospital/facility	3,230 visits

It would seem that one procedure code could subsume all this "hourly" psychotherapy with the addition of a location variant for office, hospital/facility, or home. Furthermore, a number of the procedures that could be used only by physicians were never or no longer used. Some streamlining for the group therapies and the brief forms of psychotherapy also appears readily achievable.

Although there are procedure codes for both telephone consultation (92855) and biofeedback (92890), they were never billed, since apparently they were not allowable procedures. Certainly a phone consultation can be supportive, even incisive, while the effectiveness of biofeedback is increasingly being demonstrated. Behavior therapy is viewed by many as the treatment of choice for certain conditions, such as phobias, but there was no procedure code for it. It is just not credible that *no* phone consultation, biofeedback, or behavior therapy was provided by any psychiatrist in 1981. If those procedures were billed simply as psychotherapy in order to avoid difficulties in reimbursement, then valuable information on the real diversity of the treatment provided is lost (McGuire and Frisman, 1983). And, as pointed out earlier, psychiatrists prescribe and review medications for a number of their patients, but of 355,543 visits only 1,501 were for chemotherapy management (90862) and 673 for individual medical psychotherapy (90841). It would be valuable to know the extent to which psychoactive medication is used in conjunction with or instead of psychotherapy.

It was noted earlier that between 1975 and 1981 there was a 12.6 percent decline in the proportion of outpatient visits to psychiatrists, a decline more than taken up by psychologists and social workers. Indeed, in six of the nineteen states where all visits exceeded 1 percent of the total visits nationally, the number of outpatient visits to psychologists in 1981 exceeded the number to psychiatrists. Hourly psychotherapy was the predominant, the modal, procedure, and in nine of these nineteen states in 1981, there were more such visits to psychologists than to psychiatrists. Clearly, psychiatry is facing a challenge to its once preeminent position in psychotherapy, and psychoanalysis is no longer a billed procedure.

Although psychiatry's preeminence in one-on-one psychotherapy is on the wane, it appears, at least as of 1981 in this nationally representative program, that it has consolidated and is strengthening its control over inpatient services, carrying 82 percent of all such services. Indeed, in some states, such as Virginia, psychiatry has a virtual monopoly over inpatient care. But the number of CHAMPUS inpatient visits dropped sharply between 1975 and 1981. In addition, Congress set a sixty-day cap on such services, beginning in January 1983, and, where necessary, is encouraging increased ambulatory and alternative care. With inpatient services coming under heavy cost constraints, it may be that what psychiatry is gaining in its fight to keep the hospital door closed to all other mental health practitioners is more and more control over less and less practice. It may also be that psychiatry is painting itself into a visible hospital corner, to be met with antitrust action for restraint of trade, refusal to deal, and boycott; a curtailment of hospital psychiatric benefits in group health plans; and a growing emphasis on alternatives to hospitalization.

The rise of CHAMPUS costs for mental health benefits from $121.4 million in 1980 to $146.9 million in 1981, a 21 percent increase in one year, underscores that cost will be a major factor and in the short term will force program changes. The CHAMPUS is actively exploring alternatives. In fall 1981 CHAMPUS-CHOICE was initiated: in Houston, Minneapolis, and Portland the program contracted with local HMOs as an alternative choice. Early experience indicated a reduction in program costs. Potential cost reduction was also a factor in the recognition of clinical social workers on an independent basis. All inpatient and outpatient services, when extended, have been brought under peer review through methods developed by the American Psychological and Psychiatric associations under contract with the CHAMPUS. Because it can exert pressures on practitioners, peer review, one objective of which is utilization review, is not universally popular. But something must be done to control cost, and if it is not done by one's peers, it will be done externally. That is the political reality (Willens and DeLeon, 1982). The American Psychological and Psychiatric associations could not agree on the terms of a single joint contract and so bid separately; the contract was awarded to the American Psychiatric Association. For an earlier discussion of CHAMPUS peer review, see Rodriguez (1983).

Peer review is not achieved without its own costs. The average cost of psychiatric peer review in 1983 was $156, psychological $269. It should be obvious, then, that not only because of the cost involved and the high volume of low-frequency visits, it is impractical to put other than high-volume claims to such scrutiny. The high user or the user of high-cost services (hospitalization) can therefore expect increasing attention the greater the use.

As we have seen, the recent growth in number of psychologists (Dörken and Webb, 1981, and Chapter One) has been phenomenal. Social workers and psychiatric nurses are now recognized as CHAMPUS providers without referral, and we read of the mounting "physician glut." In these procompetition days such "surplusage" is fertile ground for the negotiation of alternative or discounted rates or capitated at-risk contracting with organized entities. Another model for cost containment, quite familiar to government, is the public utility model with rate setting. So long as the number of beneficiaries does not decrease significantly, and Congress faces a massive budget deficit, it would be unrealistic to assume that the cost per visit can continue to keep increasing along the merry UCR way.

Perhaps the most salient fact evident from this analysis of mental health services utilization is the minimal (1.41 percent) utilization in 1981, even a slight decline since 1975, in the face of an extensive benefit. Although some insurers or government officials may allege that coverage of mental health services is unaffordable or will involve runaway costs, the facts in this national, comprehensive, and open fee-for-service benefit under consumer/patient choice underscore just the opposite.

References

CHAMPUS: CHAMPUS/CHAMPVA Mental Health Update, Blue Cross of Washington and Alaska, Apr.–June 1985.

DeLeon, P., VandenBos, G., and Kraut, A., "A Review of Federal Legislation Recognizing Psychology." *American Psychologist,* 1984, *39,* 933–946.

Dörken, H. "CHAMPUS Ten-State Claim Experience for Mental Disorder: Fiscal Year 1975." *American Psychologist,* 1977, *32,* 697–710.

Dörken, H. "CHAMPUS Ten-State Claim Experience for Mental Disorder: Fiscal Year 1975." In C. Kiesler, N. Cummings, and G. R. VandenBos (eds.), *Psychology and National Health Insurance: A Sourcebook.* Washington, D.C.: American Psychological Association, 1979.

Dörken, H. "Mental Health Services to Children and Adolescents Under the CHAMPUS: Fiscal Year 1975." *Professional Psychology,* 1980, *11,* 12–14.

Dörken H., and Webb, J. T. "Licensed Psychologists on the Increase: 1974–1979." *American Psychologist,* 1981, *36,* 1419–1426.

Kiesler, C. "Mental Hospitals and Alternative Care: Noninstitutionalization as Potential Public Policy for Mental Patients." *American Psychologist,* 1982, *37,* 349–360.

McGuire, T., and Frisman, L. "Reimbursement Policy and Cost Effective Mental Health Care." *American Psychologist,* 1983, *38,* 935–940.

Rodriguez, A. "Psychological and Psychiatric Peer Review at CHAMPUS." *American Psychologist,* 1983, *38,* 941–947.

U.S. General Accounting Office. *Extent of Billings by Nonpsychiatric Specialty Physicians for Mental Health Services Under CHAMPUS.* Pub. No. HRD-80-113. Washington, D.C.: U.S. General Accounting Office, 1980.

Wells, K., and others. *Cost Sharing and the Demand for Ambulatory Mental Health Services.* Santa Monica, Calif.: Rand Corp., 1982.

Willens, J., and DeLeon, P. H. "Political Aspects of Peer Review." *Professional Psychology,* 1982, *13,* 23–26.

Patrick H. DeLeon
Gary R. VandenBos
Alan G. Kraut

5

Federal Recognition of Psychology as a Profession

Psychology is still a new and evolving profession. During the past decade, the profession has accomplished a number of legislative objectives that place it in a good position to continue to influence the development of our nation's health care and social policies. However, its educators and practitioners are just beginning to appreciate the significance and nuances of the legislative process. As the profession's training institutions, in particular, continue to broaden their horizons, the prospects for future legislative successes are enhanced.

The relative youth of psychology as a profession is not fully recognized, even within psychology. It was only in 1977 that the Missouri psychology licensure act finally allowed psychology to claim statutory recognition in all fifty states and the District of Columbia (DeLeon, Donahue, and VandenBos, 1984). As the profession of psychology has matured, it has become increasingly interested in obtaining statutory and administrative recognition for its services under the various federal health care programs. Primarily because of this "professional youth," however, psychology has only begun to achieve the type of legislative and administrative recognition that it desires.

Not only are its practitioners relatively young (Pallak, 1985), but the field is still in the early stages of developing its own legislative agenda, and professional psychologists are also just beginning to appreciate the extent to which various elements of their profession have different legislative priorities and agendas.

99

In this chapter we provide a broad overview of the federal legislative issues of concern to professional psychology. In enumerating psychology's successes, we also hope to suggest targets for future legislative efforts. Although we will not discuss state legislation in any depth, many of the federal issues we will discuss have state counterparts.

Psychology's Public Image

In the public's mind *psychology* is synonymous with *mental health*. For the lay public, and especially for the elected politician, *psychology* conjures up the image of a clinician testing or providing psychotherapy. As such, the public perception of the profession is quite limiting, for professional psychology is considerably broader in scope than diagnostic testing and psychotherapy. During the past decade, for instance, an increasing number of psychologists have become involved in the new subfield of health psychology (DeLeon, 1979; Matarazzo and others, 1984). The importance of the psychosocial aspects of health care is gaining increasing recognition (Inouye, 1985; Yates, 1984). As another example, in the legal and judicial arena approximately a dozen schools have established joint psychology/law programs (Melton, 1983). Further, increasing numbers of psychologists are becoming involved in public service, especially as high-level policy administrators or policy formulators. These developments notwithstanding, psychologists still have to overcome their stereotype as testers or "shrinks," an image that is all too limiting.

The Federal Government as a Purchaser of Care

During the 1970s there were considerable public expressions of congressional concern about perceived inequities in access to, quality of, and availability of health care (DeLeon and VandenBos, 1980). For example, Senator Ribicoff, the sponsor of a Carter administration health-related bill, pointed out that "only about 2 million of the 12 million children who are eligible for Medicaid are appropriately screened and that 22 percent of those who are found to be in need of treatment do not in fact receive it" (DeLeon, 1977,

p. 750). The same type of health statistics exists in the 1980s, as evidenced in the 1985 Congressional Budget Office report *Reducing Poverty Among Children,* but the major policy focus has shifted from equity to cost containment (Chapter Twelve). Recent statistics show that in 1984 our nation spent $387.4 billion, or 10.6 percent of our gross national product, on health care. This was the highest expenditure in our history, but the rate of increase had begun to drop and was the lowest in twenty years.

There are four, possibly five, major programs in which the federal government acts as a purchaser of health care: the Civilian Health and Medical Program of the Uniformed Services (CHAM-PUS), the Federal Employees' Health Benefit Program (FEHBP), the medical expense deduction provisions of the Internal Revenue Code, and Medicare and Medicaid (Titles XVIII and XIX of the Social Security Act). Mainly because these programs come under the jurisdiction of different congressional committees and subcommittees, psychology has been accorded significantly different status under each of the programs (DeLeon, VandenBos, and Kraut, 1984).

CHAMPUS. CHAMPUS provides reimbursement for the health care expenses of 7.9 million military dependents and retirees for services that they cannot obtain at military health care facilities. For fiscal year 1985 the CHAMPUS budget request was $1.4 billion.

Since the congressional deliberations on the fiscal year 1976 appropriations bill (P.L. 94-212), "clinical psychologists" have been expressly enumerated as autonomous providers under the program. But during the following year's appropriations deliberations, the descriptive phrase *psychologically necessary* was deleted in an effort to shorten and clean up the appropriations bill. The Department of Defense (DOD) used this modification as a rationale for a requirement of physician referral and supervision. Accordingly, the following year the Congress again included language making clear its intent that psychologists were to be deemed autonomous providers.

Subsequent Senate reports have clarified for DOD a number of professional issues involving psychologists. For example, the phrase *clinical psychologist* was to include any doctoral-level psychologist licensed by the appropriate state authorities, psychological services were to be peer-reviewed, and there was to be no federal restriction on the scope of psychological practice—that is, psychologists were to be deemed independent providers on both an inpatient and an outpatient basis, as well as in residential treatment facilities.

From 1977 to 1985 DOD contracted with both the American Psychological Association and the American Psychiatric Association to provide national peer review systems. After that period, the systems were combined into one, again at congressional direction. Presently, the only statutory difference between the ways psychologists and their medical colleagues are treated is that a physician must supervise the services of marriage and family counselors. However, this is a responsibility or professional opportunity that psychology has never requested.

During the congressional deliberations on the Department of Defense Authorization Act of 1985 (P.L. 98-525), the armed services committees incorporated the basic psychology appropriations language into the CHAMPUS authorization statute (10 U.S.C. secs. 1071-1093). The previous year, in drafting the 1984 Authorization Act (P.L. 98-94), the armed services committees incorporated language, which had been enacted during a prior session (P.L. 97-377), that instituted an annual sixty-day limitation on inpatient mental health care but provided an express waiver for "extraordinary medical or psychological circumstances."

Other than the express references to psychological services described above, the CHAMPUS authorization statute is quite broad and permissive in nature and, as far as psychology is concerned, gives the secretary considerable discretion to develop the CHAMPUS benefit package that he or she deems appropriate.

Federal Employees' Health Benefit Program (FEHBP). In 1974 P.L. 93-363 included "clinical psychology" under the FEHBP direct-recognition (or "freedom of choice") provision, which now provides that "when a contract . . . requires payment or reimbursement for services which may be performed by a clinical psychologist . . . an employee, annuitant, or family member covered by the contract shall be free to select, and shall have direct access to, such a clinical psychologist . . . without supervision or referral by another health practitioner. . . . The provisions . . . shall not apply to group practice prepayment plans." The accompanying

Senate report made clear that it was the intent of Congress that all doctoral-level psychologists licensed for independent practice by the appropriate state authorities should be considered "clinical psychologists" under FEHBP.

Although a specific mental health benefit is not mandated by the generally permissive statute (5 U.S.C. secs. 8901–8913), the Office of Personnel Management, which has responsibility for annually negotiating the various contracts under FEHBP, has consistently included mental health care. The various mental health disciplines, including psychology, express concern that the negotiated mental health benefit has not been sufficiently comprehensive. However, we are not aware of any incident since enactment of P.L. 93-363 in which psychology as a profession has been treated differently than its medical counterparts.

Internal Revenue Code. Under both the corporate and personal provisions of the Internal Revenue Code (26 U.S.C. secs. 162 and 213) there has to date been surprisingly little interest in legislatively defining what constitutes bona fide "medical expenses" (DeLeon, 1981), even though for fiscal year 1984 the Office of Management and Budget estimated that the U.S. Treasury lost $28.5 billion as a direct result of these provisions. The implementing IRS regulations and the various tax court decisions have been quite consistent in attempting to draw a distinction between services that are targeted toward ameliorating a particular psychological or physical deficit (deductible) and those that might instead be considered to be merely beneficial to one's general health or sense of well-being (nondeductible). Since 1973 the personal federal income tax instructions have expressly stated that the services of psychologists may qualify under this provision of the law.

Thus, under each of the three federal health programs described to this point in the chapter, psychology is treated in exactly the same manner as its medical counterparts.

Medicare and Medicaid. From their very inception, the congressional committees with jurisdiction over these two programs have stressed their intention that these were to be health, not social welfare, programs. As such, both have always had an express and deliberate "medical" orientation, and both have included the requirement that only services that are "medically necessary" should be reimbursed.

Of considerable historical importance to psychology is the fact that the Senate report accompanying the original bill (the Social Security Amendments of 1965, P.L. 89-97) expressly stated that "the committee's bill provides that the physician is to be the key figure in determining utilization of health services" (Sen. Rpt. #89-404). In response to subsequent efforts by various nonphysician health care providers to broaden the basic orientation of the programs, the Congress directed the Department of Health, Education, and Welfare to conduct a formal study of the possibility of expanding the availability of various types of health services (P.L. 90-248). In December 1968 the department submitted its "Independent Practitioners Study" (Cohen, 1968) to the Congress. The report specifically stated that the services of clinical psychologists should be reimbursed when they are provided in an organized setting and when there has been physician referral. Further, it was recommended that a physician should establish a plan for the patient's total care and also retain overall responsibility for patient management. Finally, the report recommended that reimbursement be to the agency, not directly to the individual psychologist. The report was never implemented.

With this orientation being prevalent in the congressional committees with jurisdiction over Medicare and Medicaid, it should not be surprising to psychologists that early efforts to include them as autonomous practitioners were not successful (DeLeon, Kjervik, Kraut, and VandenBos, 1985; Inouye, forthcoming). In 1972 psychology achieved its first statutory recognition under either Medicare or Medicaid when P.L. 92-603 authorized the secretary to determine "whether the services of clinical psychologists may be made more generally available . . . in a manner consistent with quality of care and equitable and efficient administration" under Medicare. This provision eventually resulted in the "Colorado Medicare study" and formal hearings before the Senate finance committee in August 1978 (Bent, Willens, and Lassen, 1983; Inouye, 1983; McCall and Rice, 1983).

During the congressional deliberations on the Omnibus Reconciliation Act of 1980 (P.L. 96-499), psychological services were expressly enumerated under several Medicare provisions authorizing payment for rehabilitation services. However, an express requirement was also included that every patient must be under the care of a physician and, further, that there must be a formal treatment plan, established and periodically reviewed by a physician. Of interest, it was not until nearly five years later that organized psychology, including the authors, became aware of these particular provisions of the Medicare statute.

During the 98th Congress (1983–1984) professional psychology made three rather significant advances under separate programs of the Social Security Act. The first was a modification of the Medicaid statute to ensure that programs or facilities being reimbursed under the Medicaid "clinic" provisions did not have to be administered by a physician. At the time, the Health Care Financing Administration (HCFA) was in the process of issuing regulations for physician administration. The proposed HCFA regulations would have affected most community mental health centers. However, Senator Daniel K. Inouye, by emphasizing the inherent inconsistency of this requirement with the statutory provisions providing professional autonomy for certified nurse-midwives, was successful in having language incorporated into the Deficit Reduction Act of 1984 (P.L. 98-369) to prevent this effect.

The second accomplishment was achieved in the same bill, also at Senator Inouye's request and with the support of organized psychology. Psychologists were included in the Medicare health maintenance organization (HMO) provisions as autonomous providers. Nurse-practitioners had achieved this status in 1982, and the senator was again able to utilize the nursing profession's earlier legislative success in his efforts to further the psychological profession. Presently 17 million Americans are enrolled in HMOs. This was the first time that psychologists were recognized as autonomous providers under any of the Medicare or Medicaid provisions and directly followed up on the recommendations presented at the 1978 "Colorado study" hearings.

The final major legislative accomplishment was the express inclusion in the Social Security Disability Benefits Reform Act of 1984 (P.L. 98-460) of statutory language ensuring that "qualified psychologists" would be allowed to evaluate mental impairments for purposes of determining whether a beneficiary should be eligible for disability benefits. It came after two years of work involving organized psychology, mental health consumer groups, the Social Security Administration, and Congress. The same bill also included "psychological abnormalities" as a valid cause of pain.

Other Federal Initiatives

For professional psychologists involved in forensic work, the 98th Congress represented an especially good two years. Before that session, the Federal Rules of Criminal Procedure expressly stated that federal courts must use the expertise of psychiatrists when mental health evaluations or examinations were desired. Psychologists were not mentioned anywhere in the federal rules, which reflected the provisions of the federal criminal statute (Title 18). Although the federal rules are not binding on the various state courts, there can be little question that they have major precedent value.

By way of background, the Congress, in 1966, had created the National Commission on Reform of Federal Criminal Laws expressly to review the possible need for any major legislative overhaul of the federal criminal statute. The commission's recommendations were submitted to Congress in 1971, and in the U.S. Senate alone, over 12,000 pages of testimony and commentary were subsequently received. In January 1978 the Senate passed its version of a comprehensive reform bill, but both houses of Congress were unable to develop similar proposals until the 98th Congress.

In the beginning of the legislative process, the Senate proposals included reference to "clinical psychologists" but with a requirement that a medical doctor also be involved. However, subsequent Senate judiciary committee recommendations provided for the autonomous functioning of psychologists. President Reagan's proposed Criminal Code Reform Acts of 1982 and 1984 also provided for complete parity between psychology and psychiatry. In the closing hours of the 98th Congress, P.L. 98-473 (the Fiscal Year 1985 Continuing Resolution) was passed, providing complete parity for psychologists with their medical colleagues throughout all aspects of the federal Criminal Code. In addition, the Criminal Justice Mental Health Standards adopted by the American Bar Association's House of Delegates (American Bar Association, 1984) provided complete parity for professional psychology.

Since these developments, all recommendations from the National Conference of Commissioners on Uniform State Laws have also included complete professional parity. In essence, professional psychologists who are involved with the judicial or criminal justice system now possess a firm body of support from both the Congress and the American Bar Association that their expertise is comparable to that of their medical colleagues.

Professional psychologists who are employed within the federal service (for example, in the Veterans Administration, the U.S. Public Health Service, or the Department of Defense) have their own unique legislative priorities. The Veterans Administration (VA), the largest employer of psychologists in the nation, currently employs more than 1,400 doctoral-level psychologists in its Department of Medicine and Surgery. Presently, there is considerable disagreement among members of the VA psychology corps on whether they wish to be hired under the authority of Title 38 (Veterans' Benefits) or Title 5 (Civil Service) of the U.S. Code. P.L. 95-151 (Veterans Health Program Extension and Improvement Act of 1979) placed the statutory requirement for psychology licensure under Title 38, but individual psychologists are currently hired under the broad Title 5 civil service authority, which mentions the profession of psychology only under a very minor provision. The VA Health Care Program Amendments of 1980 (P.L. 96-330) directed the VA to conduct a comprehensive study of the possibility of including psychology and various other health care professions under Title 38. However, the perceived possibility of losing their current private-practice authority has made many psychologists very hesitant to be transferred to Title 38. Nevertheless, the concerted efforts by the Reagan administration to implement the various recommendations of the Grace Commission (Grace, 1983), which proposes a reduction of 2 percent in federal midlevel managerial positions, has raised considerable interest in the possible transfer, especially among the VA chief psychologists. Presently, the VA has been able to exempt all Title 38 employees (mainly physicians and nurses) from the reduction, and the projected effect on psychology would be a 7 percent reduction in 1985 alone (Lips, 1985). On a more positive note, the Veterans Health Care Amendments of 1984 (P.L. 98-528) provided new authority for the administrator to grant a special pay bonus, similar to that currently being received by VA physicians, to psychologists who have gained diplomate status.

In the closing hours of the 97th Congress (1981–1982), as a provision of the Orphan Drug Act (P.L. 97-414), psychologists were authorized to serve in the U.S. Public Health Service Regular Corps. Until then, an estimated twenty-five psychologists were serving in the corps under the broad, generic statutory authority of the Department of Health, Education, and Welfare. Of interest, membership in the Regular Corps is the only legislative requirement for being appointed surgeon general of the United States.

The approximately 400 clinical or health care psychologists serving in the Department of Defense have unique legislative needs, for there is every indication that they are treated in a second-class manner by the department. In August 1978, at the request of Senator Inouye, the principal deputy assistant secretary for health affairs issued a memorandum urging each of the armed services to systematically address the utilization of psychologists. The memorandum indicated that there were problems and suggested that administrative and promotional opportunities for psychologists should be enhanced.

In August 1982 the Defense Audit Service of DOD surveyed the morale of military psychologists and selected other nonphysician health care providers. Its report (U.S. Defense Audit Service, 1982) concluded that there was evidence of factors that "seriously affected morale." Since the congressional deliberations on the fiscal year 1981 Department of Defense appropriations bill (P.L. 96-527), the Senate appropriations committee has expressed its concern about this matter. The fiscal year 1984 appropriations bill (P.L. 98-212) directed the assistant secretary for health affairs to establish a special task force on nonphysician morale. The task force has been meeting since that date and has made a number of recommendations, which, if adopted, would significantly improve the morale of military psychologists.

However, as reflected in the March 1984 DOD inspector general's audit report, the three services appear to be resistant to modifying the status quo. Nevertheless, one element of the problem that the Senate appropriations committee initially raised has been addressed. At the committee's request, DOD has instituted a requirement that psychologists (and several other health care professions, including physicians) be licensed. During the House of Representatives floor deliberations on the 1986 Department of Defense Authorization Act, an amendment was accepted that would codify this requirement. This is a first step in providing military psychologists with professional recognition. Legislation is also currently pending in the Senate that would provide military psychologists who obtain diplomate status with a special pay bonus, comparable to that currently authorized for military physicians. However, much remains to be done to significantly improve the professional status of military psychologists.

In the long run, perhaps the most important development for all of professional psychology has been the extent to which its educational institutions have recently begun to expand their horizons. Traditionally, departments of psychology have relied almost exclusively for student support on the resources of the National Institute of Mental Health, state hospitals, and the VA. This is steadily changing, however, and a number of leaders in the professional school movement have publicly called out for psychology to establish its own service delivery programs and institutions (Fox, 1982; Fox and Bent, 1984; Rodgers, 1980).

Within the last two sessions of Congress, psychology has begun to make a concerted effort to have its training institutions and their students deemed eligible for support under the various professional school initiatives. As a direct result, psychology has now been included under the Indian Education Act Fellowship provisions (P.L. 98-511), the National Health Service Corps

Scholarship program (P.L. 97-35), and the Individual Federal Insured Loan program (P.L. 97-35).

Public Law 97-35 (the Omnibus Budget Reconciliation Act of 1981) also included clinical psychologists under the section of the health professions training authority that directs the secretary to collect data on health professions personnel. This accomplishment will eventually provide the Congress with objective data on the possible "substitutability" of psychologists for psychiatrists under the various federal training and service delivery programs. These data should allow psychology to modify the present "psychiatric health manpower shortage area" designations to more accurately reflect the present state-of-the-art generic "mental health" orientation. The data should also allow psychology to effectively demonstrate to the department and to the Congress the extent to which its health care practitioners actually function in a considerably broader arena than mental health care.

During the 98th Congress, President Reagan vetoed the proposed Public Health Service Act Amendments of 1984, which would have made psychology programs also eligible for the Health Careers Opportunity Program (Educational Assistance to Individuals from Disadvantaged Backgrounds) and the Health Professions Student Loan program. Both these initiatives are expected to be enacted into public law during the 99th Congress (1985–1986).

Future Directions

Health policy psychologists who have examined their profession's legislative growth have consistently observed that psychology has been successful when we have taken it on ourselves to see that either one individual or a cohesive group is readily available to systematically provide psychological expertise to our nation's health policy leaders (Bevan, 1980; DeLeon, O'Keefe, VandenBos, and Kraut, 1982; Forman and O'Malley, 1984; Hosticka, Hibbard, and Sundberg, 1983; Payton, 1984). For example, under the federal worker's compensation program designed for federal employees, clinical psychologists are expressly included in the definition section both for "physician" and for "medical, surgical, and hospital services and supplies" (5 U.S.C.

secs. 8101(2) and (3)). At one of the APA Public Policy dinner discussions held several years later, the Senate staff member who helped draft that provision made it quite clear that one psychologist, Gene Shapiro, had singlehandedly convinced the chairman of the committee with jurisdiction over the program that psychologists should indeed be recognized as autonomous providers (Goldberg, 1980).

A recent comprehensive review of the extent to which the various congressional committees have expressly provided for coverage of psychological services within statutes under their jurisdiction concluded that "psychology has probably received its greatest legislative recognition under those federal programs that have been developed specifically to address the unique needs of our nation's handicapped individuals" (DeLeon, Forsythe, and VandenBos, forthcoming). In the 1983 hearings held by the Senate (authorization) Subcommittee on the Handicapped, when it was overseeing the Vocational Rehabilitation Act and the Education of the Handicapped Act, seven of the thirteen public witness panels included psychologists or persons with doctoral degrees in related fields. Further, both the president and the president-elect of APA's Division of Rehabilitation Psychology submitted formal testimony for the record. Is it any wonder that the authorization statutes addressing the problems of the handicapped reflect the importance of behavioral science?

There appears to be little question that psychology does in fact have considerable scientific and clinical expertise that can be of definite assistance to our nation's health policy leadership (Bevan, 1982; Kiesler, 1982). The crucial issue is how to ensure that it is attended to (DeLeon, 1983; Masters, 1984; Reppucci, forthcoming; Saxe and Koretz, 1982; Weick, 1984).

For whatever reasons, historically psychologists appear to have actively avoided participating in the political process. A survey of the approximately twenty-five psychologists who have served on Capitol Hill during the past decade found that only two had decided to remain on either the House or the Senate staff for more than three years (DeLeon, Frohboese, and Meyers, 1984). During the Senate Appropriations Committee hearings on the fiscal year 1984 appropriations bill for the Departments of Labor, Health and

Human Services, and Education, only 4 of the approximately 155 public witnesses testifying were psychologists, and only 2 of these individuals identified themselves as psychologists (DeLeon and VandenBos, forthcoming). This is indeed in sharp contrast to the concerted advocacy of the rehabilitation psychologists but, unfortunately, is far more typical.

Professional psychologists simply do not appreciate the significance of the reality that our nation's health policy is established by politicians, not by health care professionals. They also do not appreciate that the vast majority of politicians do not have a personal background in health and thus they must, and do, rely very heavily on outside public witnesses for advice and programmatic recommendations. In our judgment, psychology's own hesitancy to participate actively in the political process has been the most significant obstacle to greater legislative success to this point.

During the next decade, psychology will undoubtedly pursue legislative agendas on two distinct levels. The first will stress the more immediate, short-term (or perhaps even crisis) agendas. Simply stated, psychology must systematically strive to ensure that its practitioners and scientists are expressly included in every appropriate phase of every legislative development. If psychology really wants its professional expertise to be appreciated by our nation's health policy leadership, the profession must ensure that its views are consistently considered.

In essence, psychology must become part of the underlying process. A concrete example: When one thinks about research related to dental care, much of what immediately comes to mind is essentially behavioral or psychosocial (that is, research on patient compliance and on anxiety). Accordingly, behavioral psychologists should begin to testify routinely on behalf of the research programs of the National Institute of Dental Research. Similarly, although psychology was successful in modifying the Medicare HMO provisions to include express reference to its practitioners, psychology has still not been able to modify the basic HMO authorization statute to include express reference to psychologists. Presently, the more than 400 psychologists employed in HMOs function under the broad statutory authority of "other health

professions—as the case may be—licensed to provide such services"
(42 U.S.C. 300e-1(2)). In the same manner, psychology must work
to ensure that its practitioners are appropriately recognized under
the Medicare and Medicaid rural health clinic provisions, the
Medicare hospice benefit, and the Medicaid recertification
provision, especially as the latter applies to care in mental hospitals.
Nurse-practitioners have already been expressly included under
each of these latter initiatives (DeLeon, Kjervik, Kraut, and
VandenBos, 1985).

To some professionals these legislative goals may not seem
especially meaningful, chiefly because they cannot see the direct
relevance to their daily lives and professional practices. However,
we can assure the reader that unless psychology is willing to commit
itself over the long haul to the effort that will be necessary to obtain
this type of legislative recognition—which to some, admittedly, is
mainly of symbolic importance—the psychological profession will
never develop the necessary legislative presence to have a significant
impact on such programs as Medicare, with its evolving Prospective
Payment System. If we are not resolved to accomplish what can be
done, we will never realize our full potential.

The second approach, and one that psychology is just
beginning to develop, is to generate one's own legislative agenda.
During the 98th Congress, for example, our nation's twenty-three
schools of public health capitalized on the recommendations of the
U.S. surgeon general in *Healthy People* (U.S. Department of
Health, Education, and Welfare, 1979) and succeeded in having
legislation enacted (P.L. 98-551) to authorize the establishment of
a network of health promotion and disease prevention centers across
the nation. The Health Promotion and Disease Prevention
Amendments of 1984 clearly indicate that each of the eventual
thirteen centers will be established in conjunction with a school of
public health, but they also make express reference to the
contributions of psychology. In the 99th Congress, the schools of
public health have generated considerable interest in the
committees with jurisdiction over Medicare and Medicaid in the
possibility of establishing similar demonstration authority under
these programs. If this latest proposal also becomes public law,

psychology may once again benefit from an open door through the foresight of the schools of public health.

In its own behalf, psychology has begun to develop some forward legislative planning, but it needs to do more. For example, as of this writing legislation has passed the House and Senate that reauthorizes the National Institutes of Health (NIH)—fourteen separate agencies, including eleven institutes, that support about $6 billion in mostly biomedical research. In 1984 only $137 million in behavioral research was funded. The pending legislation is likely to significantly increase the behavioral figure. It emphasizes health promotion and disease prevention activities and mandates that behavioral scientists shall be eligible to serve on all NIH national advisory councils. There are numerous areas in which psychology can play a major role. Psychology could take the lead in developing quality nursing home care and its alternatives, in developing programs for the homeless, in improving employee productivity, and perhaps even in furthering international peace. Over the next decade, we expect psychology to begin to truly shape its own legislative agendas.

References

American Bar Association, Standing Committee on Association Standards for Criminal Justice. *Proposed Criminal Justice Mental Health Standards.* Washington, D.C.: American Bar Association, 1984.

Bent, R. J., Willens, J. G., and Lassen, C. L. "The Colorado Clinical Psychology/Expanded Mental Health Benefits Experiment: An Introductory Commentary." *American Psychologist,* 1983, *38,* 1274–1278.

Bevan, W. "On Getting in Bed with a Lion." *American Psychologist,* 1980, *35,* 779–789.

Bevan, W. "A Sermon of Sorts in Three Parts." *American Psychologist,* 1982, *37,* 1303–1322.

Cohen, W. J. *Independent Practitioners Under Medicare: A Report to the Congress.* Washington, D.C.: Department of Health, Education, and Welfare, 1968.

DeLeon, P. H. "Psychology and the Carter Administration." *American Psychologist,* 1977, *32,* 750–751.

DeLeon, P. H. "The Legislative Outlook for Psychology: A Health Care Profession." *Academic Psychology Bulletin,* 1979, *1,* 187–192.

DeLeon, P. H. "The Medical Expense Deduction Provision— Public Policy in a Vacuum?" *Professional Psychology,* 1981, *12,* 707–716.

DeLeon, P. H. "The Changing and Creating of Legislation: The Political Process." In B. Sales (ed.), *The Professional Psychologist's Handbook.* New York: Plenum, 1983.

DeLeon, P. H., Donahue, J., and VandenBos, G. R. "The Interface of Psychology and the Law." In J. R. McNamara (ed.), *Critical Issues, Developments, and Trends in Professional Psychology.* Vol. 2. New York: Praeger, 1984.

DeLeon, P. H., Forsythe, P., and VandenBos, G. R. "Federal Recognition of Psychology in Rehabilitation Programs." *Rehabilitation Psychology,* forthcoming.

DeLeon, P. H., Frohboese, R., and Meyers, J. C. "Psychologist on Capitol Hill: A Unique Use of the Skills of the Scientist/ Practitioner." *Professional Psychology: Research and Practice,* 1984, *15,* 697–705.

DeLeon, P. H., Kjervik, D. K., Kraut, A. G., and VandenBos, G. R. "Psychology and Nursing: A Natural Alliance." *American Psychologist,* 1985, *40,* 1153–1164.

DeLeon, P. H., O'Keefe, A. M., VandenBos, G. R., and Kraut, A. G. "How to Influence Public Policy: A Blueprint for Activism." *American Psychologist,* 1982, *37,* 476–485.

DeLeon, P. H., and VandenBos, G. R. "Psychotherapy Reimbursement in Federal Programs: Political Factors." In G. R. VandenBos (ed.), *Psychotherapy: Practice, Research, Policy.* Beverly Hills, Calif.: Sage, 1980.

DeLeon, P. H., and VandenBos, G. R. "Health Psychology and Health Policy." In G. C. Stone and others (eds.), *Health Psychology: A Discipline and a Profession.* Chicago: University of Chicago Press, forthcoming.

DeLeon, P. H., VandenBos, G. R., and Kraut, A. G. "Federal Legislation Recognizing Psychology." *American Psychologist,* 1984, *39,* 933–946.

Forman, S. G., and O'Malley, P. L. "A Legislative Field Experience for Psychology Graduate Students." *Professional Psychology: Research and Practice,* 1984, *15,* 324–332.

Fox, R. E. "The Need for a Reorientation of Clinical Psychology." *American Psychologist,* 1982, *37,* 1051–1057.

Fox, R. E., and Bent, R. J. "Current Status and Future Directions of Professional Psychology." In J. R. McNamara (ed.), *Critical Issues, Developments, and Trends in Professional Psychology.* Vol. 2. New York: Praeger, 1984.

Goldberg, M. "Worker's Compensation Legislation." Address presented at American Psychological Association Public Policy dinner, Montreal, Canada, Sept. 26, 1980.

Grace, P. J. *The President's Private Sector Survey on Cost Control.* Washington, D.C.: U.S. Government Printing Office, 1983.

Hosticka, C. J., Hibbard, M., and Sundberg, N. D. "Improving Psychologists' Contributions to the Policymaking Process." *Professional Psychology: Research and Practice,* 1983, *14,* 374–385.

Inouye, D. K. "Mental Health Care: Access, Stigma, and Effectiveness." *American Psychologist,* 1983, *38,* 912–917.

Inouye, D. K. "Saving Health Care Dollars Through Psychological Service." *Congressional Record,* 1985, *131,* S8656–S8659.

Inouye, D. K. "Psychology and Medicare: The Final Hurdle." *Psychotherapy in Private Practice,* forthcoming.

Kiesler, C. A. "Mental Hospitals and Alternative Care: Non-institutionalization as Potential Public Policy for Mental Patients." *American Psychologist,* 1982, *37,* 349–360.

Lips, O. Testimony of the Association of VA Chief Psychologists and the American Psychological Association before the U.S. Senate Committee on Veterans' Affairs, May 7, 1985.

McCall, N., and Rice, T. "A Summary of the Colorado Clinical Psychology/Expanded Mental Health Benefits Experiment." *American Psychologist,* 1983, *38,* 1279–1291.

Masters, J. C. "Psychology, Research, and Social Policy." *American Psychologist,* 1984, *39,* 851–862.

Matarazzo, J. D., and others (eds.). *Behavioral Health: A Handbook of Health Enhancement and Disease Prevention.* New York: Wiley, 1984.

Melton, G. B. "Training in Psychology and Law: A Directory." *Division of Psychology and Law Newsletter,* 1983, *3* (3), 1–5.

Pallak, M. S. "Report of the Executive Officer: 1984." *American Psychologist,* 1985, *40,* 605–612.

Payton, C. R. "Who Must Do the Hard Things?" *American Psychologist,* 1984, *39,* 391–397.

Reppucci, N. D. "Final Report of the BSERP Task Force on Psychology and Public Policy." Washington, D.C.: American Psychological Association, forthcoming.

Rodgers, D. A. "The Status of Psychologists in Hospitals: Technicians or Professionals." *Clinical Psychologist,* 1980, *33* (4), 5–7.

Saxe, L., and Koretz, D. (eds.). *Making Evaluation Research Useful to Congress.* New Directions for Program Evaluation, no. 14. San Francisco: Jossey-Bass, 1982.

U.S. Congressional Budget Office. *Reducing Poverty Among Children.* Washington, D.C.: U.S. Congressional Budget Office, 1985.

U.S. Defense Audit Service. *Survey of the Morale of Nonphysician Health Care Providers.* Project No. 2FM-011. Washington, D.C.: U.S. Department of Defense, 1982.

U.S. Department of Defense, Inspector General. *Audit Report: Utilization of Health Professionals in Executive/Management Positions and Special Pay Compensation.* No. 84-052. Washington, D.C.: U.S. Department of Defense, 1984.

U.S. Department of Health, Education, and Welfare. *Healthy People: The Surgeon General's Report on Health Promotion and Disease Prevention.* DHEW Pub. No. (PHS) 79-55071. Washington, D.C.: U.S. Government Printing Office, 1979.

Weick, K. E. "Small Wins: Redefining the Scale of Social Problems." *American Psychologist,* 1984, *39,* 40–49.

Yates, B. T. "How Psychology Can Improve Effectiveness and Reduce Costs of Health Services." *Psychotherapy,* 1984, *21,* 439–451.

Part Two

New Perspectives on Training and Practice

The purpose of Part Two is to encourage clinical psychology to take a hard look at itself. Issues of training, professionalism, competency, and broader horizons are raised. Not simply a where-to-from-here dialogue, this part points to the need for reformation of professional training and with it a practitioner orientation.

The traditional training of clinical psychologists as scientist-practitioners split between graduate study and formative training in facilities under the direction of another profession is past due for major change. The need is not simply for a proliferation of professional schools but that training be focused toward the general practice of psychology and be undertaken in psychological service centers, as proposed in Chapter Six. These concepts underlie training at the Wright State University School of Professional Psychology, one of psychology's foremost professional schools, situated in a health sciences university together with the schools of other health professions but with its own psychological training center. The orientation is that of a practitioner-scholar. All too many practitioners, as poignantly elaborated in Chapter Seven, function as technicians or technologists defined by their techniques or knowledge base, rather than as professional practitioners defined by the field of need they serve. The increasing numbers of licensed psychologists and their expanding scope of practice raise concurrent issues addressed in Chapter Eight—issues of public protection and benefit. Requirements for competency assurance must be backed by laws that state clear, behaviorally specific, and enforceable standards for regulating the practice of psychology.

Psychology's potential contributions to the health care system are described in Chapter Nine. The literature on both contributions to the process of health care and solutions of health problems since 1980 is reviewed. Many opportunities remain to be exploited by psychology as the profession becomes progressively more involved in cost-effective general health care, as in anxiety reduction in coronary care units, psychological approaches to pain control, and presurgical counseling. As of today, clinical psychology has but touched the surface of a range of opportunities in general health care that exceeds by far the full range of mental health services.

6   *Ronald E. Fox*

Professional Preparation: Closing the Gap Between Education and Practice

I believe that psychology has the potential to become a major health service profession with an enormously important role in the social, economic, and political arenas of our nation. Furthermore, if psychology were properly organized to deliver the best services that we now know how to provide, using the organizational structures that we know to be the most efficacious, I believe that we could (1) significantly reduce the enormous drain on society's financial resources that has resulted from an overly "medicalized," illness-driven approach to health care and health care financing, (2) change the basic structure of the current health care delivery system, including the nature and types of health care facilities and the methods for financing that care, and (3) open markets for psychological service of such magnitude that the size and influence of our profession would be profoundly and permanently changed.

Admittedly, these are strong assertions. I do not believe them to be unrealistic, given the proper development of our profession. However, it is unlikely that psychology will even begin to develop properly unless some significant impediments to professional practice and training are removed—namely, the artificial restrictions on access to our services in major portions of the existing health care system (hospital services, for example) and the general lack of availability of the effective treatment alternatives that our profession should be providing. The major focus of this chapter is a discussion of these impediments, why their removal is crucial to adequate training in our profession, and how the needed changes might be accomplished.

To those persons who do not believe that psychology can—or should—play the kind of central role in the future health care of our society to which I have alluded, I can only assert that I believe them to be sadly mistaken. It is not my intention to argue the broader issues in this forum. Rather, the aim of this paper is to examine selected elements of current education and practice that prevent our profession from assuming what I think should be its proper role.

Defining the Profession

The subsequent discussion is based on certain assumptions about the scope of our profession, and the nature of professional education is a function of how we choose to define ourselves. I therefore propose the following definition of professional psychology:

> Professional psychology is that profession which is concerned with enhancing the effectiveness of human functioning; therefore, a professional psychologist is one who has expertise in the development and application of quality services, based on psychological knowledge, attitudes, and skills, and offered to the public in a controlled, organized, and ethical manner in order to enhance the effectiveness of human functioning.

This definition is quite broad in terms of the area of responsibility it claims as the proper domain of psychological practice. Some of the implications of the definition need further elaboration.

First, when defined as broadly as is proposed above, the profession of psychology is neither identical to nor coextensive with the science of psychology. A profession should be defined by the area of need that its practitioners meet, not by a body of scientific knowledge or a collection of scientifically validated methods (see

Chapter Seven). Professions are not limited to the routine application of the findings of their basic science(s). Once applications become routine, technicians are used and a professional extender is defined. Any professional who restricts himself or herself to the routine application of confirmed findings is, in fact, behaving as a technician rather than as a professional. It is precisely the point at which uncertainties exist that the services of a professional are required. One does not need a lawyer to draw up a standard will or to draft a simple and uncontested divorce agreement; collecting blood samples does not require a physician.

A professional is required when judgment is needed to determine which assessment procedure to use or which intervention strategy appears most probable of success or when the precise nature of the problem itself is ambiguous. The professional makes educated guesses and tries to resolve the particular problem at hand in the most reasonable manner, given the current state of knowledge. Professional psychology is not restricted to applying the verified findings of the science of psychology; rather, it is concerned with using knowledge from its basic science to enhance the effectiveness of human behavior. Physicians assume responsibility for managing physical problems for which the sciences have discovered no cures. So, also, does the professional psychologist assume responsibility for helping people resolve problems in the absence of definitive data on which to base the solutions. While the scientist is trained to proceed only on the basis of established facts, the professional often must act with imperfect information.

A second implication of the proposed definition is that a particular problem domain cannot define the profession as a whole. The ultimate concern of the professional psychologist is all problems involving human coping skills. Subdomains (specialties) of practice that are defined by the type of client complaint (such as emotional problems), by the techniques used (such as behavior therapy), or by the organizational settings in which the service is delivered (such as a clinic) must not be confused with professional practice as a whole.

A third implication is that, in its professional aspects, psychology is more concerned with general health issues than with mental disorders. A profession devoted to enhancing the effective-

ness of human behavior and human coping skills must be
concerned with all human functioning and the ability to cope with
all types of health conditions. Psychologists are concerned not only
with helping people to cope with anxiety or emotional disturbances
but also with helping them to cope with such physical health issues
as chronic illness, impending surgery, heart attacks, and
unhealthful habits and life-styles (Fox, 1982).

It may be objected that the proposed definition is too broad
and impinges on the legitimate work of other disciplines and
professions. Although it is true that many social and biological
sciences are involved in the study of some aspects of human
behavior, psychology is the only discipline that has both a
comprehensive science of human behavior and an established
professional arm. Social work and the ministry, for example, are
professions that attempt to help clients improve the effectiveness of
their behavior, but neither profession is rooted in a comprehensive
science of human behavior. There is no basic science unique to
ministerial practice. The basic science of sociology, though focused
on social institutions and social processes, is not a comprehensive
science of human behavior. Many types of scientists study various
aspects of human behavior, and many types of professionals are
concerned with improving people's behavior. But it remains my
contention that psychology is the only established profession with
a comprehensive discipline base that is concerned with the entire
spectrum of human behavior; whether the subject is individual
behavior or group behavior or social systems behavior, it falls
within the scope of the science and the profession of psychology. As
a medical specialty, psychiatry is certainly concerned with
improving the effectiveness of human behavior. However,
psychiatry is based not in a comprehensive basic science of human
behavior but, rather, in the biological and physical sciences, which
deal with disease and illness. There is no basic science of psychiatry
that takes as its subject general human behavior. Indeed, the
teaching of behavioral science in most departments of psychiatry is
done by psychologists (Matarazzo and Carmody, 1981; Lubin,
Nathan, and Matarazzo, 1978).

Professions should be liberal and expansive in defining the
boundaries of their legitimate area of concern and responsibility.
Medicine had absorbed all physical illnesses and diseases into its

orbit well before the discovery of reliable diagnostic and treatment techniques for most of those illnesses and diseases. In its applied aspects, psychology should be as broad as the basic science that supports it. Since the science of psychology is concerned with the totality of human behavior, the territory for the profession of psychology is broad indeed.

Professional psychology encompasses far more than the provision of health care services. For instance, the professional practice specialties of school psychology and industrial psychology are not concerned, as a rule, with provision of health care services. In this chapter, however, the discussion is concerned solely with training young psychologists for effective functioning as health care providers.

Scope of Health Care Psychology

Enhancing the effectiveness of human coping skills in the context of general health care services involves working with an extremely broad array of problems and illnesses and cooperating with an equally broad array of health care specialists.

The most common cause of illness in the United States is psychological stress. The migraine headache, the peptic ulcer, the anxiety reaction or depressive reaction from situational upset, the psychophysiologic skin lesion, essential hypertension, functional bowel disease, functional back pain, and a bewildering array of conversion reaction complaints that can mimic almost any known disease symptom are but a few examples of the conditions which contribute almost three-fourths of all problems brought to physicians and which are caused, in large part, by psychological stress (Crombie, 1963; Mazer, 1967; Spiegel, 1974). An even more devastating group of illnesses with indirect psychological causes are those that are consequences of purposive, voluntary, or even deliberate behavior. Examples in a long list include lung disease from smoking, heart disease from overeating and underexercising, liver disease from excessive alcohol consumption, venereal disease from sexual activity, and assorted penetrating wounds and broken bones from aggressive behavior of various forms.

All these conditions, in their end stages, should be treated medically *and* psychologically, as outcomes either of less-than-ideal behavior patterns or of less-than-ideal ways people have of viewing themselves and their responses to stress. Probably the most desirable treatment approach, from the standpoints of both reducing human misery and being most cost-effective, is psychological help before the illnesses occur to correct patterns of behavior or attitudes that have high potential for producing illness. The next most ideal approach is a collaborative one of medical care for the illness after it occurs and psychological care to ameliorate the behavior or psychological state that gave rise to the illness. It is to this large array of problems that psychology, the science and profession of understanding and influencing human behavior, relates itself as a health care profession.

Psychology is not a medical specialty, but it does have a vitally important health care role in the treatment of conditions such as those described above. In this view, the psychologist relates to numerous medical specialties through dealing with inappropriate behavior of which various illnesses are the outcome. Thus, even though, and partly because, psychology is not a medical specialty, it is an important, even critical, health care specialty.

To bring their skills and expertise more directly into the health care delivery system, health care psychologists should receive portions of their professional training in conjunction with medical students and residents in various health specialties. As medical and psychological professionals learn more directly about the expertise each has to offer, they are more likely to use each other's services to the benefit of the public and to develop the comprehensive health care delivery systems that are needed. A logical outcome of sound training in health care psychology would be an increased incidence of psychologists establishing practices in conjunction with primary-care medical specialists such as pediatricians, family practitioners, and internists.

A very superficial survey of some additional health problems with which psychology can or should be associated strongly suggests a large potential demand for psychological health care services. Some examples with which pediatricians are confronted are bruxism, obesity, the battered child, encopresis, the refusal of oral medication necessary to sustain life, a variety of learning problems, various behavioral/developmental problems, and the emotional residuals of various medical disorders. All these are high-incidence problems that are costly to society and are demonstrably responsive to psychological intervention techniques (Wright, 1976).

The family practitioner deals with a host of problems having psychological implications. Conversion reactions and psychophysiological disorders are often caused or maintained by family tensions and/or inappropriate expectations or behavior patterns. In addition, the family physician is often the specialist who has the responsibility for long-term medical management of patients with chronic diseases. Psychological counseling has helped post-heart-attack patients to adhere better to an exercise program and a weight control program, to reduce smoking, and to realistically adjust work and outside activity schedules. All these effects contribute to a lower rate of reinfarction (Rahe, O'Neil, Hagan, and Arthur, 1975). In a well-designed and carefully controlled experiment, Gruen (1975) demonstrated that brief psychological counseling is an effective addition to the hospital treatment of heart-attack victims. Patients who received counseling spent less time in the intensive care unit, had fewer cardiac emergencies while in the hospital, used less pain medication, and resumed normal activities significantly earlier than heart-attack patients who did not receive psychological help.

Internists, along with family physicians and pediatricians, also face a vast array of illnesses and diseases that have strong psychological components: ulcers, migraine headaches, functional bowel disorders, and certain skin diseases, to mention a few. Hypertension, which is the leading cause of death in the United States as well as a major factor in the incidence of stroke (which, in turn, is the third leading cause of death), is an example of one commonly confronted problem. In some studies many patients with elevated blood pressure show significant reduction in blood pressure with appropriate psychological intervention. The interested reader should consult Wertlieb (1979) for a discussion of some of these illnesses from a biopsychosocial perspective.

The specialist in obstetrics and gynecology is confronted with functional dysmenorrhea, depression, symptoms associated with premenstrual tension, postpartum psychosis, and a variety of sexual problems, all of which have strong psychological components that should be treated using psychosocial and family interventions.

There is a great deal of evidence (Olbrisch, 1977) that improved response to surgery follows very brief counseling interventions. The improvement is manifested by patient reports of less pain, by the need for less medication, and by measurably faster recovery rates to normal functioning than among patients who did not receive counseling. Pre- and postsurgery counseling has been especially useful in reducing the high rate of postoperative psychosis following cardiac surgery.

Chronic pain centers are being established in major centers around the country. The basic research and the practical applications of various behavioral approaches in the management of pain were developed by psychologists (Fordyce, 1976). Pain centers rely heavily, if not exclusively, on psychological principles and techniques to increase the functional effectiveness of persons afflicted with chronic pain who are largely unable to profit from further medical intervention (DeGood, 1979).

Persons with alcohol problems often incur very high medical costs. In addition to high utilization of medical services, these individuals cost their employers a great deal through absenteeism and lost production. Research findings suggest that active intervention programs not only reduce medical care utilization but actually result in a profit to the employer funding the intervention program (Olbrisch, 1977). Inappropriate utilizers and overutilizers of medical services are reduced through the addition of psychological services to the health care delivery system, which results in more efficient medical treatment. Geriatric patients, who tend to be overutilizers of certain medical services, benefit from psychological care, as evidenced by being rated as healthier by their physicians and nurses and by using smaller amounts and fewer types of medication than before the psychological care was introduced (Schulz, 1976).

Few of the problem areas discussed in this section involve clients with mental disorders. For all their ubiquity, mental disorders still involve only a small segment of the general population of this country. In contrast, the general health problems outlined in this section touch almost the total population at one time or another. The growth potential for psychology with respect to this still largely unserved group is staggering to contemplate, and the potential financial rewards are considerable. It is precisely this general population that we must train young psychologists to serve, rather than concentrating our efforts on teaching them to work almost exclusively with persons who have mental disorders.

The following example illustrates the need for services in the general health area and the huge amounts of money associated with some of our current care systems. The Industrial Commission of Ohio claims to be the largest underwriter of work-related health and accident insurance in the world. In support of this claim, the commission points to the fact that the interest on its capital funds at the end of calendar year 1981 was accumulating at the rate of over $50,000 per minute. Over 75 percent of the chronic cases on the rolls of the commission are workers with low-back pain who have not responded sufficiently to medical treatment to return to work. Because the treatment of choice for such persons is a psychosocial program developed by psychologists, the commission's Rehabilitation Division is in the process of establishing a series of treatment centers throughout the state. The Rehabilitation Division will soon be the largest employer of psychologists in the state of Ohio. From the commission's viewpoint, it is not essential that psychology be able to help all the disabled workers suffering from low-back pain. Even if only a stable minority are returned to work, the cost/benefit advantages of the intervention are still likely to be considerable. A worker stricken at age forty, with twenty-five years of productive work ahead, can consume a large amount of cash benefits if he or she is unable to return to work. Similarly, the early disability retirement of city and state law enforcement officers often carries a cost of $1 million per person, and such retirements are becoming more frequent. Increasingly, psychologists are being engaged to provide return-to-work counseling and to develop and conduct stress management training programs for this target population.

The opportunities for psychologists in these and other health problem areas are tremendous, but our professional training has been slow in developing explicit programs for teaching students to assume the roles that will be opened to them.

Although health care is broader than mental health care, the latter is by no means excluded. However, as is true of health care in general, our training programs are not always producing students capable of delivering the services that are the most needed. For example, many clinical psychology programs still devote most of the intervention portion of their curriculum to teaching students how to do psychotherapy—but psychotherapy is not the service that is most needed by the large segment of the mentally disturbed who are confined to hospitals. Doctoral students in our program recently conducted a clinical service needs analysis survey of all the patients in the Dayton Mental Health and Developmental Center (DMHDC) (Drude and Mayer, 1981). DMHDC is a large, fairly typical, state-operated mental hospital. The largest single unmet need for patients in the facility was not medication or psychotherapy but transition services to help them reenter the community and maintain themselves outside the hospital. Patients were leaving the hospital quickly, to be sure. But they were also returning quickly because of inadequate or completely lacking transition services of various types. It is true that transition services may be provided by any of several professions. But halfway houses, community-based patient support groups, and various other programs aimed at keeping mental patients out of hospitals (the most expensive form of mental health care) are ones in which the profession of psychology has played a pioneering role (Fairweather, Sanders, Maynard, and Cressler, 1969).

If the roles described in this section are the ones for which health care providers should be trained, why is so little specific training for such roles being provided? In my opinion, the training of health care providers in psychology is severely hampered by a general lack of availability of autonomous professional role models in much of the current health delivery system. The following section addresses the issue of impediments to psychological training in health care service, as I see them. Impediments to the growth and development of the profession of psychology as a whole were discussed in an earlier article (Fox, Barclay, and Rodgers, 1982).

Some Impediments to Health Care Training

The primary vehicle for training students in the practical and applied aspects of most professions is role modeling by experienced practitioners of that profession. Students observe their mentors applying the skills of their profession to real situations and problems. Later in training, students begin to practice themselves under the critical eyes of their teachers. The crucial element in tutorial learning of this type is that the teacher must be practicing the skills that the student is expected to learn. Far too often, practicing professionals are not available as role models for psychology students across the range of problem domains outlined in the preceding section. This statement is not meant to demean the considerable services that psychology provides or to criticize the progress that psychology has made in the health care system. But the fact is that students must have access to role models who are practicing the full breadth and range of their profession, and such access is currently rare for our students. In part, this circumstance is due to the newness of our profession and to the rapid growth in the discovery of new applications for our skills, and in part to regulations governing major elements of the health care system (such as hospitals), which have failed to change with the changing realities of the development of new knowledge from newer professions such as psychology.

One problem with current practices in hospital settings is that psychology does not have the independence and autonomy vital for proper role modeling. Hospital regulations typically require that a physician be in charge of all professional care for the patient and that other professional services not be provided without the physician's request or consent. However, a proper profession cannot flourish or develop without independence and autonomy in defining when its services are needed and what those services are to be. The professional must have the responsibility for delivering the services that he or she believes necessary as well as for modifying those services on the basis of the client's response. For psychologists, this situation is rare with respect to most of the services in a hospital. Practically speaking, patients' access to the services of one profession, psychology, is controlled by another profession, medicine. Just as a psychologist is not qualified to make medical decisions, however, so is a physician inadequately trained to be the judge of when a patient should see a psychologist. To change this state of affairs will be a complex task requiring regulatory modification, new legislation, new mechanisms for interprofessional cooperation, changes in public perception and awareness, and structural changes in the delivery system itself.

Eventually, psychology must become capable of providing services independently and autonomously both in existing human service delivery systems (such as hospitals) and in new "homes" of our own that do not yet exist. While a psychology center should include services not related to health, it should also have provisions for services that require "in-house" residential care for certain clients, such as certain types of transition services, emergency care service for people in crises, substance misuse programs, a chronic-pain program using psychosocial approaches, and some portions of a treatment compliance unit.

Psychology needs to develop comprehensive psychological service centers that are the profession's counterpart to medicine's teaching hospitals or regional medical centers. Albee (1964) detailed some of the basic elements of a comprehensive service center. However, developments in recent years would require a much broader array of services than he envisioned. It should go without saying that the small psychology clinic or university counseling service, which is typically the only treatment service owned by a psychology training program, does not meet the need for a comprehensive psychological service center in which the full range of professional services is offered. A truly comprehensive center of the type that psychology really needs for the proper training of its students would be large, visible, and expensive; it would not fit into the basement or one wing of anything else. To develop such centers will require large sums of money from both the public and the private sectors. However, if psychology intends to become a truly major profession capable of delivering a range of services as broad and as varied as human behavior itself, and if the profession truly intends to make a significant impact on the nature of health care delivery in this country, then we must all begin to think in such terms. If we think we have something to offer and services that are worth providing, then we must expect to have the means for delivering those services, including the appropriate institutional settings.

The advantages of having psychological centers of the type mentioned above are great, both for the profession and for the public. Once numerous persons with particular classes of problems begin to seek services at centers operated by professionals who are sanctioned by society to help with those problems, the opportunities and demand for more knowledge and better treatment are enhanced. This has been the history of most university medical centers. Persons with cancer go to such centers for services even though cures may not be available. As more and more cases appear and as treatment results remain equivocal, the public and professional demand for better knowledge escalates, thus promoting research endeavors. The stimulation of research efforts and the emphasis on the latest developments in practice make such settings ideal environments for the education and training of young psychologists. At present there is no center in existence that even approaches the range and complexity of services that are needed.

Building the kinds of centers needed by psychology will require a great deal of money and the concentration of large numbers of psychologists within single organizational entities. There is, of course, no formula for securing the funding that such a major undertaking would require. However, our profession is not without resources. In the remainder of the chapter I will briefly outline some of the methods by which psychology could direct its knowledge and skills toward the creation of comprehensive psychological service centers.

Obviously, public funding is a natural source of funds for our centers. Public involvement in various aspects of health care financing has been increasing almost exponentially over the past two decades. It has become obvious to most people that individuals' habits and attitudes (behaviors) play a critical role in preventive health care. Further, the shaping of certain habits and attitudes is obviously the approach with the greatest potential to reduce skyrocketing costs. Thus, psychology is a profession whose time seems to have come. We are in the right place, at the right time, with the knowledge and skills for which demand is likely to increase rapidly over the next few years. If we represent ourselves properly and vigorously, we have a good chance of being able to win public support in both state and national legislatures for the kinds of institutions and programs that are needed.

I do not subscribe to the school of thought that urges restraint for new ventures during times of economic difficulty. In fact, I believe that an economic recession creates the most favorable climate for us to mount compelling arguments for increasing access to our services.

Psychology has been quietly, but effectively, building strong political bases in several states over the past twelve to fifteen years. The knowledge and contacts developed through these activities could be highly useful to the profession for securing public support to fund, at least partly, our service centers. For those who might scoff at such an assertion, a brief history of the School of Professional Psychology at Wright State University, in Ohio, may be instructive. The school was created by the Ohio legislature in 1978 through the efforts of a small committee formed by the Ohio Psychological Association that utilized the political knowledge and skills that psychology had acquired through a vigorous legislative effort over a period of several years. Not only was the school created over the vigorous objections of eight large state-supported universities with traditional Ph.D. programs in clinical psychology as well as the objections of the Ohio Board of Regents, but $900,000 in start-up funds were appropriated; and this was in the midst of a sharp decline in the state's economy. Psychology has a great deal to offer, and the public will buy, if we sell ourselves properly. As one further sequel, the Ohio legislature in 1985 was persuaded to appropriate $3 million to the Wright State University School of Professional Psychology for construction of its new Psychological Services Center! This school of professional psychology, situated on a health sciences university campus amid schools of other major health professions, has the natural environment in which interdisciplinary training for health care on a collegial basis is possible.

Another element in the funding resources for a comprehensive center should be organized faculty group practice plans. Medical and dental faculties in university training programs have frequently used organized practice plans not only to augment salaries but also to help secure needed funds to support the expensive teaching costs commonly associated with teaching hospitals and comprehensive dental clinics. Although faculty practice plans are common in other professions, they are almost nonexistent in psychology training programs.

Faculty practice plans can generate funds for a service center in several ways. First, the service center can assess overhead charges to the practice plan to help meet operating expenses. Second, the plan can provide a patient referral pool for new faculty members, thus aiding the growth in the size of the faculty and the expansion of services offered. This is a significant point in that it is extremely difficult, if not impossible, to add new or expanded services in a training program when the academic budget must cover staff costs and when the number of students in the program remains stable. Through service activities, needed growth and development are provided largely by purchasers of services rather than by the academic program budget. Third, and most important, through organized group practice activities, the faculty could develop and offer a variety of programmatic services, which then would attract public and private contracts and fee-for-service funds and also establish a natural environment for the attraction of applied research funds.

It is possible to conceive of several types of programmatic services which a faculty group could offer and which are beyond the capabilities of our typical solo practitioner. I will briefly outline only a few such services.

An obvious example of a programmatic service is a psychometric laboratory using computer-assisted interpretation and scoring, as well as the services of psychological extenders, for a variety of assessment and problem-definition purposes. The Psychometric Laboratory at the Ohio State University Medical Center is one of the largest earners of fee-for-service income in the Department of Psychiatry there. With such a service, assessment fees to consumers can be drastically reduced while the income for the psychologists who provide the professional oversight and responsibility is significantly increased. Even though the technology and knowledge base for such services were developed by psychologists, few laboratories exist in training programs so that students can learn to incorporate the laboratory concept into the practices they will be establishing. Instead, the greater portion of time is still devoted to teaching students to administer the highly specialized, individual tests that are not only expensive but also of relevance to a small segment of the total population. We should be spending the bulk of our time in teaching students to deliver affordable services to the many rather than expensive services to the few. Psychometric laboratories exist, but typically they are housed in medical centers, drug houses, or independent mail-order establishments rather than in psychology centers where they could be used for student learning and to help associate the service with our profession in the public's mind.

Another example of a programmatic service that could be offered is a cooperative federation of fee-for-service providers, similar to a foundation for medical care, with the peer review and data collection function administered or provided by the faculty practice plan and with psychology practitioners in the immediate geographical region constituting most of the panel of providers. A somewhat similar program has already been operated successfully in the Delaware Valley Psychological Clinics (Chapter Eleven). The psychology school at Wright State University was recently approached by a large insurance underwriter to explore our interest in using the school's faculty practice group to provide peer review and program control functions for a psychology panel on contract with the insurance company. Since the faculty plan already incorporates a peer review program, and students are trained in it as well, the practice group could easily organize and monitor a peer review function as well as provide several administrative services that are difficult for solo practitioners. Not only is such a concept marketable, but it allows our profession to gain access to a large population that is presently receiving few services from us. What the public most needs is services in the preventive mode that bear on general health (and thus health care costs) rather than services for those suffering from mental disorders. As a profession, we have tended to focus the bulk of our efforts on securing increased access to our services by the emotionally disturbed. If psychology were to concentrate its efforts on increasing the general population's access to brief, inexpensive care, a virtual revolution in the manner and mode of psychological practice would result.

A third example of the kind of service that an organized practice plan could offer is the creation of a wide variety of therapeutic "modules" that maximize the use of extenders, group procedures, and standard service routines. Some typical modules might include a thought/attention control program, a relaxation program, a cognitive restructuring program, a treatment compliance program, and a family-group program specifically aimed at the reduction of "enabling" behaviors in drug abusers. These modules are being created by the faculty at Wright State initially to serve as elements in a larger chronic-pain management program. Later on, some of these modules may be combined with others to meet the needs of a different client group (stress reduction/ management being one example). Such program modules are not only more cost-effective than individual, one-on-one services but also more often suitable to that large segment of the general population who could benefit from psychological services but who do not need the highly specialized individual services that our profession has tended to emphasize.

In effect, the ability to establish large, comprehensive psychological service centers lies within our grasp. In order to attract the public and private training and building funds and the applied research funds, as well as the large fee-for-service markets from which we have largely excluded ourselves, we must first begin to organize ourselves to offer the services that are likely to offer the greatest benefit at the lowest cost to the most people. The model of a psychological practitioner that is most visible to the public should not be the individual psychotherapist treating the emotionally disturbed but, rather, one who uses a variety of interventions, programs, and strategies to help people cope with ordinary problems in living.

The idea of a general practice model offered by an organized group of psychologists, each of whom specializes in one or more brief, specialized techniques, in an organizational setting that requires case transfer and group consultation has been elaborated in some detail by Cummings and VandenBos (1979). These authors detail the advantages of such an approach and encourage its adoption by private practitioners. Their model is also an ideal one for faculty private practice groups. Training programs should organize their faculties into group practices offering brief, demonstrably effective interventions designed to meet particular conditions or problems that arise throughout a client's life span. Such plans will provide the means for building a house of our own for public service and training as well as for modeling the best services that the profession has to offer.

Fox, Kovacs, and Graham (1985) look to no less than a "comprehensive overhaul of the entire system by which professional psychologists are trained, identified, licensed and encouraged into specialties" and describe a series of eighteen principles to this end. They note that the current fourteen fully approved schools of professional psychology accredited by APA's Committee on Accreditation already enroll about 50 percent of all doctoral students in clinical psychology. Thus, to a large extent, the shift from traditional departments to schools of psychology has already occurred.

Summary

Psychology is capable of becoming a major health care profession whose proper domain of responsibility is the improvement of the effectiveness of human behavior. Since human behavior is inextricably intertwined with health problems of almost all varieties, health care providers in psychology must be trained through direct experience with the full range of patients in comprehensive health care delivery systems. This can be achieved on a widespread basis only when autonomous access to the health care system is accomplished and when truly comprehensive psychological service centers are established. Until such changes are accomplished, psychology will not be able to fully teach the skills that it already has the knowledge to provide. Such accomplishments would require massive changes in the profession as it now exists and in the basic structure of our nation's health care delivery system.

The accomplishment of such changes is a goal worthy of a major profession. It is a goal that can shape our efforts for years to come. In the words of Shaemos O'Sheel:

> He whom a dream has
> possessed
> Knoweth no more of doubting . . .
> And never come darkness down
> But he greeteth a million morns.

References

Albee, G. "A Declaration of Independence for Psychology." *Ohio Psychologist,* June, 1964, pp. 60–64.

Crombie, D. L. "The Procrustean Bed of Medical Nomenclature." *Lancet,* 1963, *1,* 1205–1209.

Cummings, N. A., and VandenBos, G. R. "The General Practice of Psychology." *Professional Psychology,* 1979, *10,* 430–440.

DeGood, D. E. "A Behavioral Pain-Management Program: Expanding the Psychologist's Role in a Medical Setting." *Professional Psychology,* 1979, *10,* 491–502.

Drude, K., and Mayer, T. "Continuity of Care of 'Revolving Door' Patients at Dayton Mental Health Center." Dayton, Ohio: School of Professional Psychology, Wright State University, 1981. (Mimeographed.)

Fairweather, G. W., Sanders, D. H., Maynard, H., and Cressler, D. L. *Community Life for the Mentally Ill: An Alternative to Community Care.* Hawthorne, N.Y.: Aldine, 1969.

Fordyce, N. E. *Behavioral Methods for Chronic Pain and Illness.* St. Louis, Mo.: Mosby, 1976.

Fox, R. "The Need for a Reorientation of Clinical Psychology." *American Psychologist,* 1982, *37,* 1051–1057.

Fox, R., Barclay, A., and Rodgers, D. "The Foundations of Professional Psychology." *American Psychologist,* 1982, *37,* 306–312.

Fox, R., Kovacs, A., and Graham, S. "Proposals for a Revolution in the Preparation and Regulation of Professional Psychologists." *American Psychologist,* 1985, *40,* 1042–1050.

Gruen, W. "Effects of Brief Psychotherapy During the Hospitalization Period on the Recovery Process in Heart Attacks." *Journal of Consulting and Clinical Psychology*, 1975, *43*, 223–232.

Lubin, B., Nathan, R. G., and Matarazzo, J. D. "Psychologists in Medical Education: 1976." *American Psychologist*, 1978, *33*, 339–343.

Matarazzo, J. D., and Carmody, T. "Psychologists on the Faculties of United States' Schools of Medicine: Past, Present and Possible Future." *Clinical Psychology Review*, 1981, *1*, 6–10.

Mazer, M. "Psychiatric Disorders in General Practice: The Experience of an Island Community." *American Journal of Psychiatry*, 1967, *124*, 609–615.

Olbrisch, M. "Psychotherapeutic Intervention in Physical Health." *American Psychologist*, 1977, *32*, 761–777.

Rahe, R. H., O'Neil, T., Hagan, A., and Arthur, R. J. "Brief Group Therapy Following Myocardial Infarction: Eighteen Month Follow-up of a Controlled Trial." *International Journal of Psychiatry in Medicine*, 1975, *6*, 349–358.

Schulz, R. "Effects of Control and Predictability on the Physical and Psychological Well-Being of the Institutionalized Aged." *Journal of Personality and Social Psychology*, 1976, *33*, 563–573.

Spiegel, J. P. Statement before the Subcommittee on Retirement, Insurance, and Health Benefits of the Post Office and Civil Service Committee, U.S. House of Representatives, by the American Psychiatric Association, Oct. 8, 1974.

Wertlieb, D. "A Preventive Health Paradigm for Health Care Psychologists." *Professional Psychology*, 1979, *10*, 548–557.

Wright, L. "Psychology as a Health Profession." *Clinical Psychologist*, Winter 1976, pp. 16–19.

7

David A. Rodgers

Psychologists as Practitioners, Not Technicians

The rapid and impressive empirical growth of psychology as a profession is well documented in the preceding chapters. Careful reading of those chapters will also reveal the considerable diversity of both conception and application of this supposedly unitary, young, and vigorous profession. Indeed, the suspicion arises that psychology is not *a* profession but is *many* professions.

The conceptualization or definition of a field is far from trivial. There must be a central unifying practitioner conception that serves as a stable and guiding core for the profession, one that gives it unity and purpose. This enters fundamentally into the nature of desirable public regulation through laws or statutes, the design of training programs for professionals, and the actual and appropriate structures for the delivery of services to the public. The current conceptualizations of psychology strongly influence the nature of the American Psychological Association and other professional and related scientific societies. They even determine the appropriate direction, or lack thereof, of supportive research emphases.

The primary shaping of the modern profession of clinical psychology came during World War II, when the increased numbers of young persons entering service, the increased stress of a high-technology war, and the increased societal sensitivity to psychological dimensions of disability coalesced to present the society with a

141

perceived major need for new approaches to dealing with unsolved emotional problems. Psychological scientists were turned to as an alternative source of possible solutions because of their pursuit of basic understanding of behavior patterns, emotional responses, and cognitive processes. Although the science of psychology was far from perfect in its inputs, the psychologists trained in that science proved to be remarkably effective in working with the war casualties, so that they became a major secondary profession dealing with exactly that group of problems with which psychiatry was struggling at the time.

Interestingly, one of the earliest impacts of psychology as a science on the professional treatment of these war casualties was to shift emphasis toward restoring the casualties to normal functioning as quickly as possible, often by returning them to the front lines, rather than "regressing" them into an invalid or sickbed role. This emphasis on improving effectiveness of functioning of the person rather than on removing behavioral responsibility from the patient and taking charge of the pathology as though it were an entity in its own right, independent of the person, has usually characterized psychology and distinguished it from medical treatment.

Before World War II, there was, of course, an existing tradition of professional psychology, mostly identified with mental testing and vocational or personal-effectiveness counseling. These two approaches continued, evolving essentially into the present specialties of school psychology and counseling psychology. After World War II, clinical psychology emerged largely independent of these approaches, as the field of greatest demand, of greatest numbers, and of greatest dominance in professional psychology. For example, in the 1983 APA Census of Psychological Personnel (Stapp, Tucker, and VandenBos, forthcoming), 44.4 percent of respondents listed clinical psychology as their major field. The next most common listings were counseling psychology, at 11.2 percent, educational psychology, at 5.9 percent, and industrial/organizational psychology, at 5.5 percent. For comparison, experimental psychology was listed by 3.2 percent and physiological psychology by 1.3 percent. Clinical psychology began primarily as a hybrid cross between scientific psychology and psychiatric or medical practice, with some limited input from counseling and mental measurement practice. It fit uncomfortably into the scientific norms, which were not really oriented toward direct delivery of service to the public in areas of great need but professional ignorance. However, it did fit comfortably into the broader medical perspective, as a "technology field" or "limited practice of medicine" that expanded the services of the physician, well within the tradition of midwives, nurses, lab technicians, and medical social workers.

This new approach had typical hybrid vigor, which the conceptualizers at the Boulder Conference (see Raimy, 1950) sought to ensure by defining the new area as a "scientist-practitioner" field in which the pragmatics of professional work would be blended with or grafted onto the rigors of scientific training. On the delivery side, services were rendered primarily in medical settings. Patient "safety" was ensured by extending primary responsibility to the physician, under his or her license for the "unlimited" practice of medicine, the psychologist retaining secondary responsibility for those areas in which he or she was "technically competent." The scientific background of the psychologist lent itself well to this concept of high-level technologist, since the scientist-practitioner model had been built substantially on the concept that psychologists should not deliver services of unestablished validity but only services of validated effectiveness, for which their own skills had been established by rigorous training. This concept is essentially that of a technologist or technician, however, not of a "practitioner-professional."

The societal need at the end of World War II was great, and the bureaucratic structure of the Veterans Administration self-consciously and economically supported the development of clinical psychology as a major profession. A major influence on the emerging profession of clinical psychology during this period was the blurring of distinctions among mental health professionals. There are two threads that have led to confusion about the nature of clinical psychology.

First, a known technique that accomplishes known outcomes can be learned by different kinds of professionals, and one may not need to undergo the rigors of comprehensive professional training in order to deliver that technique. Examples are psychoanalysis (which Freud himself recognized as not requiring a "medical professional" background, and, indeed, it has been learned by many lay analysts who do not superimpose it on conventional professional training), interpretation of various psychometric instruments, including the Rorschach (developed by a physician) and the TAT, biofeedback, and behavior modification. Professionals other than psychologists can and do learn all these techniques, as do nonprofessionals (including master's-level psychologists who may not qualify for professional licensure). Even "average laypersons" learn many psychological techniques, such as hypnotherapy or sensitivity training. To the extent that psychologists are known by the techniques they deliver, therefore, they must either monopolize their techniques, through legal psychological practices acts, or be only one kind of participant in a field that is shared widely with others who do not identify themselves as psychologists. In general, psychology has not tried to monopolize its techniques, having been sensitized to the offensiveness of such an approach by being on the "other side" of medical practices acts. Even the most sophisticated psychological techniques are therefore often accessible by other, nonpsychology professionals, such as physicians, social workers, psychiatric nurses, and substance abuse counselors, to name a few. This technique focus and sharing of techniques has been one factor contributing to the concept of "mental health professionals" and the blurred professional identities of clinical psychologists, psychiatrists, nurse practitioners, and clinical social workers.

A second thread that contributes to the confusion of "mental health professionals" is the fact that emotional and behavioral problems are without definable solutions that could withstand careful scientific scrutiny. To the extent that the profession of psychology subscribes to an honest scientific underpinning, it cannot claim any uniqueness of a scientifically validated sort in many of these areas. From a scientific perspective, therefore, psychology can be seen as having no essentially unique role as a profession to differentiate it definitively from other professions.

These and multiple other pressures have led to identity confusion in psychology. The growth of the profession has been substantially shaped by the concept of a "scientist-practitioner," a person who is rigorously trained in research methodology and who then learns how to deliver the fruits of the wisdom and knowledge of that scientific training to a needy public. This is, of course, a carrying forward of the same model of merging scientific knowledge with practical need that seemed to have proved so effective in the crisis of the Second World War. In actuality, there have been several practical outcomes that may have contributed more to identity confusion than to identity clarification. First, professional training in psychology, until quite recently, has occurred exclusively in academic departments of universities rather than in professional schools (see Fox, Barclay, and Rodgers, 1982, for one review of this background). Academic departments generally are not geared to manage direct interface with a consuming public. Direct professional apprenticeship training in clinical psychology, the biggest "psychology profession," has consequently tended to be in medical institutions. As a result, clinical psychologists during their apprenticeship training seldom learn how to assume primary responsibility or how to differentiate primarily psychological problems from medical (including psychiatric) problems. Instead, they learn how to function in medical institutions, as medical extenders, essentially in a high-level technology rather than a primary-professional role. Medical centers are, of course, designed to use medical extenders, who function on the medical team, "on referral from and under the general direction of" a physician who is designated the chief of the team. As a consequence, psychologists in their apprenticeship training are at risk of learning how to be technicians for psychiatrists or "limited-practice-of-medicine technologists" rather than independent professionals—"they do the same things a psychiatrist does, except they can't give drugs or write prescriptions." For example, the *Diagnostic and Statistical Manual* of the American Psychiatric Association (1980), *DSM-III,* a psychiatric/medical nomenclature, is regarded as the primary diagnostic nomenclature of *clinical psychology,* which does not have an accepted categorization of its own of the problems it presumably uniquely addresses. This statement is not meant as a criticism of medicine or of academic programs; rather, it identifies what is almost an inevitable consequence of the pattern of professional training that has characterized clinical psychology over the past thirty years.

Second, the model of academic training that has traditionally existed in academic departments has, not surprisingly, been transferred to professional training as well. That model is one of increasingly high specialization and increasing individuality of training as one approaches the doctorate. The concept of "learning more and more about less and less until one knows everything about nothing" has been considerably blunted but still leads to American Psychological Association recognition of specialties in at least four different "professions of psychology"—clinical, counseling, school, and industrial—each with its clearly separate training track. In addition, waiting in the wings are neuropsychology, forensic, community, human factors, and a variety of other specialties that divide rather than unify the field of professional psychology. This divisiveness is due largely to the academic pattern of specialty training at the subdoctoral level. It contrasts with the more typical pattern in professional schools, such as those of medicine, law, and dentistry, of generic training to a professional journeyman level, followed by postgraduate specialization beyond that generic base. Even within the specialties, training in professional psychology may differ markedly from one university to another, based on the principle of "academic freedom" to teach individualized excellence, a freedom that is fundamental for academic pursuit of basic knowledge but is potentially devastating for professional identity and public protection from individualized professional caprice.

In a brief and somewhat exaggerated summary, "professional psychology" can be said to consist, by APA policy, of four professions, not one, and does not have a "house of its own" in any particular specialty except possibly counseling psychology. Clinical work takes place in medical settings or in the restricted confines of private practice, which depends heavily on medical referrals and medically oriented third-party payment arrangements. School psychology exists mostly in school systems under professional educators, and industrial psychology either is often indistinguishable from and housed in management consulting firms or is of an applied science rather than a practitioner-professional type. This leaves control of most of the training of professionals in the hands of the academic rather than the professional community, so that the professionals often look to techniques, as technologists and technicians do, for identity and justification of their existence and share their techniques broadly with multiple other professionals and nonprofessionals. These conditions lead to struggles both within the legal structure of state statutes and within the professional structures of the American Psychological Association. In short, an identity crisis is almost pandemic in professional psychology and threatens to spawn fragmentation rather than maturation.

Alternative Kinds of Professionalism

As this brief history of professional psychology illustrates, the translation of a scientific field into professional skills that can be delivered with benefit to a consuming public may have many dimensions. No professional movement in history has been more systematically oriented to the concept of a scientific base for professional practice than psychology. The diverse ways in which this translation can be made are therefore basic to understanding the nature of professional psychology.

There are at least three distinct conventional pathways linking a scientific field to professional application: that of the applied scientist, that of the scientist/practitioner, or technologist, and that of the practitioner. All these are represented in psychology, often intermingled.

First, consider the *applied scientist*. A clear-cut model is the professional chemist, working in industry. The applied scientist is little different from the academic scientist, except that the problems toward which his or her investigations are directed are chosen because of their practical value to a consuming public. The scientific methods of precise and rigorous investigation are applied to problems of a practical sort in areas where scientific knowledge is lacking. The only translation from normal scientific method is the restricted definition of the problem toward which the investigative method is directed. In psychology, much of the work of industrial and organizational (I and O) psychologists and of human factors psychologists is of this sort. Careful research can identify the appropriate complex of characteristics. Subsequent application of the findings, however, normally does not call for a professional psychologist, since the contribution of the psychologist is to derive the general scientific knowledge on which application is based. Such psychologists, in a technical sense, are not scientist/practitioners but, rather, applied scientists. Such applied scientific work is usually embedded within institutional needs and institutional controls in ways that do not require scientific or extensive regulation by state law. Adequacy of the work is usually self-evident, manifested by the success or failure of the scientific investigation to elucidate the problems toward whose solutions it is directed.

Next, consider the *scientist/practitioner,* or *technologist.* The technologist is one who applies a body of certain knowledge that has been previously elucidated by adequate scientific or technical investigation and whose practice essentially does not go beyond established procedures or a defined knowledge base. It is this conception that best fits the scientist/practitioner formulation. Two linkages are required between the technologist and the consuming public. One is a determination that the particular techniques involved are applicable and appropriate. The other is a management of situations or problems that arise when the technique or its application does not work as expected. These are the problems of diagnosis and of professional responsibility for the presenting problem. A simple and common solution to the problems of diagnosis and professional responsibility is for the technologist to work "under the direction of or on referral from" a practitioner-professional, who takes responsibility for both the initial evaluation and the professional management of unexpected complications or failure of the technique. Such a technologist is an extender, basically, of the competencies of the practitioner who assumes ultimate professional responsibility. Many psychologists function as technologists in this capacity, doing psychological testing, group therapies, defined psychotherapies, behavior modification programs, or many other highly technical tasks on professional assignment from another psychologist or a physician who determines that such technical skills are called for (by assigning patients) and who assumes ultimate responsibility for making sure other procedures are followed if the technologist's work turns out to be inappropriate or insufficient to manage the problem.

Technologists can function independently as well as in an extender capacity, although problems remain of diagnosis and professional responsibility for treatments that do not work. Diagnosis is usually handled by a referral system, including self-referral, and professional responsibility is usually handled by specifying the contract between technologist and consumer. An example of a person functioning as an independent technologist would be an optometrist, specializing, with highly standardized techniques, in measuring visual characteristics and fitting corrective lenses. Optometrists may see patients on referral from ophthalmologists or on self-referral. Their contract with the consumer is an explicitly delimited one of providing corrective lenses according to standard criteria that allow minimal subjective application of the "professional arts" and require predominantly use of defined technical skills. The defining characteristics of technologists is that they serve only those needs that fit their techniques and do not (or should not) attempt to extend their techniques beyond their established skills or beyond the domain for which those skills are relevant.

Many psychologists function in this "independent technologist" status, essentially seeing clients who are appropriate to their particular methodological approach, either on self-referral by a knowledgeable consuming public or "on referral from" but not "under the direction of" a physician or an agency or another psychologist. If client-centered therapy or phobic deconditioning or assertiveness training turns out to be ineffective, then the client returns to the original referral source or independently seeks help elsewhere for further work.

Technologists' services are clearly important, require a high level of competence and ethical behavior, and are accompanied by pride in professional identity. Nevertheless, the technologist's service is usually bounded by the "practitioner profession" that does the initial diagnosis and manages the problems that do not fit the particular technologist's techniques. It is always bounded, by definition, by the limitations of the techniques used. The technologist, then, even a high-level independent technologist, is an extender of a basic practitioner profession rather than an independent professional.

Practitioner professions basically arise not because of a well-substantiated knowledge base but rather, because of a public need. Medicine is a clear example. Historically, people with illness found that they could not be sure of survival through using their own knowledge and their own skills. They therefore turned to others for help. These early helpers, whether they were physicians or oracles or priests or witch doctors, were turned to because they offered to try to do the best they could with problems that no one knew how to solve, not because they had technologically competent solutions.

The various practitioner approaches—oracle, priest, physician—were differentiated not so much in the beginning on the basis of effectiveness in dealing with the problems (none of them was very effective) as on the basis of hypothesized cause/effect/cure linkages. Medicine, for example, was built on the protopostulates that illness is a physiological process (rather than a spiritual or magical process), that normal physiological processes exist, that illness is an aberration of these normal processes, and that cure involves restoring physiological functioning to normality. It is this type of mythology that explains depression as a physiological aberration rather than as a coping skills deficit and therefore as a medical rather than a psychological problem (from the medical perspective), to be treated with medication to correct the physiology rather than with behavioral coaching to improve coping processes. At issue is the attempt by medicine to define an exclusive province rather than recognize overlap in practice consequent to the use of different approaches.

The true "turf battles" between practitioner professions most constructively arise over the issue of whose protopostulates are most likely to have practical payoffs for the needy public. For example, is alcoholism better approached as aberrant physiology or as aberrant self-regulated coping behavior or as aberrant moral behavior or as aberrant social behavior? It can be (and has been) looked at in all these ways. Each perspective has had some success and some failure in dealing with an as yet unsolved major problem area. The perspective with which the problem is approached, of course, determines whether societal resources toward solution are placed mainly behind medicine, psychology, religion, or law enforcement. The issues are obviously not trivial, either for the professions involved or for the consuming public, which must gamble its resources on uncertain outcomes.

To continue the foregoing emphasis, medicine became defined as a practitioner profession by its willingness to *seek* physiological causes and physiological corrections for all physical illnesses, not primarily because it offered effective cures. Before knowledge about infectious processes existed, physicians nevertheless assumed responsibility for trying to cope with the plague. Physicians still assume responsibility for trying to cope with the problems of cancer, even those forms of cancer that are essentially incurable even by the best of today's methodology. They assume responsibility for managing patients with acquired immune deficiency syndrome (AIDS), a condition with *no* known cure. It is worth noting that 1918 is sometimes set as the date afer which the survival chances of the ill patient were probably improved rather than decreased by entering a hospital. Physicians' willingness to attempt as best they can to solve the problems in their field of assumed responsibility has thus been the defining characteristic of medicine, not its technological adequacy for the task and not the scientific knowledge base underlying such service (Rodgers, 1980). This also is the modal pattern of professional practice in clinical psychology.

Indeed, professional practitioners are most needed in those transitional areas between complete ignorance and complete certainty. When knowledge in an area of human need reaches the level of scientific certainty, then services based on that knowledge can usually be delivered by a professional technologist. At the other extreme, when there is *no* sound knowledge base in an area, "oracles" can serve that field of human need as well as the professional practitioner, whose cultural role thus lies somewhere between complete ignorance and complete science. Professional practitioners survive as effective professionals to the degree that they can minimize harm and maximize gain in areas of ignorance while still making available the benefits of whatever knowledge exists and stimulating rapid growth toward increasing degrees of certainty of effective solutions.

Since the practitioners' techniques of effective solution are often powerful, their potential for doing harm is often even greater than the potential of the complete charlatan for doing harm. An example is the probable killing of George Washington by excessive bleeding by his physician, for a probable infectious condition, from which he might have recovered had he been exposed merely to the ministrations of a "snake-oil salesman" with his bitter teas and ineffective nostrums. The need for balance between a high potential for doing harm and a high promise for doing good cannot easily be regulated by the public but is of clear public importance. The solution has been to license and identify such practitioners, to set broad boundaries on their practice, and to depend on complex legal and quasi-legal structures for protection of the public. These structures consist of guild-enforced professional ethics, of exposure of students to rigorous training programs that are credential-based as well as competency-based (even though competency is basically undeterminable in fields of ignorance but reflects the "conventional wisdom" of the guild), and of a complex system of malpractice law that is designed, however ineffectively, to penalize obviously or demonstrably deliberate charlatanism or incompetence. The public clearly has a large stake in stimulating attention to its major areas of need while protecting itself as best it can from grossly incompetent tampering with those needs by any except a "selected few" who are best equipped to help the culture stumble forward in its ignorance. These "selected few" are the professional practitioners whose skills must be fully as great in coping with ignorance during a time frame that simply does not allow clarification by underlying knowledge as they are in knowing when true solutions do exist for definable problems and knowing both how to define the problems and how to apply the solution under such conditions.

The characteristics of a practitioner profession are vastly different from those of an applied science profession. Breadth of knowledge about known solutions can be far more critical than highly specialized knowledge about narrow areas of scientific concentration; ways to handle problems with unknown solutions in spite of the presence of ignorance is usually more critical than capacity to identify clearly the presence of ignorance or to withhold recommendation in the absence of certain knowledge. Public regulation of the profession, in close interaction with intraprofessional regulation, is far more critical than for the applied scientist, because the practice itself does not always contain intrinsic evidence of its effectiveness. The differences between the professional practitioner and the professional technologist tend to be more subtle in practice than in conception or theory. Confusion of these approaches is central to many identity issues in professional psychology.

The most "efficient" model of the practitioner-professional is a person to whom a consumer comes with an undiagnosed problem in a particular area of need, who diagnoses the problem by determining whether it is scientifically understood and responsive to known techniques, who refers such problems to appropriate technologists, and who struggles as best she or he can with those conditions or those dimensions of the problem that are identified as not responding to the work of an extender or technologist. Thus, the practitioner-professional paradoxically tends to be the steward of the cultural ignorance base more than of the cultural knowledge base in the particular area of need that is served, appropriately and efficiently utilizing technologists as primary appliers of the available techniques that are based on sound knowledge.

This point is critical enough to warrant further analogous description. Consider the field of law. Lawyers exist not because they know all the legal answers but because people have need of legal advice. They, too, have extenders who are technologists. Law clerks will routinely search library files for related cases or draw up simple wills and trust deeds and the like. Lawyers tend to reserve their primary time and input for issues of unknown legal outcome. For example, it is in the complicated court trial where there is no clear-cut legal precedent or where the precedent tends to run contrary to the needs of the attorney's client and therefore contrary to the established knowledge base of the field that the attorney may spend primary time and effort preparing and presenting the case. Again, it is in the area of nonstandardized and nonroutinized application that the services of the practitioner-professional are most needed. The practitioner-professional thus is the primary steward of the cultural need for help in the face of ignorance, certainly a common enough human problem with enough human risk that it is undoubtedly deserving of a human institution to ensure that such problems receive attention that will maximize potential for gain and minimize potential for loss. It is for such reasons that practitioner professions tend to be designed around such maxims as "First do no harm, and then try to do good."

Those who doubt this view of the practitioner-professional as dealing more with ignorance than with knowledge might consider the question, Who *does* deal with the numerous human problems that have no clear-cut solutions? Who treats the AIDS patients, the cancer patients, the intractable-pain patients, the schizophrenics, the acute anxiety states; who deals with the problems of the difficult adolescent, the difficult marriage, or the difficult legal issue? The idea that all these problems have known solutions and that professionals deliver, or *should* deliver, only validated services is a gross distortion of reality.

Psychology as a Practitioner Profession

The question arises whether psychology is a practitioner profession. More specifically, and this point needs to be understood quite explicitly, the question arises whether one facet is a practitioner practice, since clearly there are facets of psychological work that are extender technologist, independent technologist, applied science, and pure science practice. Use of the same term, *professional psychology*, to apply to all these activities is conceptually confusing but is, nevertheless, the reality of our present nomenclature.

If psychology is to be a practitioner profession, then it will be so because it serves an essentially unique field of human need, whether or not such needs have known solutions. This issue has been previously discussed (see Rodgers, 1980, 1981a; Fox, Barclay, and Rodgers, 1982). As the science of psychology is focused on codifying knowledge about purposive behavior and especially human purposive behavior, then I suggest that a field of practitioner psychology can and does exist that deals with problems arising out of ineffectual human purposive behavior, problems arising out of less-than-optimal patterns of behavioral coping. An example of such problems will illustrate: One type of migraine headache results from vascular dilational spasm in the head, following a prolonged period of vasoconstriction that is secondary to autonomic nervous system arousal in response to perceived threat or challenge. In psychological terms, a person stays physiologically highly mobilized in order to achieve personal achievement goals, to a level and in a manner of mobilization that results in a side effect of a migraine headache. If that person could reduce the chronic mobilization of tension, by "learning to relax" (for example, through biofeedback training) or by getting out of a chronically stressful situation (for example, by changing jobs) or by any one of a variety of other coping strategies or changes in patterns of purposive behavior, then the incidence of migraine headache could also be reduced, directly as a result of improving the effectiveness of behavioral coping. These approaches, it is worth noting, are minimally intrusive—no drugs, no lab tests, no hospitalization, no surgery—and, for this reason, could well be the initial treatment of choice.

Although the relevance of coping patterns to migraine headaches is clear, such relevance by itself does not establish psychology as a practitioner profession, even if psychology assumes responsibility for working with behavioral effectiveness. Since there are other types of headaches and other causes of headaches, someone must clearly "diagnose" whether a coping skills approach would be useful. It is not usually indicated, for example, in a tumor-induced headache. If a psychological approach is useful, someone must further diagnose what particular behavioral approach would be best—biofeedback relaxation training, vocational counseling, marriage counseling, and so on. Suppose the assumption is made that since the headache is a form of pain, the initial diagnosis is primarily the responsibility of a physician, and suppose the physician refers the patient to a psychologist for biofeedback treatment. The psychologist who treats the coping dimension is essentially a high-level technologist, dealing with the problem after it has been prediagnosed by and referred from a physician for a particular approach. Unfortunately, if all headaches are assumed to be exclusively in the domain of the medical practitioner, most physicians are poorly trained in psychology and tend to pursue physiological causes and physiological cures, according to medicine's underlying protopostulates, even for headaches that are primarily side effects of coping skills problems. Indeed, within the medical model, strong vasoconstrictors that block the vasodilation that precipitates migraine headaches are routinely prescribed and do reduce the incidence of headaches.

Suppose, however, that a true practitioner profession of psychology exists. If the consumer makes the assumption that the headache may represent a psychological problem, he or she can come to a psychologist, who will make the primary diagnostic determination that it is or is not the side effect of a coping skills deficit. Then the psychologist is a true practitioner-professional, as here conceived, not simply a technologist. This, of course, raises the counterrisk to the physician's dilemma that the psychologist needs to know enough physiology *and* enough psychology to differentiate between stress-induced migraine headaches and headaches that are not of psychological cause. There can be errors of diagnosis from the psychological side, just as there can be and indeed *are* numerous errors of diagnosis from the medical side. In the ideal world, for most problems of uncertain nature that might straddle practitioner boundaries of expertise, cross-referrals and cross-consultation would be routine.

Four related assertions are often made about professional psychologists vis-à-vis physicians. Comment about these will further clarify the nature of practitioner professions in general and the practitioner field of psychology in particular. These assertions are that psychologists (1) are but limited licensed practitioners, (2) can make only a partial diagnosis, (3) cannot assume full responsibility for care, and (4) cannot determine what care is necessary.

First, consider these statements as they might apply to *any* practitioner profession, such as medicine. The physician has an unlimited license to practice *medicine* but not to practice *anything*, such as law. In this sense, all professionals of whatever sort are limited licensed practitioners. Their "unlimited licenses" at best are for practice only within their own professional domain.

In the same sense, all practitioners can make only partial diagnoses. For example, the physician may diagnose the extent of the trauma and the potential for recovery of function of a hand mutilated by a punch press but cannot make the diagnosis that the injury represented gross neglect by the worker's employer (a legal "diagnosis") or that it is grounds for divorce by the worker's spouse (a personal "diagnosis" by the spouse) or that it requires reassignment of the worker to another job at identical pay (a management-labor-agreement "diagnosis"). Even in a more restricted sense, no professional is in fact skillful enough to make complete diagnoses even within the domain of her or his legal license. For example, the endocrinologist is not competent to make comprehensive psychiatric diagnoses, just as the psychiatrist is not competent to make comprehensive proctological diagnoses. Thus, all professionals in fact make only partial diagnoses within the range of potential diagnoses.

In a directly parallel sense, no professional can assume full responsibility for all care or determine all care that is necessary in all instances, both because each professional's license is limited to one field of endeavor and because his or her knowledge and skills are limited. The psychiatrist does not assume full responsibility for the brain surgery undertaken on the "psychiatrist's patient" by the brain surgeon consulted. Similarly, the ophthalmologist does not determine what care is necessary for a skin condition diagnosed by a dermatologist consulted. If the ophthalmologist did try to countermand the prescriptions of the dermatologist, it would ultimately be the patient who would have legal and practical responsibility for choosing what care is "necessary" or "whom to believe."

Taken in their broadest sense, then, all the foregoing statements apply to all professionals. The "unlimited license" and the "full responsibility" practitioners are conceptual myths and practical fictions. As specifically applied to psychologists, the statements may highlight two additional problems, however. The first problem is the failure to understand the nature of the true practitioner field of professional psychology. The second problem is the tendency for one profession to monopolize societal resources that another profession may need in order to function appropriately.

The first problem is reflected in the context in which the statements are usually made. They usually refer to clinical psychologists functioning in a medical setting, treating psychiatric or other medical problems or at least problems that are conceived and diagnosed within the framework of *DSM-III,* a psychiatric/ medical nomenclature. The context for the statements is thus medical, predominantly a nonpsychology domain and thus one in which a psychologist's license, skills, and responsibilities are all limited rather severely. In this context, the statements either misidentify psychology as a medical specialty, which it is not, or refer to the professional technologist role of the psychologist serving the practitioner field of medicine, which, as already noted, is a limited type of activity to which the statements could accurately be applied. The statements that the psychologist is a limited licensed practitioner, can make only a partial diagnosis, cannot assume full responsibility for care, and cannot determine what care is necessary do not apply any more to the *practitioner* field of psychology *functioning in the professional domain of psychology,* however, than to any other practitioner profession functioning in its own domain. When viewed in the context of another profession's field, all other professionals are never more than "limited practitioners." For example, both the attorney and the physician are "limited practitioner psychologists," limited to the overlap between law or medicine and psychology, just as the psychologist is a "limited medical specialist" or "limited legal specialist." These are simply examples of the fact that all practitioner licenses are limited to one domain of problems, a domain that may overlap other professional domains and therefore appear "limited" when viewed in the context of the other domain, which it does not fully encompass.

These statements do highlight a second problem in the emerging practitioner field of psychology. Resources that any profession uses in its practice are often determined by, controlled by, or limited by law. In the treatment of psychological problems that are conceptualized within the framework of medical diagnoses, psychologists would often find it advantageous to use societal resources that are also used by physicians. Hospitals are a prime example. Their history should be recalled.

Hospitals developed out of a nonmedical, religious tradition that is as relevant for the care of the psychologically distressed as for the care of the medically ill. As described by Dolan, Fitzpatrick, and Hermann (1978, p. 52), "From the moment the significance of Christ's teachings penetrated the thinking of the early Christians, special places were set aside in their homes for hospitality and the actual care of the sick. These were called *Christrooms*, or *diakonia*, reflecting a literal interpretation of the words of Christ: 'I was a stranger and you took me in.'" Bullough and Bullough (1984, p. 87) elaborate: "hospitals . . . emerged in the medieval period to care for those who had no home or family—the traveler away from home, the orphan, the destitute, the soldier, the sick monk or nun, and even some of those who were mentally ill. These early hospitals . . . served a combination of roles: hostel, hotel, and hospital, all three derived from the French word *hôtel*." This tradition of hospitals being primarily nursing facilities for the care of those in need for whatever reason, rather than medical facilities for the exclusive care of medical patients, continued late into the last century. Indeed, it was not until 1918 that the College of Surgeons set medical standards for hospitals. This set of standards was the forerunner of the set established by the Joint Commission on Accreditation of Hospitals and marked the beginning of the "capture" of hospitals by the medical profession. (Paradoxically, current trends in third-party payment for illness treatment threaten to reverse the control relationships in the symbiotic tie between medicine and hospitals, as major hospital corporations assume more and more control of medical practice.)

Hospitals are extremely useful in medical practice, but they could also be highly useful in many aspects of psychological practice. Indeed, hospitalization of the emotionally distressed, a common practice, generally reflects psychological need much more than medical need. Although hospital treatment of the emotionally distressed seldom meets sophisticated standards of psychological, as opposed to medical, care, it is well within the tradition of the hospital movement. To the extent that the medical profession can capture by law exclusive use of the hospital system and to the extent that alternative societal resources are not available to serve the same function, then this legal fact will limit, through medical monopoly, the psychologist's ability to assume full responsibility for all aspects of even the psychological care of clients. As seen from the perspective of practitioner psychology, such arbitrary societal limitations are unfortunate, and their removal through legislative and regulatory processes should and will be fought for. This does not differentiate practitioner psychology from any other practitioner field, however. For example, physicians are greatly restricted in their attack on lung cancer by not being able to close down all cigarette factories, but the law decrees that that activity lies outside the domain of medical practice.

These last problems, of the shared use of societal resources and the overlapping of professional domains, raise many important conceptual issues. Some with respect to medicine are the extent to which psychological services do not simply overlap with but can substitute for medical health care services, the way they can or should be complementary to and complemented by the work of medical practitioners or technologists, and the degree to which interprofessional competition is beneficial or harmful both to the professions involved and to the public served. There is some literature on each of these issues, which tends to suggest the obvious: society tends to be best served by open competition between qualified and publicly regulated competitors; by the marketplace or a "disinterested" public body rather than by monopolistic control of societal resources used in professional practices; and by mutually respectful collegial interaction and integration of effort when professional activities are focused on overlapping problems.

The concept of a practitioner profession clearly does not mean an error-free approach to problems. Rather, it means someone who is knowledgeable and skillful enough to assume professional responsibility for dealing with the raw material of human need, for sorting it into workable categories, and for either rendering appropriate services or referring to an appropriate alternative source of services. From this perspective, there is fully as much need for a practitioner field of psychology, dealing with human purposive behavior, as there is for a practitioner field of medicine, dealing with problems of physiological aberration. There will be errors when self-regulated behavior is pursued at the expense of physiological intervention or at the expense of necessary legal advice, social agency service, or education. However, those errors are no more profound or more costly to the public than the errors involved in erroneously pursuing physiological solutions to human coping problems—for example, by prescribing addicting drugs, unnecessary operations, protracted nonfunctional hospitalizations, or unnecessary medications that carry risks of grave behavioral or physiological side effects. Similarly, there are errors when solvable marriage problems are inappropriately handled by legal divorce proceedings or when social problems that could be dealt with by helping a person become behaviorally effective (for example, by helping overcome a workplace phobia) are instead handled by placing people on permanent disability status or welfare or when problems of tobacco abuse or alcohol abuse or sexual abuse are treated as merely matters calling for education of the public. What is being emphasized here is that psychology as a practitioner profession will not be without its faults and errors, any more than other practitioner professions are free of faults and errors when dealing with complex human problems that often have no "clean" solutions. However, the absence of psychology as a practitioner profession contributes greatly to faults and errors by others who are incompetent in psychology's general domain of expertise but are tempted to function there when that absence leaves a vacuum.

"Knowledge" and "Failure" in the Practitioner Professions

It is clear that practitioner-professionals must be sufficiently familiar with the knowledge base in a particular domain of human need to be able to distinguish between what is known and what is not known, what can be dealt with effectively by current techniques and what cannot. The true practitioners are thus usually "gatekeepers" or "triage" persons, who must be broadly knowledgeable about all alternative approaches to a particular area of human problems.

The deceptive dilemma of all practitioner professions is that the professional's failure to achieve results with his or her own techniques does not automatically alert the practitioner to the inappropriateness of those techniques. Although practitioner work requires a substantial and broad competency in the solid knowledge base of the field, this knowledge may be used mainly to channel people toward technologists who provide the known solutions, while the practitioner may concentrate attention on problems that do not yield readily to these techniques, because they are the "leftover problems" that technologists cannot manage. "Failure" may therefore appropriately be more common than "success" for many practitioners, because they may concentrate largely on the problems that do not have known solutions. The difference between "inappropriate" and "appropriate" failure is not always obvious, as any psychologist working with obesity or alcohol or smoking or other substance abuse syndromes will assert.

The use of a broad knowledge base in order to triage to technologists calls for an entirely different kind of training in knowledge for the practitioner than for the scientist (see Rodgers, 1964). The scientist is looking for the unique and individualized angle that will allow going beyond the previous knowledge base, often a knowledge base with a very narrow focus. In contrast, the professional must typically make conventional and nonunique decisions that will consistently have the same meaning. In factor-analytic terms, the practitioner has to be trained in the commonality of the knowledge base, not in specificity. A scientist advancing the frontier of knowledge can be intensely ignorant of fields that lie outside her or his area of specialization without great harm to the consumer of the resulting scientific products. However, if a primary value of the practitioner is to make an initial diagnosis that assigns to the appropriate technologist problems that are drawn from a wide range of potential diagnosable categories, then breadth of knowledge across the field and awareness of the multiple options are critical. Furthermore, the practitioner need not necessarily be highly skilled in the technical application of procedures of a technologist sort in order to be a highly effective practitioner. Physicians are seldom as skilled as nurses or lab technicians in hitting a vein on the first thrust of a hypodermic needle. Similarly, practitioner psychologists need not be as highly skilled in biofeedback techniques or assertiveness training techniques or even the details of giving a WISC-R as are the specialists on whom they may depend. The technologist and even the scientist, in contrast, will often have to know techniques and equipment thoroughly in order to deal with the subtle nuances of these procedures as they affect results or outcomes in "critical hairsplitting" situations or comparisons.

The importance of knowing what one knows and of knowing what one does not know but what others might know is therefore critical, and the importance of identifying the boundaries of one's "turf" in a practitioner sense is essential to both the welfare of the public and the welfare of the profession. Patients have become permanent iatrogenic invalids from unnecessary surgeries for conversion reaction complaints. Patients have ended up with severe organic brain syndromes from blood clots thrown by heart catheterization studies for chest pain complaints that grew out of psychological stress syndromes rather than clogged arteries. These circumstances are partly effects of the complexities of the problems of "knowledge" and of "failure" in the practitioner field, where the practical meanings of these terms are quite different from their meanings in the fields of technology and of science. They also illustrate the societal hazard when there is no clearly recognized practitioner field of psychology across whose boundaries another practitioner steps only at severe risk of being accused of "practicing psychology without a license" or of being charged with "psychological malpractice."

A purist might raise the question whether there is a functional difference between ineffective approaches, regardless of the motivation of the practitioner. From the societal perspective, there is indeed an important difference. It is of two orders. First, there are degrees of ignorance and of success. The "success rate" for treating acute adult leukemia was only 15 percent in 1980, certainly a measure of ignorance in this medical field—but the same rate was only 3 percent in 1970. Thus, even profound ignorance may not be complete ignorance, and even if expert help is only slightly better than no help at all, that can be a substantial gain overall to the society. Second, part of the ground rules and indeed part of the practice of any competent practitioner profession is a constant sifting of its ignorance for increasingly effective approaches, so that even the failures become the experience out of which future success is slowly developed. This constant attention to the process of pushing back the curtain of ignorance again distinguishes the true practitioner-professional from the fanatic, charlatan, or quack.

Not only is there persistent pressure to push back the curtain of ignorance, but also the particular nature of the practitioner field tends to determine how that progress is likely to be made. As has been suggested, practitioner fields are based on broad protopostulates that structure the way their successes or failures are appraised. Medicine, for example, assumes that medical correction comes from beneficially altering physiological process. The medical perspective attempts to understand how physiology was altered in successful treatment and how it was either altered or left unaltered in unsuccessful treatment. For example, medicine has pursued the understanding of brain chemistry and neurotransmitter biology as the prime way of understanding "psychiatric" depression. Practitioner psychology, in contrast, has pursued the understanding of expectations, learned patterns of behaving, goal orientations, and similar coping processes as the prime way of understanding "psychological" depression. Because of such differences in the impact on the shaping of future knowledge, clear differentiation of practitioner fields, each with its own protopostulates and its own directions for growth, is important even in areas of relative ignorance, before any practitioner field has functionally adequate approaches to the particular problem.

It is the slow progress toward knowledge and effectiveness that differentiates practitioner approaches from magical or superstitious or fanatical ones, that makes worthwhile the heavy investment of the public—through regulatory laws, professional fees, construction of supporting public institutions, and so on—in the "special privileges" of the practitioner fields to dabble, in their ignorance, with their own, often ineffective "professional arts," even when those are not well grounded in scientific understanding at the time. Medicine as a field did not know how to deal with the plague in past centuries, but persistently attempted to, in ways that gradually led to the evolution of a physiological knowledge base that now makes the plague and many other infectious conditions essentially trivial public health menaces. There is in this sense an extremely critical difference between the ineffectiveness of a true practitioner profession and the ineffectiveness of others dealing with the same problem: the practitioner profession mainstreams our ignorance toward ultimate understanding and knowledge. In a more technical sense, the profession becomes the cultural custodian of pushing toward significant solutions. It is seldom (although occasionally) the physician who makes the basic scientific discoveries that advance the field of physiological knowledge on which effective medical practice is based. However, it is indeed the medical establishment and the recognition and support by the public, by science, and so on of the mission of medicine as a practitioner field that enables medicine to focus strongly on the advancement of knowledge. This stance has an applied and highly functional purpose. Then too, organized medicine maintains perhaps the largest lobbying force and political action committee in the country and is especially sensitive to addressing concerns that advance its guild functions, channel research funds to medical endeavors, and otherwise advance its guild orientation while promoting the advancement of the societal concerns it serves.

Recognition of the implications of the foregoing characteristics of a practitioner field should alert all basic scientists to be strong supporters of their appropriate practitioner extensions, just as such recognition should also alert the practitioners to be strongly supportive of their underlying basic science support structures. In present-day psychology, there is little evidence of appreciation for or practical attention to this crucial *symbiotic*—as opposed to similarity—tie between practitioner and scientist and little evidence of respect for the importance of the critical *differences* between them. As a result, we are currently experiencing the problem of a large medical practitioner field stimulating research on physiological and biological processes in the absense of a similarly vigorous, accepted, or effective "behavioral science practitioner" field that can stimulate the channeling of similar cultural supports toward understanding of psychological processes and dimensions of behavioral coping effectiveness, processes that are far more critical to public welfare at the present stage of history than are biological ones, as important as those are.

A practitioner field that can "mainstream ignorance" is thus quite different from quackery and quite different from hard science as well. Unfortunately, it is often superficially difficult to distinguish in its practices and in its immediate outcomes from less societally useful approaches. George Washington probably *was* bled to death by a conscientious physician using the best technology available to medicine at the time. That specific event is hard to justify, although it undoubtedly was one very small piece of the continuing struggle of the medical field to find workable answers, a struggle that has led to our essentially magnificent medical "technology" of the present era, in which, fortunately, large segments of medical practice are indeed technologically sound and not entirely dependent on medicine as a "healing *art*."

The foregoing discussion highlights two dimensions of the relation between science and practitioner work. One is that the work of the practitioner, though heavily dependent on sound knowledge, is very often scientifically indefensible simply because it is dealing with areas of need that science has not yet adequately elucidated. Thus, the practitioner simply cannot practically be held to the same standards as the scientist, cannot be trained in the same way, and cannot be judged by the same criteria. Second, because the ultimate service of the practitioner to the public must come from pushing back the curtains of ignorance, ignorance that is the reason for the practitioner's presence to start with, there can be no more critical partisan to support scientific advance in relevant areas than the practitioner. The practitioner thus becomes, or should become, an advocate for science, of the highest order, drawing on a tremendous reservoir of societal need and societal importance to support the channeling of resources to the scientific efforts. Consider, for example, how little societal support there might be for the biological sciences if it were not for the practitioner field of medicine. If there were a similarly respected and vigorous practitioner field of psychology, concerned about the mammoth problems of behavior and human coping effectiveness, then similar massive infusion of support for basic research in psychology (and indeed in sociology and anthropology and the biological bases of behavior) might also be expected. As already noted, this symbiotic tie between the practitioner and research fields is based on *differences* between the two approaches, not similarities. This principle is little understood in psychology, in its training programs, its implementation programs, its public relations programs, and its professional society (especially APA) structures. The misunderstanding works to the disadvantage of both the basic science and the practitioner field. Each should be strongly supporting the development of the other, in its own symbiotic best interest, not belittling or undercutting the other. By the same token, each will have most respect for the other if the differences as well as the similarities are clearly recognized, appreciated, and respected.

Psychology as a Practitioner Field

There are three fields of need that psychology as a practitioner profession might serve: (1) the behavioral dimensions of illness, or "health psychology," (2) behavior modification in which behavior is shaped to fit predetermined conceptions or models, and (3) coping skills enhancement in which self-regulated behavior is optimally managed to accomplish self-determined goals.

The traditional de facto definition of *clinical* psychology as a practitioner field has been the psychological treatment of psychiatric disorders. The field still uses *DSM-III*, of the American Psychiatric Association, as its primary nomenclature. Most clinical psychology sections in institutional settings are in departments of psychiatry. APA talks about practitioner psychology, or at least a large branch of it, as a "mental health field," and psychiatry is seen as the primary "competition." Clearly, the behavioral dimensions of and behavioral approaches to psychiatric illness constitute an important area of societal need, since medicine does not prepare physicians well for attending to behavioral dimensions of these or other medical problems. Historically, it was psychology's attention to the psychological dimensions of the "psychiatric" casualties of the Second World War that provided the major cultural impetus for the growth of professional psychology. In some respects, then, the most accurate description of what clinical psychology, the major branch of professional practitioner psychology, seems to deal with could well be the behavioral dimensions of "psychiatric illness."

As a defining characteristic of a technology field, such a conceptualization would be defensible, but not as a defining conceptualization of a practitioner field. Among other considerations, it would be extremely limiting, in at least three major dimensions. First, psychiatric illness, precisely defined in medical terms, is not a very broad spectrum of human problems. Since anxiety, depression, and emotional distress of various sorts are normal responses to common life situations, these conditions become illnesses only when they somehow depart from normal response and perhaps especially when they depart from normal physiological processing of stimulus information. If psychology as a practitioner field were truly to limit its concerns to this narrow range of pathology, then the opportunity for its practitioners to broaden their understanding of normal stress and normal distress conditions would be lost. The parent who is "understandably" distressed about how to deal with a teenage son who is acting out is trying to deal with a son who is not technically ill in either a medical or a psychiatric/medical sense. Such parents might, nevertheless, benefit greatly from attention to their own behavioral patterns used to deal with the son and currently could receive benefit from clinical psychology as it is now practiced, even though they do not have a psychiatric illness either. Thus, a rigorous conceptualization of psychiatric illness would certainly draw the boundaries too narrowly, if practitioner psychology were to be limited to behavioral dimensions of such states. Of course, to the extent that "psychiatric illness" is extended to cover every human reflex in the behavioral repertoire, as has tended to be the grandiose pattern of the past, then such a definition of psychology might not be so limiting, but it is conceptually tortuous. Furthermore, such an "unlimited" definition of psychiatric illness is indefensible, this probably being one of the primary conceptual dilemmas that have led to the self-conscious "remedicalization" of psychiatry over the past decade and a half.

Second, under such a definition, psychology would become basically a limited practice of medicine, rather than an independent field in itself. The parameters on which psychology focused would be defined by the profession of medicine rather than by the profession of psychology, and psychology's techniques would be a subpart of the unlimited practice of medicine available to the psychiatrist, rather than anything unique, simply because the physician always assumes the responsibility for trying to do everything that is necessary to deal with the medical condition he or she is trying to treat. Such a definition of psychology practice would clearly lend validity to a common distinction that psychiatrists and psychologists do the same things, except that psychiatrists can prescribe medicine and use medical procedures but psychologists cannot. If the field were to be defined thus, it probably would be conceptually cleaner to define psychologists as high-level psychiatric technologists rather than as independent practitioner-professionals. This, essentially, is the argument psychiatry now uses for insisting that psychologists should not have independent privileges in hospitals or other privileges appropriate to a practitioner profession.

Third, as already suggested, this conceptualization would leave untouched an extremely important and extremely large domain of human need that could and should benefit from the attention of *some* practitioner field, and psychology is the logical profession to attend to that extended area of need. Psychology's primary approaches to behavioral dimensions of psychiatric illness involve self-understanding, self-management of relaxation techniques, learned patterns of assertiveness or communication or coping, adjustment of expectations to external realities or internal skill capacities, and development of interpersonal skills or patterns that reduce tension and build support. These same approaches are also useful in a variety of conditions that should not be characterized as "psychiatric illness." The parent of the acting-out teenager is one example. The executive with a pattern of expressing anger that alienates him from others and reduces his promotability would be another, as would a young couple who find themselves in a marriage that is not working well. The definition of psychology as a subfield of psychiatry is, therefore, an anachronism that may have served an important need during World War II but is long outdated and too limiting.

Even if the concept is broadened beyond psychiatric problems to all behavioral dimensions of health, there are difficulties. Within APA, there has been a proposal in recent years to limit definitions of practitioner work in psychology (for example, requirements for licensure) to "health" psychologists. To the extent that the concept of "health" psychology refers to the behavioral dimensions of illness, medical disability, injury, physiological sensory loss, and medically at-risk life-styles, it is only a more elaborate or extended variation of the concept of practitioner psychology as dealing with the behavioral dimensions of psychiatric illness, except that the subject matter is broadened to the behavioral dimensions of all illness. To the extent that *health* means, in a non-medically oriented sense, "degree of living equilibrium," then, from a psychological perspective, it is indistinguishable from effectiveness of psychological, or behavioral, coping. This concept of effectiveness of behavioral coping, as a definition of the practitioner field of psychology, will now be considered.

Another possible definition of psychology as a practitioner field, with some historical roots, is that of a behavior-shaping profession. If psychology is the science of behavior, then the profession of psychology might be able to shape behavior to fit some predetermined goal or ideal. Psychologists might be able to decriminalize the criminal, socialize the child, shape the worker into an effective producer, modify the behaviors of chronically institutionalized patients into more satisfactory conformity to institutional needs such as dressing themselves and toileting themselves. Although this is certainly a conceptually defensible focus of a practitioner field of psychology, it has a primary limitation: the hazard of determining whose model is to be used to shape behavior. This, of course, is the specter of *Brave New World* or *1984*. Behavior control, in which the person's behavior is subjected to modification according to the will of another, always carries at least some threat of slavery, in which the gain of the behavior modification is to the person who sets the model for the behavior, at the expense of the person whose behavior is modified. In a culture that is as self-consciously committed to individuality and individual freedom as the American culture at this point in history, such a definition seems precluded. Both scientific and professional psychology may well explore and at times implement aspects of behavior modification or behavior control to moderate self-destructive, highly deviant, or ineptly focused behavior. This is not a central focus of present professional work, however, and does not seem likely to become so.

The idea of a practitioner field of psychology dealing with problems of human purposive behavior, focused on enhancing coping effectiveness through the alteration of patterns of self-regulated behavior, has been repeatedly suggested throughout this chapter. It seems a defensible, a needed, a viable, and even an ongoing enterprise. This view has been elaborated elsewhere as it would relate to licensing laws (Rodgers, 1981b), professional education (Fox, Barclay, and Rodgers, 1982), and public need (Rodgers, 1981a). Self-regulated purposive behavior is an exquisitely useful tool that has allowed the human animal to adapt to an incredibly varied range of environments. Effective use of the adaptive skills of purposive behaviorism is critical for the well-being and even the survival of both individuals and groups. Human goals can often be more effectively achieved by shifting from a "lower level" to a "higher level" of behavioral sophistication. For example, shifting from either passivity (which is often adaptive but at considerable price to personal goals) or aggressiveness (which is often more effective for achieving personal goals but often at considerable risk and often with loss of group support) to assertiveness (a term implying an optimal balance that avoids as much as possible the problems of both passivity and aggressiveness while still maximizing chances of achieving one's own goals) is one such way of improving human effectiveness by modifying the pattern of coping. It is the role of assisting people in achieving more competent levels of self-regulation that I suggest as a defining role for the practitioner field of psychology.

Such an approach is directed toward maximizing the effectiveness of the human being in every sphere of important human endeavor, whether that endeavor is regulating behavior so as to minimize the risks of physical illness or maximize the potential for recovery from physical illness, altering management skills to improve the effective coordination of a work group, facilitating more meaningful regulation of intimacy relationships, or altering life-style patterns so as to improve satisfactions of living. It is a broad field that is not well approached by any other profession.

The primary scientific underpinning of the field would be comprehensive understanding of the nature of human behavior, which, of course, is the defining concept of scientific psychology. The techniques of the field, at our present level of sophistication, are mainly those which professional psychologists now know and which psychology students are currently taught. Approached in systematic fashion, the field would no doubt expand into numerous new areas of application and numerous new techniques of approach, while largely absorbing and encompassing nearly all the present activities regarded as typical of professional practitioner psychology. In a broad sense, it would deal with the problems in the behavioral dimensions of life parallel to the way medicine deals with the problems in the physiological dimensions of life.

References

American Psychiatric Association. *Diagnostic and Statistical Manual of Mental Disorders.* (3rd ed.) Washington, D.C.: American Psychiatric Association, 1980.

Bullough, V. L., and Bullough, B. *History, Trends and Politics of Nursing.* East Norwalk, Conn.: Appleton-Century-Crofts, 1984.

Dolan, J. A., Fitzpatrick, M. L., and Hermann, E. K. *Nursing in Society: A Historical Perspective.* (15th ed.) Philadelphia: Saunders, 1978.

Fox, R. E., Barclay, A. G., and Rodgers, D. A. "The Foundations of Professional Psychology." *American Psychologist,* 1982, *37,* 306–312.

Raimy, V. C. (ed.). *Training in Clinical Psychology.* Englewood Cliffs, N.J.: Prentice-Hall, 1950.

Rodgers, D. A. "In Favor of Separation of Academic and Professional Training." *American Psychologist,* 1964, *19,* 675–680.

Rodgers, D. A. "The Status of Psychologists in Hospitals: Technicians or Professionals." *Clinical Psychologist,* 1980, *23,* 5–7.

Rodgers, D. A. "Proposal for the Creation of a 'New' Profession of Psychology." Position paper prepared for the Policy and Planning Board of the American Psychological Association, 1981a.

Rodgers, D. A. "A Proposed Model Psychology Licensing Law." *Professional Practice of Psychology,* 1981b, *2,* 47–71.

Stapp, J., Tucker, A., and VandenBos, G. "Census of Psychological Personnel: 1983." *American Psychologist,* forthcoming.

8

Arthur N. Wiens
Herbert Dörken

Establishing and Enforcing Standards to Assure Professional Competency

Although we can assume that one of the characteristics of a profession is the concern its members show for the general welfare of the public, that assumption probably does not account fully for the interest that most professions have shown in being statutorily recognized and regulated. Psychology is no exception. We must recognize that licensure has promoted the economic well-being of our profession and has enhanced our reputation. Statutory recognition is a symbol of respectability and of having become established as a profession. In addition, the status of psychology as a licensed profession has attracted increasing numbers of qualified persons into its practice (see Chapter One). With specification of practice standards, statutory recognition also helps to define the profession of psychology more clearly and makes it a legal entity.

In establishing its practice standards, some argue, the profession has sought to enshrine elitist or ultimate standards. Not so. Psychology has sought to establish the minimum standards considered by wide consensus to be sufficient for acquisition of the education, training, and experience necessary to begin practice. These standards have to be such that the public may have reasonable assurance of basic competence but have to be attainable

by a sufficient number of would-be practitioners that the profession
will have the human resources to serve the public need. Havighurst
(1984, p. 65) summarizes the current trend toward balancing quality
standards with competition from alternatives while minimizing
malpractice yet encouraging consumer choice. In his view, "We live
in an era of limits . . . alternatives to the previously dominant style
and methods of practice have begun to seem acceptable . . . we are
gradually accepting the fact that we can't have it all, that the highest
quality is not necessarily worth its high cost, and that trade-offs
must be made. The belief that the same high standards should
prevail everywhere . . . is seen as more and more unrealistic and
emphasis is placed instead on raising standards where they are
unacceptably low." That is the philosophy of this chapter, that
minimum professional standards should be not only established but
enforced.

The clear purpose of professional and occupational
licensure, including certification statutes, is to protect the public
from harm. This worthy purpose has led to the licensing of over 500
professions or occupations in the United States and to the
development of licensure statutes for the practice of psychology in
all of the United States and most of the provinces of Canada. These
licensure statutes include three major provisions: (1) specification
of entry requirements for membership in the profession, (2)
establishment of standards and regulations for practice and for
disciplining practitioners who do not adhere to these practice
standards, and (3) establishment of the authority to prevent
unlicensed practice or title use by persons who have not met the
entry requirements of the licensed profession. This last provision
gives the professional or occupational group a "privileged" status
in that persons deficient in the requisite knowledge and skills are
denied an opportunity to pursue that profession or occupation. It
is generally assumed that the members of a profession possess
special knowledge and that the greater the impact a profession has
on society through the normal exercise of its knowledge, the greater
the need for its practice to be regulated by the state.

Society, through its legislators, has given statutory
recognition to the practice of psychology and now expects an
accounting of whether the public's expectations for establishment

and enforcement of practice standards and the avoidance of harm have been fulfilled. The licensure process is the vehicle with which we as a profession seek to provide these "quality assurances."

In this chapter we briefly discuss the basic nature of the licensure process in psychology. We then go on to assert that the practice of psychology should be licensed and regulated because when practiced by unqualified practitioners, it is a hazard to the public health and welfare. One important component of continuing competency assurance among psychologist practitioners is to define practice standards and regulations explicitly and hold psychologists to them. In fact, as psychology defines ever more specialized practice areas, issues of competent practice will become increasingly important because of the implied and generally accepted assumption that those with special training and/or experience adhere to a higher standard of conduct. Finally, in this chapter we list some behavioral specifics of unacceptable practice as these have been defined in state statutes.

The Licensure Process in Psychology

The licensure process in psychology has three phases. In the first phase, the applicant is evaluated for evidence of a doctoral degree in psychology and the necessary one to two years of supervised experience as a psychologist—that is, the entry requirements for membership in the profession. In this first phase of licensure the applicant takes the national Examination of Professional Practice in Psychology to verify acquisition of basic knowledge in psychology. In this phase representatives of the *profession* wish to verify that the applicant for licensure possesses minimum knowledge which all psychologists are expected to have and which defines the generic discipline of psychology. It is assumed that this body of knowledge is large and can be acquired only through the long, intensive educational process leading to the doctoral degree in psychology.

Similarly, in this first phase, representatives of the *public* served by psychologists wish to be assured that members of the profession share and apply a common body of psychological knowledge relevant to professional practice. The public assumes that a licensed psychologist will have sufficient breadth of training to recognize the parameters of a variety of problem situations and provide safe, effective, and appropriate help or make referral to another professional practitioner who can. Essentially, this first phase of the licensure process examines what the applicant has done in the past, although that obviously does not necessarily predict competent practice in the future. Even so, it is assumed that the person educated in psychology is best prepared to offer competent services in psychology. Thus, knowledge is presumed to be necessary, but not sufficient, for competent practice.

The second phase of the licensure process identifies the areas of professional competency in which the applicant expects to practice. The applicant is asked, typically through oral or essay examination, to describe past focus of study and experience and to establish, to the profession's satisfaction, competency in a specific practice area. The oral examination may be conducted by peers who practice in the same competency area and who can present actual practice situations in that specialty area for the applicant to consider. Such examinations test for specific practice knowledge and are clearly related to the projected practice of the applicant. The examinations in this second phase of the licensure process do have a prospective view and are designed to increase the probability that the applicant will be a competent practitioner in a particular area of practice. Yet we must recognize that competent practice is a complex combination of knowledge, skill, ability, and personal characteristics and that even competency definitions vary among professions and among specialties within a profession. Given this much variability in the definitions of competency (making it an elusive criterion variable), one cannot seriously expect that we will soon develop an examination procedure to *predict* competent professional practice with much accuracy. We are still dealing with probabilities of competency in this phase of licensure.

This brings us to the third phase of the licensure process, which is the assurance of competency of the individual practitioner for the individual consumer of psychological services. Such competency assurance is, in fact, the theoretical basis of licensure, which is predicated on the assumptions that the practice of psychology can have negative as well as positive impact on the consumer and that the consumer cannot be expected to evaluate the special and unique professional knowledge that the practitioner is expected to possess (Wiens, 1983). Fortunately, the licensure process does have the potential for competency assurance, but only through a system of practice regulations and discipline/enforcement procedures. The competency assurance that licensing boards can provide to consumers of psychological services is directly proportional to the vigor and dispatch with which a state licensing board disciplines, remediates, or removes the license of an incompetent, unethical, negligent, dishonest, or unprofessional practitioner.

Practice of Psychology as a Hazard to the Public Health and Welfare

If the incompetent practice of psychological procedures were not hazardous, there would be no public value in licensing the profession of psychology. Clearly, however, the incompetent, unethical, negligent, dishonest, or unprofessional practice of psychology *is* hazardous to the public. Not only are members of our profession aware of this potential for harm, but evidence of consumers' concern is mounting. In general, the public has become increasingly dissatisfied with both the cost and the quality of many professional services. The number of malpractice suits against physicians, psychiatrists, psychologists, lawyers, and other professionals has grown dramatically during the last decade. Juries' financial awards have escalated in size. In addition, the public has begun to demand a role on licensing boards and in the formulation and implementation of regulations involving the professions (Hogan, 1979). Concern is increasing that professional licensure, because of inadequate monitoring by state boards, does not guarantee the public protection from harm, that licensees rarely have their licenses revoked, and that people practicing without a license are rarely prosecuted.

Society has traditionally sought to inhibit incompetent professional practice through licensure, self-regulation through professional associations, and malpractice suits. When any one of these measures proves less than fully effective, the other two must be made capable of taking on an added burden of public protection. One concern is that psychologist licensing boards and professional association ethics committees have not been sufficiently vigorous in enforcing regulatory and ethical standards of practice. If this is true, then we may well expect the remaining control mechanism of malpractice suits against psychologists to increase in frequency and financial severity.

The medical profession faced this very situation during the malpractice crisis of 1974-75, when physicians demanded malpractice relief from legislators. When legislators, in turn, demanded closer monitoring of physician practices and more vigorous enforcement of practice standards, physicians began to confront issues of definitions of practice standards and tougher disciplinary strategies. As a result, various statutory steps to promote stricter enforcement of practice standards have been taken, including providing legal immunity for physicians who report colleagues to disciplinary boards; making such reporting mandatory for physicians and, in some states, for hospitals, medical societies, and malpractice insurers; adding new grounds for disciplining physicians, including definitions of incompetence; making penalties more flexible; putting discipline in the hands of new agencies that are independent of the licensing boards; and giving the disciplinary boards new power, such as subpoenaing records and invoking summary license suspension. The impact of these changes is reflected by the fact that actions against physicians by state disciplinary boards increased almost 500 percent between 1971 and 1977, annual license revocations alone more than quadrupling in that period. The actual number of revocations, 198, is less impressive and is probably just a drop in the bucket in light of estimates that 5 percent of the country's 287,000 physicians are impaired in some way (Rosenberg, 1979). Have we even begun in psychology to approach the level of professional discipline and enforcement represented by these changes in the medical profession?

Probably very few psychologists have seriously considered the fact that the basis of licensure is the legislative expectation of enforcement of practice standards by the profession or the assumption that the unlicensed practice of psychology poses a serious risk to the consumer's life, health and safety, or financial well-being. Psychologists must think seriously about whether the practice of psychology may be hazardous to the public health and welfare or whether, in fact, we believe that our services to the public are so innocuous that they require no supervision or licensure for practice. Is psychotherapy, for example, simply the purchase of friendship, as Schofield (1964) once proposed? If it is nothing more, we probably should not try to license its practice or bill the consumer for it. The demand for regulation rests on the assumption that there is a degree of risk and danger involved in the psychotherapeutic process and in other psychological practices, such as psychodiagnosis. In general, the therapeutic process, with the blind trust and confidence that many patients place in their therapist, offers many opportunities for unethical activities and other abuses. Anecdotal evidence to support these assertions is probably known to all psychotherapists.

Many therapies stimulate anxiety as a motivation for change, and some patients may experience panic anxiety and destructive psychological decompensation. Some active and directive therapists tend to abuse their patients, both verbally and physically, in ways that may result in serious emotional disturbance. Poorly handled transference relationships may result in lasting dependency. Given the potential and actual abuses in our profession, one wonders why there have been so few malpractice suits against psychotherapists. A major reason may be that psychotherapy has been seen as unique to each individual practitioner and client, and as a consequence it has been difficult to define the duties that should be required for therapists in general (Karson, 1978). It is also a private and confidential procedure and therefore generally shielded from an outside evaluation. However, we may be seeing the development of some standard expectations of psychotherapists and the development of practice standards that will provide the basis for litigation for a conclusion of negligence in practice if such expectations and standards are not met. For example, a newly licensed practitioner might be ill advised to begin treatment with a severely troubled patient who would be better served by an experienced practitioner. In this case, ignorance or disregard for professional limitations could be the basis for litigation. Improper diagnosis is a common source of medical malpractice; similarly, proper assessment and diagnosis or problem determination before psychotherapy is begun is necessary in order to avoid a charge of diagnostic negligence. Proper operational diagnosis (of the problem, not the symptom) and consultation continue to be necessary throughout therapy, and a therapist could be negligent by failing to reevaluate the original diagnosis or by failing to seek necessary consultation. A therapist could also be negligent by choosing a type of therapy inappropriate for persons with certain personality traits—for example, not providing support for the decompensating patient or prolonging the treatment for a patient with mild, transient neurotic symptoms. Of course, the patient has a right to full and complete information about the treatment. Failure to provide such information might result in a charge of negligence. Engaging in a course of therapy without an individualized treatment plan based on informed consent might result in charges of coercion, violation of civil rights, or unprofessional practice.

A therapist may also behave unethically by failing to maintain appropriate objectivity necessary to resolve the patient's problem. Personal contact with the patient may confuse the therapist's personal goals with professional obligations. A therapist also has a duty to be available during a patient's crisis. If a patient's condition can be shown to have worsened because of lack of care at a time of crisis, the therapist can be held responsible. An extension of a therapist's duty is to monitor the patient's behavior and emotional response during various life events—that is, during the other twenty-three hours of each day. Negligence or incompetence may also be charged when a therapist prolongs treatment longer than necessary (Cummings, 1979) or discharges a patient prematurely. If in doubt, the therapist should seek consultation.

These are only a few examples of the forms that unethical or hazardous practice may take. When psychologists begin to treat a patient, they represent themselves as having the skills and knowledge common to psychologists. Generally stated, a psychologist who lacks ordinary knowledge and skills or neglects to apply those possessed may be found liable for an injured patient (or his or her family) in a malpractice action (Karson, 1978).

In addition to the experiential evidence we probably all have, the work of Strupp, of Hadley, and of Bergin documents the existence of specific problems in psychotherapy (reviewed in Bergin and Lambert, 1978). Bergin's evidence for deterioration effects in psychotherapy is accumulating and offers empirical support for concern about the dangers of psychotherapeutic practice. Given these data, we believe the profession should publicly recognize that unqualified or incompetent psychologist practitioners pose a serious risk to the consumer's life, health, safety, and financial well-being. Clearly, we can document that unqualified practitioners pose a hazard to the public. Do we want to do so and thereby call attention to ourselves and raise questions about why we have not been more vigorous in self-discipline procedures? We have no choice. We have started to spell out the educational preparation that psychologists must have for licensure, and we must now attend to the other phases of licensure and spell out more vigorously the boundaries for acceptable psychological practice.

Zemlick (1980) has argued vigorously that a major challenge facing psychology today is that of effecting a viable self-regulatory program or else chancing ever-increasing external restraint, regulation, and legislative and judicial controls. He believes that the recent flurry of sunset legislation is only one of a number of indicators reflecting the disenchantment and dissatisfaction of the consumer with the profession's failure to maintain high standards of accountability. The energy, costs, and interference with personal goals implied in effective self-regulation are much more than most psychologists seem to have been willing to pay. Thus, as Zemlick points out, psychologists on ethics committees have offered various excuses for lack of vigorous enforcement: the costs of enforcement exceed the budget, there is the threat of suit, psychologists should not be judgmental, the committee/board violated its own procedures or was not sufficiently self-informed, and so on. Finally, he concludes that this self-excusing behavior convinces no one we are doing all we can and should and that psychology should take the increasingly proactive leadership role that society has a right to expect from the profession.

Practice Standards and Boards of Examiners

We have emphasized the assumption that psychologists' practices can be hazardous to the public because we think we must accept this assumption and sensitize ourselves to it before we can proceed to define the boundaries of acceptable psychological practice. In fact, some state boards are taking the lead in this direction. For example, the state of Virginia has passed legislation that requires the Virginia Board of Psychology to see that inspections of each practitioner are undertaken in order to ensure that each practitioner is conducting his or her practice in a competent manner and within the lawful regulations of the board. Because the Virginia board distributes summaries of state statutes that relate to the practice of psychology, its licensees cannot claim ignorance of relevant laws. The Virginia board has also established disciplinary guidelines to ensure uniformity in handling disciplinary cases.

In a similar vein, the Ohio Psychology Licensing Board has designated a number of psychological procedures as potentially serious hazards to mental health that require professional expertise in psychology in their application. The Ohio board, which based its decision on research evidence and public testimony, designated the following procedures as restricted in that they constitute a hazard if inappropriately used: sensitivity training; confrontation groups; hypnosis; individual intelligence testing; psychological diagnosis and personality evaluation; individual and group psychological psychotherapy; psychological behavior therapy such as, but not limited to, implosive therapy, aversive therapy, and desensitization; couples and family psychological psychotherapy; and psychological psychotherapy for sexual dysfunctions. Although this list is quite extensive, the reader might wish to expand it even further.

The licensing board of Minnesota also proposed new rules of conduct for its licensees. These rules represent an effort to specify unacceptable practice behaviors in less ambiguous terms than are often found in codes of ethics.

These states are trying to find clear-cut language that details a range of incompetent, unethical, negligent, dishonest, or unprofessional practices in such a fashion that enforcement of practice standards can be achieved directly and with dispatch.

Client Complaints. In order to enforce the newly developing standards, psychologists and licensing boards must consider how to facilitate the receipt of consumer complaints. Clients may not know that complaints can be filed or how to do so. We may also have a significant problem with psychologist practitioners themselves in this regard in that there have been some informal tales of practitioners who explicitly threaten a client with reprisal if the client makes it known that a complaint may be or has been filed. Both practitioners and clients need to know that there must be no reprisal if a complaint is made in good faith. In fact, a number of psychologists are now purchasing pamphlets for their waiting rooms describing procedures for evaluating services and for addressing complaints.

Minnesota, in its proposed rules of conduct, has again addressed some of these issues. The proposed rules state, for example, that psychologists shall make available as a handout to clients a statement of practice competencies submitted to the Psychology Licensing Board. Furthermore, the Minnesota board has proposed a "Client's Bill of Rights," which states that consumers of psychological services offered by psychologists licensed by the state of Minnesota have the following rights:

1. To expect that a psychologist has met the minimal qualifications of training and experience required by state law.
2. To examine public records which contain the credentials of a psychologist.
3. To receive a copy of the Rules of Conduct of the Board of Psychology from the Document Section of the State of Minnesota.
4. To report complaints to the Board of Psychology.
5. To be informed of the cost of professional services prior to receiving these services.
6. To be guaranteed confidentiality as defined by rule and statute.
7. To be free of discrimination on the basis of race, religion, sex, or other unlawful discrimination while receiving psychological services.

An article entitled "How to Complain About a Lawyer" (Daggett, 1979) has been disseminated in Oregon as one way of educating the public about that process. It includes a description of the complaint process, grounds for a complaint, and possible outcomes of complainant actions. This handout could easily be adapted by psychologists and would be a worthwhile adjunct to the kind of information handouts developed by the Minnesota board. The point of such materials is to reassure the public that we as a profession are serious about maintenance of practice standards and willing to submit ourselves for review.

Enforcement. Stated simply, we need explicit criteria for defining and identifying "bad apples." We also need explicit mechanisms for getting them out of the "barrel."

It is true that the very low malpractice insurance rates for professional psychologists reflect the fact that few claims have been adjudged against them. However, we should not take idle comfort in this tranquility. There has been a dramatic increase in the number of licensed psychologists over only the past decade (see Chapter One and Dörken and Webb, 1981), from about 20,100 in 1974 to 25,250 in 1977 to 45,683 by mid-1985. This, coupled with an equally dramatic shift to full-time private practice (Dörken and Webb, 1979, and Chapters One and Two), plus the recent expansion into new markets of practice based on new federal and state legislation, broadening the practice of psychology (Dörken, 1976), increases our "exposure to risk" as professionals/practitioners by geometric proportions. The days of isolated practitioners and others functioning as a cottage industry are essentially in the past, albeit the recent past. We had best establish clear procedures for the control of psychological practice before there is a more dramatic need to "clean up our act."

From the public protection standpoint, the weakest aspect of psychology licensure/certification laws appears to be the relatively ineffective procedures for stopping unlicensed practice, curbing unprofessional conduct by a licensee, and revoking, restricting, or suspending a license for cause. Most licensure laws provide that the administrative board will adopt rules and regulations whose violation can lead to some form of censure. Regulations, as we know, have the force of law, but they tend not to be as widely

known. There is probably greater "sentinel" effect by having the
specifics "up front" in the law itself.

The fact that psychology licensing laws are badly in need of
teeth was recently demonstrated vividly by the great difficulty and
expense that the California Psychology Examining Committee
encountered as it attempted to revoke a license for assault and
battery and another for procedures hazardous to life. In the first
instance, after the practitioner was found guilty and his license
revoked, he moved to another state and now practices there—as
what? a licensed psychologist! In the other case, death of a patient
finally brought license revocation—but the practitioner continued
to practice as an unlicensed counselor and has since petitioned for
relicensure.

If we are unable to make disciplinary sanctions "stick" in
these dramatic instances of unethical behavior, it is clear that state
boards have much work to do in articulating practice standards and
enforcing adherence to them. Concern about the issue of sanctioned
psychologists' simply moving to another state was reflected in the
discussions at the Executive Committee meeting of the American
Association of State Psychology Boards in the spring of 1980.
Participants in that meeting were concerned about how little
information is available on actions taken against psychologists and
about the lack of any explicit format for evaluating the performance
of a licensing board. Among other things, there needs to be a process
for sharing information on disciplinary actions taken by boards—
revocations, suspensions, denials, stolen or lost certificates, fines,
and so on. More important, however, there needs to be a systematic
effort among psychology boards to communicate with one another
in order to develop effective means of ensuring the public's safety
by assuring the quality of psychological practice. Fortunately,
communication mechanisms are now in place so that state boards
can be informed when a psychologist's license is revoked in another
jurisdiction.

Perhaps many psychologists have assumed that the
profession's code of ethics would guarantee that psychologists
would practice ethically and within their area of competence.
However, to begin with, it must be recognized that the ethical codes
of professional societies, with their potential for peer condemnation

and dismissal from the professional society, are essentially without effect on nonmembers. The threat of being dropped from membership has also not been a sufficient deterrent to prevent the involvement of members of professional groups in unprofessional, unethical, or incompetent practice.

Many psychologists have shifted the area of their specialization postdoctorally (see Dörken and Webb, 1979). Some of these psychologists have followed the APA guidelines for reeducating themselves in the area of the new specialty; other psychologists have simply relabeled themselves and started practice in an area other than the area of their graduate education. The courts in Ohio recently addressed this specialty dilemma by finding that if one practiced as a "clinical psychologist," one should be held to the standards of expertise expected of that specialty (*Midwestern Psychological Services, Inc.* v. *Potts and Potts,* No. 79, AP-338 and 339, Dec. 13, 1979). The implications of this court decision include the following: professional associations' code of ethics do not adequately control professional practice; society is concerned about the competence of psychologist practitioners; and the courts and other legal bodies will define our practice standards if we fail to define them proactively.

Wellner and Abidin (1981) make the point that as society's demands for services grow and as professional services and practices become more directly involved in governmental regulatory systems, it is evident that there are substantial burdens on the professions to clearly establish their regulatory or enforcement procedures for the maintenance of quality control and for demonstrating the effectiveness of these procedures for the public good. Wellner and Abidin discuss the need to establish an effective communication and jurisdictional system or network within the profession to facilitate the responsiveness of all the available enforcement resources regardless of the consumer's initial contact point. Contact points might the APA Committee on Scientific and Professional Ethics and Conduct, the state psychological associations' committees on ethics, the state boards of examiners in psychology, the Council for the National Register of Health Service Providers in Psychology, or other committees or organizations. Identifying areas of responsibility and linking the various enforcement components could provide a needed mechanism to ensure public accountability. Wellner and Abidin conclude that if psychology as a profession does not accept responsibility for self-regulation of practice, we can only accept the inevitable outside regulatory system that will be imposed on us.

False Advertising and Misrepresentation. From time to time articles appear in the professional literature reporting on reviews of "yellow pages" phone directories that find that as many as a quarter of the persons listed under "Psychologists" simply are not licensed as such (Goebel and Beach, 1981). Some hold lesser licenses, but the majority are unlicensed. All, of course, have misrepresented themselves to the public. Some state boards take systematic "cease and desist" action, but a number seem to take the view that the nonpsychologist is not a priority jurisdiction.

Assorted counselors, self-styled psychotherapists, even mediums, more regularly than we like to admit, hold themselves forward as psychologists, even as clinical psychologists. There are also persons who claim to be psychologists and who have actually had some graduate training in psychology but have not completed the level of preparation held necessary for professional practice. Finally, there are some psychologists who, even though they do private work that requires a license, hold themselves above the law.

All these parties undermine licensure standards *and* public confidence. In California, for example, about half the complaints to the Psychology Examining Committee are about persons not licensed as psychologists; yet, the committee claims it does not have the resources or time to prosecute. Amending the licensing law to enable the state or local psychological association to proceed might be one solution. In any event, it is far from sufficient to establish minimum standards for licensed psychologists and then hold them to those standards. Those who falsely advertise and misrepresent themselves as psychologists should be enjoined and prosecuted. The more active and prompt the prosecution, the fewer offenders there will be. In the process of enforcement, those practicing without a license but presumably licensable should be obliged to become licensed or cease their practice.

Peer and Utilization Review. In the course of practice a series of standards is coming to the fore. It is no longer sufficient that the practitioner alone be satisfied. Increasingly, third parties and others are demanding that the services rendered have a specified purpose and that they be acceptable to the consumer. The era of the treatment plan based on informed consent by the patient has arrived. This fits well with the philosophy that people, including patients, must be responsible for their behavior. Such a self-determination role is an essential first step away from the dependency of the sick role and toward a coping model. This necessary dialogue with the patient will oblige the practitioner to consider alternatives and to be more explicit and detailed in treatment planning. If this regular coming to terms with a number of patients does not prompt a practitioner to consider different treatments for different conditions, peer review will. The same treatment for everybody, as has been the penchant of therapy schools, is a mockery of individual differences. In requiring that treatment plans, typically after some level of service has been rendered, be subject to external/peer review, there is an implicit consultation on a best approach. This process of oversight and at times justification facilitates identification of the incompetent or marginal, in the public interest, and also serves as a time when alternatives may be considered and treatment plan objectives revised.

Given that resources are finite—those of most patients and the limits of most third parties—utilization review is increasingly being turned to. There is no doubt that cost as well as quality is a consideration here. What exactly can be done predictably within the available limits? Health insurance was never intended as an annuity policy for the therapist; it was intended to assist insured in resolving their health problems and in maintaining their employability and productivity. Group health insurance, though seen simply as a fringe benefit by many beneficiaries, was, after all, originally provided by employers with that motive. In this multistage process, practitioners increasingly, then, must face and answer the questions of who will benefit from what treatment, for what presenting problem, in what time, under what circumstances. These specific questions must always be addressed, and practitioners must develop the flexibility and capability for using them (see Chapter Eleven). The increasing pressure for such specificity and predictability will bring order out of laissez faire. To the extent that psychological intervention does not make a difference, then to that extent it is neither beneficial nor necessary.

Practice Standards of Law. It may come as a surprise, perhaps even a shock, to many psychologists to learn of the various ways in which their professional practice is being legally recognized yet circumscribed. As a first step in this self-informing we will present details of practice standards derived from four sources in California law: the California licensing law, California law that applies to psychologists among other practitioners, adaptations possible from the Medical Practice Act of California, and enforcement specifics that might be drawn from other laws. No attempt is made to rank these specifics for importance or severity, and the list is surely not exhaustive, though quite extensive. It should be noted, though, that many of the behavioral specifics of unacceptable practice to follow apply not only during practice hours but continuously during one's professional life.

I. Enforcement Specifics of the California Psychology Licensing Law
    1. Conviction of a crime substantially related to the qualifications, functions, or duties of a psychologist.
    2. Use of any narcotic or any alcoholic beverage to an extent or in a manner dangerous to oneself, any other person, or the public or to an extent that such use impairs one's ability to perform the work of a psychologist with safety to the public.
    3. Fraudulently or neglectfully misrepresenting the type or status of license actually held.
    4. Impersonating another person holding a psychology license or allowing another person to use one's license.
    5. Using fraud or deception in applying for a license or in passing the examination provided for in the licensing law.
    6. Accepting commissions or rebates or other forms of remuneration for referring persons to other professionals.
    7. Willful, unauthorized communication of information received in professional confidence.

8. Violating any rule of professional conduct promulgated by the committee and set forth in regulations duly adopted under the licensing law.

9. Being grossly negligent in the practice of one's profession.

10. Violating any of the provisions of the licensing law or regulations duly adopted thereunder.

11. Aiding or abetting any person to engage in the unlawful practice of psychology.

12. The suspension, revocation, or imposition of probationary conditions by another state of a license or certificate to practice psychology issued by the state to a person also holding a license issued under the California law if the act for which the disciplinary action was taken constitutes a violation of the California law.

13. The commission of any dishonest, corrupt, or fraudulent act or any act of sexual abuse, or sexual relations with a patient, or sexual misconduct that is substantially related to the qualifications, functions, or duties of a psychologist or psychological assistant.

14. Functioning outside one's particular field or fields of competence as established by one's education, training, or experience.

15. Failure to post in a conspicuous location a notice that reads as follows:

   Notice: The Department of Consumer Affairs receives questions and complaints regarding the practice of psychology. If you have any questions or complaints, you may contact this department by calling (insert appropriate regional number) or (insert appropriate telephone number) or by writing to the following address: Board of Medical Quality Assurance, Allied Health Complaints, 1430 Howe Avenue, Sacramento, California 95825.

II. Other California Law that Includes Licensed Psychologists

1. A psychologist may not be employed by a proprietary or nonprofit hospital (except a philanthropic corporation

serving its members) on a salaried basis to render psychological services if the hospital bills and collects a fee for these services.

2. No professional corporation may be formed so as to cause any violation of law or any applicable rules and regulations relating to fee splitting, kickbacks, or similar practices.

3. No psychologist may employ persons known as cappers or steerers to obtain business.

4. Any price advertised shall be exact and shall not be fraudulent, deceitful, or misleading and shall contain no statements of bait or discount.

5. Repeated acts of clearly excessive treatment, or clearly excessive use of diagnostic procedures, or clearly excessive use of diagnostic or treatment facilities as determined by the standard of the local community of licensees are unprofessional conduct.

6. Whenever psychologists in the course of practice acquire evidence of child abuse or have reason to believe a client has suffered from child abuse, they shall report the same to a child protective agency within thirty-six hours. Failure to do so is a misdemeanor.

7. Similar law requires the reporting of elder abuse.

8. Prior to appointment of any physician, clinical psychologist, or the like to the medical staff of a health facility or the granting of clinical privileges, the facility will ascertain from the licensing board that the applicant possesses an unrestricted license. When any facility revokes, suspends privilege, or places the practitioner on probation, it must notify the licensing board.

9. The Psychology Examining Committee may require any licensee who is placed on probation or whose license is suspended at committee discretion to obtain additional training and to pay the necessary examination fee. The examination may be written or oral or both and may include a practical or clinical examination by peers at the option of the committee.

III. Specifics Adaptable from the Medical Practice Act
1. Knowingly making or signing any certificate or other document directly or indirectly related to the practice of psychology that falsely represents the existence or nonexistence of a state of facts constitutes unprofessional conduct.
2. Altering or modifying the clinical record of any person, with fraudulent intent, constitutes unprofessional conduct.
3. Any false or misleading advertising constitutes unprofessional conduct.

IV. Some Provisions Found in Other Psychology Licensing Laws
1. Persons, including psychologists, who report possible violations of law or malpractice by a psychologist, in good faith, shall be immune from damages.
2. A psychologist shall not abandon a patient or client in need of immediate professional care without making arrangements for the continuation of that care.
3. A psychologist shall not abandon professional employment without reasonable notice or under circumstances that seriously impair the delivery of professional care to patients.
4. Failing to exercise appropriate supervision over persons who are authorized to practice only under the supervision of the licensee is grounds for suspension of the license.
5. Failing to make available to a patient or, on a patient's request, to another licensed practitioner, consistent with that practitioner's scope of practice, copies of summary reports regarding the patient constitutes a misdemeanor.
6. Failing to complete forms or reports required for the reimbursement of a patient by a third party (reasonable fees may be charged for such forms) is unprofessional conduct.
7. Submissions of fraudulent claims for services to Medicaid or to a health insurance or health care service plan is actionable fraud.
8. Failure to establish and to keep systematic and dated

records for each client that accurately reflect the services provided is professional negligence.

9. Failure to promptly submit an itemized account statement or receipt on the request of the patient or a third party is unprofessional conduct.

10. Exercising undue influence in such a manner as to exploit the client for the financial gain of the practitioner or a third party is grounds for revoking the license.

11. Willfully harassing, abusing, or intimidating a patient physically or verbally is grounds for revoking the license.

12. A psychologist changing his or her service specialty or entering an additional area of specialization must undertake such study, training, or supervision as to yield competence comparable to those held by graduates at the doctoral level from university programs, including this specialty area.

13. A psychologist shall not give anything of value to or compensate the media in expectation of or in return for news publicity.

14. A psychologist shall not provide or offer to provide services to a client who is known or should be known to be receiving services of a related nature from another professional without notifying the latter.

15. A psychologist shall assume responsibility for the preservation and security of clients' records for a period of at least six years after the date of the last entry.

16. A psychologist shall not charge a fee to a client who is entitled to his or her services free of charge unless the client has been made aware by the psychologist of such services and nonetheless has elected in writing to be seen by the psychologist for a fee.

This iteration of forty-three expressions of the behavioral specifics of what can be regarded as acceptable and as unacceptable practice warrants serious consideration among the states and throughout the profession. Since the model psychology licensing law of the American Psychological Association dates back to 1976 and is in serious need of modernization, it may be more productive to focus on specific aspects of licensure for which consensus can more readily be obtained, such as enforcement. However, the methods for establishing practice standards and regulations and effectively enjoining unacceptable professional practice will, of course, vary according to state law.

In some states it may be necessary to establish more severe penalties for infraction of practice standards. Both to toughen the misdemeanor infraction in the California law and to establish a basis for enjoining the unlicensed practice of psychology, new powers were adopted in legislation in 1982, as follows:

1. "Any person who violates any of the provisions of this chapter shall be guilty of a misdemeanor punishable by imprisonment in the county jail not exceeding six months, or by a fine not exceeding two thousand dollars ($2,000), or by both."

2. "Whenever any person other than a licensed psychologist has engaged in any act or practice which constitutes an offense against this chapter, the superior court of any county, on application of the committee, may issue an injunction or other appropriate order restraining such conduct. Proceedings under this section shall be governed by the Code of Civil Procedure except that it shall be presumed that there is no adequate remedy at law, and that irreparable damage will occur if the continued violation is not restrained or enjoined. On the written request of the committee, or on its own motion, the Division of Allied Health Professions may commence action in the superior court under the provisions of this section."

Another complex issue is the identification of individual psychologists whose practice may be unprofessional, unethical, or negligent. Even though such a practitioner may be known to other psychologists, they may be reluctant to act on that knowledge because of the privileged communication concept embodied in most, if not all, state psychology statutes. That privilege, with few exceptions, belongs to the patient. Without the patient's consent, the psychologist's records are inviolate. Thus, there would have to be a patient complainant who would have to carry the burden of a specific practice complaint against a given practitioner. But the numbers of such complainants, though few, are increasing.

From another perspective it may be the unethical practitioner who is the "patient" invoking privileged communication. Some states, such as California, have laws that prevent the proceedings of hospital staff review committees, medical care foundations, and professional standards review organizations from being subject to discovery, even in a malpractice action brought by a patient of that practitioner. Interestingly, as an aside, this immunity does not hold in suits by physicians claiming wrongful or arbitrary exclusion from hospital staff privileges (Evidence Code, sec. 1157). But what about state association or APA ethics committees that claim to treat all matters brought before them in absolute confidence? Would we want to enable such groups to assist each other in the suspension of incompetent practice through the exchange of confidential information? Again, psychologists in each state will need to examine their own statutes. It might well be that ethics committee records would be readily subject to subpoena in a malpractice action, particularly if there were criminal implications.

At any rate, along with the recommendations of Wellner and Abidin (1981), we support the need for a communication network in enforcement. A professional association should be able to forward selected records of its ethics and professional standards review committees to the state licensing agency when it has probable cause to believe that a member or other licensed psychologist has engaged in unprofessional conduct or in incompetent practice. Indeed, the "Ethical Principles of Psychologists" of the American Psychological Association (1981) places a responsibility on members of the APA to attempt to resolve ethical violations of another psychologist, including, when such violations are serious, bringing them to the attention of appropriate committees on professional ethics and conduct (Principle 7, g).

Psychologists, it seems, are often timid about questioning the ethics or practices of a colleague. At least in some areas, the legal profession does not have such reluctance. Lawyers are automatically disbarred for failure to file their income tax return or for comingling of funds. We believe that greater attention must be given to the behavioral specifics of unacceptable practice and to their roles both in setting standards and in serving as bases for enforcement. Or, to quote W. B. Webb, "We have a faulty sensing system, an inadequate evaluating system, and a pitifully weak sanction system" (personal communication, Mar. 3, 1981). We do not have the means to reliably sense unacceptable practice behavior at present, that is, be made aware of it, and even then, we are without mechanisms to determine disputed facts, and, of course, without such determination we cannot require actions by other authorities. The behavioral specifics above, as adopted in California and several other states, should be helpful in this regard.

A Final Word

There is no more exact science than psychology in the area of understanding and modifying human behavior. As experts in behavior, then, we should be well equipped to delineate what constitutes unprofessional conduct and unacceptable practice. We, as psychologists, above all ought to have such restraints, prohibitions, and public protection made explicit in our own licensure laws and in behaviorally specific and enforceable practice regulations.

We have delineated many aspects of unacceptable practice above. The public expectancy should be that they apply not only during hours of practice and with clients but throughout one's professional lifetime and in all human relationships. We believe also that both the philosophy and the specifics described here are, in the main, equally applicable to other human service and health professions and that we professionals, as well as the consumers of our services, will ultimately be best served by more systematic, careful attention to both the definition and enforcement of ethical practice.

References

American Psychological Association. "Ethical Principles of Psychologists." *American Psychologist,* 1981, *36,* 633–638.

Bergin, A. E., and Lambert, M. J. "The Evaluation of Therapeutic Outcome." In S. L. Garfield and A. E. Bergin (eds.), *Handbook of Psychotherapy and Behavior Change.* (2nd ed.) New York: Wiley, 1978.

Cummings, N. A. "Prolonged (Ideal) Versus Short-Term (Realistic) Psychotherapy." In C. Kiesler, N. A. Cummings, and G. R. VandenBos (eds.), *Psychology and National Health Insurance: A Sourcebook*. Washington, D.C.: American Psychological Association, 1979.

Daggett, B. "How to Complain About a Lawyer." *Solo News*, 1979, *6*, pp. 1-2.

Dörken, H. "Laws, Regulations, and Psychological Practice." In H. Dörken and Associates, *The Professional Psychologist Today: New Developments in Law, Health Insurance, and Health Practice*. San Francisco: Jossey-Bass, 1976.

Dörken, H., and Webb, J. T. "Licensed Psychologists in Health Care: A Survey of Their Practices." In C. Kiesler, N. A. Cummings, and G. R. VandenBos (eds.), *Psychology and National Health Insurance: A Sourcebook*. Washington, D.C.: American Psychological Association, 1979.

Dörken, H., and Webb, J. T. "Licensed Psychologists on the Increase: 1974-1979." *American Psychologist*, 1981, *36*, 1419-1426.

Goebel, J., and Beach, D. "Telephone Directory Advertising: Who Is a Psychologist?" *Professional Psychology*, 1981, *12*, 535-536.

Havighurst, L. "Reforming Malpractice Law Through Consumer Choice." *Health Affairs*, 1984, *3* (4), 63-70.

Hogan, D. *The Regulation of Psychotherapists*. Cambridge, Mass.: Ballinger, 1979.

Karson, M. J. "Regulating Medical Psychotherapists in Illinois: A Question of Balance." *John Marshall Journal of Practice and Procedure*, 1978, *2*, 601-633.

Rosenberg, C. L. "Tougher Doctor-Policing Laws." *Medical Economics*, Apr. 2, 1979, pp. 108-142.

Schofield, W. *Psychotherapy: The Purchase of Friendship*. Englewood Cliffs, N.J.: Prentice-Hall, 1964.

Wellner, A. M., and Abidin, R. R. "Regulation/Enforcement/Discipline of Professional Practice in Psychology: Issues and Strategies." *Professional Practice of Psychology*, 1981, *2*, 1-14.

Wiens, A. N. "Toward a Conceptualization of Competency Assurance." *Professional Practice of Psychology*, 1983, *4*, 1-15.

Zemlick, M. J. "Ethical Standards: Cosmetics for the Face of the Profession of Psychology." *Psychotherapy: Theory, Research and Practice,* 1980, *17,* 448–453.

9

George C. Stone

❦❦❦❦❦❦❦❦❦❦❦❦❦❦❦❦❦❦❦❦❦❦❦❦❦❦❦❦

Contributions by
Psychologists to
Improving Health Care

Psychologists have much to offer within the health system, a system that includes such diverse components as waste disposal, cultural patterns of nutrition, and regulation of environmental pollutants. Within this total system, the health *care* system constitutes only a part but certainly a very important part. For purposes of this discussion, the health care system can be defined as the total complex of institutions, organizations, and persons engaged in providing "expert" health services germane to maintaining and restoring the health of individuals who directly or indirectly contract for the delivery of such service. The primary purpose of the health care system is the providing of such health care, but many of the activities that go on within it are only indirectly concerned with health care: the training of health service providers, the conduct of research to discover new approaches to treatment, and all the activities that support the actual health care transactions between experts and clients.

Health psychologists can contribute to the more effective functioning of the health system and the health care system in many ways and at many levels (Stone, 1979b, 1982). In this chapter I will consider only those aspects of their work that bear directly on the processes of health care themselves—the specific communicative and interventive acts that experts perform in their professional roles and the behavior of clients or patients in relation to those acts.

200

Psychologists contribute to health care through two broad categories of action: they are often direct providers of health services to clients, and they often act to facilitate the provision of services by other groups of professionals through research, teaching, and consultation regarding the processes of health care. Most of the other chapters of this book address the issues of psychologists as health service providers. This chapter will focus on their indirect contributions through their expertise as analysts, designers, and appraisers of health care processes. In their indirect roles, psychologists use their knowledge of the methods, facts, and principles of psychology to observe systematically the processes of health care. They identify situations where psychological factors appear to be impairing goal attainment. They develop psychological models of these situations and design modified procedures and system-level interventions to alter the situation in ways that will enable the expert to improve the quality of health care. Throughout these activities they draw on their knowledge of methods for the appraisal of individuals' characteristics and behavior to guide their analysis and design, to match individuals to alternative modes of treatment in the health care system, and to evaluate the effectiveness of the health care services. Finally, they make use of their knowledge of communication and group dynamics to increase the likelihood that knowledge can be effectively applied to the resolution of health problems. These are the kinds of contributions that psychologists are making in the health care system. A major portion of this chapter will be devoted to presenting examples of the kinds of contributions being reported in current literature.

Psychological Models of the Health Care Process

To facilitate our examination of the ways psychologists have contributed and can contribute to improving health care, it is essential that we have a framework to organize the diverse activities that occur in health care transactions. We encounter frequent references to the several variants of the "medical model" (Szasz and Hollender, 1956; Veatch, 1972) and to the problem-solving model (D'Zurilla and Goldfried, 1971) as alternative ways of construing the transaction between a health care provider and the client. These and other models can all be incorporated within a more comprehensive model of the health transaction (Stone, 1979a) and seem to be based on assumptions or prescriptions about the ways certain issues in the transaction are to be resolved. The "health transactions model" is an expanded version of a problem-solving model that makes explicit provision for the participation of two or more parties in the transaction. In fact, there are always at least three interests represented in the health transaction: (1) Those of the health care *practitioner.* (2) Those of the person to whose health the expert services are addressed. This person is often designated as the *patient* and will be referred to by that term here, even though it is not a precise fit in some transactions (preventive health education, for example). (3) The interests of the party that pays for the services, or *payer.* In some cases the patient and payer are one and the same. In other cases a parent or other personal agent for the patient contracts for the services, and in others a "third party" payer in the form of an insurance company or government agency does so. Analysis of the psychological aspects of these different interests and their interactions is important for health psychology.

The boundaries of complex social interactions, such as health transactions, are not clearly marked. Health care begins with the decision by the patient or agent to secure expert assistance, and this decision, made in a rich sociocultural matrix, is an important subject for study by health psychologists and other social and behavioral scientists. To keep this chapter within manageable proportions, however, I will limit discussion of the health care transaction to that which involves actual contact and communication between health care practitioners and patients, patients' families, and agents.

Within these bounds, the health care transaction proceeds, often episodically, through the classical stages of problem solving: (1) appraisal and formulation of the problem, (2) generation of alternative methods of treatment, (3) selection of one or more alternatives for implementation, (4) planning for and implementing the selected treatment by practitioner, patient, collateral, or some combination of these agents, (5) evaluation of the effectiveness of the treatment, and (6) return to any of the first five stages for further work if necessary or termination of the transaction. At any stage, it is possible to return to earlier stages, and more or less extensive and more or less relevant collateral activities may be undertaken from any stage. However, it is not possible to skip a stage. When the performance of a stage is not observable, I presume it to have occurred too rapidly to have been detected (as, for example, in highly routinized procedures where the elements of choice are predesignated).

The various models of health transactions that have been proposed vary in several ways: in the way the several stages are performed, in the kinds of information that are incorporated into the appraisal and subsequent stages, and in the range of alternative interventions that is considered. Let us take a closer look at the mapping of three familiar models onto the health transactions model: the medical (or biomedical) model, the biopsychosocial model, and the holistic model.

The "medical model" has been described with some variation by many writers. More often than not, of late, it is presented as a whipping boy against which the superiority of some alternative model can be demonstrated. The most essential feature of this model is that it is scientific and rational (Engel, 1977). It purports to use the scientific method of hypothesis generation followed by testing hypotheses against observations to establish the cause(s) of the patient's distress. Achievement of this diagnosis leads, through the mediation of medical expertise, to generation of a set of treatment alternatives. The means of choosing among the alternatives and presenting them to the patient give rise to most of the variability in the process aspects of the model. Evaluation of treatment effectiveness is a normal part of the process. The resemblance of this scientific/rational model to the problem-solving aspects of the health transactions model outlined earlier is obvious and is not surprising, since the problem-solving model is essentially a generalization to wider spheres of the canons of "scientific method."

The biopsychosocial model, most eloquently supported by Engel (1960, 1977, 1980), is, from a process point of view, a variant of the medical model that is quite strongly committed to the active doctor, passive patient of Szasz and Hollender (1956) (see Engel, 1977, pp. 132–133, and Engel, 1980, p. 536). What distinguishes it from the "biomedical model," which Engel uses consistently as the contrasting, dominant model of recent times, is its recognition that patients are whole, living persons. The aim of the model is not to abandon a scientific, rational approach to medicine but to expand the medical model to incorporate psychological and sociological information about the patient and to recognize that humans are embedded as components in hierarchical systems that are dynamically interactive. According to Engel (1980, p. 536), "The doctors' tasks are, first, to find out *how* and *what* the patient is or has been feeling and experiencing; then to formulate explanations (hypotheses) for the patient's feelings and experiences . . . ; to engage the patient's participation in further clinical and laboratory studies to test such hypotheses; and, finally, to elicit the patient's cooperation in activities aimed to alleviate distress. . . . The patient's tasks and responsibilities complement those of the physician."

The "holistic model" of health care is not so sharply formulated or so strongly identified with a single, influential description as the two models previously discussed. A recent, thoughtful description by a psychiatrist (Gordon, 1981) attributes the term *holistic* to Jan Smuts's philosophical concept of holism as an alternative to the analytic reductionism of the sciences of the late nineteenth and twentieth centuries. In this view, holism aspires to "comprehend whole organisms and systems as entities greater than the sum of their parts" (Gordon, 1981, p. 114) and is little different from the systems approach that characterizes the biopsychosocial model. But Gordon goes on to propose and document seventeen characteristics of holistic medicine, many of which do distinguish it. These include the incorporation of not only the psychological and social but also the spiritual. In thus going beyond the bounds of most contemporary science, the door is opened for the inclusion of many procedures whose validity is not considered to be scientifically proved, such as acupuncture, massage, and the like. Definitions of health go far beyond the absence of disease to include terms like *joy, vigor,* and *sensual pleasure.* Stress is placed on the possibility and, hence, the responsibility for self-healing by right thinking as well as right living. The practice of holistic medicine is seen as transforming its practitioners as well as its patients.

Does the holistic model go beyond the bounds that can be encompassed within the framework I have called the health transactions model? I think not, although many proponents of holistic health might disagree with that judgment. The holistic model proposes to expand significantly the range of alternative actions that will be considered as potentially useful. There is more emphasis on the activity of the client during the selection and, especially, the implementation phases of care, and the processes of evaluation may be less confined to objectively measurable effects. None of these differences appears to make the problem-solving paradigm inapplicable, however. It is simply applied with different content and different rules for reaching decisions.

The health transactions model thus appears capable of providing a conceptual place for all the issues that are stressed by those who make use of the other models. In discussing psychological aspects of health care we can therefore use this model to organize our review of the work that could be and is being done by psychologists.

The focus in this chapter is on the *process* of health care as patterned human behavior. I have identified five major subdivisions of that process in the stages of problem solving: (1) goal setting, (2) generating alternatives, (3) selecting alternatives to be implemented, (4) implementing them, and (5) evaluating their effectiveness in attaining the established goals. The psychologist who addresses these processes professionally can engage in any of five levels of activity: (1) basic research, (2) design of new interventions, (3) selection of interventions, (4) performance of the interventions, and (5) evaluation of the effectiveness of the interventions. The correspondence of these levels to the stages of problem solving is obvious. The remainder of the chapter is organized, first, according to the level of activity by psychologists, from basic research to evaluation. Within each of these categories I will seek wherever possible to give examples of work that addresses each aspect or stage of the health care process. To perform this review exhaustively is beyond the scope of this presentation. I have limited myself to examples from the recent literature, specifically articles listed in *Psychological Abstracts* for four years (1979–1981 and 1984) in the section "Health Care Services" and under the index headings

"Health Care" and "Health Care Services." Altogether, I found 201 publications reporting or discussing specific kinds of contributions, not including direct care, that can be or are being made by psychologists in health care settings. In carrying out this review, no special effort was made to verify that the work reported was actually performed by a psychologist as long as the activities were such that they might customarily be a part of a psychologist's repertoire. Table 9-1 shows the distribution of topics discussed. The total of 229 entries in the table reflects the fact that some of the papers dealt with more than one topic. From this total set, I have selected a smaller number that are most relevant to practicing psychologists. These are described briefly and cited so that they can be examined by the reader who wants more detail.

The literature from 1982 through 1984 was scanned at a later date to determine whether the trends observed in the initial survey had continued. The number of articles listed in the section "Health Care Services" declined sharply between the middle of 1980 and the middle of 1982 and then rose sharply again to equal or surpass the rate observed in 1979 and the first part of 1980. No obvious changes in *Psychological Abstracts,* such as change in editorship or in the categories used, occurred during that time. In 1984 there were 380 entries in this section, of which 264 were judged to fit the criteria for selection that were used in the earlier review. These studies were also classified in Table 9-1. The results were very similar; differences could be due to shifts in subjective boundaries between the two occasions of classification or to a genuine shift in the focus of work. The greatest change was the nearly threefold increase in the number of studies concerned with research on outcomes. Comment is made in the appropriate section on this increase. Also noteworthy was a substantial increase in the amount of work addressed to the total process of a health care situation, commonly research proposals or critiques concerning communications, interactions, organizational structure, or philosophy of the service providers and their programs. Interestingly, no cell that was empty in the first survey had an entry in 1984.

The succeeding sections describe a few of the unusually significant articles from 1984 as well.

Table 9-1. Publications on Psychological Interventions by Phase of the Health Care Process.

Level of Psychological Intervention	Total Process (a)	Goal Definition (b)	Generating Alternatives (c)	Selecting Alternatives (d)	Implementation (e)	Evaluation (f)	Sums
1. Conduct basic research	7	23	25	15	19	19	108
	15	24	26	27	14	55	161
2. Design intervention	3	11	15	11	16	5	61
	17	11	5	3	7	8	51
3. Select intervention	0	0	0	0	0	0	0
	0	0	0	0	0	0	0
4. Implement intervention	X	X	X	X	X	12	12
						20	20
5. Evaluate process	7	10	8	12	7	4	48
	13	6	1	3	2	6	31
Sums	17	44	48	38	42	40	229
	45	41	32	33	23	89	263

Note: Data are numbers of articles listed in *Psychological Abstracts* for the years 1979–1981 and 1984 in the section "Health Care Services" that describe work in selected categories. Upper figure in each cell is for 1979–1981, lower figure for 1984. Cells marked "X" were not included in the survey.

Basic Research on Health Care Processes

The difficulty of distinguishing basic from applied research and the questionable value of doing so have been discussed in many places. Those arguments have special cogency in the field of health psychology, which, as a whole, is concerned with the application of psychological knowledge and principles to psychological problems of the health system. I have elsewhere discussed the possibility not only of validating our basic knowledge in the setting of the health system but of augmenting it there (Stone, 1981). Such augmentation is one component of what is here included in the category of basic research. Also included is work that is purely descriptive of psychological phenomena as they can be observed in health care settings even though such descriptions are often intended to be ancillary to the development of particular applications. Whenever a publication stopped short of explicit proposals concerning how the descriptions could be put to work in health care, although the authors might speculate on applications in their final discussion, it was classified here. A great deal of research on the psychophysiology of falling sick and on biobehavioral treatments of illness has not been considered in this review. Examples are studies on the Type A personality pattern and heart disease and on stress and susceptibility to cancer. These topics represent psychological *components* of health care rather than psychological *aspects* of the health care process.

Basic Studies of the Provider/Patient Interaction as a Whole (1a). Seven papers addressed the overall process of the provider/patient interaction. Detailed observational study of such interactions revealed patterns associated with some aspect of the success of the interaction. Wurster, Weinstein, and Cohen (1979), for example, observed interactions between senior medical students and child patients and were able to identify strong transitional probabilities, such as a probability of .85 that Directive Guidance would be followed by Cooperation and a probability of .67 that Permissiveness would be followed by NonCooperation.

Basic Studies of Goal Setting in Health Care (1b). Psychologists can contribute to health care by helping providers and patients discover what patients need and by examining the processes whereby goals are made more or less explicit and contracts negotiated. In identifying studies directed to this aspect of health care, I found ten that focused specifically on "needs" without implications for the specification of treatment. Some used psychological methods to identify undetected needs of special groups of clients. Others were concerned with the evaluation of patients' reports of their symptoms in relation to a number of other variables. Wood (1980) used psychophysical methods with patients suffering from obstructive lung disease to appraise the relation between their thresholds for detecting a resistive load to breathing and their self-reported severity of symptoms. In terms of signal detection theory, patients with a greater *response bias* toward reporting resistance were likely to report their symptoms as more severe, although these patients showed no greater *sensitivity* to resistance. In a similar study, Nailboff, Cohen, Schandler, and Heinrich (1981) found that chronic respiratory patients and patients with chronic back pain actually had higher pain thresholds to radiant heat than control subjects, and these authors argued for an adaptation model rather than a hypochondriasis model for chronic-pain patients. Lunghi, Miller, and McQuillan (1978) reported that patients suffering from osteoarthritis of the hip were more likely to report high symptom scores if their lives were relatively impoverished in either pleasant or unpleasant life events (Hoeper and others, 1980). These studies of patients' reports of symptoms can provide a refined basis for working with them to establish realistic and attainable goals.

Studies in the later sample were mostly quite direct in their approach to discovering needs. Coffman (1983) obtained responses from 203 parents of children in a cerebral palsy clinic to the statement "It would help me and my children to talk to a nurse about this." A large majority of parents identified one or more topics of concern, but only a third of them identified topics for their children to discuss. Topics concerned the disease and its implications for the children's social and physical development. Other studies investigated the degree to which health care providers perceived needs in the same way as their patients did. Phillips, Seidenberg, Heald, and Friedman (1983) compared predictions made by seventy members of the Society for Adolescent Medicine of teenager's preferences regarding having a chaperone present during genital examination with teenagers' self-reported preferences. Providers were generally accurate, although they somewhat underestimated the adolescents' reticence to have health providers of the opposite sex present or performing such examinations and the desire of some age and gender groups to have a parent present. Roth, Heffron, and Skipper (1983) compared lists of medical and psychosocial problems submitted by 100 patients against material entered in their charts by family practice residents. The two problem lists agreed completely 65 percent of the time.

Some studies span the processes of goal formation and the generation of alternatives and sometimes extend to include the consideration of choice among alternatives. Altogether, such topics correspond approximately to what is commonly called "diagnosis." Psychologists' basic contributions here most often took the form of detailing or expanding the statement of the problem to include some consideration of what might be at the base of it and thus, implicitly at least, what might be done about it. Typical of such studies was a report by Wender, Palmer, Herbst, and Wender (1977) that young children with chronic, nonspecific diarrhea had significantly more problems in a number of areas than age- and sex-matched controls. These findings led the authors to propose that this group of children was manifesting temperamental traits based on physiological factors reflecting, perhaps, an imbalance of the autonomic nervous system. More research to establish more clearly the contributions of innate psychological factors and secondary patterns of reaction to the psychosocial environment would provide a basis for determining when to work on the development of special coping skills for children of various autonomic balance types and when to look toward environmental changes to help resolve medical problems.

Another kind of contribution from basic studies of diagnosis is some prognosis of the degree of rehabilitation possible for patients with a particular problem. Such work differs from the attempt to predict response to a particular treatment, which I have classified as research on the selection process (1d). Several studies drew rather explicit implications from their findings. Byrne (1979) suggested that liaison psychological services to coronary care units might sensitize the staff to identifying patients at greatest risk for adverse emotional problems following myocardial infarctions. Lown and colleagues (1980) discussed the evidence for involvement of psychophysiological factors in the development of ventricular fibrillation (the cause of sudden cardiac death) and suggested the possibility of incorporating such information in the design of patient management procedures for patients subject to this form of risk. Philip, Cay, Vetter, and Stuckey (1979) traced the course of anxiety during the period following myocardial infarction and showed how this information could be used to assist in rehabilitation of persistently anxious patients. Hall and Havassy (1981) reviewed factors contributing to the greater incidence of obesity in women than in men and recommended treatment strategies that reach beyond traditional sex roles.

Although the number of these studies of patients' needs and goals is relatively large in proportion to the number of studies found, it is surely very small against the potential that exists for psychologists to use their expert knowledge of appraisal in all the myriad diseases and patient populations to assist patients and providers alike in identifying attainable objectives of care that will bring maximum satisfaction to participants.

Generation of Alternatives (1c). Within the ideal plan of classification that underlies this chapter, the present section would include both basic studies of the psychological *processes* involved in the discovery of alternative methods of approaching health care for particular situations and the development and mobilization of psychological *knowledge* as a stimulus and support for the generation of new alternatives. Among the publications identified in this review, however, no studies of the process appeared. One group (Horowitz and others, 1980) investigated the impact of alternative ways of informing patients about their risks of manifesting coronary heart disease, thus, presumably, inducing patients to generate different alternatives in their personal confrontation of these risks. These authors did, in fact, demonstrate that the group receiving more frequent reminders of risk reported much higher levels of "coping experiences" than a group with less frequent reminders.

Providing the basis for generation of new alternatives by elucidating psychological aspects of etiology was the most common focus of the papers classified here. Articles that are specific proposals for new forms of treatment or case management are classified at the level of design; those grouped here did not take the step of drawing implications for treatment but, rather, sought to identify causal factors that could lead to the development of new treatments. Two kinds of reports in this category are so numerous and so familiar that I have chosen not to include examples of them in this review. These are the studies attempting to demonstrate the presence and nature of a relation between stressful life events and illness and those of coronary-prone (Type A) behavior. Each of these areas has itself been the subject of extensive recent reviews.

A variant on the topic of Type A behavior was offered by Kahn and associates (1980), who compared blood pressure elevations during coronary bypass surgery of persons classified as Type A and others not so classified. These authors found evidence of autonomic hyperactivity in the Type As, which they suggested might contribute to the association between Type A behavior and coronary heart disease. Another relationship between cardiovascular disease and the function of the nervous system is found in the report by Zamir and Shuber (1980) that hypertensives have higher thresholds for pain (produced by stimulation of tooth pulp) than normotensives. The authors suggested an interrelation between blood pressure and pain regulation that could ultimately provide a basis for new treatment approaches.

Several studies of behavioral correlates of particular diseases offer some preliminary leads to understanding those conditions in new ways and thus to finding new modes of treatment. Adatto, Doebele, Galland, and Granowetter (1979) studied voiding and sexual habits of female university students subject to recurrent urinary tract infections. Voluntary urine retention was implicated as a likely factor in these patients. The authors suggested that a behavioral approach might be effective. Wolkind and Zajicek (1978) interviewed seven women who had recently given birth to first children about their experiences during pregnancy, seeking correlates of severe nausea and vomiting. Social difficulties and particular views of the woman's role were found to be associated with these symptoms. In a well-controlled study of postoperative pain control, Lim and colleagues (1983) found that subjects given transcutaneous electrodermal stimulation (TES) required 25 percent less morphine than placebo subjects but that in a covariance analysis TES contributed only 19 percent to the explained variance in morphine use, while a measure of neuroticism accounted for 80 percent. A potential role for psychological interventions is apparent.

Studies that take outcomes of treatments as dependent variables can also, at times, contribute to the generation of new alternative treatments by demonstrating inadequacies of those currently available. Other outcome studies conducted in a context of reasonably well-developed treatment alternatives offer promise of providing guidance in the choice of treatments. Ramani, Quesney, Olson, and Gunnit (1980) investigated the value of simultaneous video and EEG monitoring in documenting the diagnosis of hysterical seizures in epileptic patients. In a study quite similar to those cited earlier concerning the role of anxiety in postsurgical patients, Kuperman, Osmon, Golden, and Blume (1979) showed that MMPI variables were successful in predicting outcomes of neurosurgical procedures a year or more after surgery. The authors drew implications for the incorporation of psychological interventions before surgery for selected patients.

A final example of the investigations of the utility of psychological measures for generating and selecting among alternative treatment approaches is given by Stone and Neale (1981), who showed that the relation between self-reports of life events and physical symptoms was significantly stronger in married couples who scored low on measures of hypochondriasis and tendency to enter the sick role readily than in high-scoring couples. Their contribution is to point out a factor that needs to be taken into account in evaluating the role of life events in planning for a patient's care—a second-order, or mediating, factor.

Selection of Alternatives (1d). This category also has two subdivisions, one concerned with the process of treatment selection and one with the development of information to aid in the choice among treatments. Work by Brick and Swinth (1980) exemplifies studies of the process itself. They interviewed professionals in several mental health disciplines, inquiring about the attributes they used in making client placement decisions regarding developmentally delayed children. Although respondents mentioned many attributes, a few readily observed attributes, such as age, presence of physical disabilities, place of residence, and source of referral, were sufficient to predict accurately what decisions would be made. The authors developed a computer model to simulate the decisions on client referral and showed significant correspondence between the model and the actual decisions made by professionals. Marcy, Brown, and Danielson (1983) found that a method of counseling based specifically on knowledge of adolescent development led to more effective practice of contraception than conventional counseling. Surprisingly, counseling was no more effective when given at the time of a negative pregnancy test than at a routine medical visit.

Five studies were directed at identifying patient characteristics predictive of one or another aspect of responses to treatment. Three examples are given here. Lange (1978) studied factors predictive of headache as a side effect from the medical diagnostic procedure of lumbar puncture, showing that patients with high neuroticism scores who expressed fears and complaints about the operation itself were more likely to report the problem of headaches as well. Sobel and Worden (1979) examined the value of MMPI scales to predict psychosocial adjustment in cancer patients. The expected result, that high ego strength was associated with effective coping strategies, supports the view that this psychological variable can be of value in identifying patients able to contend with more demanding treatments. In a related study, one of a substantial series, Kinsman, Dirks, and Jones (1980) showed how patients' coping styles are related to illness-specific attitudes, symptoms, and experiences in asthma. These authors have elsewhere demonstrated how physicians vary their medical decision making on the basis of their perception of patients' coping styles (Kinsman, Dirks, and Jones, 1982).

In the 1984 sample there were several examples of this type of study. Singh and Williams (1983) studied attitudes and behavioral intentions about abortion, using data from a 1977 national survey. Sex, religious behaviors, and beliefs about fertility, sexual permissiveness, and freedom of expression all influenced attitudes and intentions. Concerned about unnecessary caesarean deliveries, Morford and Barclay (1984) questioned 149 women who had recently given birth to discover differences between those who had delivered vaginally and those who had delivered by caesarean section. The best predictors of vaginal birth were high desire to learn self-assertion, clear understanding of informed consent, low trust, and noncompliant behavior. The authors present a five-point counseling plan for pregnant women based on their findings.

In this area, as in the previous one discussed, one gains the impression of vast opportunities awaiting exploration by psychologists to put their skills to work in aiding health care.

Implementation of Treatment (1e). There are at least three subcategories of basic research on the implementation of treatment. One category is mainly descriptive of the processes and problems that arise in the course of treatment, the second is concerned with preparing patients for stressful medical procedures, and the third is concerned with identifying any factors associated with patients' ability to cope successfully with their treatment. In the first category there were three observational studies in which staff behaviors were recorded and, in some cases, related to patient behavior and treatment outcomes. Marton, Dawson, and Minde (1980) recorded the types of physical contact received by premature infants during intensive and postintensive care. No correlates of such behavior were reported. Two groups studied the incidence and consequences of independent and dependent behaviors by residents in nursing homes (Baltes, Burgess, and Steward, 1980; Barton, Baltes, and Orzech, 1980). In both studies it was found that independent behavior, such as eating, dressing, grooming, and toileting, was not reinforced or supported by staff behavior, while dependent behavior (asking for assistance with the behaviors listed above) was reinforced.

Most studies of the preparation of patients for their encounters with the treatment process fall into the category of design studies, since they take the form of tests of actual psychological interventions. Among basic studies it is appropriate to mention a critical review of the literature on the effect of preparation for childbirth. As a result of their review, Beck and

Siegel (1980) concluded that although some of the cited studies reported findings suggestive of the value of such psychological support, methodological shortcomings of the prior work pointed to the necessity for further research. This review underscores a risk for the field of health psychology that some fad of treatment that has face validity only may be widely adopted.

The majority of studies of implementation were concerned with factors associated with success or failure of patients in dealing with the exigencies of treatment. Several of these demonstrated in one way or another that psychological distress was associated with difficulty in following through with demanding treatment programs. This effect was seen in control of hypertension (Brody, 1980), diabetes (Bradley, 1979), and home dialysis treatment (Lowry and Atcherson, 1980; Steidl and others, 1980). Smoking cessation was also found to be less successful when there was marital discord or depression (Daughton, Fix, Kass, and Patil, 1980). Such studies suggest the hypothesis that professional assistance in dealing with life stresses may be repaid by increased effectiveness of medical treatments. No direct tests of this hypothesis were found in this review.

Two recent studies bring psychological theory to bear: Lowe and Frey (1983) extended Ajzen and Fishbein's "theory of reasoned action" to encompass joint intentions of father and mother regarding completion of Lamaze childbirth intentions. Gastorf and Galanos (1983) investigated the role of physicians' dogmatism/ authoritarianism in its interaction with a disease orientation versus a patient orientation as an influence on the attribution of noncompliance.

Evaluation (1f). In this category are placed not the actual evaluations of treatments leading, at least potentially, to decisions about whether to continue to use the treatment but studies that could be considered ancillary to such evaluations. In these studies, novel outcome variables, other than health outcomes, are examined for their possible implications for evaluation. Such implications fall into three subcategories: (1) simple descriptions of unwanted outcomes, (2) attempts to explain their occurrence, and (3) information that could enhance evaluation.

In some cases these noncentral variables are seen as possible "side effects"—associated effects whose values need to be added into the total computation of the cost/benefit ratio in evaluating a treatment. In the sample of studies included here, five simply described outcome variables with no attempt to identify predictive factors. Payk-Rahiff and Payk (1978) used a battery of psychological tests to appraise psychological costs associated with implantation of pacemakers, finding signs of hysterical symptoms, hypochondriacal fears, and depressive reactions. Two studies reported on the physical and emotional impact of mastectomy on women's lives—pain, loss of arm strength, changes in body image, sense of loss, and so on (Meyerowitz, 1981) and on their sexual behavior (Frank, Dornbush, Webster, and Kolodny, 1978). Brackney (179) described the impact of home dialysis on married couples. Hollenbeck and others (1980) documented serious effects of separation, both behavioral and physiological, observable in hospitalized children as a result of separation from the parents.

Parker and colleagues (1983) looked for improvement on mental status tests following carotid endarterectomy but failed to find it.

The second subcategory includes studies in which psychological variables are identified that are *predictive*, or prognostic, of the favorability of the primary outcomes of health care. In the absence of recognized alternative approaches to treatment, a patient's status in these studies could not be used to choose among treatments, nor would it be likely that a decision to treat or not to treat would be made on the basis of any but the strongest of predictors. Thus, one presumed value of these studies seems to be their potential for permitting satisfaction or dissatisfaction to be associated with intermediate outcomes in terms of deviations from a regression line. They provide an amplification of outcome evaluations. Perhaps more important is their potential for leading to modifications of the treatment program to address the needs of those with poor prognoses.

Two examples in this subcategory stressed psychosocial outcomes but considered what lay behind them. Roeske (1978) described psychological reactions of women following hysterectomy, having worked with them. She stressed their "mourning process" and sought to explain variations in their reactions using a variety of factors ranging from organic pathology to attitudes toward menses, childbearing, and many other aspects of life. Gundle and others (1980) interviewed thirty patients just before coronary artery surgery and again one to two years later. They reported a marked discrepancy between physiological recovery, which was generally good, and psychosocial recovery, indexed by employment and sexual functioning, for example, which was generally poor. This important observation, made without systematic documentation by many authors, points to a need for psychological assistance in postcoronary rehabilitation, especially in view of these authors' further observation that self-concept appears to be a crucial mediating factor.

A recent study (Metzger, Rogers, and Bauman, 1983) investigating the effects of age and marital status on emotional distress after mastectomy came up with findings contrary to expectations: being married, generally regarded as a stress-buffering social support, was found to provide little or no protection. In fact, never-married subjects were less likely to worry about recurrence or experience depressions.

Two papers investigated the possibility of using personality measures to predict pain variables. Smith and Duerksen (1979), using a battery of tests, including the Rorschach, the Street-Gestalt Completion, and the MMPI, described personality patterns of chronic-pain patients for whom surgery is unlikely to bring relief. Clum, Scott, and Burnside (1979) found that the amount of information cholecystectomy patients had before surgery was negatively related to both subjective and behavioral measures of outcomes (the more information, the more pain) in persons who were "internals" on the Health Locus of Control Scale. "Externals" showed a significant relation of the same kind only with regard to the subjective measures. However, the number of subjects (forty-eight) was too small to warrant interpretation of this difference between internals and externals.

Blank and Perry (1984) found that the psychological content of delirium in hospitalized burn patients was predictive of the severity of psychological symptoms after the delirium was resolved.

Four studies addressed medical outcomes, using as dependent variables subjective report of overall satisfaction with the results of pacemaker implantation (Goble, Gowers, Morgan, and Kline, 1979), measured occlusion of coronary arteries in repeated angiograms (Krantz, Sanmarco, Selvester, and Matthews, 1979), and one-year survival of melanoma patients apparently in remission (Rogentine and others, 1979). In each of these studies there was some indication of the value of psychological predictors. The potential value of accurate and efficient predictors of outcomes is an interesting question to consider in the absence of alternative treatments. No data-based studies relating to this question were found. What impact might there be from knowing, for example, that one's personality was predictive of relapse in melanoma?

The third subcategory attempts to provide information that can improve the process of evaluation. One study sought to establish a psychological variable as a convenient *index* of clinical outcome. The electrodermal response (EDR)—level and change of skin conductance during the valsalva maneuver—was demonstrated to differ markedly between patients on renal dialysis and normal controls, and a correlation was established between renal function and the EDR in renal patients (Doerr, Follette, Scribner, and Eisdorder, 1980). Woodson and da Costa-Woodson (1980) showed that the impact of obstetric analgesia on infant behavior needed to be evaluated in light of other maternal, labor, and infant variables, which contributed as much to outcome as the analgesia did. Byrne and Whyte (1978) factor-analyzed data gathered largely from questionnaires and interviews to identify eight factors in the illness behavior of survivors of myocardial infarction (for example, somatic concern and sick-role acceptance). They discussed these factors in terms of their implications for treatment and thus, potentially, of their value in evaluating outcomes.

Psychological Designs for Health Care Processes

Until this time, psychologists have been much more prone to gather data and elaborate theories to increase our understanding of health care processes than to venture into actually designing and testing new ways of delivering service. Let me remind readers once again that this statement is not made in reference to direct psychological services, which are excluded from this review. In the previous section I noted that some studies went beyond the gathering of data to propose specific implications of those data for the design of treatments. In this section are reviewed or exemplified only the twenty-seven articles in which the presentation and/or testing of a new design was the primary purpose. Two of these addressed the total context of the therapeutic transaction (2a). One, whose author had been a cancer patient as a child, drew on that experience to suggest that more hospitals should provide organized support teams to work with hospitalized children (Aronson, 1978). Barofsky (1978) examined the entire sequence of processes involved in the development of a pattern of self-care through the mediation of health care providers and recommended a program that facilitates such an outcome. The program is based on having patient and provider jointly author the medical record in order to enhance communication and direct attention to self-care behaviors. The program includes a self-teaching component and a continual monitoring of the correspondence between the patient's subjective reports of well-being or symptoms and objective findings from clinical tests. A continuing negotiation of diagnosis and treatment is fostered.

Other recent descriptions of programs include one aimed at prevention and early intervention delivered in an obstetrics/ gynecology service (Callahan, Desiderato, Heiden, and Pecsok, 1984), a program of secondary psychosocial care in a health maintenance organization (Adams and Kagnoff, 1983), and a program of training, research, and clinical service in behavioral pediatrics (Christophersen, Cataldo, Russo, and Varni, 1984).

Designs in the area of goal setting (2b) included recommendations to health care providers about the sexual needs of persons previously hospitalized for strokes (Humphrey and Kinsella, 1980), a recommendation, based on interviews with parents of children scheduled for surgical treatment of cleft palate, that counseling programs be established to bring parental expectations into line with reality (Pannbacker, 1977), and presentation of a "Health Needs Assessment Questionnaire" for use by family physicians to determine patients' perceptions of their health needs (Brunn and

Trevine, 1979). Krantz, Baum, and Wideman (1980) described the development of the Krantz Health Opinion Survey, which measures patients' preferences for information and active participation in medical care. The instrument is designed for use by physicians and others in planning programs of care with their patients. Beaber and Rodney (1984) reported that a hypochondriasis questionnaire showed that no patients with high scores were identified in medical records as suffering from hypochondriasis. The authors recommend routine use of a "very short, non-symptom-oriented measure of somatization" to enhance detection and early management efforts with such patients. Lowman (1979) reported the development and preliminary evaluation of a program in which public health nurses were trained to provide a "grief intervention" for parents who have lost a child to alleviate the profound guilt that is prone to develop in such couples. The article's emphasis on the system level of intervention qualifies it for inclusion here.

Designs for the generation of alternatives (2c), as represented in the sample, took the form of proposals for new kinds of treatments to be added to or to replace the alternatives conventionally used. As it happened, the two papers in this category that were selected for their relevance to the practicing psychologist were both recommendations concerning the behavioral treatment of tension (Philips, 1978) and migraine headache (Adams, Feuerstein, and Fowler, 1980), which appear promising on the basis of research to date. Both papers also stressed the need for more research and for caution in making claims.

Dirks, Fross, and Evans (1977) described and recommended two instruments for use in assessing the disposition of asthma patients to suffer from panic and fear during attacks and offered suggestions for how these measures can help physicians in their management of such patients (2d). Gross and Huerta (1980) recommended psychological consultation to pediatricians evaluating children for possible epilepsy on the basis of two years of experience showing the possibility of functional pathology. Nineteen such cases were found out of an unspecified total reviewed. Millon, Green, and Meagher (1979) offered a general-purpose self-report inventory for use in a variety of medical settings and described how it can be used in medical decision making.

Designs for the implementation of treatments (2e) were almost always presented in the form of descriptions of programs that appeared to the authors to be highly successful. Two of these were concerned with the management of pedodontic patients. Klorman and others (1980) reported that young patients' disruptiveness could be reduced by modeling appropriate coping and mastery behaviors. Stokes and Kennedy (1980) described how modeling had reduced uncooperative behavior in most of a group of forty second-grade children. Eight children whose behaviors were still too disruptive for effective dentistry were brought under control with the use of tangible reinforcers. Reisinger and Lavigne (1980) described how patient training and skills development programs could assist pediatricians in managing a variety of problems that frequently confront them. Taylor, Pfenninger, and Candelaria (1980) reported a case in which treatment contracts were used to reduce Medicaid costs of a patient who made "frequent and unnecessary outpatient and emergency room visits." Bowler and Morisky (1983) reported improved compliance behavior among 200 hypertensive patients who participated in brief, structured small groups.

Wakeman and Kaplan (1978) documented positive results from the use of hypnosis with burn patients. Explicit or implicit recommendations for the use of counseling interventions were made in other articles. Droske (1978) described ways in which hospital staff members can help parents deal with their children's posthospital adjustment. Counseling and anticipatory guidance is helpful, both before admission and before discharge, about the kinds of changes in children's behavior that can be expected. The ubiquity and the temporary nature of such changes are important information for parents.

Similar kinds of recommendations have been made for support of couples following intestinal bypass surgery for one of the pair (Neill, Marshall, and Yale, 1978), implantation of cardiac stimulators (Adamovic, Jevremovic, and Knezevic, 1975), caesarean deliveries (Lipson and Tilden, 1980), and cancer patients (Gordon and others, 1980). Winstead (1978) described illness behavior of men who had contracted filariasis in the Pacific theater of World War II and reported on generally successful preventive psychiatric treatment in such cases. The value of psychological support for patients, siblings, parents, and members of the medical team involved in bone-marrow transplantation procedures with child patients was described by Patenaude, Szymanski, and Rappeport (1979). Horman (1980) endorsed the value of the relatively simple expedients of flexible visiting policies and living-in accommodations for parents to reduce stress involved in hospitalization of young children.

Recommendations on methods for evaluating treatment outcomes (2f) were surprisingly infrequent. One paper recommended the use of direct observation of patient behaviors (for example, "inappropriate," "repetitive," "relating to people") during occupational therapy on a psychogeriatric ward as a means of evaluating the effectiveness of the sessions (Burton, 1980). Smith and colleagues (1979) described a scale for evaluating the degree of recovery from severe head trauma, and Eson, Yen, and Bourke (1978) reported on a procedure designed for serial assessment of neuropsychological recovery after serious head injury. Marin (1980) described a set of precoded response categories for analyzing consumer feedback in the evaluation of health service delivery.

Krol and Nordlund (1983) described use of a patient satisfaction instrument to provide feedback to residents about their physician/patient relationships and needs-assessment data for the behavioral science portion of a family medicine program.

Psychologists' Contributions to Selection Among Health Care Alternatives

In a landmark paper often used to date the emergence of health psychology as a recognized field of study, Schofield (1969) included as a potential contribution of health psychologists the appraisal of patients as an aid to health care providers in selecting among available treatments and treatment approaches. Schofield further elaborated on this potential in later writing (for example, Schofield, 1979), and others have also pointed to this possibility (Hunt and MacLeod, 1979). It is surprising, therefore, that in the four years included in this survey no specific reports of such activity were discovered. Surveys of the activities of psychologists working in medical settings refer to psychological testing as an important component of their work (Berger, 1978), and it must be assumed that activities in the arena of selection are occurring. There would seem to be value to be drawn from a fuller reporting of such work. Indeed, Cummings and Dörken in Chapter Eleven point to the viability of using specific procedures for specific disorders, while Dörken and Bennett in Chapter Thirteen underscore that progress and refinement in this direction are essential to cost-effective care.

Psychologists' Implementation of Health Care Services

In defining the scope of this review, I have deliberately excluded descriptions of the provision of direct psychological services to patients (4e) in view of the extensive coverage of this topic in other chapters of this book. In this section it would be appropriate to refer to reports of psychologists' participation in goal setting, treatment planning, and evaluation of outcomes. Here again, the choice to classify a report as falling into the group of basic studies or of design proposals or include it here was somewhat arbitrary. Where the emphasis was on the discovery of effects not intended, I put the report with the basic studies. When the description of the activity and the demonstration that it was possible and worthwhile were emphasized, I called it a design study. Only those reports that focused on the substantive and expected output from the process are presented here. None of the articles on goal setting (4b) or treatment planning (4c, 4d) seemed to me to have this focus. There were, however, a number of evaluative studies (4f) that did.

Field and Widmayer (1980) compared infants delivered by caesarean section under general anesthesia with vaginally delivered infants for whom, at most, local anesthesia was given to the mothers. Evaluations were made at birth, four months, and eight months on the basis of obstetric medication and complication scores, maternal and infant blood pressures, ratings of infants' temperaments and adaptability, and maternal attitudes. By eight months, differences were mainly in the mothers' perceptions of their infants. Infants in the two groups were indistinguishable at this time by the measures used in the study.

An interesting example of psychological evaluations in health care involved a psychometric method based on S. S. Stevens's approach to ratio scaling. Words descriptive of pain were presented in randomized orders on each trial to test the effectiveness of a short-acting analgesic for pain produced by stimulation of tooth pulp. This psychologically sophisticated method permitted detection of a reduction in intensity of pain when there was no change in rated unpleasantness of the stimulus (Gracely, Dubner, and McGrath, 1979).

Most evaluative studies made use of data gathered by interviews and questionnaires. Examples of such studies in the present sample include an evaluation of sexual function following treatment of prostatic cancer with radioactive iodine (Herr, 1979), leading to the conclusion that this new treatment was much less impairing than previous forms. An investigation of attitudinal and behavioral outcomes following laparoscopic sterilization in an outpatient clinic (Turner-Bonk, Penfield, and Driscoll, 1978) provided a profile of the patients and indicated that a very high proportion (96 percent) had "no regrets." A similar study of psychosocial recovery following myocardial infarction was reported with implications for improvement of routine management of such patients (Mayou, Foster, and Williamson, 1979; Mayou, Williamson, and Foster, 1978). Although there were few reports of studies in this subcategory, verbal self-report is probably the most frequently used approach to evaluation. A critical review of the quality of the methods used might reveal an area to which well-trained psychologists could make important contributions.

Evaluations of Health Care Processes

In Table 9-1 the term *evaluate* or *evaluation* appears both on the right-hand end of the dimension of health care processes and at the bottom of the dimension of psychological activities. This fact reflects the comparable underlying structure of problem solving that characterizes both health care and psychologists' work. In classifying the reports of empirical work of a psychological nature, I found occasion to use both regions of the chart. When psychologists or psychological activities were contributing in some

way to the devising and performance of evaluations of health care
services—that is, when they constituted an integral component of
those services—they were classified in the cells on the right margin.
In the present section studies are reported of the *processes* of health
care—critiques of the system, its models of care, and the like. This
topic was second only to basic studies in the amount of work
reported during the years reviewed.

 Evaluations of the Overall Process (5a). Two reports
addressed the question of the overall impact of patients' being
engaged in the system of health care delivery. Goldberg, Comstock,
and Graves (1980), as part of a study of psychosocial factors
associated with high blood pressure, reported that, among a sample
of persons encountered in a communitywide screening program,
treatment for hypertension was associated with an excess of
psychosomatic symptoms that the authors thought were best
explained as a result of being labeled hypertensive. The need for
learning more about "other elements in the cost-benefit equation,"
beyond the recognized benefit of medical treatment of hypertension,
was pointed out. Drotar, Malone, Negray, and Dennstedt (1981)
reviewed the charts of thirty infants hospitalized for "nonorganic
failure to thrive." They found three major shortcomings in system
performance: underutilization of psychosocial services, insufficient
emphasis on treatment planning as opposed to diagnosis, and
inadequate charting of information concerning follow-up.
Corrective suggestions were offered.

 Becker and Poe (1980) studied the effects of involving users
in the design of a hospital wing. "Cosmetic" and inexpensive
changes, such as painting, rearranging furniture, and installing
new carpets, were found to have positive effects on mood, morale,
and perceived quality of health care. Use of public areas increased,
especially during evening visiting hours. Curiously, however,
visitors reacted negatively to the changes. The improved staff and
patient morale following the changes were taken to indicate that
small environmental details can have significant effects.

 A more focal critique of a system variable demonstrated a
significant positive association between the time patients were
required to wait for their first appointment in a community mental
health clinic and the number of failures to keep the appointment

(Folkins, Hersch, and Dahlen, 1980). Evaluations of overall clinical competence of physicians are an important topic in this area, to which only a single paper in the sample was addressed. Brockway (1978) tested a system of four measures to assess completeness of data collection, accuracy of problem identification, interview skills, and patient and physician assessment and showed that the system was able to detect appreciable gains during the first year of a family residency program.

Evaluations of the Goal-Setting Process (5b). Five rather heterogeneous papers addressed and challenged the goals of health care and the ways these goals are established. Ludwig (1981), for instance, pointed out unwanted social and individual outcomes, such as delay of recovery and sustained vocational impairment, associated with the availability of benefit payments for disabled persons. Although this paper might have been classified as a demonstration of unintended side effects from an established treatment approach, it seems to challenge and call for reexamination of the basic goals of organized medicine in the treatment of disability. Two papers appraised the goal of "normalization" for handicapped persons (Briton, 1979; Thurman and Fiorelli, 1979). Both potential benefits and pitfalls were seen in taking normalization as a major goal.

Morgan (1978) investigated the "prestigious defeatism" of physicians and psychologists regarding the incurability of disorders that they typically treat. He invited his respondents to submit examples of "incurable disorders" that they frequently encountered in their practice. Examples of "incurable conditions" cited by psychologists included schizophrenia (8 percent of those responding) and "trauma-induced mental aberration" (2 percent). Some physicians included substance addictions on their list of incurable conditions (percentage not reported). From the number of conditions nominated as incurable, he estimated that one in two psychologists, three in four psychiatrists, and nine in ten nonpsychiatric physician specialists exemplified iatrogenic defeatism.

Evaluations of the Diagnostic Process and the Presentation of Options (5bc). It was not always possible to separate clearly evaluations of different components of the health care process.

Several studies emphasized to varying degrees the range of activities from goal setting to selection of treatment. Silvestre and Fresco (1980) used interviews to appraise parental reactions to the experience of and the knowledge obtained from the procedure of amniocentesis. Various impacts were identified. Grodin (1978) discussed ethical issues that arise in perinatal and neonatal care with regard to extent of intervention, iatrogenicity, and prognostication. Potential contributions of psychologists were discussed. In relation to a somewhat later period in a child's development, Plomin and Foch (1981) questioned the validity of pediatricians' diagnoses of "hyperactivity." Using both psychological tests and parental ratings of behavior, they showed that the diagnoses were related to parental assessment but not to laboratory findings. The issue of patients' knowledge of the severity and prognosis of their condition was examined by Howard (1976). Generally, patients knew their diagnosis but not its severity or prognosis. Physicians tended to inform patients only when they believed that patients already had the information from some other source. These studies make clear the need for close attention to the psychological meaning of diagnostic processes in the lives of patients and health care providers. Such meaning influences not only the impact of the diagnosis on patients but also, apparently, the actual diagnoses that are made.

Evaluation of the Selection of Interventions (5d). Exemplifying studies in the area of evaluation of the treatment selection process is a paper by Hammond (1979) that argues that physicians fail to prescribe medication for pain in a great many cases when it would be appropriate to do so. The author asserts that physicians act out of their fear of addicting their patients to opiates, which would represent a symbolic loss in a power struggle with the patients. In a somewhat similar, critical vein, Messerli, Garamendi, and Romano (1980) report results of a survey indicating that mastectomy patients felt that their surgeons had left many of their questions unanswered, implying that they had not been adequately involved in the decision about the surgical treatment plan. A third critique of the decision making of health care providers is presented by Dowell and Jones (1980), who studied referrals among twelve human service agencies. Their data suggested that the agency personnel referred as much by "habit" as by rational evaluation of the clients' problems.

Evaluations of Health Care Activities (5e). In this section we consider the few reports that evaluate not the direct health outcomes of health care activities but other aspects of their impacts. Seltzer (1981), studying environments of residential treatment facilities for mentally retarded persons, identified five descriptive dimensions and demonstrated significant differences among six program types on these dimensions. He then used multiple regression analysis to investigate the relation between the environmental characteristics and the clients' postrelease adjustment in the community, their retention of skills learned in the residential program, and the satisfaction they reported with their experiences there. Many significant associations were found. Among the strongest were those on the dimensions of "in-house responsibilities" and "autonomy," which showed essentially linear increases over the six types of living arrangements from state institutions to independent apartments. The responsibility variable also accounted for a significant proportion of variance in a composite "Performance Index of Community Living Skills." "Autonomy" was significantly associated with residents' satisfaction.

Zawatski, Katz, and Krekeler (1979) reported on the use of a Likert scale to appraise the satisfaction expressed by spouses of patients in a coronary care unit with the nursing care that had been given. Generally, the care was perceived as good, but there was less satisfaction with the amount of information about patients that had been given to spouses. O'Brien (1980) studied patterns of interaction between chronic dialysis patients and their families and friends, using two series of structured interviews given three years apart. The amount of interaction increased over this time period, but the quality deteriorated. Patients who expected more of their families tended to report better social functioning. An implication of need for more support to such patients and their families could be drawn from the results of this study. Such an implication was drawn more directly for patients and their families following myocardial infarction: Mayou, Foster, and Williamson (1979) interviewed 100 such patients in the hospital and two and twelve months after the beginning of the episode. Patients and families frequently did not recall or understand what they were supposed to be doing in the way of care. Physicians underestimated the negative impact of the extended recovery phase on these families. On the basis of this evaluation, the authors concluded that there were both medical and economic reasons for instituting better rehabilitation programs.

Evaluations of Evaluations (5f). This review of psychologists' activities in relation to health care is completed with two examples of reports that asked how well the evaluations of health outcomes are performed. The validity of introspective memories of pain accompanying neurosurgical procedures was examined by comparing responses to the McGill Pain Questionnaire given one and five days after the procedure (Hunter, Phillips, and Rachman, 1979). Reports made after five days were "surprisingly accurate," providing reassurance about their value.

Krop, Hall, and Mehta (1979) questioned 100 postcoronary patients after discharge from a VA hospital to evaluate the degree to which they had communicated any concerns to their physicians about the impact of their illness on marital relationships and sexual function. Few patients had done so at all, and when they did, the discussions were usually initiated by patients rather than physicians. Thus this study points to a deficit in the normal procedures of evaluating the patient's preparation for the rehabilitative phase of postcoronary illness.

Discussion and Conclusions

In this chapter I have first set forth a framework for consideration of the work being done by psychologists in relation to the health system and, more particularly, the health care system. The health system, as here conceived, is that portion of our total environment and of our adaptation to it that has impact on the health of our minds and bodies. Thus defined, the health system cannot be separated out from the total environment; it interpenetrates the environment and must be seen as an aspect of that totality. The health *care* system is that part of the health system that involves the provision of specialized health services through direct or indirect contracting.

The framework for analysis of psychologists' contributions is based on a conception of behavior as problem solving. Individuals seeking to maintain, enhance, or restore their health engage in problem solving with regard to the health hazards of the environment (including the internal environment of the body) and to the health problems that result from interactions with those hazards. Health care professionals engage with clients or patients in joint problem solving to prevent or overcome health problems. Health psychologists may act as providers of health care, but they may also act as researchers, engineers, consultants, and evaluators for the health care system to enhance the capacity of that system to provide effective services.

The second major portion of the chapter consists of a survey of approximately four years' output of publications (abstracted in *Psychological Abstracts* for 1979, 1980, 1981, and 1984) on the indirect contributions from psychology and related fields to the enhancement of health care, classified according to the dual problem solving of health care provider and the psychologist acting as consultant to the health care system. It might be asked whether the work being described in the publications found by the survey is representative of the work actually being done. We know that many psychologists heavily invested in specific applications find little time or incentive to describe their work in published reports. Holding in mind the caution indicated by this question, there are, nonetheless, questions of more substantive interest that could be raised concerning the distribution of effort reflected in Table 9-1. What has guided psychologists in their choice of topics for study? Do they make rational choices based on estimates of costs and benefits of their work for the functioning of the health care system? Are they guided by the availability of support for the work or simply by the fortuities of opportunity?

All the factors mentioned and many others are no doubt operative. As we move into the second decade of endeavor in health psychology, it will behoove us to look at the whole range of opportunities available in order to identify those where our effort may produce the greatest return. In a world occupied by a plethora of health care providers—physicians, nurses, public health specialists, health educators, clinical pharmacists, and so on—

psychologists are uniquely qualified by their training to draw from the core body of psychological research. We need to appraise the activities of the health care system and identify in them the basic psychological processes involved—learning, decision making, motivation, perception, and attribution, for example. We need to appraise the effectiveness of current practices in achieving social and individual goals of health care for patient and practitioner alike. We need to use our knowledge and skills to propose innovative approaches and to document their value. We need to use our skills for appraising individuals in tailoring treatments to meet their needs and capabilities. We need to use our competence in groups and organizations and our understanding of communication processes in dealing with the problems that arise in the course of health care delivery. And we need to build on our methods for the study of values and preferences to improve the ability of health care providers to measure the impact of their work on the quality of lives.

The studies cited in this survey give some promise that we are making a beginning in this domain of opportunities. I hope that the survey may also stimulate some readers to undertake work that is not being done and to describe work that is being done but not reported.

References

Adamovic, V., Jevremovic, M., and Knezevic, M. ["Psychosomatic and Psychological Aspects of Implantation of Cardiac Stimulators."] *Anali Zavoda za Mentalno Zdravlje,* 1975, 7(4), 59–66.
Adams, H. E., Feuerstein, M., and Fowler, J. L. "Migraine Headache: Review of Parameters, Etiology, and Intervention." *Psychological Bulletin,* 1980, *87,* 217–237.
Adams, J., and Kagnoff, M. "Development of Pediatric Secondary Psychosocial Care in a Health Maintenance Organization." *Children's Health Care,* 1983, *12*(1), 4–10.
Adatto, K., Doebele, K. G., Galland, L., and Granowetter, L. "Behavioral Factors and Urinary Tract Infection." *Journal of the American Medical Association,* 1979, *24*(23), 2525–2526.

Aronson, J. "I May Be Bald but I Still Have Rights." *Journal of Clinical Child Psychology*, 1978, 7(3), 181–184.

Baltes, M. M., Burgess, R. L., and Steward, R. B. "Independence and Dependence in Self-Care Behaviors in Nursing Home Residents: An Operant-Observational Study." *International Journal of Behavioral Development*, 1980, 3(4), 489–500.

Barofsky, I. "Compliance, Adherence and the Therapeutic Alliance: Steps in the Development of Self-Care." *Social Science and Medicine*, 1978, 12(5), 369–376.

Barton, E. M., Baltes, M. M., and Orzech, M. J. "Etiology of Dependence in Older Nursing Home Residents During Morning Care: The Role of Staff Behavior." *Journal of Personality and Social Psychology*, 1980, 38(3), 423–431.

Beaber, R. J., and Rodney, W. M. "Underdiagnosis of Hypochondriasis in Family Practice." *Psychosomatics*, 1984, 25(1), 39–46.

Beck, N. C., and Siegel, L. J. "Preparation for Childbirth and Contemporary Research on Pain, Anxiety, and Stress Reduction: A Review and Critique." *Psychosomatic Medicine*, 1980, 42(45), 429–447.

Becker, F. D., and Poe, D. B. "The Effects of User-Generated Design Modifications in a General Hospital." *Journal of Nonverbal Behavior*, 1980, 4(4), 195–281.

Berger, M. "The Role of the Clinical Child Psychologist in an Endstage Renal Disease Program." *Journal of Clinical Child Psychology*, 1978, 7(1), 17–18.

Blank, K., and Perry, S. "Relationship of Psychological Processes During Delirium to Outcome." *American Journal of Psychiatry*, 1984, 141(7), 843–847.

Bowler, M. H., and Morisky, D. E. "A Small Group Strategy for Improving Compliance Behavior and Blood Pressure Control." *Health Education Quarterly*, 1983, 10(1), 56–69.

Brackney, B. E. "The Impact of Home Hemodialysis on the Marital Dyad." *Journal of Marital and Family Therapy*, 1979, 5(1), 55–60.

Bradley, C. "Life Events and the Control of Diabetes Mellitus." *Journal of Psychosomatic Research*, 1979, 23(2), 159–162.

Brick, H. J., and Swinth, R. L. "A Process Model of Group Decision Making in a Multidisciplinary Health Care Agency." *Journal of Pediatric Psychology*, 1980, *5*(3), 305–321.

Briton, J. "Normalisation: What Of and What For?" *Australian Journal of Mental Retardation*, 1979, *5*(6), 224–229.

Brockway, B. S. "Evaluating Physician Competency: What Difference Does It Make?" *Evaluation and Program Planning*, 1978, *3*, 211–220.

Brody, D. S. "Psychological Distress and Hypertension Control." *Journal of Human Stress*, 1980, *6*(1), 26.

Brunn, J. G., and Trevine, F. M. "A Method for Determining Patients' Perceptions of Their Health Needs." *Journal of Family Practice*, 1979, *8*(4), 809–881.

Burton, M. H. "Evaluation and Change in a Psychogeriatric Ward Through Observation and Feedback." *British Journal of Psychiatry*, 1980, *137*, 566–571.

Byrne, D. G. "Anxiety as State and Trait Following Survived Myocardial Infarction." *British Journal of Social and Clinical Psychology*, 1979, *18*(4), 417–423.

Byrne, D. G., and Whyte, H. M. "Dimensions of Illness Behaviour in Survivors of Myocardial Infarction." *Journal of Psychosomatic Research*, 1978, *22*(6), 485–491.

Callahan, E. J., Desiderato, L., Heiden, L., and Pecsok, E. H. "Prevention and Intervention Through Obstetrics and Gynecology." *Behavioral Medicine Update*, 1984, *5*(4), 11–19.

Christophersen, E. R., Cataldo, M. F., Russo, D. C., and Varni, J. W. "Behavioral Pediatrics: Establishing and Maintaining a Program of Training, Research, and Clinical Service." *Behavior Therapist*, 1984, *7*(3), 43–46.

Clum, G. A., Scott, L., and Burnside, J. "Information and Locus of Control as Factors in the Outcome of Surgery." *Psychological Reports*, 1979, *45*(3), 867–873.

Coffman, S. P. "Parents' Perceptions of Needs for Themselves and Their Children in a Cerebral Palsy Clinic." *Issues in Comprehensive Pediatric Nursing*, 1983, *6*(1), 67–77.

Daughton, D. M., Fix, A. J., Kass, I., and Patil, K. D. "Smoking Cessation Among Patients with Chronic Obstructive Pulmonary Disease (COPD)." *Addictive Behaviors*, 1980, *5*(2), 125–128.

Dirks, J. F., Fross, K. H., and Evans, N. W. "Panic-Fear in Asthma: Generalized Personality Trait vs. Specific Situational State." *Journal of Asthma Research,* 1977, *14*(4), 161-167.

Doerr, H. O., Follette, W., Scribner, B. H., and Eisdorfer, C. "Electrodermal Response Dysfunction in Patients on Maintenance Renal Dialysis." *Psychophysiology,* 1980, *17*(1), 83-86.

Dowell, D. A., and Jones, T. "A Study of Coordination of Services: Referrals." *Journal of Community Psychology,* 1980, *8*(1), 61-69.

Droske, S. C. "Children's Behavioral Changes Following Hospitalization—Have We Prepared the Parents?" *Journal of the Association for the Care of Children in Hospitals,* 1978, 7(2), 3-7.

Drotar, D., Malone, C. A., Negray, J., and Dennstedt, M. "Psychosocial Assessment and Care for Infants Hospitalized for Non-Organic Failure to Thrive." *Journal of Clinical Child Psychology,* 1981, *10*(1), 63-66.

D'Zurilla, T. J., and Goldfried, M. R. "Problem Solving and Behavior Modification." *Journal of Abnormal Psychology,* 1971, *78,* 107-126.

Engel, G. L. "A Unified Concept of Health and Disease." *Perspectives of Biological Medicine,* 1960, *3,* 459-485.

Engel, G. L. "The Need for a New Medical Model: A Challenge for Biomedicine." *Science,* 1977, *196*(4286), 129-136.

Engel, G. L. "The Clinical Application of the Biopsychosocial Model." *American Journal of Psychiatry,* 1980, *137*(5), 535-544.

Eson, M. E., Yen, J. K., and Bourke, R. S. "Assessment of Recovery from Serious Head Injury." *Journal of Neurology, Neurosurgery and Psychiatry,* 1978, *41*(11), 1036-1042.

Field, T. M., and Widmayer, S. M. "Developmental Follow-up of Infants Delivered by Caesarean Section and General Anesthesia." *Infant Behavior and Development,* 1980, *3*(3), 253-264.

Folkins, C., Hersch, P., and Dahlen, D. "Waiting Time and No-Show Rate in a Community Mental Health Center." *American Journal of Community Psychology,* 1980, *8,* 121-123.

Frank, D., Dornbush, R. L., Webster, S. K., and Kolodny, R. C. "Mastectomy and Sexual Behavior: A Pilot Study." *Sexuality and Disability,* 1978, *1*(1), 16-26.

Gastorf, J. W., and Galanos, A. N. "Patient Compliance and Physicians' Attitude." *Family Practice Research Journal,* 1983, *2*(3), 190-198.

Goble, R. E., Gowers, J. I., Morgan, J. C., and Kline, P. "Artificial Pacemaker Patients: Treatment Outcome and Goldberg's General Health Questionnaire." *Journal of Psychosomatic Research,* 1979, *23*(3), 175-179.

Goldberg, E. L., Comstock, G. W., and Graves, C. G. "Psychosocial Factors and Blood Pressure." *Psychological Medicine,* 1980, *10*(2), 243-255.

Gordon, J. S. "Holistic Medicine: Toward a New Medical Model." *Journal of Clinical Psychiatry,* 1981, *42*(3), 114-119.

Gordon, W. A., and others. "Efficacy of Psychosocial Intervention with Cancer Patients." *Journal of Consulting and Clinical Psychology,* 1980, *48*(6), 743-759.

Gracely, R. H., Dubner, R., and McGrath, P. A. "Narcotic Analgesia: Fentanyl Reduces the Intensity but Not the Unpleasantness of Painful Tooth Pulp Sensations." *Science,* 1979, *203*(4386), 1261-1263.

Grodin, M. A. "Ethical Issues in Perinatology: The Rights of the Fetus and Newborn." *Journal of Clinical Child Psychology,* 1978, *7*(3), 184-187.

Gross, M., and Huerta, E. "Functional Convulsions Masked as Epileptic Disorders." *Journal of Pediatric Psychology,* 1980, *5*(1), 71-79.

Gundle, M. J., and others. "Psychosocial Outcome After Coronary Artery Surgery." *American Journal of Psychiatry,* 1980, *137*(12), 1591-1594.

Hall, S., and Havassy, B. "The Obese Woman: Causes, Correlates, and Treatment." *Professional Psychology,* 1981, *12*(1), 163-170.

Hammond, D. "Unnecessary Suffering: Pain and the Doctor-Patient Relationship." *Perspectives in Biology and Medicine,* 1979, *23*(1), 152-160.

Herr, H. W. "Preservation of Sexual Potency in Prostatic Cancer Patients After 125I Implantation." *Journal of the American Geriatrics Society,* 1979, *27*(1), 117-119.

Hoeper, E. W., and others. "Diagnosis of Mental Disorder in Adults and Increased Use of Health Services in Four Outpatient Settings." *American Journal of Psychiatry,* 1980, *127*(2), 207–210.

Hollenbeck, A. R., and others. "Children with Serious Illness: Behavioral Correlates of Separation and Isolation." *Child Psychiatry and Human Development,* 1980, *1*(1), 3–11.

Horman, E. "Children in Hospitals." *Infant Mental Health Journal,* 1980, *1*(2), 123–127.

Horowitz, M., and others. "News of Risk for Early Heart Disease as a Stressful Event." *Psychosomatic Medicine,* 1980, *42*(1), 37–46.

Howard, A. R. "Patients' Attitudes Toward Treatment Approaches." *Newsletter for Research in Mental Health and Behavioral Sciences,* 1976, *18*(2), 7–9.

Humphrey, M., and Kinsella, G. "Sexual Life After Stroke." *Sexuality and Disability,* 1980, *3*(3), 150–153.

Hunt, E. B., and MacLeod, C. M. "Cognition and Information Processing in Patient and Physician." In G. C. Stone, F. Cohen, N. E. Adler, and Associates, *Health Psychology—a Handbook: Theories, Applications, and Challenges of a Psychological Approach to the Health Care System.* San Francisco: Jossey-Bass, 1979.

Hunter, M., Phillips, C., and Rachman, S. "Memory for Pain." *Pain,* 1979, *6*(1), 35–46.

Kahn, J. P., and others. "Type A Behavior and Blood Pressure During Coronary Artery Bypass Surgery." *Psychosomatic Medicine,* 1980, *42*(4), 407–414.

Kinsman, R. A., Dirks, J. F., and Jones, N. F. "Levels of Psychological Experience in Asthma: General and Illness-Specific Concomitants of Panic-Fear Personality." *Journal of Clinical Psychology,* 1980, *36*(2), 552–561.

Kinsman, R. A., Dirks, J. F., and Jones, N. F. "Psychomaintenance of Chronic Physical Illness: Clinical Assessment of Personal Styles Affecting Medical Management." In C. J. Coreen and R. Meagher (eds.), *Handbook of Clinical Health Psychology.* New York: Plenum, 1982.

Klorman, R., and others. "Effects of Coping and Mastery Modeling on Experienced and Inexperienced Pedodontic Patients' Disruptiveness." *Behavior Therapy,* 1980, *11*(2), 156–168.

Krantz, D. S., Baum, A., and Wideman, M. "Assessment of Preferences for Self-Treatment and Information in Health Care." *Journal of Personality and Social Psychology*, 1980, *39*(5), 977–990.

Krantz, D. S., Sanmarco, M. I., Selvester, R. H., and Matthews, K. A. "Psychological Correlates of Progression of Atherosclerosis in Men." *Psychosomatic Medicine*, 1979, *4*(6), 467–475.

Krol, R. A., and Nordlund, D. J. "Patient-Satisfaction Data and Residents' Physician-Patient Skills." *Journal of Family Practice*, 1983, *17*(1), 141–142.

Krop, H., Hall, D., and Mehta, J. "Sexual Concerns After Myocardial Infarction." *Sexuality and Disability*, 1979, *2*(2), 91–97.

Kuperman, S. K., Osmon, D., Golden, C. J., and Blume, H. G. "Prediction of Neurosurgical Results by Psychological Evaluation." *Perceptual and Motor Skills*, 1979, *48*(1), 311–315.

Lange, H. U. ["Anxiety and Neuroticism in the Development of Headache After Lumbar Puncture Operation."] *Nervenarzt*, 1978, *49*(1), 47–49.

Lim, A. T., and others. "Postoperative Pain Control: Contribution of Psychological Factors and Transcutaneous Electrical Stimulation." *Pain*, 1983, *17*(2), 179–188.

Lipson, J. G., and Tilden, P. "Psychological Integration of the Caesarean Birth Experience." *American Journal of Orthopsychiatry*, 1980, *50*(4), 598–609.

Lowe, R. H., and Frey, J. D. "Predicting Lamaze Childbirth Intentions and Outcomes: An Extension of the Theory of Reasoned Action to a Joint Outcome." *Basic and Applied Social Psychology*, 1983, *4*(4), 353–372.

Lowman, J. "Grief Intervention and Sudden Infant Death Syndrome." *American Journal of Community Psychology*, 1979, *7*(6), 665–677.

Lown, B., and others. "Psychophysiologic Factors in Sudden Cardiac Death." *American Journal of Psychiatry*, 1980, *137*(11), 1325–1335.

Lowry, M. R., and Atcherson, E. "Home Dialysis Dropouts." *Journal of Psychosomatic Research*, 1980, *24* (3–4), 173–178.

Ludwig, A. M. "The Disabled Society?" *American Journal of Psychotherapy*, 1981, *35*(1), 5-15.

Lunghi, M. E., Miller, P. M., and McQuillan, W. M. "Psycho-Social Factors in Osteoarthritis of the Hip." *Journal of Psychosomatic Research*, 1978, *22*(1), 57-63.

Marcy, S. A., Brown, J. S., and Danielson, R. "Contraceptive Use by Adolescent Females in Relation to Knowledge, and to Time and Method of Contraceptive Counseling." *Research in Nursing and Health*, 1983, *6*(4), 175-182.

Marin, B. V. "Use of Consumer Feedback in Planned Change and Evaluation Activities." *Journal of Community Psychology*, 1980, *8*(4), 308-313.

Marton, P. L., Dawson, H., and Minde, K. "The Interaction of Ward Personnel with Infants in the Premature Nursery." *Infant Behavior and Development*, 1980, *3*(4), 307-313.

Mayou, R., Foster, A., and Williamson, B. "Medical Care After Myocardial Infarction." *Journal of Psychosomatic Research*, 1979, *23*(1), 23-26.

Mayou, R., Williamson, B., and Foster, A. "Outcome Two Months After Myocardial Infarction." *Journal of Psychosomatic Research*, 1978, *22*(5), 439-445.

Messerli, M. L., Garamendi, C., and Romano, J. "Breast Cancer: Information as a Technique of Crisis Intervention." *American Journal of Orthopsychiatry*, 1980, *50*(4), 728-731.

Metzger, L. F., Rogers, T. F., and Bauman, L. J. "Effects of Age and Marital Status on the Emotional Distress After a Mastectomy." *Journal of Psychosocial Oncology*, 1983, *1*(3), 17-33.

Meyerowitz, B. E. "The Impact of Mastectomy on the Lives of Women." *Professional Psychology*, 1981, *12*(1), 118-127.

Millon, T., Green, C. J., and Meagher, R. B. "A New Inventory for the Psychodiagnostician in Medical Settings." *Professional Psychology*, 1979, *10*(4), 529-539.

Morford, M. L., and Barclay, L. K. "Counseling the Pregnant Woman: Implications for Birth Outcomes." *Personnel and Guidance Journal*, 1984, *62*(10), 619-623.

Morgan, R. F. "The Iatrogenic Psychology of Practitioner's Defeatism and Other Assertions of the Null Hypothesis." *Psychological Reports*, 1978, *43*(3), 963-977.

Nailboff, B. D., Cohen, M. J., Schandler, S. L., and Heinrich, R. L. "Signal Detection and Threshold Measures for Chronic Back Pain Patients, Chronic Illness Patients, and Cohort Controls to Radiant Heat Stimuli." *Journal of Abnormal Psychology,* 1981, *90*(3), 271-274.

Neill, J. R., Marshall, J. R., and Yale, C. E. "Marital Changes After Intestinal Bypass Surgery." *Journal of the American Medical Association,* 1978, *240*(5), 447-450.

O'Brien, M. E. "Effective Social Environment and Hemodialysis Adaptation: A Panel Analysis." *Journal of Health and Social Behavior,* 1980, *21*(4), 360-370.

Pannbacker, M. "Parental Preoperative Ideas of Speech After Surgical Management of Cleft Palate." *Rehabilitation Literature,* 1977, *38*(11-12), 352-358.

Parker, J. C., and others. "Mental Status Outcomes Following Carotid Endarterectomy: A Six-Month Analysis." *Journal of Clinical Neuropsychology,* 1983, *5*(4), 345-353.

Patenaude, A. F., Szymanski, L., and Rappeport, J. "Psychological Costs of Bone Marrow Transplantation in Children." *American Journal of Orthopsychiatry,* 1979, *49*(3), 409-422.

Payk-Rahiff, H., and Payk, T. R. ["Psychology of Patients with Pacemakers."] *Zeitschrift für Psychosomatische Medizin und Psychoanalyse,* 1978, *24*(4), 368-378.

Philip, A. E., Cay, E. L., Vetter, N. J., and Stuckey, N. A. "Short-Term Fluctuations in Anxiety in Patients with Myocardial Infarction." *Journal of Psychosomatic Research,* 1979, *23*(4), 277-280.

Philips, C. "Tension Headache: Theoretical Problems." *Behavior Research and Therapy,* 1978, *16*(4), 249-261.

Phillips, S., Seidenberg, M., Heald, F. P., and Friedman, S. B. "Health Professionals' Predictions of Teenagers' Preferences Regarding Chaperones During Physical Examinations." *Journal of Adolescent Health Care,* 1983, *4*(4), 241-245.

Plomin, R., and Foch, T. T. "Hyperactivity and Pediatrician Diagnoses, Parental Ratings, Specific Cognitive Abilities, and Laboratory Measures." *Journal of Abnormal Child Psychology,* 1981, *9*(1), 55-64.

Ramani, S. V., Quesney, L. F., Olson, D., and Gunnit, R. J. "Diagnosis of Hysterical Seizures in Epileptic Patients." *American Journal of Psychiatry*, 1980, *137*(6), 705–709.

Reisinger, J. J., and Lavigne, J. V. "An Early Intervention Model for Pediatric Settings." *Professional Psychology*, 1980, *11*(4), 582–590.

Roeske, N. C. "Quality of Life and Factors Affecting the Response to Hysterectomy." *Journal of Family Practice*, 1978, *7*(3), 483–488.

Rogentine, G. N., and others. "Psychological Factors in the Prognosis of Malignant Melanoma: A Prospective Study." *Psychosomatic Medicine*, 1979, *1*(8), 647–655.

Roth, P., Heffron, W., and Skipper, B. "Patient, Physician Problem Lists: A Comparative Study." *Family Practice Research Journal*, 1983, *2*(3), 164–170.

Schofield, W. "The Role of Psychology in the Delivery of Health Services." *American Psychologist*, 1969, *24*, 555–584.

Schofield, W. "Clinical Psychologists as Health Professionals." In G. C. Stone, F. Cohen, N. E. Adler, and Associates, *Health Psychology—a Handbook: Theories, Applications, and Challenges of a Psychological Approach to the Health Care System.* San Francisco: Jossey-Bass, 1979.

Seltzer, G. B. "Community Residential Adjustment: The Relationship Among Environment, Performance, and Satisfaction." *American Journal of Mental Deficiency*, 1981, *85*(6), 624–630.

Silvestre, D., and Fresco, N. "Reactions to Prenatal Diagnosis: An Analysis of 87 Interviews." *American Journal of Orthopsychiatry*, 1980, *50*(4), 610–617.

Singh, B. K., and Williams, J. S. "Attitudes and Behavioral Intentions About Abortion." *Population and Environment: Behavioral and Social Issues*, 1983, *6*(2), 84–95.

Smith, R. M., and others. "A Functional Scale of Recovery from Severe Head Trauma." *Clinical Neuropsychology*, 1979, *1*(3), 48–50.

Smith, W. L., and Duerksen, D. L. "Personality and the Relief of Chronic Pain: Predicting Surgical Outcome." *Clinical Neuropsychology*, 1979, *1*(3), 35–38.

Sobel, H. J., and Worden, J. W. "The MMPI as a Predictor of Psychosocial Adaptation to Cancer." *Journal of Consulting and Clinical Psychology*, 1979, *47*(4), 716-724.

Steidl, J. H., and others. "Medical Condition, Adherence to Treatment Regimens and Family Functioning: Their Interactions in Patients Receiving Long-Term Dialysis Treatment." *Archives of General Psychiatry*, 1980, *37*(9), 1025-1027.

Stokes, T. F., and Kennedy, S. H. "Reducing Child Uncooperative Behavior During Dental Treatment Through Modeling and Reinforcement." *American Journal of Applied Behavior Analysis*, 1980, *13*(1), 41-49.

Stone, A. A., and Neale, J. M. "Hypochondriasis and Tendency to Adopt the Sick Role as Moderators of the Relationship Between Life-Events and Somatic Symptomatology." *British Journal of Medical Psychology*, 1981, *54*(1), 75-81.

Stone, G. C. "Patient Compliance and the Role of the Expert." *Journal of Social Issues*, 1979a, *35*, 34-59.

Stone, G. C. "Psychology and the Health System." In G. C. Stone, F. Cohen, N. E. Adler, and Associates, *Health Psychology—a Handbook: Theories, Applications, and Challenges of a Psychological Approach to the Health Care System*. San Francisco: Jossey-Bass, 1979b.

Stone, G. C. "Training for Health Systems Research Consultation." In A. Broskowski, E. Marks, and S. H. Budman (eds.), *Linking Health and Mental Health*. Beverly Hills, Calif.: Sage, 1981.

Stone, G. C. "*Health Psychology:* A New Journal for a New Field." *Health Psychology*, 1982, *1*, 1-6.

Szasz, T. S., and Hollender, M. H. "A Contribution to the Philosophy of Medicine: The Basic Models of the Doctor-Patient Relationship." *Archives of Internal Medicine*, 1956, *97*, 585-592.

Taylor, C. B., Pfenninger, J. L., and Candelaria, T. "The Use of Treatment Contracts to Reduce Medicaid Costs of a Difficult Patient." *Journal of Behavior Therapy and Experimental Psychiatry*, 1980, *11*(1), 77-82.

Thurman, S. K., and Fiorelli, J. S. "Perspectives on Normalization." *Journal of Special Education*, 1979, *13*(3), 339-346.

Turner-Bonk, M. F., Penfield, A. J., and Driscoll, D. L. "Laparoscopic Sterilization at an Outpatient Clinic." *Public Health Reports,* 1978, *93*(1), 55–59.

Veatch, R. "Updating the Hippocratic Oath." *Medical Opinion,* 1972, *8,* 56–61.

Wakeman, R. J., and Kaplan, J. Z. "An Experimental Study of Hypnosis in Painful Burns." *American Journal of Clinical Hypnosis,* 1978, *21*(1), 3–12.

Wender, E. H., Palmer, F. B., Herbst, J. J., and Wender, P. H. "Behavioral Characteristics of Children with Chronic Nonspecific Diarrhea." *Annual Progress in Child Psychiatry and Child Development,* 1977, *10,* 455–467.

Winstead, D. K. "Filariasis Bancrofti and Chronic Illness Behavior." *Military Medicine,* 1978, *1143* (12), 869–871.

Wolkind, S., and Zajicek, E. "Psycho-Social Correlates of Nausea and Vomiting in Pregnancy." *Journal of Psychosomatic Research,* 1978, *22*(1), 1–5.

Wood, M. M. "The Perception of Symptoms: An Experimental Study of Breathlessness." *Australian Journal of Psychology,* 1980, *32*(1), 53–58.

Woodson, R. H., and da Costa-Woodson, E. M. "Covariates of Analgesia in a Clinical Sample and Their Effect on the Relationship Between Analgesia and Infant Behavior." *Infant Behavior and Development,* 1980, *3*(3), 205–213.

Wurster, C. A., Weinstein, P., and Cohen, A. J. "Communication Patterns in Pedodontics." *Perceptual and Motor Skills,* 1979, *48*(1), 159–166.

Zamir, N., and Shuber, E. "Altered Pain Perception in Hypertensive Humans." *Brain Research,* 1980, *201*(2), 471–474.

Zawatski, E., Katz, B., and Krekeler, K. "Perceived Needs and Satisfaction with Nursing Care by Spouses of Patients in the Coronary Care Unit." *Perceptual and Motor Skills,* 1979, *49*(1), 170.

Part Three

Economics
and Competition

Part Three describes ways that clinical psychologists can compete more effectively in the health care marketplace. Success will depend not only on competence but on market penetration. States traditionally have had sovereign roles in education, professional licensing, and insurance, all central to the future of clinical psychology. The renewed emphasis on state autonomy in recent years only highlights the necessity of having state-level statutory recognition as the basis for practice. Chapter Ten illustrates what can be accomplished, market by market, demonstrating the essential role of advocacy. The systemic changes underway in health care oblige practitioners to look ahead, plan for, and shape their future if they are to have one. Several viable and operational private-sector models for practice are described in Chapter Eleven: the California Psychological Health Plan, Biodyne Centers of America, the Delaware Valley Psychological Clinics, and Treatment Centers of America. Each is an organized entity that can network and contract in the marketplace to deliver a range of services.

Cost has become a major force in the reforms of health care now underway. We have entered an era of limits. The best at any cost is no longer affordable. The closer scrutiny of health care services is bringing heightened demands for evidence of effectiveness. The central role of cost as a force in reform is discussed and illustrated in Chapter Twelve. In Chapter Thirteen we conclude with an extensive consideration of new directions for clinical

245

practice and forces behind these changes. The heightened competition between and within professions, the shrinkage of solo practice, the increasing importance of health care as distinct from mental health care, the focus on therapeutic effectiveness with specific treatments for specific disorders—all are a part of the industrialization of health care and new market strategies.

The destiny of health care is no longer being left solely to practitioners. It is big business, and the laws of economics will apply. We have documented some of the great strides achieved by professional psychology today. We point also to the organized strategies necessary for effective competition if professional psychology is to continue into tomorrow to fulfill its potential as a major health care profession.

Herbert Dörken
Lewis G. Carpenter, Jr.

10

How State Legislation
Opens Markets for Practice

Most psychologists come to learn, during the years after graduation, that there are often opportunities for which they had no formal training. And most psychologists with an active clinical practice come to discover another irony: there are services they are competent to provide on an independent basis except that the law does not allow it or does not recognize them for reimbursement. The enterprising will view the former situations as solvable and will take steps to seize the opportunity. The latter quandaries, however, are not resolvable by individual initiative, training, or ability; they require statutory authorization and change.

Laws or regulations that limit or restrict psychological services are obvious barriers. When the law is silent regarding psychologists, however, that is not necessarily helpful or an open avenue. A principle of statutory construction, "Expressio unius est exclusio alterius," holds that what is not expressly included is excluded. The main barrier to progress is neither the restriction nor the lack of specification; it is the inertia within the profession to deal with a historical mass—the laws of the state—to come to know it, to use it to advantage when it is supportive, and to amend it when it is not (DeLeon and others, 1984). It is all there for anyone to know, to use, and to be guided by. We are a nation living under published and public law. Our laws, however, except in a few instances in recent years, were promulgated without any thought of or input from clinical psychology (DeLeon, 1984).

In an early attempt to describe the parameters of the effect of
state law, Dörken (1977b) noted that the effect does not simply come
directly from the passage of state law but from the interactive effect
of federal on state law, the enabling state regulations, and the
posture of the state administration. In an earlier book, Dörken and
associates (1976, chapters 3 to 5) gave an account of federal
legislation recognizing the practice of psychology and the advocacy
that was necessary to achieve it. In the same work, Shapiro, Dörken,
Rodgers, and Wiggins (1976) outlined some of the techniques for
achieving legislative success. The legislative process is a system, and
the many steps to be taken to "work the system" have also been
described (Dörken, 1981a), together with a summary of the gains
achieved in California in the 1979–80 biennium. Later in that year
Dörken (1981b) also described the laws and regulations and the set
of new laws achieved, recognizing the hospital practice of
psychology in the state, at the time a pioneering advance.

What underlies any such achievement, of course, is
determined advocacy, not simply by the legislative advocates but by
the supporting organization that they represent (Dörken, 1983a).
This support requires not only consensus so that there is a unity of
purpose (not always easy to achieve among psychologists) but also
funding both for expenses and for professional time (often difficult
to raise to a realistic level). Even by 1984, with ample evidence of
the fruits of such investment, the California State Psychological
Association (CSPA) still invested only minimally in its legislative
program.

DeLeon (1983) underscored the need to become involved if
one has any thought of changing or creating legislation and, with
others, outlined how public policy can be influenced (DeLeon,
O'Keefe, VandenBos, and Kraut, 1982) and how the training and
skills of psychologists can be applicable to the legislative process
(DeLeon, Frohboese, and Meyers, 1984). But he lamented how
transitory their involvement has been: "Although approximately
twenty-five psychologists have had the opportunity of serving on
congressional staffs during the past decade, only two individuals
have remained more than three years" (DeLeon, Frohboese, and
Meyers, 1984, p. 697).

There have been some accounts of legislation across the states. In 1967 the Committee on Legislation of the American Psychological Association sought to guide states in establishing or revising practice legislation by publishing a model for such actions ("A Model for State Legislation," 1967). From the passage of the first state licensing law for psychologists, in Connecticut in 1945, to the fiftieth, in Missouri in 1977, it took more than three decades before psychology could aver that its practitioners were licensable in all states. Clearly, the profession has not rushed into success, nor has it applied its research and communication skills with anywhere near the level of resolve or sophistication of which it is capable.

In 1970 Dörken sought to document the law and regulation base, bringing increased recognition to psychologists in positions of responsibility in public mental health services. Separate aspects have been summarized across the states, such as commitment procedures (Dörken, 1977a; Drude, 1978) and competency determination before the courts (Sobel, 1978). Sales and others of the law/psychology graduate training program at the University of Nebraska at Lincoln have sought to review implementation in the states of various federal laws, such as the Education for All Handicapped Children Act of 1975 (P.L. 94-142), and state laws as they delineate the role of psychologists in, for example, the disposition of sex offenders (Brunette and Sales, 1980). Dörken and Associates (1976) sought to document the recognition of clinical psychology under federal law at the time and under state insurance codes. Later, Dörken (1983b) provided an update on these state "freedom of choice" laws. He also described the very limited statutory base for worker's compensation (Dörken, 1979b) and hospital practice (Dörken and Webb, 1979; Dörken, Webb, and Zaro, 1982). For perhaps the most comprehensive current account of "laws affecting professional practice," see section V, by that title, in Sales (1983) and, of course, Chapter Five here by DeLeon, VandenBos, and Kraut.

A California Perspective

For close to twenty years CSPA has been active in the state legislature and state government, seeking its rightful place under

the California sun. The intensity of the effort and the amount of
resources devoted by CSPA have, with better appreciation of reality,
increased over recent years. We shall describe the entire legislative
history of psychological practice in California, giving emphasis to
the decade 1975–1984.

In early years the struggle was only to assure basic rights—
a license, confidentiality, some third-party reimbursement, and the
like. The effort, intense at times, tended to be single-purpose. It was
only a "one front at a time" battle because psychologists simply did
not perceive the whole territory. This meant that psychology
neither tried to move on several fronts nor was a target for others.
Life was simple and inexpensive. Psychologists' sphere of activity,
their influence, and their income were correspondingly small.

As time went on, CSPA expanded the role of California
psychologists, opening new opportunities—insurance reimbursement, Medi-Cal, nondiscrimination in county mental health,
worker's compensation (Dörken, 1981b), various forensic services,
hospital staff membership, mixed professional corporations, and
police psychology, to name only some of the more important. With
more opportunity came more psychologists. The number licensed
in California has grown apace (Dörken and Webb, 1981).
Concurrently, the number of faculty members involved in teaching
and training psychologists has also expanded and the subject matter
diversified.

What CSPA has accomplished is the envy of some, is being
copied by other associations, and is attracting growing resistance
from medicine and psychiatry. Yet, the future is bright. Every
psychologist, regardless of specialty or place, has benefited. The
advances of any segment of psychology have a ripple effect on all
other segments, be it in status or pay or jobs. And the same applies
to what is hurtful to any one segment. Momentum and recognition
in the legislature and administration have developed, and
psychology can now expect both to defend itself successfully and to
expand its condition. However, this requires a unity and continuity
of understanding and purpose by psychologists—qualities, alas,
that do not seem to be endemic to the species!

Today psychologists can be seen in places they did not dream of occupying fifteen years ago, began to perceive only a decade ago, and, in some settings, became broadly involved in only a few years ago. Some markets are still only under development.

These successes have come at a price. As more and more difficult and far-reaching measures are undertaken, it costs more money to run the necessary assertive legislative program, and psychology now finds itself frequently under attack by those who want some of its territory or by those who want to reduce or contain it. With any expansion of one health profession, interprofessional "turf" issues among the others intensify.

The message ought to be very clear. What you have today is not necessarily what you will have tomorrow. If you fail to protect your interests, you will see components of your practice legislated out of existence. The legislative process is a two-way game. You can win and you can lose. If you don't play, you can hardly win, but you can certainly lose.

In 1984 an Assembly Select Committee on Mental Health was formed and charged to review mental health services statewide and formulate major recommendations for change. The climate is one of bipartisan support for constructive change together with support of the administration. The extent to which psychology succeeds in presenting its case will determine the extent of its recognition as a health/mental health profession in mental health services, public and private, for years to come.

There are forty state senators and eighty members of the assembly and their staffs and an array of committees in both houses as well as majority and minority caucuses. There are, of course, the administration and all the government agencies and departments as well. Given such an armada, you find what you might expect—a lot of action.

In the 1983–84 biennium almost 6,400 bills were introduced. Given that bills, except urgency measures, can be introduced only during the first sixty days of the legislative year—nine weeks—they are introduced at an average rate of 400-plus a week. This is the prime time to identify bills which pose a threat, which are supportive, or which might be constructively amended. Unless you screen *all* bills, you will not know the extent to which you may be affected. From this screening, CSPA in recent years has usually followed some 100, taking active positions on about half. Each bill goes to its policy committee in its house of origin, and then, if it has fiscal implications for the state—and about three-quarters do—to a fiscal committee in that house, then to the floor and transfer to the other house, where the process is repeated, then back to the house of origin or conference if differences between houses must be reconciled, and then to the governor with power of veto. For fifty bills there are, then, 175 committee hearings to follow or at which to testify ($50 \times 2 + 50 \times .75 \times 2$) in a span of eight months. Obviously, to achieve the desired outcome, you must get at least a majority vote in your favor in each committee (average size, eleven). You may need to contact only 75 percent of the legislative committee members or their personal staffs on a bill. You always have to contact the committee staff. The contacts involved, then, come to over 1,600 in a year, not even including the occasions when you have to go back a second or third time ($175 \times 11 \times .75 + 175$)!

Another view of the complexity of the legislative process is provided by consideration of the government codes (laws) that you want to amend, add to, or delete. The various California codes, when shelved together in bound volumes, occupy a space seven and three-fourths feet wide by seven feet high. Some codes are not of concern to psychologists as a profession (for example, election, vehicle, and water codes). Others are more central, and legislation of concern to psychology frequently appears in bills affecting the Health and Safety Code, Insurance Code, Welfare and Institutions Code, Business and Professions Code, and Penal Code and at times the Civil Code, Code of Civil Procedure, Labor Code, Unemployment Insurance Code, Government Code, and Evidence Code. In summary, an effective legislative program is not a casual endeavor; it requires both knowledge and know-how—and a lot of legwork and contacts.

CSPA has had nineteen years of continuous representation in Sacramento, the state capital, although for the psychologists involved it was on a voluntary basis, except for expenses, until 1976. Since 1966 Carpenter has been a legislative advocate, joined by Dörken in 1973. The governmental action program of CSPA has been cheap, not only for what it has produced for psychologists but also compared with what other health professions spend in like efforts. Even in 1984, CSPA devoted less than 15 percent ($62,700) of the association's budget to legislative advocacy (Dörken, 1983a).

With occasional legal consultation and expert supportive testimony, the authors have conducted essentially all the direct lobbying to carry CSPA's legislative program from 1974 through 1984. Over this period, Dörken drafted twenty-one of the CSPA bills enacted into law.

Until 1976 CSPA's legislative pace was essentially a single bill in some years. In that year an annual proactive program designed to open up new markets for practice was implemented. During the nine years from 1966 through 1974, CSPA had gained passage of six bills, and over the 1975–1984 decade, twenty-six more of its bills were enacted into law, not to mention the many constructive amendments gained in other bills. This has yielded a very substantial cumulative effect, not only establishing psychology's presence before the legislature but materially opening and expanding areas of practice. It is fair to say that generally the practice of psychology in California lags behind the scope of its legislation. Perhaps the clearest way to delineate its scope is by topic.

Licensing

In 1967 a licensure law with a definition of *practice* was enacted (S.B. 1158–Beilenson, chapter 1677) to replace the certification law of 1957. Since then CSPA has sought to strengthen its licensing law. This has meant adding elements to practice, such as behavior therapy and biofeedback (A.B. 3618–Duffy, chapter 734, 1976), and increasing qualifications, such as an M.A. degree for psychological assistants. The definition of *fee* was broadened from any charge, monetary or otherwise, to include "whether paid directly or paid on a prepaid or capitation basis by a third party, or a charge assessed by a facility for services rendered" (S.B. 2105–Stull, chapter 1208, 1978). Then, under A.B. 1072 (Rosenthal), chapter 955, 1979, acts of sexual abuse or relations with a client became cause for suspension or revocation of license. Further grounds for denial or revocation of license were added in 1982 (A.B.

2199–Frizelle, chapter 462), and the Psychology Examining Committee was empowered to seek injunction of the unlicensed practice of psychology. The Psychology Licensing Law provides for the licensing not only of individuals but also of corporations. A 1977 amendment (S.B. 629–Presley, chapter 1126) enabled physicians to practice medicine in a psychology corporation provided their shares or memberships are always less than 50 percent. A comparable amendment was made to the Medical Practices Act enabling psychologists to practice their profession in a medical corporation. Four years later provision was made for the establishment of mixed-profession corporations (A.B. 845–Moorhead, chapter 621) so that not only physicians but also podiatrists, nurses, and optometrists could practice their profession within a psychological corporation. Traditionally, professional corporations have been unidisciplinary. But this innovative legislation, believed to be a first among states, sought to enable the delivery of comprehensive health care through a psychological corporation or corporations of the other named professions, positioning the profession to be competitive in the trend to shift from the solo practitioner to organized entities. Psychologists have taken little advantage of this opportunity.

CSPA has striven to make application of the licensing law broader. Until 1979 the public sector was exempt, but with enactment of S.B. 230 (Carpenter), chapter 996, state and local health facilities must meet the same licensing standards as private health facilities, eliminating this dual standard of care too widely prevalent across the country and thereby clarifying and expanding upon the single, statewide, all services standard, public or private, that was first introduced the prior year (S.B. 212, chapter 321, 1978). Psychologists providing direct mental health care or working in a facility providing direct mental health care must be licensed; this includes not only hospitals and nursing homes but also the entire Short-Doyle (community mental health) program and student health services. In 1984 this principle was applied to the California Youth Authority and the Department of Corrections (S.B. 1621–Torres, chapter 1123).

Within the Psychology Licensing Law, CSPA sought to establish a definition and title protection for the "clinical psychologist" specialty in 1981. The legislature agreed that it would be helpful to clients to be able to identify among the licensees those with clinical experience, but the governor vetoed the bill, no matter that, under another code relating to hospital practice, clinical psychologists were already defined in state law.

The mandate of training by the legislature rather than the professions (which tend to resent and oppose it) is not entirely new. Back in 1976, psychologists and other psychotherapists except physicians found that as of July 1979 they would be required to have ten contact hours of training in human sexuality as a condition of licensure (A.B. 4178-Vasconcellos, chapter 1433). Physicians found later that they were required to have training in human nutrition, and in 1984, S.B. 1796 (Rosenthal), chapter 1149, sought to require thirty contact hours of training in alcoholism for all health professions as a condition of licensure or relicensure. Generated by the public concern over the extent of alcoholism, drunk drivers, industrial accidents, and familial strife, the bill was nonetheless opposed by CSPA in its original form on the grounds that the profession, not the legislature, should determine the content of professional training. The outcome requires those matriculating after August 1985 to have "completed training in the detection and treatment of alcohol and other chemical substance dependency." It would be prudent for university and professional school training programs to take cognizance of these new mandated training requirements.

In 1983 the Psychology Examining Committee sponsored a bill to mandate thirteen contact hours of training in cross-cultural issues as a condition of licensure or relicensure. On CSPA objection, A.B. 1637 (Harris) was amended to apply only to new licensees and to take effect only in 1985. The bill was later vetoed by the governor.

The mounting public concern about and reports of child abuse have culminated in legislation introduced in 1985 (A.B. 141-Molina) to require that for any physician, psychologist, clinical social worker, or marriage, family, and child counselor to be licensed or relicensed after January 1, 1986, evidence will be required of a minimum of ten contact hours of training in child-abuse assessment and reporting completed after 1982. As other special problems emerge, legislators may well again seek a training mandate for the professions involved.

Insurance

CSPA sought recognition for third-party reimbursement for covered benefits under health insurance and gained passage of A.B. 111 (Ryan), chapter 296, in 1969. Not until after the fact was it understood that the Insurance Code section amended applied only to the indemnity benefit plans of the commercial (for profit) health insurance industry, the disability (health) policies. Progressively it became apparent that we would need to gain recognition for psychologists under all types of "health insurance," actually prepaid health care coverage.

This has required a long-term and persistent strategy, and it has been a difficult road to travel, as it has been opposed by the other underwriters, the state, and the California Medical Association. It was not until five years after Ryan that the "freedom of choice" principle was extended to the self-insured employee welfare benefit plans (since preempted by ERISA), nonprofit hospital service plans (including Blue Cross, the largest single underwriter in the state), and health care service plans (Blue Shield and health maintenance organizations such as Kaiser) in S.B. 2002 (Petris), chapter 958, 1974. Before that psychologists were qualified under Medi-Cal (Medicaid) through chapter 577, 1971, in A.B. 949 and retained in all subsequent amendments such as S.B. 970 (Gregorio), chapter 1005, 1975, and A.B. 4431 (Rosenthal), chapter 914, 1976, for outpatient services. Through A.B. 991 (Ingalls), chapter 913, 1975, prepaid health plans offering mental health services (California has mandated availability—mental health services must be offered—not mandated mental health coverage) are to "provide the services of a psychologist and psychiatrist" such that the "enrollee may be seen initially by either a physician or a psychologist." But there seems almost no end to the loose ends requiring attention.

In 1980, S.B. 1811 (Carpenter), chapter 1235, was passed, requiring all health care service plans, including individual practice associations (IPAs) that offer mental health benefits, to make reasonable efforts to make available to their members the services of licensed psychologists. Largely, the law has been ignored, indeed even defied by some IPAs. Thus, CSPA was pleased to support A.B. 2947 (Bane), chapter 977, in 1984, requiring that any health care service plan that negotiates or enters into a contract with professional providers to provide services at alternative rates shall give "reasonable consideration to timely written proposals for affiliation" from all nonmedical professional providers and, likewise, proposals for "contracting" by professional providers with disability insurers and nonprofit hospital service plans. Now, in 1985, the same author has introduced legislation (A.B. 526) so that the provisions of chapter 977, 1984, would apply to *every* health care service plan, disability insurer, or nonprofit hospital service plan. Passive and not-so-passive resistance can continue beyond legislation designed to correct it. Eventually the message gets across.

Policies or plans written or issued for delivery in California are one thing, those from out of state quite another. Out-of-state policies/plans such as those in national or regional coverage had typically refused reimbursement to psychologists for service to California residents even when they paid for physician services, arguing that they were not bound by California FOC law or that the California psychologist was not licensed in their state. Although several states, such as Massachusetts, New Jersey, and Ohio, have managed to gain extraterritorial legislation so that their law applies to covered residents regardless of the state of issue, such a proviso is usually strongly opposed by the insurance industry. The compromise enacted in California (S.B. 693–Petris, chapter 558, 1981) deems a reciprocal intent to recognize psychological services among all states (currently thirty-nine, covering about 92 percent of the national population) having direct-recognition or freedom-of-choice laws.

CSPA also supported S.B. 940 in 1983 (McCorquodale, chapter 1259), requiring all forms of group "health insurance" to communicate to their policy holders or members the availability of outpatient coverage for nervous and mental disorders. Then, although legislation enacted in 1978 created a new class of health facility, the psychiatric health facility, or PHF (twenty-four-hour residential, acute care nonhospital), which requires clinical psychologists in the basic services, the state had failed to write the impending regulations by 1984. Catch-22: no regulations, no private sector PHF could apply for license; no license, no recognition for third-party reimbursement. CSPA accordingly was pleased to support S.B. 2160 (Garamendi), enacted in 1984 as chapter 1367, so that where policies/plans provide coverage for inpatient mental health services in a hospital, they shall cover services in a PHF.

Every year, it seems, new arrangements emerge to deny payment for psychologist claims in some form or another. They have to be addressed. The complexities of "health insurance" are discussed at greater length in Dörken (1983b).

Disability evaluation and health care under worker's compensation is an entirely separate jurisdiction in most states and in California is regulated under the Labor Code, not the Health and Safety or Insurance Code. Nor is it served by the disability (health) carriers, but rather by insurers in the casualty/liability field and the State Compensation Fund. Until a compensation settlement is awarded, the health/medical care coverage provided under worker's compensation is typically more extensive (all necessary health and medical care in California) than under health insurance and is without the deductibles and copayments common in the latter. The size of this market was at two-thirds the premium volume of all accident and health insurance in California in 1976 and growing at a faster rate. All employed persons must be covered.

Few states have gained recognition for psychologists in this very major market. Only Montana (1971) and Ohio (1974) had gained recognition in worker's compensation before enactment of S.B. 311 (Carpenter) in 1977 as chapter 1168. The recognition in Montana, however, was gained through its provider freedom of choice legislation, while, by negotiation, psychologists in Ohio gained recognition in their state compensation fund. Thus, S.B. 311 was the first legislation to gain direct statutory revision of worker's compensation law, in this case, the Labor Code. (For a more extensive discussion of worker's compensation, see Dörken, 1979b.)

This recognition was not easy to achieve. Four previous attempts in California had failed, three in committee and one by gubernatorial veto. In 1977 the bill was finally supported by the administration through the Division of Industrial Accidents and by the California Applicants' Attorneys Association (trial lawyers, who had established favorable court law), the United Farm Workers, and the California State Firemen's Association. The Association of California Insurance Companies (as distinct from the Association of California Life Insurance Companies, whose members underwrite disability/health insurance) finally concurred that psychologists meeting standards more stringent than licensure (licensure plus doctorate plus two years' clinical experience in a recognized health setting) would be amended into the definition of *physician*. By cross-reference this new recognition also applied to disability evaluation under the state Unemployment Insurance Code. In 1985, psychologists in Hawaii gained recognition as "health care providers" along with physicians and others in a broad revision of the state's worker's compensation law (HRS, 386-1).

Thus, California has gone well beyond the direct-recognition or freedom-of-choice law for health insurance and has a recognized role in the federal/state medical assistance program (Medicaid) and in the casualty/liability insurance field under worker's compensation and unemployment. Additionally, a Participating Providers' Agreement was negotiated and implemented with Blue Shield of California in 1978, which also applies to the new Blue Shield Preferred Plan, first offered in 1984.

Under cost containment pressures, both the federal and state governments have, especially lately, been pressing for prepaid and capitated coverage under health maintenance organizations for Medicare and Medicaid beneficiaries. Within this fast-developing category is the individual practice association, typically a federation of physicians forming a group practice and offering a prepaid health plan, often developed with input from the county medical society. Pressure is mounting from the administration in California to have Medi-Cal patients served by capitated health systems.

In 1974 the Waxman-Duffy Prepaid Health Plan Act (A.B. 586–Waxman, chapter 983) included psychological services within provisions allowing the director of health to contract with single-service prepaid health plans. As a harbinger of events to come, this act enabled the director to require that services be provided on an "at risk" basis. While this legislation made provisions for Medicaid, it did open a new concept for health care delivery in the state. Specialized health care service plans of optometry, dentistry, and psychology began to emerge.

Initially sponsored by CSPA's Division of Clinical and Professional Psychology, the California Psychological Health Plan (CPHP) gained its license as a single-purpose (specialized) health care service plan under the Knox-Keene Law in 1976. Although it reimburses its participating providers as a preferred provider organization on a uniform contracted fee-for-service basis and requires peer review, its revenue is received on a capitated basis of a fixed dollar amount prepaid monthly per family or per employee beneficiary regardless of use. As of October 1985 CPHP was providing outpatient mental health coverage for about 200,000 lives under multiple contracts with such employers as cities, school districts, and private corporations. It is, we believe, the first operational psychological IPA in the country.

It will behoove psychologists in the near future to develop service delivery organizations in other states, even nationally, since it is expected that solo practice will soon be seriously undercut, if it does not all but vanish, in the industrialization of health care (Dörken, 1983a). It is therefore of great importance that psychologists have access to all prepaid health plans, preferred provider organizations, individual practice associations (IPAs, a type of HMO), and any other organization that delivers mental or behavioral health services. It is not acceptable that mental health services in an IPA or other organization be delivered only through a psychiatrist, as gatekeeper, who may or may not refer, abrogating patient choice of provider while restraining the practice of psychology, whether under the guise of quality control or monopoly protection.

Forensic Practice

Until 1974 psychologists in California were scarcely aware of forensic practice. Of course, they read in the newspapers of psychiatric testimony, but there was no basis for participation by psychologists. Beginning with that year, CSPA's legislative planning laid out a strategy to include forensic mental health, competency determination, disability evaluation, commitment, and the like as part of the recognized practice of psychologists. Codes were searched and legislative tactics developed, and for the past ten years CSPA has sponsored forensic legislation and, by amendment, included psychologists in such legislation of other parties. Now, few significant segments remain for which psychologists do not qualify under the Penal Code and the several related civil codes. Many psychologists now make a large part of their living from this work, which was unthinkable ten years ago.

Contrary to the stories about "Murphy's Law," while A.B. 1529 (Murphy), chapter 154, 1974, was in final makeup, CSPA gained a parity amendment under the Penal Code so that when there is a question of mental competence in a criminal proceeding, the court shall appoint a psychiatrist or licensed psychologist. In any case where "the defendant is not seeking a finding of mental incompetence, the court shall appoint two psychiatrists, licensed psychologists, or a combination thereof." This provision established a pattern for future amendments of the law.

In 1976 A.B. 4285 (Brown), chapter 1101, recognized psychologists on parity with psychiatrists in the evaluation of mentally disordered sex offenders (MDSOs), and in the next year under S.B. 1178 (Presley), chapter 164, the court was enabled to appoint the "necessary psychologists or psychiatrists" when MDSO defendants had pleaded not guilty by reason of insanity or diminished capacity in criminal proceedings. The Berman bill of 1978, however, A.B. 3665, chapter 391, brought more comprehensive recognition to "court psychologists" and really established the basis of their court practice. When any defendant in a felony case pleads not guilty by reason of insanity, "the court must select and appoint two, and may select and appoint three, psychiatrists, or licensed psychologists . . . to examine the defendant and investigate his sanity." Additionally, for certification of mental disorder under civil commitment (involuntary hospital admission), two signatures are required. The first must be the professional person in charge of the agency or facility providing the evaluation services "or his designee." The designee must be a physician or licensed psychologist, while the second person must be a physician (psychiatrist if possible) or a licensed psychologist. Thus, the two signatures may be those of psychologists, physicians, or a combination (remember the Murphy bill). For a person to be recertified in the facility providing the fourteen-day intensive treatment, the same two-signature certification process is repeated.

CSPA had adopted as policy a definition of *forensic psychologist* substantially more stringent than licensure, on the thesis that where life or personal liberty is at stake, the task warrants an advanced level of competence. This standard—licensure, doctoral degree in psychology, and "at least five years of postgraduate experience" (since interpreted by the attorney general as postdoctorate) "in the diagnosis and treatment of emotional and mental disorders"—was introduced throughout the Berman bill for the first time. Thus, without amending the generic licensing law, that bill established a specialty standard in the Penal Code and Welfare and Institutions Code, since extended to the Code of Civil Procedure, Civil Code, and so on.

Additionally, the Berman bill provided that the judge shall appoint not fewer than two or more than three clinical psychologists or psychiatrists to make a personal examination of an alleged mentally disordered sex offender directed toward determining whether the person is an MDSO. In the next year, Berman (A.B. 122, chapter 245) amended another law to ensure that actions brought for the purpose of declaring any person under the age of eighteen free from the custody of one or both parents because of their inability to support or control the child due to their "mental deficiency or mental illness" shall be based on the testimony of two psychiatrists or qualified psychologists.

Ordinarily, the privilege resides with the patient in a psychotherapist/patient relationship. However, in enabling minors over twelve to directly consent to mental health treatment, A.B. 657 (Imbrecht), chapter 657, 1979, conveyed the privilege to the therapist, amending the Evidence Code to this effect. Involvement of the minor's parent/guardian is encouraged, unless in the opinion of the therapist it would be inappropriate.

In 1980 S.B. 1688 (Maddy), chapter 1206, further advanced psychology's standing before the court when it enabled the court, in a civil action where a person's mental condition is in controversy, to order a mental examination by a physician or clinical psychologist. This amendment has an interesting history. CSPA had not been aware that only a physician could be called in such a civil proceeding until the American Psychiatric Association, in an *amicus* brief in 1979, cited a case in San Diego County in which a psychologist, not being a physician, could not be recognized by the court. It was helpful to learn of this anomaly and be able to rectify it in the next year!

The Maddy bill also provided that the probation officer shall furnish the court-appointed psychiatrists *and* psychologists pertinent information of the circumstances surrounding a crime and the prior record and history of a person at issue. Further, it recognizes that a qualified psychologist may have provided the intensive treatment of a person detained for court-ordered involuntary treatment.

In 1980 the mounting public concern over child abuse prompted legislative action. S.B. 781 (Rains), chapter 1071, was the first to be enacted in what by 1985 became a torrent of bills. The Rains bill mandated the reporting of child abuse by both medical and nonmedical practitioners. Psychologists, after some continued advocacy, were listed in the "medical" class. However, the Penal Code had defined *child* as a person under eighteen years of age and *sexual assault* as unlawful intercourse with an unmarried person under that age. It quickly became apparent to the practitioners who had to report and the child protective services receiving an inundation of reports that in this respect, at least, the new law was behind the times. Given the extent to which young men and women of high school age had become sexually active, it became necessary to lower the age for intercourse, as an offense, to under fourteen. Thus, heterosexual intercourse was deleted from the Code, as a form of sexual assault, on an urgency basis in 1981 (S.B. 322-Rains, chapter 29). A.B. 518 (Kapiloff), chapter 435, 1981, made further clarifications in the immunity from liability of those reporting and the confidentiality of the reports. With the mandated reporting, some televised and scandalous court suits and other media reports have occurred regarding incest, pornographic photography, and molestation by child-care custodians. The extent of the problem brought to front-page news led to a torrent of new child-abuse bills in 1984 and 1985. Fines are being increased and abuse conditions clarified to an extent too detailed to review here.

The ability to determine whether parents were incapable of supporting their child was accorded to psychologists for determinations made in-state back in 1979 (A.B. 122–Berman, above), but recognition of the profession to make such decisions on an out-of-state basis was not achieved until S.B. 14 (Presley), chapter 978, in 1982.

Authority for psychologists to undertake a rather more dramatic competency determination was initiated by the sole physician legislator with an amendment from CSPA. A.B. 3522 (Filante), enacted as chapter 1183 in 1982, enables the licensing board of any healing arts profession to order an examination by one or more physicians or psychologists when any licensee appears unable to safely practice his or her profession because of impairment due to mental illness.

The other end of the abuse continuum is elder abuse. CSPA supported S.B. 1210 (Carpenter), chapter 1273, when it mandated the reporting of elder abuse by psychologists as medical practitioners, among many others, in 1983. Neglect, as one index of abuse, included failure to provide for the mental health needs of an elder. It is grounds for reporting, then, when a practitioner reasonably suspects that mental suffering has been inflicted on an elder. The extent of the mandated reporting, determinate sentencing, and the like may be viewed as part of a public swing toward being more conscious of the rights of victims than of perpetrators.

Controversy has surrounded the use of hypnosis-induced recall in the courts. A.B. 2669 (Sher), chapter 479, 1984, would permit such recall before a court if the hypnosis had been performed by a licensed physician or psychologist.

Even before passage of S.B. 147 (Petris) as chapter 188, 1983, some 72 percent of police departments in California had psychologists on staff or under contract. To the extent that they were evaluating the mental condition of applicant or entrant peace officers, however, such evaluation was not authorized by law. S.B. 147 corrected this in requiring that a "peace officer" shall be found to be free from any emotional or mental condition that might adversely affect the exercise of the powers of the office as determined by a physician or licensed psychologist meeting specified standards. Although we may think of "peace officers" as members of police departments, sheriffs' offices, and the highway patrol, the number of classes so designated by the state has proliferated in recent years to include over eighteen personnel classes, such as state park rangers, airport safety inspectors, and foresters. In effect, this legislation has formally opened up and given further impetus to the rapidly developing new field of police psychology. It also carried a minor amendment to the Penal Code such that the sentence of any person convicted of a lewd act with a child under fourteen shall not be suspended until the court first obtains a report from a "reputable" psychiatrist or psychologist.

Health Facility Practice

Before 1978, psychologists' practice in health facilities was limited to that of employee status or, for a very few, minimal clinical functions at the pleasure of the medical staff on an informal basis. Psychologists had no formal rights either to practice or to sit on policy committees of the hospital or other health facility. Further, psychologists treating patients on an outpatient office basis were essentially compelled to surrender their patients to a psychiatrist when the patients required hospitalization.

It became clear to CSPA that these limitations constituted both an economic and a professional liability, and a long-term legislative strategy was developed to resolve the problem. The difficulties of accomplishing this soon became apparent. Opposition from the medics was expected, health facilities being their castles, and this occurred. But opposition from numerous other quarters, such as the hospital association, health plans, and state administrative rulings, was not expected to such an extent, and the combined opposition was formidable.

Gaining state law to recognize the hospital practice of psychology in California was no overnight task. After nine years of planning and preparation, including a preliminary failure in 1975, S.B. 259 (Carpenter) passed in May 1978 as chapter 116. A landmark among state laws regarding the practice of psychology, it defined *clinical psychologists* for purposes of hospital practice, enabling their appointment to the *professional* staff on determination by the health facility. Two years later, this permissive legislation was strengthened (S.B. 1443–Carpenter, chapter 735). The law now "may enable the appointment . . . [to] the *medical* staff" (emphasis supplied). Nothing shall require a facility to offer a particular health service, but "if a health service is offered by a health facility with both licensed physicians . . . and clinical psychologists on the medical staff, which both . . . are authorized by law to perform, such service may be performed by either, without discrimination." Thus, S.B. 259 was permissive and S.B. 1443 nondiscriminatory legislation, a significant distinction, as we shall see later.

This legislation played a part in obliging the Joint Commission on Accreditation of Hospitals (1979) to revise its medical staff standards to broaden medical staff membership beyond physicians so that it may include other licensed individuals permitted by law and by the hospital to provide patient care services independently. The matter is by no means finished, as psychologists still do not have the full status and privileges they warrant. Meanwhile, health facilities are authorized to grant staff membership and clinical privileges to psychologists. The attorney general has ruled that this may include admitting and in-hospital independent practice within the scope of the psychology license. In practice, health facilities will require, at minimum, a physician having the ultimate responsibility for the medical aspects of patient care. Thus, medical collaboration in admission is required. However, by amendment to the Nurse Practice Act, A.B. 2002 (Moorhead), chapter 406, 1980, made it possible for nurses to implement a treatment regimen ordered by a clinical psychologist. The complex interplay among vested interest, law, and resolution in this matter in California is summarized through 1980 in Dörken (1981a). But the issues continue.

Legislation enabling the appointment of psychologists to the medical staff is a local option to which many hospitals have reacted negatively. Broad resistance is illustrated by Blue Cross. In marketing its Prudent Buyer plan to hospitals throughout the state, it has sought to contract with physicians and has also allowed dentists and podiatrists to contract. But for several years it has steadfastly refused to contract with psychologists—and has even attempted to persuade some they are better off without a contract. This refusal has even applied to psychologists who are members of the active medical staff. Beginning in January 1986, Blue Cross officials have promised that contracts will be available to psychologists who are staff members, but nothing is in writing. Legal action may well be necessary.

Passing legislation is one thing; getting the regulations necessary to implement the law can be something else. It is the regulations under Title 22 of the California Administrative Code that set forth the specifics and standards for health facility licensure. The original legislation had become law in May 1978. Under increasing pressure from psychology and the bill author, the director of the Department of Health Services finally sent a circular notice to all hospitals and other health facilities in July 1981, directing their attention to the provisions of law (which override regulation) and the fact that facility licensing regulations would need to be changed to "harmonize" with the statutes, specifically citing the regulation by which only a psychiatrist can be responsible for the diagnostic formulation and individual treatment plan. A public hearing on the proposed regulations was not held until April 1982. As presented, those regulations did provide that a psychiatrist or clinical psychologist could be responsible for the diagnosis and treatment plan.

The California Medical Association (CMA) and the California Psychiatric Association (CPA), which had lost the battle in the legislature, opened fire, claiming unwarranted expansion of practice, gross interference with facility administration, the quality of patient care would be jeopardized, psychologists were not competent to assume such responsibilities, and so on. Moreover, their attorneys sent out "instructional" memoranda to all hospital administrators. Physicians by the hundreds wrote letters of complaint and concern to the Department of Health Services (all of which had to be answered). At the eleventh hour, just before transfer of the amended regulations to the agency responsible for their adoption, psychology was removed from the diagnosis and treatment planning regulation, and the somewhat castrated regulations were adopted on February 12, 1983, almost five years after passage of the law. The regulatory change was not all that could reasonably be expected, but it did include some very positive gains. The new regulations acknowledged that in hospitals psychologists may be allowed to admit their patients and that licensure and degree cannot be used as a basis for determining level of membership in the medical staff or denying voting or other rights.

The response from psychology was twofold. CSPA submitted legislation enabling psychologists to independently perform these two functions in keeping with their licensure, while the California Association of Psychology Providers (CAPP) filed suit against the department. CSPA's bill cleared the Senate in 1983 and its Assembly committees in bitterly contested and heavily lobbied hearings but was finally tied up on the assembly floor by the CMA and became a two-year bill. CSPA made a concerted effort to directly lobby all eighty members of the Assembly but let the bill die in August 1984 when a majority vote of forty-one could not be guaranteed. (The last head count was thirty-nine for, though several seemed equivocal; seventeen opposed; two would "take a walk" (be absent); and the balance, twenty-two, would not commit.) The odds were favorable but not certain, and CSPA concluded that a loss would jeopardize the CAPP suit.

After review of the complaint, both the department and CAPP moved for a summary judgment (decision on the legal questions) before the California Superior Court. In June CPA sought to enter the lawsuit as an *amicus curiae,* but CAPP succeeded in persuading the court to deny the CPA motion. On July 30, 1985, the Los Angeles Superior Court overturned the Title 22 regulations in question and ordered the department to write new regulations within sixty days.

The word *may* in the context of S.B. 1443 allows two interpretations. Physicians have been inclined to view it as a basis for excluding psychologists from the medical staff, and therefore the nondiscriminatory provisions would simply not apply. The intent was quite different: that discrimination is not permitted where services may be provided by clinical psychologists or physicians. The facility does not have to offer a particular service, but if it offers one that both psychologists and physicians can legally provide, then the nondiscriminatory provisions apply. For instance, despite the law, the Department of Health Services, which licenses hospitals, had steadfastly refused to revise the regulations giving authority to formulate diagnoses or treatment plans solely to psychiatrists (in psychiatric facilities or units). By Superior Court action in July 1985, the department was obliged to issue emergency regulations effective November 12, 1985, which gave to both psychiatrists and clinical psychologists the responsibility of diagnosing and formulating treatment plans.

While the new regulations state clearly that clinical psychologists can be responsible for diagnosis and treatment planning, it is also expected that the CMA/CPA will introduce legislation in 1986 to restrict psychological practice in hopsitals and nursing facilities, if not excluding psychologists from the medical staff altogether. Further, it is expected that CSPA will introduce legislation clearly mandating psychological practice, with full participation, in all health facilities.

We have elaborated on this issue at some length because it is fundamental to psychology as an autonomous health profession and because it illustrates well the forces and complexities involved when you tackle a major issue. But tackle such issues psychology must. For another account of the level of professional mobilization and resources required to have psychology amended into the hospital licensing law in the District of Columbia, see Tanney (1984), a splendid effort and succinct account.

Two other developments related to health facilities are of note. In 1978, S.B. 1496 (Gregorio), chapter 1234, described in Chapter Eleven, created a new class of health facility with CSPA support, the psychiatric health facility, which mandates clinical psychologists in its basic services. The psychology clinic made possible by A.B. 2409 (Bates), chapter 1315, 1980, was also recognized as a new category of health facility, one to be directed by a clinical psychologist. Psychology clinics may provide services in the home when related to those at the clinic. Psychological assistants can be employed by these clinics, and, of course, clinic services may be vendorized, thus providing a nonprofit entity from which to deliver mental health services.

Clinical Practice

Clinical practice can exist without necessary relation to hospitals, courts, or insurance as previously discussed. CSPA has consistently sought to broaden the scope of psychological practice and to be alert to new markets. Previously described was the legislation enabling the formation of a mixed-profession psychological corporation on a for-profit model and the nonprofit psychological clinic as a state-licensed health facility. CSPA supported A.B. 1406 (Bates), chapter 478, 1979, which exempts speech and hearing clinics from facility licensure laws if all patients are referred by a physician, dentist, or psychologist. In fact, CSPA also supported S.B. 1418 (Alquist), chapter 454, 1980. This law broadened the exemption from clinic licensure from five designated professions to any place "operated as a clinic or office by one or more licensed health care practitioners and used as an office for the practice of their profession." Support had also been given to S.B. 1394 (Beverly), chapter 1297, 1978, enabling professional societies, including psychological associations, to establish and provide a referral service at no charge and to be exempt from liability from its operation.

While supporting improved standards in the public sector, CSPA has usually encouraged the privatization of health care and the contracting out of specified services. Consistent with this policy, CSPA supported the Right to Compete Act of 1979, A.B. 210 (Goggin), enacted as chapter 653. Under guidelines of integrity and accuracy, this act encouraged the freedom of price and product advertising of health services.

Efforts by many to mandate benefits for the treatment of alcoholism have not succeeded. However, in 1984 CSPA supported a compromise that required employers of twenty-five or more persons to "reasonably accommodate" any employee wishing to voluntarily enter and participate in an alcoholic rehabilitation program (A.B. 2490–Agnos, chapter 1103).

The passage of A.B. 3480 (Robinson) in 1982 as chapter 329 set off a chain reaction that is being heard around the country. By giving insurers the authorization to negotiate and enter into contracts with professional providers charging "alternative" or reduced/discounted rates, the legislature gave impetus to preferred provider organizations (PPOs) and conveyed its intent to dramatically change the rates for health services and how they are paid. Practitioners of any profession committed to solo independent practice were essentially eclipsed, as corporations and major practice groups are staffed not only to negotiate contracts but to deliver volume services on a twenty-four-hour basis. Thus, the new law provided fertile ground for the formation of organized entities. Repeated efforts by the California Medical Association, together with CSPA in some instances, to rescind or undo A.B. 3480, were shot out of the water by the combined opposition of management, the unions, government (state and local), elder citizen groups, and others. The mere sight of such extensive opposition was usually sufficient to have committees take such bills off the calendar and not even bring them to a vote. The CMA even did all that it could with political action funds to unseat one of the authors in the 1984 elections, but he was reelected. The provisions of A.B. 3480 are here for the foreseeable future and will spread across the country. By joining with other provider groups, however, CSPA is having some success with amendments to assure the participation not just of physicians but of other providers willing to participate, as in the Bane legislation referred to earlier (A.B. 2947, 1984). This may be the silver lining.

Increasingly, peer review has become an added aspect of clinical practice. Though heralded as a means of achieving quality control—and it will usually weed out the very few grossly incompetent or fraudulent practitioners—it is more commonly implemented with the objective of utilization control. However controversial, psychologists generally agree that if it is undertaken, it should be done by peers. The peers, though, want immunity from liability for their actions. Accordingly, CSPA supported bills extending immunity to psychologists on hospital review panels and, beyond peer review committees, to their professional society (A.B. 2700–Alatorre, chapter 705, 1982, and A.B. 463–Alatorre, chapter 1081, 1983).

Public Services

CSPA's effort has long been concerned with and involved in mitigating the relatively dependent condition of the psychologist in the public sector. Such psychologists are employees, working under salary schedules and rules of various agencies over which they have little influence. It follows that the legislation successfully accomplished and attempted for public-sector services has been quite different in character from that in other areas.

S.B. 1560 (Petris), chapter 726, 1978, CSPA-initiated, was the culmination of eight years of effort and three prior bills by the same author. As the several laws now stand, psychologists in local mental health services and in state hospitals cannot be denied any administrative, professional, or technical position for which their training and competence qualify them. Moreover, positions of responsibility must be "equally open" to the several mental health professions, whether program director or chief of local mental health services or program director within a state hospital. An exception is hospital director of a state hospital for the mentally disordered. The hospital director of a state hospital for the developmentally disabled may be (and is in two of them) a psychologist. Indeed, the Department of Developmental Disabilities in the former administration was directed by a psychologist, and the clinical director of Napa State Hospital, the largest and most complex state hospital program in the state, is also a psychologist.

CSPA's legislative strategy in this sector aims to raise salaries and to create a higher status and a more independent function within the institutions. The tactics for these goals are to broaden the scope of practice (for example, to program direction), to force salary setters to recognize and pay for higher functions, to recognize career-ladder opportunities, to modify the rules for health facility organizations, enabling medical staff membership and clinical privileges (see "Health Facility Practice"), to upgrade qualification requirements, to defend against persons with lesser job titles performing the work of psychologists, and to move psychology into the medical classifications encompassing physicians, dentists, and podiatrists. The collective thrust of establishing more and higher standards is to promote higher classification and salary differentials, with higher ceilings, based on more complex services. This will be a long struggle, with the unionization of state employees in recent years bringing an added complication. In professional classes, the qualifications of the employee are considered in determining classification and pay in the federal government; not so in California, where pay is according to the job, no matter how well qualified the incumbent.

CSPA sought to create law that would enable alternative salary ranges to be established on the basis of differential qualifications recognized in state law; thus, for psychologists, unlicensed, licensed, clinical psychologist, "forensic" psychologist, and board-certified would form a hierarchy. The principle, however, applied to all professional personnel. CSPA's bill was moving, but in the closing days of the session, the bill on comparability of pay for women was locked in committee. By consent of the author, essentially that entire bill was married into the CSPA bill and passed. Since the governor was a known supporter of this women's issue and since three government departments were opposed to CSPA's (although they "lost" in every committeee hearing), CSPA reasoned that the expansion, valued and endorsed by psychology in its own right, would also provide a measure of insulation from a veto. S.B. 459 (Carpenter) was enacted as chapter 722, 1981, with the comparability principle and with the original objective intact.

As one expression of CSPA's concern for standards, it sponsored S.B. 230 (Carpenter), chapter 966, 1979. The measure requires the same professional standards in the public as in the private sector. Psychologists who provide direct health or mental health care, whether as staff or on contract, or who work in entities, state, or county, that provide direct health care must be licensed. A time waiver is given to psychologists from out of state and to new graduates sufficient to allow transition to licensure. For psychologists employed before enactment of the law, there is a grandparent provision, but it precludes promotion or transfer without licensure. This law eliminated what had been a long-standing dual standard between public and private mental health services.

Until passage of S.B. 1621 (Torres), chapter 1123, 1984, certain functions in facilities of the Department of Corrections were restricted by regulation to the direction of or performance by physicians. With passage of this legislation these "medically or psychologically necessary" services can be provided by psychologists employed by or under contract to the department: prescreening of mental disorders, determination of mental competency of inmates to participate in classification hearings, evaluation of parolees during temporary detention, determining whether mental health treatment should be a condition of parole, and such other services as may be required consistent with their licensure. This bill also provides that clinics of the department shall be under the direction of a psychiatrist or psychologist and that all mental health treatment or diagnostic services shall be provided under the direction of a psychiatrist or psychologist licensed in California. This one bill has very materially changed the opportunities and professional standing of psychologists in correctional facilities throughout the state. It has, in effect, opened an employment or contract market for psychologists just at a time when major prison construction is underway. It also permits psychologists employed by a prisoner to assist in his or her defense to visit while the prisoner is in custody.

The rapid deinstitutionalization of state hospitals in California was implemented without any adequate provision for follow-up or alternative facilities. The county jails have become one alternative, and the population of vagrants has increased. CSPA was moved to lend strong support to passage of A.B. 3052 (Bates), chapter 1233, which in 1978 established a community residential treatment system whose case managers were to be supervised by a psychologist, psychiatrist, or clinical social worker. Subsequent legislation gained some entitlement to third-party reimbursement, and funding was gained for independent living centers. This issue, alternatives to hospitalization, is being addressed in the Mental Health Services Reform Act of 1985 and 1986.

In 1980, S.B. 1742 (Speraw), chapter 1237, brought state law into conformity with the federal definition of *developmental disability* and included mental disabilities originating before age eighteen and expected to continue indefinitely. Services include but are not limited to diagnosis, treatment, mental health referral, and follow-along services—a potential major expansion of services to the developmentally disabled.

Throughout California there is a network of community college districts, each with student health care service employing clinical psychologists and/or psychiatrists. In response to the appeal of one district, urgency legislation applying to all was enacted in 1979 with CSPA support. S.B. 1177 (Carpenter), chapter 462, enabled clinical psychology interns to be employed and provide mental health services under the direction of a licensed clinical psychologist or psychiatrist. This opened a new and funded training resource at a time when internships appeared to be shrinking.

Legislation has been introduced in 1985 by a senior senator to establish the California Probation Classification and Case Management System Act of 1985. The bill seeks an empirically based system and carries the potential for major reform and professional opportunity—another window of opportunity to be cultivated.

Swords of Damocles

With the national "sunset" movement promoted by Common Cause came A.B. 46 (McCarthy), a bill by the speaker of the assembly, a bill that would have eliminated the psychology licensing law (along with licensing laws for some other nonmedical professions) if that law was not reenacted. We chose not to suffer through a "sunset" review but to seek the removal of psychology from the bill or its defeat. CSPA succeeded on both counts, California being the only state to attempt such a direct confrontation (Dörken, 1979a.) Defeating the bill of such an influential legislator, even after removal of psychology, required not only presence and pressure at the time but a history of constructive relationships with legislators to draw on. A.B. 46 was not the first serious attack on psychology, nor will it be the last. Visible are other measures that could be as destructive.

Thus, a great deal of CSPA's legislative effort goes toward protecting psychology as well as toward advancing and strengthening its frontiers. Were these defensive aspects neglected, psychology would effectively cease to be a major profession within a few short years. Every year there may be as many bills to oppose as to support. These are not always in themselves dramatic, but the cumulative effect of these antagonistic bills would be disastrous. Others, such as A.B. 46, are dramatic in their ability to kill with a single stroke.

Another example: In 1982 and 1983 the state administration, both through legislative proposals and through administrative rules, sought to consolidate all fee-for-service practice under Medi-Cal (California's Medicaid program) into its Short-Doyle programs (county mental health, named after the authors of the original legislation). Additionally, the administration made several attempts to gain federal approval of the waivers (variance from federal plan requirements) necessary to implement this "Short-Doyle/Medi-Cal" consolidation. CSPA led the opposition. The legislation was amended down to a possible few pilot projects, the federal waivers were not granted, and the rule changers were not adopted. Opposition on three fronts over two years succeeded in achieving a stalemate and preserving fee-for-service practice for psychologists under the state plan. The annual collective reimbursement by the state to psychologist practitioners at the time exceeded $12 million—hardly incidental. Concurrently the state was implementing major changes in its Medi-Cal plan, negotiating hospital per diem rates, reducing fees across the board, allocating the medically indigent to counties, and so forth. A medical necessity requirement had also been imposed on all Medi-Cal services. In the Medi-Cal "trailer" bill, however, S.B. 2021 (Maddy), chapter 1550, 1982, mental health services were exempted from the medical necessity requirement on CSPA urging.

State agencies commonly hold that they provide better service at less cost than the private sector. There are many who would disagree, particularly in the health field. The key argument advanced in the Short-Doyle/Medi-Cal dispute was "Why replace a service at half the cost with one at twice the price, of lower quality, and without limits? Where are the savings the state is seeking to offset its deficit?" At the time of the dispute, the state was paying about $27 an hour for psychological services, maximum two visits a month, and $33 an hour for psychiatric services, limited to eight visits in 120 days but with prior authorization available for additional visits on an urgency basis. On the other hand, many if not most Short-Doyle services are delivered by individuals who are not physicians, and there are often no specific limits on the number of services. Indeed, a patient could "doctor shop" to all three concurrently! The next year, the county programs were limited, for state reimbursement, to 125 percent of the statewide average, $78. Where are the savings? It appears that if counties were to contract outpatient mental health services out to licensed personnel at competitive costs, everyone would be the better, including government and the patients.

A third example: In 1980 the California Medical Association sponsored A.B. 1031 (Rosenthal), which CSPA opposed and which failed. This bill proposed a Health Occupations Council to develop uniform licensing standards and examinations. The aim was to coalesce the overlaps in the practice acts of the mental health disciplines. The result would have been little distinction among psychologists, clinical social workers, and marriage, family, and child counselors. It was consistent with the view of the administration at the time that a single "psychotherapy" profession was to be preferred. Obviously, this bill would have stifled the future opportunities of psychologists, clouded the identity of the profession, and probably removed it from the field of behavioral health. Also introduced was a Senate concurrent resolution (S.C.R. 18-Wilson), which CSPA opposed and which failed. The latter proposed a committee to examine the scope of practice and licensing of health care providers; meanwhile, no new licenses or expansion of existing licenses—perils much as in A.B. 1031 above.

Where the grass appears greener, it is necessary to protect one's "turf." Almost every year there is a proposal that, if not amended or defeated, would seriously impair some aspect of the practice of psychology. A.B. 3290 (Alatorre), in 1980, also opposed by CSPA and defeated, would have eliminated the use of psychological tests, among other things, in employment situations.

Each year the legislative climate differs, and with each unique climate there will be windows of opportunity and special hazards. Perhaps because of the state's recovery from its fiscal deficit situation—although we could never establish such an attribution—several professions sought to define or redefine their practices in 1984, each, as it happened, to intrude into the practice of psychology. Consider the collective damage had there been no effective opposition. Legislation to license polygraph examiners was amended so that the restriction in the use of polygraph instruments (which are really biofeedback instruments, and the use of biofeedback is an explicit part of the practice of psychology in California) did not apply to psychologists, whether in clinical practice or for research. To eliminate the unfair practices of some employment counseling services, legislation was introduced to set standards and require licensure as an employment agency; however, an amendment gained exempted licensed psychologists or psychological corporations. The clinical social workers sought to expand their practice to include the diagnosis of mental disorder and the formulation of treatment plans. CSPA opposition saw this amended to "psychosocial evaluation." The bill later died in the inactive file. Then, in seeking title protection, occupational therapists proposed a substantial range of functions, a number of which clearly overlapped the practice of psychology. Most of these provisions were amended out on CSPA objection, and then the bill was later sent to interim study, never having cleared its first policy committee.

In Retrospect

Many factors impinge on legislative endeavors. Briefly, legislative proposals have a better chance of success when they are well planned and researched; reflect a legitimate professional interest; are likely to be of public benefit; are consistent with the climate of the times and the mood of the legislature; are authored by legislators who have established their credibility in the subject area; and are systematically advanced and represented by association advocates who are known and respected.

Over the years more than thirty-two legislators have carried bills for CSPA that have been enacted into law or have accepted major amendments reflecting the proactive and reactive components of the association's program. It is perhaps not surprising that one legislator, Senator Paul Carpenter (1983), a Ph.D. psychologist and for a year a member of the APA Committee on Health Insurance, has carried somewhat more "freight" for psychology than any other, eight bills that became law. However, another senator has carried five, three legislators have carried three, five have carried two, and twenty-two have carried one each. This represents thirty-two CSPA bills and twenty-two major amendments enacted into law. Having involved that many legislators directly in psychology's affairs says something for the scope of working relations that CSPA's advocates have established in Sacramento.

Despite all its action at the state level, CSPA has yet to develop a systematic federal aspect to its legislative program. Although it may seem only natural to try to put one's house in order before venturing afield, the federal law/Congress—and California has forty-five members in the House of Representatives—has a very major effect on professional affairs in the states. One has only to think of the restrictions on psychology practice in Medicare and Medicaid and the preemption of state FOC law by ERISA in self-funded health plans to appreciate that federal law can have a very restrictive effect on psychological practice. Conversely, the recognition under CHAMPUS, the federal employee health plans, and, more recently, the inclusion of clinical psychology in the Health Professions Educational Assistance Act and in the Criminal Code Reform Act late in 1984 are of very positive benefit. (Chapter Five presents a current account of the extent to which federal law bears on clinical practice.) No state legislative program is really comprehensive until it sustains some representation and presence in Congress as well.

We have described the main highlights in CSPA's legislative history, although there were other details/bills too numerous to mention that added to the positive outcomes. Then, too, some of the past threats that were set aside are not necessarily dead. They may readily come to life again in another form, next year, the year after, and so forth. Eternal vigilance is an essential way of life in an arena of which it has been alleged that "no man's life, liberty, or property is safe while the legislature is in session."

References

Brunette, S., and Sales, B. "The Role of Psychologists in State Legislation Governing Sex Offenders." *Professional Psychology,* 1980, *11,* 194-201.

Carpenter, P. "The Personal Insights of a Legislator/Psychologist." *American Psychologist,* 1983, *38,* 1216-1219.

DeLeon, P. "The Changing and Creating of Legislation: The Political Process." In B. Sales (ed.), *The Professional Psychologist's Handbook.* New York: Plenum, 1983.

DeLeon, P. "Federal Legislation Recognizing Psychology." *American Psychologist,* 1984, *39,* 933-946.

DeLeon, P., Frohboese, R., and Meyers, J. "Psychologist on Capitol Hill: A Unique Use of the Skills of the Scientist/Practitioner." *Professional Psychology,* 1984, *15,* 697-705.

DeLeon, P. H., O'Keefe, A. M., VandenBos, G. R., and Kraut, A. G. "How to Influence Public Policy: A Blueprint for Activism." *American Psychologist,* 1982, *37,* 476-485.

Dörken, H. "Utilization of Psychologists in Positions of Responsibility in Public Mental Health Programs: A National Survey." *American Psychologist,* 1970, *25,* 953-958.

Dörken, H. "The Formal Involvement of Psychology in the Commitment Process for Mental and Developmental Disorders." *Clinical Psychologist,* 1977a, *30,* 5-6.

Dörken, H. "Avenues to Legislative Success." *American Psychologist,* 1977b, *32,* 738-745.

Dörken, H. "Why the Sun Didn't Set in the West." *Clinical Psychologist,* 1979a, *33,* 16-17.

Dörken, H. "Workers' Compensation: Opening Up a Major Market for Psychological Practice." *Professional Psychology,* 1979b, *10,* 834–840.

Dörken, H. "Coming of Age Legislatively: In 21 Steps." *American Psychologist,* 1981a, *36,* 165–173.

Dörken, H. "The Hospital Practice of Psychology." *Professional Psychology,* 1981b, *12,* 599–605.

Dörken, H. "Advocacy and the Legislative Process: Representation in a Changing World." *American Psychologist,* 1983a, *38,* 1210–1215.

Dörken, H. "Health Insurance and Third-Party Reimbursement." In B. Sales (ed.) *The Professional Psychologist's Handbook.* Plenum, New York: 1983b.

Dörken, H., and Associates. *The Professional Psychologist Today: New Developments in Law, Health Insurance, and Health Practice.* San Francisco: Jossey-Bass, 1976.

Dörken, H., and Webb, J. T. "The Hospital Practice of Psychology: An Interstate Comparison." *Professional Psychology,* 1979, *10,* 619–630.

Dörken, H., and Webb, J. T. "Licensed Psychologists on the Increase: 1974–1979." *American Psychologist,* 1981, *36,* 1419–1426.

Dörken, H., Webb, J. T., and Zaro, J. S. "Hospital Practice of Psychology Resurveyed: 1980." *Professional Psychology,* 1982, *13,* 814–829.

Drude, K. "Psychologists and Civil Commitment: Review of State Statutes." *Professional Psychology,* 1978, *9,* 499–506.

Joint Commission on Accreditation of Hospitals. *Accreditation Manual for Hospitals.* Chicago: Joint Commission on Accreditation of Hospitals, 1979.

"A Model for State Legislation Affecting the Practice of Psychology, 1967." *American Psychologist,* 1967, *22,* 1095–1103.

Sales, B. (ed.). *The Professional Psychologist's Handbook.* New York: Plenum, 1983.

Shapiro, A. E., Dörken, H., Rodgers, D. A., and Wiggins, J. G. "The Legislative Process." In H. Dörken and Associates, *The Professional Psychologist Today: New Developments in Law,*

Health Insurance, and Health Practice. San Francisco: Jossey-Bass, 1976.

Sobel, S. "Professional Psychologists and State Statutes on Practical Competency: A Review." *Clinical Psychologist,* 1978, nos. 3 and 4, 26–29.

Tanney, F. "Hospital Privileges Legislation and the Political Process." Paper presented at annual meeting of the American Psychological Association, Toronto, Ontario, Aug. 1984.

11

Nicholas A. Cummings
Herbert Dörken

Corporations, Networks, and Service Plans: Economically Sound Models for Practice

Two men were on a mountain trek through the high Sierra Nevada of California when they were confronted by a ferocious grizzly bear. Neither man was armed. As one stood frozen in fear, the other quickly removed his hiking boots and began to put on his running shoes. "You don't really believe you can outrun that bear," jeered his companion, somewhat out of contempt but mostly out of fear. "I don't have to," replied the first. "All I have to do is outrun you."

Psychologists are ill prepared for the competition that is heating up and will soon permeate all of health care delivery. This chapter offers some examples of successful practice models that can guide psychologists who are willing to change from traditional approaches to survive the new competition. But first it may be well

Note: The Biodyne model and part of this chapter were presented by Cummings in his award address, "The Dismantling of Our Health Care System: Strategies for the Survival of Psychological Practice," at the annual meeting of the American Psychological Association, Los Angeles, August 25, 1985. The descriptions of the Delaware Valley Psychological Clinics and the California Psychological Health Plan were presented in part at the Panel on Future Markets under the egis of the APA Committee on Professional Practice during the August 1983 annual meeting in Los Angeles by Janice Kenny and Donald D. Marsh, respectively.

283

to sketch briefly how the new climate of competition came about and some of its characteristics.

During the Great Society era of the Lyndon Johnson presidency, the government began to fuel our health economy, first through the Hill-Burton legislation and then through Medicare and Medicaid. The important fact is that the government was fueling a *noncompetitive* health economy, because the medical profession had the clout to prevent a more competitive model of funding. The rest is history. Health care costs escalated at several times the inflation rate of the rest of the economy and currently account for 11 percent of our gross national product.

For several years government struggled in vain to slow down the rate of inflation in our health economy. Finally, in the early 1980s those who pay the bills for our health care, the employers, decided they had had enough. Overnight the industrial might of our nation formed health consortia in all our major cities, and these organizations included not only our largest corporations but also unions, farmers, consumers, and senior citizens. These consortia are effecting the changes in rapid succession that the government alone was powerless to bring about, and the American Medical Association is coming to realize it is unable to slow down the momentum for change. This climate is stimulating the mushrooming of health maintenance organizations (HMOs) and preferred provider organizations (PPOs), and large health corporations are applying their efficient management techniques and staking out increasingly larger market shares of our patient population. Meanwhile the employer is turning from payer to buyer and is doing so with data on use, cost, and benefits. It is industrial corporation to health corporation, industry to health dealing through negotiated contracts. As these health corporations, through consumer choice (selection and use) and employer contract (negotiated rates and services), capture more of the market, independent practitioners find their practice and their influence dwindling. Such circumstances are forcing more and more physicians to make arrangements with these health corporations.

Psychology is particularly vulnerable in this new health care delivery climate. Third-party payers do not understand the nature of mental health care and are wary of the seemingly endless quality of psychotherapy. Many segments of psychiatry are abandoning psychotherapy to the psychologist and are forming hospital-based PPOs that promise mental health delivery on a medical model of drugs and hospitalization. For now this evades the competition of the nonphysician providers and captures the typically higher inpatient benefits of group health insurance policies. This "adjustment," although it will be costly, is at least understood by the accountants' mentality, whereas psychotherapy seems ethereal and unmanageable to those who must pay the reimbursement bills. For the services that psychotherapy HMOs must provide for various reasons, there is a trend to hire social workers, who are paid less, or even mental health counselors with lesser training, who are cheaper still.

Health care is not just entering a period of change but is in the throes of a revolution. It is our prediction that during the transition period quality will suffer in the interest of cost containment. Eventually, however, those HMOs and PPOs that do not maintain quality will go out of business, yielding in favor of providers that are both efficient and effective. This time competition has been deliberately built into the system. For psychologists, it is important to note that, for those predicting the extinction of the private practice of psychotherapy as we now know it (Duhl and Cummings, 1985; Dörken, 1983; Chapters Twelve and Thirteen), it is not a question of whether but when, simply because it cannot be delivered at competitive cost. There will be psychologists who will insist that the profession should fight against the formation of HMOs and PPOs. We would remind them that the might of the California Medical Association, in its 1983 attempt to undo the legislation that authorized PPOs, suffered its greatest legislative humiliation and defeat. The health revolution is here and will continue, because those who pay the bills have decided that health costs must be contained. Major changes are in the offing.

Group Practice

The solo practice of psychotherapy is clearly on the defensive. Psychoanalysis, the most cost-intensive of all the psychotherapies, is fighting a battle for survival in the face of the cost containment efforts of third-party payers. As more and more of the patient market goes into HMOs and PPOs, in an attempt to preserve their private practices many psychologists will sign up with independent practice associations (IPAs). These organizations typically limit the reimbursement to the providers and also monitor their performance in an effort to reduce utilization. The IPA increases efficiency and cuts costs, but it cannot compete with the HMO or PPO that operates on a capitation basis and provide centers where all services are delivered, as opposed to the cost-intensive, solo practitioner's private office. When the squeeze comes, the IPA will attempt to compete with the HMO and PPO by giving the provider less and less fee-for-service reimbursement. The psychologist may be an independent contractor but at that point will have become the captive of the IPA and must either accept the reduced compensation, close the office, or find other practice markets. One alternative is for psychologists to form group practices and market themselves as a psychological PPO to general PPOs and full-range HMOs that may well wish to contract out their mental health care at an efficient cost rather than struggle with something they do not fully comprehend.

It is important from the outset to stress that group practice does not mean the usual mode of several independent solo practitioners operating under one roof, sharing overhead and participating in a pooled referral system. Rather, we have in mind a small, intensive group practice wherein all the psychologists are trained in intensive, targeted brief psychotherapy and provide a range of modalities that would not be possible in the traditional "group" of solo practitioners all essentially doing the same thing. It is a well-known fact that psychologists form groups with like-minded colleagues, thus making a truly multimodal group practice unlikely (Cummings and VandenBos, 1979). The participants in a group practice as newly conceptualized here hold common goals and agree to efficient management and aggressive marketing of their product.

Certainly the large health corporations will move swiftly to capture a large market share, but these giants have one major flaw: the loss of personal care or the human touch. There will be room in the future for psychologists who would form group service delivery models that can cut costs and still maintain the quality and personal caring that are essential to the real psychological model. Unfortunately, most psychologists eschew anything that smacks of business, almost as if in their aloofness they disdain the business reality of practice in the fantasy that the public is dependent on them. But quality care is not incompatible with efficiency, and we submit that the psychotherapists who survive the 1980s will be the individuals who have mastered what has been termed "social entrepreneurship," or a melding of humanism and efficiency (Cummings and Fernandez, 1985).

Marketing

The word *marketing* seems almost obscene to many otherwise enlightened psychologists. In 1985 the Board of Professional Affairs (BPA) of the American Psychological Association instructed its innovative Subcommittee on Future Markets that the word *marketing* has an ominous quality and that another term should be used. (More than twenty years earlier the BPA had instructed the predecessor of its Committee on Health Insurance that the word *insurance* was not respectable.) The Subcommittee on Future Markets replied that it was its intention to alert the profession to the importance of marketing, and to do so, the word itself must be used. (This response was similar to the response given BPA more than twenty years earlier that the word *insurance* was not only respectable but vital to the survival of psychology as an autonomous profession.)

Even the best program will fail without proper marketing, and "Marketing or morbidity" will be the practitioner's version of the academician's slogan "Publish or perish." It will be strictly a buyer's market, in which the practitioner will have to demonstrate that better mental health care can be delivered more efficiently and at less cost (Cummings and Fernandez, 1985).

Psychologists must learn to market themselves if they are to succeed, and market research is essential to a successful marketing program. Psychologists do not possess the expertise to mount their own marketing campaign and should seek appropriate professional help. Consultant fees range from $2,500 to $5,000 per month, and research and advertising can add to the bill (Bean, 1985). The social entrepreneur who will survive the 1980s must be prepared to invest not only time but also money in his or her own future success. Even though the burden is shared in the group practice, there is little room for the timid.

Targeted Intervention

It has been said that a peculiarity of psychotherapy is that the patient receives what the practitioner has to offer rather than what may specifically be required. For example, whether one has a marital, occupational, or alcohol problem, if one goes to an orthodox Freudian, one will be put on the couch. If the patient goes to a Jungian psychologist, pictures will be painted and archetypes will be discussed. If one goes to a behavioral therapist, desensitization will be applied. This is tantamount to a physician's giving penicillin whether the patient has pneumonia or a broken leg. Such a state of affairs existed in medicine at the turn of the century. Each physician had five or six favorite medications, and if one did not work, another was tried, and so on until the physician's limited repertoire was exhausted. Since that time medicine has matured so that there are scores of *specifics:* specific treatments for specific conditions.

The remarkable thing about the state of affairs in psychotherapy is that even though the patient receives whatever the therapist has to offer regardless of the presenting condition, it does work to an extent. The problem is that it works inefficiently, and many more sessions are required to bring about amelioration than are really necessary. The number of sessions required to accomplish remediation can be drastically reduced by using targeted interventions directed to specific conditions (Cummings and VandenBos, 1979). Psychology has more "specifics" than practitioners generally acknowledge, and Cummings (1984) uses over fifty targeted interventions applied to specific conditions. The maturity of a profession is measured by the number of specifics at its disposal, and psychology must begin using these targeted modalities, for research has shown that it is not the number of persons seen in treatment that creates the inordinate cost of mental health services but the number of sessions each is seen in order to bring about the desired effect.

Magaro (1985), advocating the use of performance contracts as the most cost-effective model for securing therapist involvement in changing patient behavior, would emphasize the skills an individual needs to function in society and would direct treatment to those deficits. With reimbursement tied to outcome, rather than to time on the job or rank, this private sector orientation would focus on brief interventions and the modification of a specific behavior as the treatment product.

The Concept of Cure

It is more timely than ever that psychologists reexamine their professional conceptions of the outcome of psychological intervention. Our conception of treatment outcome might well be termed the "ultimate cure." Any contact with a former mental health patient is labeled a "relapse" and is viewed as evidence that the earlier intervention was either unsuccessful or incomplete (Cummings and VandenBos, 1979). No other field of health care holds this view of treatment outcome. Moreover, the objections that the patient had a flight into health and now has a substitution of symptoms are not warranted by research (Cummings and Follette, 1976).

Psychologists also need to reconsider the problem of "diagnosis." Brief psychotherapy is not facilitated by accepting a vague description of the patient's problem or by giving a simplistic *DSM-III* diagnosis, which characterizes the nature of the dysfunction rather than its impact on the person. We believe that central to the initial interview is the establishment of what Cummings and VandenBos (1979) called the "operational diagnosis." It stems directly from the question "What brings the individual here today?" (rather than last week, last year, or next month).

The operational diagnosis formulates the problem(s) that the brief intervention must address, and the abandonment of the concept of cure permits the patient and therapist to interrupt the treatment as soon as the problem is solved. The patient is free to come in again if another problem arises, personally or with others. Again, the operational diagnosis defines the problem to be addressed, and treatment once again is interrupted rather than terminated. This approach to the psychologist's functioning as a general psychological family practitioner, which Cummings has termed "brief, intermittent psychotherapy throughout the life cycle," is the essence of his Biodyne model (Cummings and VandenBos, 1979; Cummings and Fernandez, 1985). The salient features are that the concept of cure is abandoned, diagnosis is redefined operationally, therepy is specific and brief, and the concept of termination of treatment is eliminated. Research has shown that brief, intermittent psychotherapy throughout the life cycle involves far less treatment than is required by traditional long-term therapy and is considerably more cost-effective.

Brief Psychotherapy

Most private practitioners in independent practice today will require additional training in brief psychotherapy regardless of their previous orientation or training. Brief psychotherapy is not merely a compressed version of long-term therapy but has its own parameters and techniques. Most effective brief therapies involve a melding of dynamic, behavioral, and systems approaches, in spite of the insistence of the adherents of these "schools" of therapy that they cannot be fused into one approach. Budman and Gurman (1983) describe the integration of various approaches so that therapy will be beneficial within a well-planned, limited amount of time.

Malan (1963, 1976), working in Great Britain under socialized medicine, discovered that brief therapy works with therapists who believe in brief therapy. Cummings (1977, 1979), working for a quarter of a century at Kaiser-Permanente in San Francisco, found that therapists who believe in brief therapy are those who are trained in brief therapy, regardless of their original orientation or previous adherence to long-term practice. In fact, reporting eighteen years of research, Cummings found that when a workable brief therapy model is offered, and without any prior screening for suitability, 85 percent of the patients will select brief therapy and will improve significantly with short-term treatment.

Only 10 percent will self-select long-term therapy and will need that more protracted intervention. The implication is obvious: with 85 percent of patients profiting from brief therapy, the 10 percent who require long-term therapy and should receive it can be financed. There remains the 5 percent of the total therapy population reported by Cummings who prove to be interminable. This is the psychotherapy group that terrifies every third-party payer and provides virtually an annuity for some private practitioners. Every provider seeking to survive in the competitive health climate must develop effective techniques for dealing with the interminable patient. Otherwise, the mental health package will not be cost-effective. But even more important, the psychologist of the future must address the fact that most long-term therapy may well be, as P. Watzlawick (personal communication, 1979) has suggested, iatrogenic (provider-caused). What, then, can psychology do to survive these changes? Following are several highly viable options.

A Community Model in Minnesota

Many, especially the federally qualified, community mental health centers are, to quote Albee, "old wine in new bottles." Many lessons were learned, however, in the development of the Minnesota Community Mental Health Services network (Dörken, 1962a, 1962b). Though twenty-five years old, some of those lessons are pertinent today. Minnesota was the second state to enact a community mental health services act. At the time it had four state mental hygiene clinics. The state was very largely without any mental health services over vast regions. How to develop cost-effective outpatient mental health services statewide was the foremost question.

The act, authored in part by input from the U.S. Public Health Service, in part by the mental health association and reflecting the social conscience of this Midwestern state, established some basic principles and encoded them in law (Dörken, 1960). The program was developed center by center and was in effect an ongoing laboratory. There were no indigenous professionals to recruit, but each community was unique and had specialized needs. With funding limited, the decision was made to recruit nationally, employ the best, and pay competitively. That yielded skills, diversity, and minimal turnover. It was quickly apparent that county civil service had neither the flexibility nor the salary structure to accommodate the caliber of staff desired, and so most of the new centers were established as nonprofit corporations in the private sector outside civil service where salaries were negotiable, premiums could be paid for excellence, and conditions for national recruitment became feasible. To have a sufficient population base of 50,000 to 100,000 usually required two or three counties. They became participants, contracting jointly with the state for the center's services. Thus, marketing, contracting, local representation, and service matched to community need were key considerations.

As the program developed further, several other facts emerged. Originally, centers were staffed with a three-person team per each 50,000 of population, the basic "holy trinity" of those days: psychologist, psychiatrist, and clinical social worker. The basic unit of concern—treatment, if you will—was the community. How to resolve community problems was the prime objective rather than simply developing a caseload or treating individuals. The training of gatekeepers and other community resources became essential. Thus, the problem was not tackled one person at a time but through a community plan (Dörken, 1962a). The services addressed the contractees' problems, not so much the traditional concerns of most mental health professionals (Dörken, 1971).

A public health philosophy prevailed, with its focus on positive mental health in harmony with the American value system, wherein the capacity of the individual to achieve is fundamental. The objective was to optimize personal resources and functionality rather than to seek a "cure" for psychopathology.

In rural areas a very pertinent question was how far a center could stretch. By plotting distance and presenting clinical problems, it was discovered that beyond an hour's drive by car, about forty to sixty miles in Minnesota then, the character of the incoming patients changed dramatically from the full range of emotional, family, behavioral, and mental conditions to predominantly acute psychotic disorders (Hodges and Dörken, 1961). Of course, the latter could not be served effectively by a distant outpatient service. Consequently, a geographical limit was set.

Three full-time equivalent (FTE) staff members per 50,000 population did not leave much idle time. It was intended that they be faced with a just manageable level of work. The traditional mental hygiene clinic model of social work intake, psychological evaluation, and psychiatric diagnosis followed by a team meeting to determine a course of action—that is, no intervention until the seventh professional time unit $(1 + 1 + 1 + 3 \rightarrow 7)$—was quickly shut down as an unworkable extravagance. Rather, the private-practice model was implemented. Patients were assigned on triage by the receptionist, matching problem to professional skills. The therapist would refer or seek consultation only when needed. As the private-practice model was implemented, it became obvious that the cost per unit of patient care in this model, the higher salaries of these corporate staff members notwithstanding, was much less than in the mental hygiene clinic model. The many hours not spent in staff meetings, multiple-staff treatment decisions, and so on substantially increased the hours directed to patient care or community service. Thus, when salaries were divided by effective program hours (as distinct from overhead), it became apparent that the higher-paid private-practice model yielded a lower cost per unit of service than the traditional mental hygiene clinic. Three state mental hygiene clinics were accordingly converted to community centers under local administration, and one was terminated, this change effected one year ahead of the legislative schedule.

In the process of this development, another major lesson was learned. None of the mental health professionals were trained as administrators, and yet competent local leadership was essential. There had to be one responsible contact for the state administrator. Competence, not profession, was then adopted as the criterion for appointment of program director, with an administrative increment added to salary. The adoption of this competency principle for program direction statewide in 1960 was a first among the states and is as valid today as then. Interestingly, in those days the three professions always became program directors in about equal numbers.

To acquire an optimum mix of skills, it was often necessary to have close to or somewhat more than a double "team," five to eight FTE professionals. Further cost studies showed that the cost per unit of service dropped as staff size increased from one to five and bottomed through eight (one and two-thirds to two and two-thirds teams) and then began to climb again, rapidly. By ten to eleven the cost exceeded that of a solo professional. Reasons included the higher cost of psychiatrist salaries, exceeding the optimum ratio in economy of scale of support staff, increased housekeeping, elimination of many smaller and less costly site options, and the necessary substitution of formal administrative staff exchanges instead of the knowledge transfer by osmosis possible in a small, tight-knit organization. When an organization grows, its growth is not linear—its surface is squared and its volume is cubed. Individuality soon becomes lost. Considering necessary diversity of skills, cost, efficiency, and geographical coverage, an FTE staff of five to eight was adopted as the most effective: small enough so that everyone knew what was going on, small enough that the workload was at a just manageable level of difficulty without idle time, but substantial enough to have the diverse skills to serve the target area. Where there was a demand for growth, adjacent counties were encouraged to form a new center. Sixteen centers were developed over a three-year span (1959–1962), with a network of twenty-six projected. The full network was implemented several years later and has been operative since.

Thus, the lessons in developing new cost-effective mental health services in Minnesota community mental health have many features in common with the Biodyne model to be discussed later: highly qualified professional staff, diversity of skills pertinent to the community served, accessible location and businesslike appearance, small and close-knit staffing organization with minimal overhead, above-par competitive remuneration with realistic fringes, time commitment sufficient to assure close identity, and progressive innovation and zeal to outreach and effect change. We will not argue that Biodyne is the only model, however, space does not permit more than a mention of several other interesting models, each of which is viable in its own right.

Delaware Valley Psychological Clinics

As the community mental health centers were just beginning to emerge across the country to bring ambulatory mental health care to reachable catchment areas, a totally private-sector network was founded in Philadelphia in 1958 by Janice Kenny and Aaron Smith. Beginning in rented basement offices, it moved into its own building in 1963.

It was the first private clinic in the area owned by psychologists and employing psychiatrists. In 1975 Smith moved to Nevada, and Kenny, with the plan of a major expansion, chose a new associate, Jan Grossman. Although the idea of expansion was appealing to Grossman, the idea was new, seemed unworkable, and therefore did not take shape until 1978. However, by 1983 they had established thirteen clinics and eight branch offices throughout the greater Philadelphia area of five counties in a ten-mile radius. The Delaware Valley Psychological Clinics (DVPC) is a privately owned partnership and is the largest group of private mental health professionals in the area. It is 100 percent supported by client fees and related third-party reimbursement and by policy accepts no government funds. Responsibility for coverage of over 39,000 patients through an affiliation with the Health Maintenance Organization of Pennsylvania has led to expansion of the clinic's network into Allentown, Bethlehem, and Easton, Pennsylvania, some fifty miles from Philadelphia. Plans are presently in the offing for expansion into the Williamsport and Lewisburg area.

No one joins the staff without passing a series of rigorous interviews and background checks. All professionals are required to have a strong background in general mental health care (psychotherapy, psychodiagnostics, and consultation) as well as at least one specialty that adds a unique coverage in service available for the clinic's clientele. Any client seeing one of the clinic's professionals has ready access to the entire specialty system, and on any given day there are numerous cross-consultations taking place among staff members. There is staffing for home visitation and shut-in services, and multilingual therapists are available who speak Spanish, French, Hebrew, Yiddish, Polish, and German.

In addition to licensed psychologists and psychiatrists, the clincs have fourteen Pennsylvania-certified school psychologists geographically distributed across the Delaware Valley. Only certified school psychologists can by state law prescribe special educational programs for learning-disabled or socially or emotionally disturbed children. DVPC is a teaching clinic with working agreements for training and teaching at Hahnemann Medical College, Fielding Institute, Bryn Mawr College, and Temple University. Internship programs in adult, child, and forensic psychology saw twenty-one young professionals in training in 1985–86. DVPC also has hospitalization privileges at six area health facilities.

Within the DVPC is a forensic division with over twenty psychologists, psychiatrists, and social workers and three sections: domestic, civil, and criminal. The domestic section is involved in over 100 divorce and custody situations each year, while the civil section handles over 200 referrals for such services as Social Security disability evaluation, worker's compensation litigation, and rehabilitation agencies. In a typical year, 50 to 100 patients are evaluated and treated in the criminal section. All services are rendered with the expectation that court testimony will be required, so that there is solid documentation, and as a result DVPC has earned considerable confidence within the legal community.

The clinics advertise, maintain a twenty-four-hour phone service, provide a computer testing service, and use computerized billing and computer-ready forms. Thus, although each of the clinics and branch offices is a small, efficient unit, the network gains economies of scale through centralized support services. As DVPC's size, coverage, and reputation grew, so did its ability to attract clients. Thus, quite apart from the professional attraction of working with competent peers, there is a distinct economic advantage to the professional affiliation.

Still another advantage to organization is in-service training provided at low cost to the staff members. Last year a two-day seminar was presented by out-of-state experts at a cost of only $50 per clinic member, compared with a customary seminar fee of $300.

The other side of the symbiotic relationship between clinic and practitioner is that the organization retains a portion of the practitioner fee. For new therapists, 100 percent of their first-session fee is retained by DVPC and 50 percent of subsequent fees. However, when the new therapist attracts or transfers in a new referral, his or her share rises to 55 percent, to 60 percent with the sixth referral, and to 65 percent with the eleventh, and after twenty referrals the therapist retains 70 percent of fee. Senior staff members who then serve a clientele of $600 or more a week for at least twenty-six weeks retain 75 percent. The financial incentive for involvement and productivity is clear. A bonus of 5 percent is given to those who arrange to see patients from home offices, thereby cutting clinic overhead. All members of the staff have an equal opportunity to reach the senior staff level.

The DVPC comprehensive psychological service network sees about 1,500 patients a week, and therapists may vary their time and therefore their income. They may also trade referrals for ones they prefer. The clinics share referrals, so that if a service is needed, a determination is made about who can deliver it. When a new client calls, he or she is connected as soon as possible with a psychologist who performs an immediate assessment of the client's problem and determines when it is convenient for the client to come in and which office is closest to the client's home or business. An appointment is then set up with the appropriate specialist within days—within hours if it is an emergency. There are no waiting lists and no awkward intake procedures. The objective is to provide the finest-quality private mental health care available in the community, promptly, appropriately, and effectively. No single (solo) practitioner or even a small group can match the in-depth professional resources of DVPC, its twenty-four-hour access, and its linkages to numerous community agencies and hospitals.

California Psychological Health Plan

The California Psychological Health Plan (CPHP) is the product of a year-long study by a task force of the Division of Clinical and Professional Psychology of the California State Psychological Association (CSPA) in the early seventies. Following the recommendations of that task force in 1972, CPHP was incorporated in 1973, registered with the attorney general in 1974, and became independent of CSPA in 1975. In 1975 CPHP became the first statewide, prepaid mental health care plan licensed by the state Department of Corporations. Under California law, CPHP is a Knox-Keene licensed specialized health care service plan and, as such, must meet rigorous state standards of solvency, reserves to meet obligations, evidence of sufficient numbers of providers, and quality-of-care assurance. A nonprofit corporation, it is essentially a closed-panel program in which the contracting providers, licensed psychologists and psychiatrists, have been screened and agree to deliver services in accord with the CPHP service plan. Services are provided in the provider's own office. Donald D. Marsh, a member of the original CSPA task force, is director of professional services.

CPHP client organizations today number more than fifty, among which are fourteen municipalities, six school districts, and various corporations including, recently, Hughes Aircraft Company. Enrollment is only for organized groups of employees, and typically CPHP is marketed as the outpatient mental health arm of a comprehensive health care plan. It operates mainly on a capitation model and currently serves about 200,000 individuals. The organization is at risk to provide and pay for all required services and administration from its capitation revenue (per person per month, prepaid), although this risk is significantly reduced where employers underwrite direct treatment costs.

A geographical directory of contracting providers is distributed to all subscribers—the eligible employees of the client organization. Utilization is encouraged, and there are orienting health education sessions with members. A reverse copayment is used whereby the first five visits are without cost to the patient. There is a 15 percent copayment for the next five, 30 percent for a subsequent five, and 50 percent from the sixteenth visit. There is no deductible and no arbitrary limit on visits. Complete confidentiality from the employer is assured, and there is easy direct access to the CPHP provider of choice. There are no claim forms.

Initial capitalization of the plan was achieved through provider member contributions ranging from $300 to $1,300. Today there is a nominal annual membership fee of $25. Provider members agree by contract that their services are subject to review and that before the sixth visit, if further services are considered necessary, a written treatment plan of the case will be formulated for discussion with a district professional standards management committee (PSMC) chair. Treatment planning and review conferences are arranged at this point and usually every fifteen visits thereafter. The purpose is not peer review in the usual sense but a collaborative, educational system to assure more effective and definitive help for covered subscribers.

The current fee allowance (adopted in August 1984 and effective through 1985) for contracting providers is $60 for a forty-five- to fifty-minute sessions, which is less than UCR in most areas of the state and certainly in Southern California, where CPHP has the majority of its members. The copayments beyond the fifth visit are paid by the patient to the provider on the basis of the current ($60) rate. These are then "alternative," or negotiated discounted, rates under California law and are agreed to as payment in full. To ensure that CPHP can maintain the reserves required by the Department of Corporations, provider members also agree to defer 20 percent of their fee on each case to be withheld in reserve, until that treatment is concluded. The reserve has been paid to providers each year. Except for any copayment, the fee then is paid not by the patient but by CPHP to the provider.

It should be noted that CPHP is not an exclusive provider organization. A subscriber may go to a noncontracting provider, but that provider is paid only 50 percent of the CPHP rate (progressively less after five visits), and the subscriber is obligated to the provider for the difference from the provider's usual charge. There is also a limit per family per year on payment to noncontracting providers, ranging from $500 to $1,000 according to the contractual arrangements with the employer group. Thus, there is a substantial financial incentive for subscribers to use CPHP providers, as in a preferred provider organization. However, CPHP is more accurately described as an IPA-type HMO (individual practice association).

CPHP has been in the business long enough and with enough clients now to have accumulated some very positive outcome data. First its concept and then its results have attracted the attention of the insurance industry. In 1975 Crown Life and Massachusetts Mutual added the CPHP benefit at no cost to the policyholder in two plans, one a multiemployer trust. In the first year, the paid/loss radio dropped from 92 to 67 percent, and despite rapid inflation in health care costs, there was no rate change under the policy until after the fourth year (Mercer, 1980). Other positive experiences are briefly referred to in "Psychological Health Plan Nips Insurance Premium Increases" (1981). More definitive is the report from the city of Redondo Beach (Casey and Siegel, 1982). The city's interest was in part sparked by the high incidence of family problems among safety employees and three successive disability retirements for psychological reasons. Instead of annually rising health insurance premiums, Redondo Beach saw its premiums remain constant from 1979 to 1981 while the group health insurance plan generated $160,000 in dividend reserves. Only one public safety employee was granted a valid psychologically based disability retirement during this period, and there were no further applicants. Moreover, the rate of absenteeism due to sickness dropped from 3.2 to 1.6 percent—all very positive outcomes and clear evidence of the impact of psychological intervention in reducing total health care costs.

CPHP serves only its subscriber members—the employees of organizations with whom it has a contractual relationship and their dependents. Its provider members, of course, serve not only CPHP subscribers but their other clients as well. As CPHP has gained major new client organization contracts, several providers are known to have moved their offices so as to be more optimally located. Of course, over time, the greater the percentage of an area population that is under contract to CPHP—or to a local HMO or other plan with a lock-in or use-incentive feature—the smaller will be the number of those inclined to use noncontracting providers. Independent practitioners will face a progressive dwindling of available clients as organized entities contract into and take over the market.

The Biodyne Model

American Biodyne Centers, based in San Francisco, offers a mental health maintenance organization (MHMO) type of PPO to HMOs, PPOs, insurance indemnity plans, medical service associations (Blue Cross/Blue Shield), and large employer groups that may wish to contract for a low-cost, effective, and comprehensive outpatient mental health benefit. The Biodyne model implements the concepts described above. It is psychology's first nationwide MHMO and can serve as a model or a point of departure for future psychological PPOs. Biodyne has already contracted to establish three centers in Arizona (in Phoenix and Tucson) and another in Florida on a for-profit basis. The Arizona centers are a joint venture with Blue Cross/Blue Shield in which the Blues will market Biodyne as an exclusive. Other centers are under negotiation in a number of states. The model might best be understood through a description of its prototype center in Honolulu. Biodyne/ Honolulu, established as a subcontractor in a cooperative agreement (No. 11-C-98344/9, 10/83-9/88) between the state of Hawaii and the federal Health Care Financing Administration, is a nonprofit clinical center conducting offset research and, in the process, providing unlimited outpatient mental health care for 68,000 eligibles, 34,000 of whom are Medicaid beneficiaries and 34,000 of whom are employed or retired federal workers and their dependents.* Thus, there are two contracts for two types of enrollees: the state of Hawaii for the Medicaid population and Hawaii Medical Service Association (a Blue Shield affiliate) for the employed group.

All practitioners are indigenous and are selected for their clinical expertise, knowledge of area problems, and adaptability to the Biodyne model. For example, of the ten current professional Honolulu staff members, three are Caucasion. All are independent contractors who received 130 hours of training in the Biodyne model at the outset. This includes an extensive training manual with programs for over fifty targeted interventions for specific conditions, and participants are given the opportunity to view the hands-on application of these interventions by the clinical director and his assistant. Thereafter, there are weekly clinical case conferences that serve not only as continual on-the-job training but also as "peer review" aimed at maintaining the integrity of the model.

* N. Cummings and H. Dörken are principal and co-principal investigators for the Impact of Psychological Intervention on Health Care Utilization and Costs, 11-C-98344/9 awarded by the Health Care Financing Administration to the Hawaii Department of Social Services and Housing (state Medicaid agency) under contract with the Biodyne Institute. Any opinions expressed here regarding Biodyne are those of the authors and should in no way be attributed to either the Health Care Financing Administration or the state of Hawaii.

No investment is required of the participating practitioners. In the for-profit centers, the practitioners, at the end of the year, have the opportunity to share in the divisible surplus resulting from having performed efficiently enough to create such a surplus from the capitated dollars to Biodyne from the contractees. The practitioners work in a well-appointed center that is limited to ten or eleven practitioners. When Biodyne increases its enrollees, it forms additional centers and staffs them similarly. In this manner each center is maintained as a small, intensive, and efficient group practice.

In addition to providing an unlimited outpatient benefit with its targeted programs, house calls when appropriate, and other services not usually seen as part of a benefit package, Biodyne also provides an outreach program for the 10 percent highest utilizers of health care. Periodically, the contractee provides Biodyne with a computer printout of the utilization record of these 10 percent highest utilizers by incidence rather than dollar amount. A printout according to dollar amount would merely produce the organ transplants, the kidney dialyses, and other users of costly service rather than the somaticizer. To the 10 percent highest utilizers, Biodyne applies its program and elicits the 5.5 percent who are overloading medical resources without there being any physical basis for it. An outreach nurse or medical social worker contacts these patients and, without threatening their belief that their problems are physical, helps them to make an appointment with a Biodyne psychotherapist. About half of a center's resources are expended in providing a comprehensive, efficient, and effective mental health package, the other half in the outreach program. In this way Biodyne renders for its contractees/clients both a comprehensive, unlimited outpatient mental health package at competitive cost and an outreach to the somaticizers that results in considerable cost containment in the provision of overall health care.

Biodyne is able to maintain a low operating overhead at each center by having each of the centers connected by computer and voice lines to a streamlined corporate headquarters in San Francisco. The integrity of the Biodyne model is maintained by scheduled visits from the clinical director and the assistant clinical directors, who, during these visits, conduct clinical case conferences and further training sessions as well as arrange for the center providers to view them in hands-on therapy through one-way screens. Finally, the American Biodyne Centers are committed to providing annual research funds to the Biodyne Institute, a nonprofit research corporation, for ongoing research designed to perpetually refine the model and keep Biodyne on the cutting edge of the profession.

Biodyne operates as an HMO-type PPO; that is, a center is maintained centrally where all the providers see their contracted patients. It has been found that not only is this more efficient and cost-effective than the IPA model, where the practitioners function out of their own individual offices, but also it fosters a stronger identification with the Biodyne model. There is a tendency for practitioners to do in their own offices what they have traditionally done there. However, Biodyne is flexible enough to adapt the model in situations that warrant modification. Two examples are illustrative.

Biodyne/Honolulu serves all of the island of Oahu from its central, convenient location adjacent to the Ala Moana Shopping Center, where the island's extensive bus system converges. This location has proved satisfactory for most Biodyne enrollees. However, the residents of Waianae, a Polynesian "ghetto" northeast of Honolulu, will not come into the city. Furthermore, about one-third of the island's Medicaid population resides in Waianae. A satellite center was established that is staffed part-time by practitioners from the Honolulu center, and this has significantly increased the impact on that segment of enrollees. Similarly, a satellite has been opened in the Pearl Ridge area, where there is a high concentration of federal enrollees.

In Brevard County, Florida, it was apparent from the outset that a modification would be necessary. Brevard County, where NASA's satellite launching station is located, is a narrow county almost 100 miles long. Because of this length, the population divides itself into northern, central, and southern county areas, and the residents of the respective areas will not usually travel the distance to another area. For this reason, Biodyne in Florida is planning for a center in the central county, with satellites in the north and south counties as part of its start-up planning and costs. In the beginning, the satellites would be the private offices of two of the participating providers in the north and south sections of the county. It would be clear from the outset, however, that all practitioners would relate to the one centrally located center for clinical case conferences, meetings, the outreach program, and the other activities of the Biodyne model. This departure from the usual Biodyne Centers model is applicable not only to a 100-mile-long county such as Brevard where there are not yet enough enrollees to form three centers but also to rural settings where there will never be a sufficient cluster of enrollees to maintain one central location serving 30,000 to 80,000 enrollees.

The organizational model of the Biodyne Centers contributes to the efficiency and effectiveness of the delivery system. But to an even greater degree, this efficiency and effectiveness is attributable to the over fifty therapeutic interventions targeted for specific conditions. Empirically tested by Cummings and his colleagues over a twenty-five-year period and known collectively as the "Biodyne model," these techniques dramatically reduce the number of sessions required to achieve patient stability as they enhance the therapeutic outcomes. The literature on select interventions is scant; Stone (see Chapter Nine) found *no* such references. This specificity of treatment is a distinctive Biodyne feature.

These techniques range from necessarily tightly drawn approaches to the several types of suicidal behavior to a more open technique for dealing with midlife crises, so differentiated because the first is life-threatening and the latter requires more latitude for self-actualization. The Biodyne training manual includes a technique for getting housebound and even bedridden agoraphobics out of bed and out of the house with mostly one but sometimes two house calls. It further includes specific interventions for each of a series of addictive behaviors, which include not only alcohol and chemical abuse but also compulsive eating and gambling, anorexia and bulimia, love and sex addictions, and even therapy addiction. Because Biodyne is a capitated delivery system, it can include a number of interventions that would not normally be reimbursed in a fee-for-service practice but are, nonetheless, important to both recovery from stress and prevention of stress.

These include stop-smoking programs, stress management programs, mind-body groups, group biofeedback training, and programs designed to help the chronically unemployed find and keep a job.

The Biodyne model has melded techniques from dynamic therapy, behavioral models, and systems approaches into cohesive interventions that belie the often-stated dogma from adherents that these approaches cannot be mixed with one another. Empirical research has shown that insight is very useful in some conditions and relatively worthless in others, and the same holds true for desensitization or family systems approaches. The important consideration is that these amalgams have been empirically tested over two and a half decades and tested with Cummings' cost/therapeutic-effectiveness ratio, which requires parsimoniously that the techniques used will render the greatest benefit in the least number of sessions.

The Biodyne model employs a substantial number of group therapy techniques, not because these cost less to deliver but because empirical research has shown that clients with certain conditions (addiction and agoraphobia, as two of many examples) recover faster and sustain the recovery longer with group therapy. Biodyne has developed a group for crisis intervention: patients needing to be seen that very day are seen in a group with other such patients. The discovery that crises are best met in crisis groups, even for an initial session, was startling indeed, but the twenty-five years of empirical research that developed the Biodyne model yielded a number of surprises that challenge several therapeutic sacred cows.

For those contracting with American Biodyne Centers there are distinct financial advantages. The Blue Cross/Blue Shield contract in Arizona is illustrative and led to the opening of three centers on September 4, 1985, two in Phoenix and one in Tucson. With Biodyne paid on a capitated basis, the "Blues" have a provider that is sharing the risk. By being able to market Biodyne as an "exclusive," the Blues gain a clear marketing advantage and one likely to increase their market penetration. With capitation, there are no claims to review or reimburse and no individual providers to be qualified, all saving administrative costs. In addition, using a provider that outreaches the many high users of health care whose utilization is the result of somaticizing psychological problems produces a substantial offset of medical care costs.

Even if the joint venture between the Blue Cross/Blue Shield of Arizona and Biodyne Centers of America corporations had no direct financial advantages, it would still have distinct quality-of-care advantages. Biodyne holds quality of care paramount. All the professional staff members are licensed/certified by the state—no paraprofessionals are used. All were selected with care for clinical competence and diversity of skills. All have received intensive training in the Biodyne model. All services provided receive regular in-house oversight for appropriateness and progress in achieving the treatment goals.

From the subscribers' perspective there are also distinct advantages. There is no deductible or copayment and no arbitrary limit on the number of visits. There are also services, when appropriate, atypical of the benefits in most health plans, such as home visits, outreach, phone consultation, biofeedback, and life-style management programs. And since no claim forms and no employer approval of services are involved, the confidentiality of the practitioner/patient relationship is strengthened.

There are also distinct advantages for the members of Biodyne's professional staff. They work in new, modern offices with state-of-the-art equipment. They work with colleges whom they can respect for their training and competence. And they practice without direction by or dependence on referral from another profession. Further, as self-employed contractors, they receive a highly competitive contract income. They are also partners in the "Biodyne family" and thereby eligible to participate in each year end's divisible surplus. As a longer-term incentive, practitioners continuing to contract with Biodyne for three or more years have the option of buying a specified number of corporation shares at nominal cost.

The above describes the many four-way advantages to the participants in the joint venture: the Blues, its subscribers, Biodyne, and its practitioners. They are incentive-oriented realities that promote the enterprise while forming the catalyst that will shape the endeavor and its success.

In reflecting on all the details, reflect also on the ultimate potential. Here is a health care corporation under psychological direction in which services are delivered predominantly by psychologists. Its focus is not services to the mentally disordered but psychological intervention in the total spectrum of health care. The federal Health Care Financing Administration (HCFA) has funded a major five-year cost-offset research project with Biodyne through the Hawaii State Medicaid program. To the extent that the Biodyne psychological intervention succeeds in reducing total Medicaid health care costs, it will have major implications for psychological services in all state Medicaid programs and the operative federal law and regulations. Blue Cross/Blue Shield of Arizona has also entered into a multimillion-dollar contract with Biodyne to develop three centers to serve the subscribers of a number of its plans in two cities. The Arizona Blues are, of course, a member of the national Blue Cross/Blue Shield Association, headquartered in Chicago. To the extent that this Arizona contract proves a success, it has major implications not simply for future Biodyne contracts but also for the inclusion of clinical psychology nationally by the country's largest underwriter of health care. Thus, as a result of demonstrating the effectiveness of psychological services in the full spectrum of health care, the ultimate and not too distant potential is to gain for clinical psychology a collegial standing, recognition, and participation throughout the health care systems of the nation.

Hospitals

Hospitalization is heavily favored over outpatient care in most health insurance plans, is often without deductibles, often has a copayment of 20 percent rather than the more common 50 percent for ambulatory mental health care, and usually has a higher ceiling on days of care than outpatient visits allowed. It is therefore not surprising, even though the large majority of clients receive their care as office or clinic outpatients, that hospitalization accounts for more than half of the mental health dollar—indeed, 70 percent of the Medicaid mental health dollar, so that Medicaid is now the largest mental health program in the country. Big money usually attracts big business. The only wonder, really, is that the involvement of large corporations in psychiatric hospitals is so recent.

Levenson (1983) summarizes the recent rapidly growing ownership of private psychiatric hospitals by investor-owned hospital chains. In 1982 there were 198 nongovernmental (private) free-standing psychiatric hospitals in the country, of which 86, or 43 percent, were affiliated with for-profit (investor-owned) hospital chains. In 1980 only 41 (or 25 percent at the time) were so affiliated, and before the late sixties, the chains did not exist. The four major chains alone in 1982 owned 71 of the psychiatric hospitals affiliated with the National Association of Private Psychiatric Hospitals. The Hospital Corporation of America owned 22 psychiatric hospitals in 1982 and has since gone on to form a psychiatric division. Obviously "big business" is attracted to a major market and one it senses to be growing. Kiesler (1982b) has clearly documented that while public attention has been focused on the deinstitutionaliza- tion of the state mental hospitals, there has been since 1962 a linear increase in "psychiatric" hospitalizations into general hospitals without psychiatric units. In effect, hospitalization for mental disease has not decreased at all—quite the opposite. The locus of care has, however, changed dramatically. With third-party reimbursement, acute care in general hospitals has become feasible, while much of the chronic care at public expense is now situated in intermediate-care nursing facilities, which have lower operating costs than state hospitals. Kiesler (1982a) also found that in all controlled studies of alternatives to hospitalization none was less effective (the majority were more effective) and all were less costly. If there is to be any substantial direct reduction in the cost of mental health care (as distinct from mental health services offsetting total health care costs), it will likely be achieved by residential alternatives to hospitalization that emphasize effective and intensive treatment.

The California legislature wrestled with this issue in 1978 and established a new class of health facility, the psychiatric health facility, or PHF (pronounced "puff"), in S.B. 1496–Gregorio, chapter 1234. This law recognized a twenty-four-hour acute residential care nonhospital in which it was intended that the per diem costs would not exceed 60 percent of the average of similar services in an area general hospital. Of particular interest to psychology, the mandated basic services included "clinical psychology." Within thirty days of the effective date of the legislation (January 1979) the Department of Health Services appointed an ad hoc committee to assist in the formulation of regulations. Seven years later, in January 1986, the draft regulations were finally given public hearing. County mental health programs had established eighteen PHFs on waivers under guidelines of the Department of Mental Health, but private facilities could not be operated without a license. Without a Certificate of Need (CON) it was not possible to grant a license. Without regulations there were no licensing criteria that could be met. And, of course, third parties would reimburse only for services in a licensed facility. Double catch-22.

Legislation in 1984 (S.B. 2160, chapter 1367) resolved much of the impasse when it required that if the health insurance included coverage for services in a general acute care hospital or an acute psychiatric hospital, then the coverage must extend to a PHF operating under either state guidelines or licensure. Finally, in the spring of 1985, the new state administration, seeking to encourage private-sector development, sent word to its Office of Statewide Health Planning that applications should be granted a waiver of the otherwise required CON. Frustrated with the years of bureaucratic delay, Senator Paul Carpenter introduced S.B. 1414 in 1985 to waive the CON requirement when the Department of Mental Health determines that the applicant either will not create excess beds in the area or will deliver services in an innovative and more competitive way or at a lower cost than services at other area facilities. The state administration then moved to incorporate these provisions into the draft regulations and the bill was then converted to another purpose. Thus, finally, the stage is set for the flexible development of cost- and program-competitive acute care mental health services in twenty-four-hour residential facilities. Hospitals, psychiatric and general, will experience the competition.

The first private-sector PHF waiver was granted to Treatment Centers of America (TCA) in the spring of 1985 to open a facility in Panorama City (San Fernando Valley), California. Of its 146 beds, half will function as a PHF with acute intensive treatment. The other half are licensed by the Department of Social Services for residential treatment, much like a halfway house but with active treatment programs. Thus, TCA-Valley can offer two levels of care in a quality professional environment at rates at least 40 percent less than psychiatric hospital care in the area.

TCA also has a thirty-four-bed behavioral health treatment center for psychological conditions and chemical dependency in adults at Scottsdale, Arizona. This operation is licensed as a behavioral health specialty unit within a skilled nursing facility. Plans are underway for the development within the year of other PHF facilities in Southern California. Samuel Mayhugh, president of TCA and a psychologist, is convinced that this model not only enables the development of residential facilities accessible to psychological practice but holds the potential for behavioral health centers to emerge as the more effective alternative to psychiatric hospitalization as measured both by cost and by multilevel treatment effectiveness. Moreover, such facilities can serve as the hub for a range of psychological health services in their area.

In Retrospect and Prospect

There are, no doubt, other viable psychological organizations across the country engaged in the delivery of health care. We hope that the descriptions of community mental health centers as nonprofit corporations, a Philadelphia metropolitan area partnership network of twenty-one offices, the California Psychological Health Plan, the Biodyne model, and Treatment Centers of America will prompt other psychologists to organize new and even more effective models for behavioral health practice. We are convinced that the viable mode of future practice will be within competitive organizations and systems.

References

Bean, E. "Doctors Find a Dose of Marketing Can Cure Pain of Sluggish Practice." *Wall Street Journal,* Mar. 15, 1985, p. 27.
Budman, S., and Gurman, A. "The Practice of Brief Therapy." *Professional Psychology,* 1983, *14,* 277–292.

Casey, T., and Siegel, H. "Compensation and Benefits: Health Care Cost Containment." *Personnel Journal,* June 1982, pp. 410–411.

Cummings, N. A. "The Anatomy of Psychotherapy Under National Health Insurance." *American Psychologist,* 1977, *32,* 711–718.

Cummings, N. A. "Prolonged (Ideal) Versus Short-Term (Realistic) Psychotherapy." In C. A. Kiesler, N. A. Cummings, and G. R. VandenBos, *Psychology and National Health Insurance: A Sourcebook.* Washington, D.C.: American Psychological Association, 1979.

Cummings, N. A. *Biodyne Centers Training Manual.* South San Francisco: Biodyne Institute, 1984.

Cummings, N. A., and Fernandez, L. E. "Exciting Future Possibilities for Psychologists in the Marketplace: One Current Example." *Independent Practitioner,* Jan. 1985, pp. 19–22.

Cummings, N. A., and Follette, W. T. "Psychotherapy and Medical Utilization: An Eight-Year Follow-up." In H. Dörken and Associates, *The Professional Psychologist Today: New Developments in Law, Health Insurance, and Health Practice.* San Francisco: Jossey-Bass, 1976.

Cummings, N. A., and VandenBos, G. R. "The General Practice of Psychology." *Professional Psychology,* 1979, *10,* 430–440.

Dörken, H. "Minnesota's Progressive Community Mental Health Services." *Mental Hygiene,* 1960, *44,* 442–444.

Dörken. H. "Behind the Scenes in Community Mental Health." *American Journal of Psychiatry,* 1962a, *119,* 328–335.

Dörken, H. "Problems in Administration and the Establishment of Community Mental Health Services." *Mental Hygiene,* 1962b, *46,* 498–509.

Dörken, H. "A Dimensional Strategy for Community Focused Mental Health Services." In G. Rosenblum (ed.), *Issues in Community Psychology and Preventive Mental Health.* New York: Behavioral Publications, 1971.

Dörken, H. "Advocacy and the Legislative Process: Representation in a Changing World." *American Psychologist,* 1983, *38,* 1210–1215.

Duhl, L., and Cummings, N. A. "Mental Health: A Whole New Ballgame." Special Issues I and II. *Annals of Psychiatry,* Fall 1985.

Hodges, A., and Dörken, H. "Location and Out-patient Psychiatric Care." *Public Health Reports,* 1961, *76,* 239-241.

Kiesler, C. A. "Mental Hospitals and Alternative Care: Noninstitutionalization as Potential Public Policy for Mental Patients." *American Psychologist,* 1982a, *37,* 349-360.

Kiesler, C. A. "Public and Professional Myths About Mental Hospitalization: An Empirical Reassessment of Policy Related Beliefs." *American Psychologist,* 1982b, *37,* 1323-1339.

Levenson, A. "Issues Surrounding the Ownership of Private Psychiatric Hospitals by Investor-Owned Hospital Chains." *Hospital and Community Psychiatry,* 1983, *34,* 1127-1131.

Magaro, P. "Fourth Revolution in the Treatment of Mental Disorders: Rehabilitative Entrepreneurship." *Professional Psychology,* 1985, *16,* 540-552.

Malan, D. H. *A Study of Brief Psychotherapy.* New York: Plenum, 1963.

Malan, D. H. *The Frontier of Brief Psychotherapy.* New York: Plenum, 1976.

Mercer, W. "Mental Health and Medical Cost Containment." *Mercer Bulletin,* 1980, *6*(5), unnumbered pages.

"Psychological Health Plan Nips Insurance Premium Increases." *Employee Health and Fitness,* 1981, *3*(1), 1-2.

12

Herbert Dörken
Patrick H. DeLeon

Cost as the Driving Force
in Health Care Reform

There are several well-known adages about the relation between money and program. There is the "Golden Rule": He who has the gold makes the rules! And there is the saying that "the program follows the dollar." From a public policy frame of reference, one can see a clear shift in focus away from the vocalized concerns of the mid-1970s regarding "access" and the "right to health care" (DeLeon, 1977) to a growing concern about simply the cost of providing health care. Whereas a decade ago, organized labor and some provider groups were very concerned about pending national health insurance proposals, today representatives of management and local chambers of commerce have also become active participants in health care policy deliberations (DeLeon and VandenBos, 1983). What is beginning to emerge is that escalating costs, not philosophical concerns, may reform our entire health care system. Money is talking.

Cost Rise Too Excessive to Sustain

In July 1982, Lynn May, then associate administrator of the Health Care Financing Administration, made an informal presentation to the Division 12/38 Public Policy Forum of the

The authors wish to express their appreciation for the review and helpful suggestions of Lewis Carpenter, legislative consultant, California State Psychological Association; Mary Uyeda, National Policy Studies, American Psychological Association; and Jean DeLeon.

American Psychological Association. Mr. May made clear not only the enormity of health care costs but also their phenomenal recent increase. To illustrate, the federal government spent $6 billion in 1976 for the Medicare and Medicaid programs combined, but by 1982, only six years later, the federal level of spending had reached $6 billion per month. He stressed that such a level of spending, a twelvefold increase in six years, must be brought under control and explicitly weighed against other priorities. May reported that the administration intended, as possible solutions, to create greater consumer sensitivity to cost, to provide economic incentives for people to seek less costly care, and to create competition among providers.

Health care expenditures have risen (and are still rising) so that in 1983 they were 10.8 percent of our gross national product (GNP), an amount that is said to be close to double all that is spent on national defense (Matarazzo, forthcoming). General Motors reportedly spends more for employee health care than for steel. Private industry, which accounts for approximately 24 percent of U.S. health care expenditures, has reported that in 1983 it paid out $77 billion in health insurance premiums for employees, retirees, and their dependents. This is more than those companies paid out in dividends that year (Califano, 1983). The 10.8 percent of the GNP (or $355 billion) translates into health spending of an average of $1,459 for every American. This was the highest in our history; however, credible projections have already been made that before the year 2000 health expenditures may very well reach 15 percent of our GNP (DeLeon, VandenBos, and Kraut, 1984). This rate of escalation in the cost of health care, unless contained, will bankrupt our society.

An economist would consider this level of increase in expenditures for health care from the perspective of three fundamental observations. First, resources are scarce in relation to human wants. Second, resources have alternative uses. And, third, individuals have different perceived wants, and there is significant variation in the relative importance they attach to these wants. Thus, from an economist's frame of reference—and, we would add, also from that of a public policy analyst—the more resources health care absorbs, the fewer are available for other pressing societal needs. Further, there is growing evidence that the public's view of how resources should be allocated for health needs is increasingly divergent from that of most health care providers. Psychologists know all too well that their views and those of physicians frequently differ. However, what is perhaps not sufficiently appreciated outside medical circles is that there is considerable disagreement among physicians about health care delivery, with practicing physicians and management, university physicians and community physicians, specialists and generalists forming opposing camps. As the noted economist Victor Fuchs (1982) has pointed out, it would be only realistic for physicians to learn to live with a changing world in the control of health care—and to address the major issues without turf fighting. The message for psychologists can hardly be different.

In 1983 traditional insurers were predicting average rate hikes of 25 to 35 percent. Aetna and Prudential are presently reporting the greatest losses in their history because of health policy claims. Such costs and losses are forcing a redesign in benefit plans to encourage more frugality and discretion in their use. In fact, a recent Office of Technology Assessment report on health care competition stressed the importance of economic incentives to patients, rather than exploring provider competition as such (U.S. Office of Technology Assessment, 1982). The new insurance industry plans, in addition to raising premiums, will undoubtedly ask employees to pay a larger share of their health care costs by increasing the minimum deductibles and the copayment levels. If employees have a choice of health plan and if increased premiums go beyond what the employer will pay, it is likely that during open enrollment periods some employees will shift to less expensive plans. Although this plan shifting in itself may to some extent disrupt providers' present modes of practice, the increased awareness that employers can expect an overall reduction in utilization of health services of 40-50 percent solely because of the imposition of a copayment requirement will, without question, have a *major* impact on providers (Newhouse, 1984).

One might predict other modifications in our traditional health insurance plans, such as providing cash rebates in lieu of services used and increasing interest in the development of innovative ways, other than the traditional fee-for-service approach, of organizing the delivery of health care. For example, there will undoubtedly be increased reliance on health maintenance organizations (HMOs) and preferred provider organizations (PPOs), especially since the former have consistently demonstrated the ability to reduce total health care costs by 10 to 40 percent (U.S. Congressional Budget Office, 1982). One can also expect the development of entirely new modes of health delivery, such as urgency centers and walk-in clinics, which will have an incident-specific orientation and will actively seek transient clients, rather than focus on the development of traditional, long-term doctor/ patient relationships. Providers, especially nonphysician health care providers, must also expect that public policy officials will attempt to reduce or, at a minimum, hold constant the number and types of professionals deemed eligible to receive reimbursement for services. On at least a superficial level, doing so would logically appear to result in reduced expenditures. It has been the government's and private industry's fixed opinion (despite all the medical offset research to the contrary) that previous efforts to reduce health care costs by increasing access to "alternative" (that is, nonphysician) providers have resulted in increased costs, rather than the economic savings that were projected as a result of expected professional "substitutability."

During the 98th Congress (1983–1984) considerable attention was given to the role of federal income tax policy in encouraging health care utilization. Our present tax policies actively encourage (or subsidize) expansive benefits. For example, the individual medical expense deduction provision (Section 213) favors the 28 percent of taxpayers who itemize their deductions, in effect subsidizing these costs (DeLeon, 1981). Similarly, employee health insurance is a business expense of the employer, in addition to being treated as a nontaxable fringe benefit to the employee. Thus, for persons having group health insurance coverage these provisions have, until recently, effectively eliminated medical expenses as a matter of personal or corporate concern. The U.S. Congressional Budget Office (1982) has estimated that the current exclusion of employer contributions for health insurance from "taxable employee income" reduces the federal government's annual income tax revenue by $16.5 billion and the payroll tax revenue by $6.5 billion. These figures are projected to increase to $31.1 billion and $14.7 billion, respectively, by 1987 (compared with $2.4 billion and $0.8 billion for 1970). In effect, our current tax policy promotes the consumption of a costly commodity, rather than promoting either a prudent buyer orientation in the purchase of "illness care" or encouraging people to make the health behavior changes that will reduce the risk of subsequent disability. As noted, however, the Reagan administration and also the Congress have begun to take a closer look at these consequences of our present medical expense tax policy (Winston, 1982). Given the magnitude of the cost involved and the extent of public support for president Reagan's reelection, the administration and the Congress have been encouraged to alter the health insurance fringe benefit as part of the tax reform movement.

Industry the Buyer to Become the Controller

In the spring of 1983, an industry panel addressed the annual meeting of the United Foundation for Medical Care at Lake Tahoe, California. The panel noted that industry was just beginning to get involved in the policy of health care and that this involvement was mainly due to the perception of costs as uncontrollable. Employers seemed to believe that they had been "had" by both providers and the insurance industry; they now intended to organize and exert major control. The industry representatives conveyed a sense of impending urgency, similar to an awakening giant. Hewlett-Packard, as an example, estimated that its self-insured medical benefit plan, if continued as it was in 1981, would have absorbed all corporate profits in five years. ARCO reported that its health costs had tripled in four years. Dramatic premium changes in the past year included a 46 percent increase for the San Diego school system and a 42 percent increase for Southern Pacific Gas.

Overall, business spending on health in 1982 was equal to one-half of corporate profits, and as reported at the Lake Tahoe meeting, many firms were becoming concerned that projected government cutbacks might shift additional health costs to the private sector. For example, at least nineteen states reported making reductions in funding for their Medicaid programs in 1983 (Young, 1984). The Intergovernmental Health Policy Project reported that thirty-four states had enacted legislation addressing the health insurance needs of laid-off or terminated workers (Markus, 1983). The 98th Congress gave considerable attention to the possibility of the federal government's requiring employers to provide at least one year of health care coverage for terminated employees. Legislation did pass the House of Representatives but did not become public law. However, this Congressional focus itself may very well be a sufficient catalyst for far-reaching federal legislation to evolve in the near future (DeLeon, 1983). In the popular news media, leading economists increasingly predict that health care expenditures—and who pays for them—will be the number one social issue during the rest of this century (*The Christian Science Monitor*, September 14, 1984).

Industry representatives, in their newly acknowledged role as purchasers of health care, are beginning to refer to employees as *their* patients. This was quite evident at the Lake Tahoe conference, for example. They are clearly beginning to see health care as being too important to be left in the hands of providers, and they do not intend to allow providers to retain control. Insurance companies are coming to be viewed as vehicles for passing through costs, rather than as health policy experts. In our judgment, it is especially significant that industry is now utilizing self-generated management information and thus beginning to actively take control over *its* health care expenditures.

Private industry has recently developed a number of innovative initiatives to contain costs. These range from the establishment by the Zenith Corporation of a medical advisory program in order to advise its employees which area hospitals are less expensive to efforts by the Dexter Corporation to increase employees' awareness by directly increasing their share of health care bills (that is, by raising deductibles and premiums) while offering an HMO option. The HMO option provides broader coverage at less cost but does require the use of its own health care facilities. The Rolm Corporation of Santa Clara, California, has been able to reduce its dental insurance costs by contracting with a private corporation. Rolm now requires the use of a particular preselected group of dentists who are screened by management for cost-effectiveness and quality of service. Each dentist is paid on a capitation basis; that is, he or she receives a set amount per month for each employee, and the rate does not change with the amount of care provided. There is a clear economic incentive for the dentist to practice preventive care and no incentive to provide unneeded services. The dentist receives cash in advance, unpaid bills are eliminated, and there are no claim forms (Miller, 1983) (*San Jose Mercury News*, March 13, 1983). For Rolm, overall costs have been less, are predictable, and are controlled. The underlying approach has many overt similarities to the HMOs discussed earlier. Again, in an evolutionary sense, this active involvement in policy and management by corporate industry represents a major change. Industry used to act solely as payer; now it is beginning to act as buyer.

The heart of industry's concern is not the overall package of health benefits but, instead, the very structure by which these services are delivered and the resulting costs. For example, Rohr Industries reported that in Maryland there is a statewide rate system for hospital care costs. As a result, the average hospital day for Rohr's employees in Maryland costs $240, compared with $723 in California. Moreover, the average duration of stay was apparently one day less for Maryland employees, and the predicted duration of stay was more accurate by one day. In response to voiced concerns that industry control might lead to lower quality of care, the Rohr spokesperson noted that of all the company's employees who are hospitalized, 34 percent contract an iatrogenic illness—that is, one contracted as a result of their hospital stay—and 11 percent suffer some additional disability as a direct result of the hospitalization. Shorter hospital stays could reduce these percentages. The decision by the Saturn Corporation (a General Motors subsidiary) that the health care coverage of its six thousand employees will be exclusively handled through PPOs and HMOs—no traditional fee-for-service plans at all—further illustrates the determination of industry to alter the structure by which care is delivered.

On a nationwide basis, Wennberg (1984) has reported that geographical variations in medical practice can be substantial, with little apparent objective difference in overall health care status. For example, in Vermont the probability that resident children will undergo a tonsillectomy has ranged from a low of 8 percent in one hospital market to a high of nearly 70 percent in another. Similarly, in Iowa, the chances of male residents having undergone a prostatectomy by age eighty-five range from 15 percent to more than 60 percent; again, the key variable seems to be different hospital markets. In the field of dentistry, a similar variation in practice exists. Within New England, for example, there is a sixfold difference in whether dental surgeons do tooth extractions in their offices or in hospitals (the latter being considerably more expensive). The former secretary of the Department of Health and Human Services Joseph Califano has estimated that 27 percent of hospital days are "medically inappropriate." The Washington Business Group on Health, with represents many *Fortune* 500 firms, has testified before Congress that nearly any major private employer can reduce health outlays by 20–30 percent by adopting a concerted strategy of reimbursement design, utilization controls, and capacity constraints that reward the efficient providers (Goldbeck, 1984). During the final days of the 98th Congress, the Senate Appropriations Committee held a special hearing on the variations in health practice.

Although national health insurance has seemed a dead or dormant issue in recent years, it could soon reemerge abruptly, for if private industry's efforts to control health care costs are unsuccessful, industry spokespersons and informed consumers see total government intervention as the only logical step left. This possibility, of course, underscores the importance for psychology of gaining broad recognition in Medicare.

Psychological Services by Contract

From a public policy frame of reference, it is but a minor step forward to envision mental health services being delivered on a contractual basis. In fact, with express congressional approval, the Department of Defense Civilian Health and Medical Program of the Uniformed Services (CHAMPUS) has developed plans for testing out contracted or prepaid mental health benefits during fiscal year 1985.

Given the relative youth of the profession, a large number of practitioners do not appreciate the extent to which their predecessors had to struggle for insurance reimbursement. Presently psychological services are legislatively protected under the Federal Employees' Health Benefit Program (FEHBP), CHAMPUS, and forty state "freedom of choice" statutes. Twenty-six states have also enacted some form of mandatory mental health benefit legislation. Within the psychological profession there is the general perception that eventually psychological services will become expressly enumerated and legislatively mandated under all state, federal, and private health plans, essentially on a fee-for-service basis. However, this seems to us a naive optimism, which does not consider the escalating costs of health care or the fundamental lack of appreciation for the intricacies of mental health care by the public and consequently also by elected officials.

A recent focus of concern has been the relation between federal and state statutes that address health care and insurance regulation. It is a fundamental principle of American law that state legislation is preempted and thus null and void. In enacting the Employee Retirement Income Security Act of 1974, as amended (ERISA), the Congress intended that state legislatures should not enact laws that would affect "employee welfare benefit plans." The underlying notion was that it would not be in our national interest for multistate employers, such as Standard Oil, to be required to negotiate a different employee welfare benefit plan in every state in which they might have an office. The ERISA legislation is extraordinarily complex and contains an express exemption for state laws dealing with the "business of health insurance." The question for psychology is whether state-enacted "freedom of choice" laws and/or mandatory mental health benefit laws fall within the "business of insurance" exemption. This is a legal question, and various elements of the underlying issue have been argued before numerous state and federal courts. In October 1984 the U.S. Supreme Court agreed to review two related Massachusetts cases: *Metropolitan Life Insurance Co* v. *Massachusetts*, 463 N.E.2d 548 (Mass. 1984), and *Travelers Insurance Co.* v. *Massachusetts*, 463 N.E.2d 548 (Mass. 1984). The central issue is the relation between ERISA and the Massachusetts "freedom of choice" and mandatory mental health benefit laws. Every one of the major professional associations involved in mental health, including the American Psychological Association, filed an *amicus curiae* brief. The implications for the autonomous practice of psychology were major. Fortunately, the Supreme Court, in an 8-0 decision on June 3, 1985, held that ERISA did not preempt mandatory mental health coverage laws, FOC laws, or the National Labor Relations Act (*Metropolitan Life Insurance Co.* v. *Massachusetts, appeal granted* (No. 84-325), 53 U.S.L.W. 3169, and *Travelers Insurance Co.* v. *Massachusetts, appeal granted* (No. 84-356), 53 U.S.L.W. 3189).

Regardless of this decision in the Massachusetts cases, however, it is important for psychologists to begin to understand the basic conceptual difference between traditional fee-for-service approaches to health care and the growing interest in capitation-based or contractually negotiated group plans. Under the former, the ultimate decision maker is the individual consumer, or patient. Under the latter approach, it is the purchaser of health care, not the consumer, who retains control. And in this latter approach, psychology "freedom of choice" legislation in providing an individual, if he or she is entitled to receive mental health care, with the right to select a psychologist, if desired, is restrained.

Given the unfortunate stigma associated with receiving mental health care, there is a societal, or public policy, rationale for ensuring that a certain minimal level of mental health benefits should be made available. However, what societal, or public policy, rationale exists for requiring that the services of one particular category of practitioners must be made available? If the ultimate purchaser of health care is able to contract with a certain group of providers and, by so doing, can ensure that cost-effective and high-quality care will be made available, what rationale does a state legislature have for insisting that such a private contract must explicitly include psychologists? If there exists the freedom to contract with a group of psychologists and the buyer chooses not to do so, what role is there for a state legislature in the process? It should not be surprising, therefore, that most, if not all, of the "freedom of choice" legislation already enacted into public law expressly exempts prepaid health care plans (HMOs) and self-insurance programs from its provisions. The public policy rationale is that if the particular class of providers is truly cost-effective, then the buyer will undoubtedly contract for their services!

Fortunately, there is growing evidence in at least several states of a collective willingness within organized psychology to be responsive to the evolving trends of the health care industry. The California Psychological Health Plan (CPHP) was the first statewide prepaid mental health care program to be licensed in a state (1976). It currently provides outpatient benefits to a number of groups, in each case in conjunction with a comprehensive health plan on a capitation basis. Some outcome data and a fuller description of the CPHP model are provided in Chapter Eleven.

CPHP has now demonstrated its financial viability, it is growing, and it is competitive in the marketplace. It was designed and staffed by psychologists, and it is one alternative that preserves the essence of traditional fee-for-service practice, albeit at a discounted rate.

There are other examples of innovative successes by organized psychology. For example, the Psychological Health Plan of Massachusetts has now been formed and is actively negotiating contracts, similar to those developed by CPHP, with industry representatives in Massachusetts. In the Quad Cities area of Iowa and Illinois, local psychologists have negotiated participation in an already-established HMO/IPA, rather than establish their own independent program. Using locally licensed psychologists as core staff and following specified models of brief intervention, the American Biodyne Centers incorporated in California have established three Biodyne Centers in Arizona and are actively negotiating the development of other Biodyne Centers in Florida, California, Ohio, Utah, and other states.

The successes in California, Hawaii, Philadelphia (see Delaware Valley Psychological Clinics in Chapter Eleven) and the Quad Cities area show that much can be done through organized professional initiative. It is often advantageous, if not absolutely necessary, to have legislation enacted that clearly authorizes organized modes of psychological practice. To this end, in 1977 the California State Psychological Association amended the state's Corporations Code and Business and Professional Code to enable psychologists to practice in a medical corporation. With later amendments, physicians, optometrists, nurses, and other health care practitioners are now expressly authorized to practice through a psychological corporation. However, on a nationwide basis, only in California and perhaps, by a liberal statutory interpretation, in Nebraska can psychologists establish and practice in interdisciplinary corporations (Overcast and Sales, 1981). The California psychologists have also taken the lead in statutorily establishing an entirely new class of licensed health facility, the psychology clinic. Such clinics must by statute be under the direction of a clinical psychologist. In developing such a far-reaching legislative proposal, the psychologists in California foresaw that new organizational entities such as this would allow them to contract to deliver a range of services with government and private industry in ways and volume that individual psychologists simply could not match.

Legislative Action to Curtail Costs

In 1982 the state of California faced an unprecedented budget deficit. The state legislature concluded that the budget simply could not be balanced unless hundreds of millions of dollars could be trimmed from the Medi-Cal (Medicaid) program. Despite the escalating costs for this public program, it was also found to be responsible for major cost shifts to the private sector; that is, whatever a hospital "lost" on its Medi-Cal patients, it typically attempted to add on to the cost of private care.

The state's answer to the budget deficit was twofold. First, a negotiator, or "czar," as he was nicknamed, was appointed out of the governor's office. This person was to be free from departmental ties and was given unprecedented authority to negotiate Medi-Cal prices (or rates), as well as the basis of service with all hospitals. Institutions that were willing to meet the state's conditions, which in the main consisted of a flat per diem rate, were advanced contracts; the others were not. Without such a contract, a hospital was no longer to be paid for services provided to Medi-Cal patients, although there were certain exceptions—for example, for children's hospitals. The bidding in California was highly competitive and concluded with remarkable dispatch. It now appears that a number of the hospitals that were unable to obtain a Medi-Cal contract will eventually go bankrupt, primarily because they simply were not managed efficiently enough to compete without the traditional cost-plus arrangement. From the state of California's perspective, the results of this approach were impressive. The state experienced a savings of $200 million in 1983 and an additional $200 million savings in 1984. In effect, the days of retrospective pass-through costs for hospitals ended abruptly in California. The recent decision by Blue Cross/Blue Shield and Mutual of Northeast Ohio to enter into a similar competitive arrangement with Cleveland area hospitals suggests that this phenomenon will not be restricted to California. In this situation, hospitals were asked to propose per-case prices, and twenty-five of the thirty-four competing hospitals were approved. Patients who go to the nine losing hospitals receive 70 percent reimbursement; those who use the approved hospitals receive 100 percent reimbursement (*The Wall Street Journal,* December 28, 1984).

Following on its success with hospital contracting, the state of California began to initiate plans to contract for professional services in July 1983. The state's primary thrust was to contract with HMOs and PPOs, thereby giving Medi-Cal eligibles a private-sector choice on a flat-rate capitation basis while allowing the state to capitalize fully on its bargaining power as a major purchaser of health care. The long-term effect will be to bypass individual practitioner contracting and traditional fee-for-service care. Legislation has been introduced in the California legislature that calls for at least 50 percent of the Medi-Cal population to be served through HMOs. If this approach is enacted into law, it would effectively convert the program from fee-for-service reimbursement to prepaid capitation contracts. It is possible that soon the only psychologists seeing Medi-Cal patients will be those in contracting entities.

As made very explicit by the speaker of the California Assembly, "Mainstreaming is over." The state is in the process of developing affordable care. It is beginning to act as a purchaser of health care, not solely a payer. As one might expect, some entities, notably organized medicine, publicly contend that this approach does not provide "optimum care." Freedom of choice is clearly being limited by the state's "prudent buyer" philosophy. From a historical frame of reference, this argument is analogous to the concerns initially raised by organized medicine when various group practices and prepaid arrangements were first proposed—for example, by the Kaiser Foundation. However, it simply has never been demonstrated that there is any objective evidence that the care provided under the alternative approaches by an established HMO such as Kaiser is of lower quality. Some commentators have likened the choice to owning a Cadillac or a Toyota, but there are many HMO members (as well as Toyota owners) who will aver that not only is the cost less, but the quality is better and the service considerably more dependable. Rather than "mainstreaming being over," it may evolve that an individual who wants to continue to have complete freedom of choice of doctor or hospital will have to pay a considerable premium for such a luxury.

Another significant modification adopted by the California legislature provided the private health insurance industry with the authority to negotiate "alternative rates." Because of their large enrollment, health care plans such as Blue Shield had been able to negotiate preferred rates with hospitals and providers for years and had done so using their purchasing power to advantage. However, the California statutes had expressly prevented the commercial carriers from doing the same. To equalize the competition and thereby eliminate potential cost shifts to this element of the private sector, the California Insurance Code was amended to authorize "an insurer [to] negotiate and enter into contracts for *alternative rates* of payment with institutional providers and offer the benefit of such rates to insurers who select such providers. Alternatively, insurers may, by agreement with group policy holders, *limit* payments under a policy to services secured by insureds from institutional providers charging alternative rates pursuant to contract. . . . This section . . . shall also be applicable with respect to both professional and institutional providers" (A.B. 3480, chapter 329, 1982; emphasis added). The message? Open price competition is here: for hospitals, for physicians, and for organized health care entities. Can there really be any question that psychology, which is but one small segment of the state's health care system, will not soon find itself caught up in the currents of these changes?

Relatively unknown before the passage of this latter legislation, preferred provider organizations (PPOs) are now being actively organized throughout California by hospitals, physician groups, indemnity carriers, employer coalitions, and insurance brokers, among others. For example, in a 1983 survey, the California Hospital Association found that 30 percent of its 535 member hospitals had already contracted with or were in the process of developing PPO entities. The twenty-four California Foundations for Medical Care (FMCs) were all projected to establish component PPOs within the year and did so, thus covering the fifty-eight counties of the state. Blue Cross, the largest health underwriter in California, launched a very aggressive campaign to solicit provider contracts with the medical staffs of hospitals (physicians, dentists, and podiatrists but not psychologists, although change has now been promised before the end of 1985). By June 1983, Blue Cross announced it had reached agreement with 42 of the 144 hospitals that had submitted proposals in response to its initial targeted marketing (Trauner, 1983). After repeated requests by the California State Psychological Association, Blue Cross "agreed" in late 1985 that psychologists who are members of a medical staff could be participative providers—an informal promise for 1986. Trauner (p. 7) describes the PPO operationally as involving "acceptance of fixed rates of payment (often at levels below customary charges) and adherence to a program of utilization review. In return [the participating providers] expect to receive rapid processing of claims and to have health benefit packages with economic incentives to encourage subscribers to use their services." This PPO evolution can hardly occur without a major impact on practitioners, including psychologists.

The traditional fee-for-service reimbursement system, even with rate setting for public services, inherently carries an incentive to perform more services, which of course evades the intent of the rate control. Conceptually, there is no such incentive in a capitated HMO whose practitioners are on salary or in counties that have replaced fee-for-service with straight practitioner salaries. In capitated models, the need to function within the prepaid resources, in conjunction with the pressures of cost-conscious peer review,

328 | Professional Psychology in Transition

serves to control utilization and to encourage services that have been shown to be cost-effective.

On a national level, the U.S. Congress has also begun experimenting with innovative reimbursement approaches. For Medicare, as a provision of P.L. 98-21, the Social Security Amendments of 1983, the Congress proposed adopting the "prospective payment system" approach, modeled after experiences in New Jersey. The underlying principle is that Medicare hospital payments are to be based on a predetermined fixed charge for each case, classified according to 467 "diagnostic related groups" (DRGs) of illnesses and injuries. In its beginning stages, exemptions are provided for certain circumstances, such as for psychiatric hospitals and rehabilitation hospitals. Interestingly, California's Medi-Cal "czar" rejected the DRG approach as too complex and demanded and got a uniform per diem rate applied to all admissions, any diagnosis. In any event, it is the clear congressional intention that as the federal government obtains more experience with the DRG system, these exemptions will be eliminated. In fact, there has already been considerable congressional interest in expanding the parameters of the program to include all physician services in hospitals (DeLeon, Forsythe, and VandenBos, forthcoming). Extension to outpatient physician care, as well as to services provided in other institutions such as nursing homes, is also being contemplated. The underlying assumption continues to be that providing clear financial incentives for cost-effective care will force the inefficient institutions and practitioners to alter their practices. As an example of the magnitude of the changes contemplated, the Congressional Budget Office estimated that after two years of "budget neutrality," Medicare would be expected to save $2.0 billion by using DRGs. Similarly, the Department of Defense CHAMPUS program has projected that it could reduce annual expenditures by $170 million, even though the DRG values were established for an entirely different population (that is, for Medicare patients).

The resistance by both government and the private sector to expansion of health care expenditures is considerable and is clearly mounting. Taxpayers are resisting proposed increases, and management is steadily gaining control over its expenditures. Both are forces urging organizational change and new methods of financing health care. The slowed growth of the economy and the rapid growth in numbers of providers are key factors giving urgency to reform. With restricted health care dollars, the income of practitioners will be linked to expenditures for hospitals, drugs, and the like. For psychologists economic viability will depend both on being able to demonstrate that their unique intervention reduces total health care costs and on developing innovative methods and procedures.

Provider Negotiation of Rates and Assumption of Risk

Does any provider still doubt that rates and fees will be negotiated? Not the hospitals in California, with only a 65 percent occupancy average statewide—especially not after their experiences with the Medi-Cal "czar." The message may not have "reached" professionals yet, but 30 percent of dental hours are presently unscheduled. The state of California has an excess of physicians, albeit somewhat unevenly distributed. The growth in that state has been greater than nationally, where there was a 40 percent increase during the 1970s. The growth of licensed psychologists in California and across the nation has been simply phenomenal: 42.2 percent nationally from 1974 to 1979, 48 percent in California (Dörken and Webb, 1981), with an additional 24 percent growth in California from 1979 to 1982. This increasing supply alone establishes a basis and leverage for negotiating "alternative rates," not to mention the backdrop of the increasing number of clinical social workers, marriage and family counselors, and psychiatric nurses.

A number of other approaches to cost containment are also being explored. For example, in 1982, Arizona, which was the last state in the nation to enact a Medicaid plan, AHCCCS (Arizona Health Care Cost Containment System, pronounced "access"), adopted a statewide "gatekeeper" approach. For this system for indigent care, all physicians, hospitals, and clinics in each of the state's fourteen counties were invited to submit bids on how much they would charge the state per person per month to provide health services to public beneficiaries. In one county, initial opposition was overcome by the threat to bring in a medical-surgical group if physicians in that county declined to bid on care of the poor. Under the Arizona Medicaid approach each public beneficiary must choose a physician from a designated contracting group who then serves as his or her "gatekeeper," or health care manager. Only the gatekeeper can decide whether the patient needs to see a specialist or to be hospitalized. The financial incentive is that the gatekeeper must pay for any recommended services out of his or her own monthly fee received from the state. This has had the effect of severely controlling the utilization of expensive specialists. The State has now decided to open up its health plan, initially aimed at the poor and needy, to any private or public employee who wishes to join. As stated above, the services of specialists—which includes psychologists—have been brought under the control of primary-care physicians. It is somewhat disconcerting for psychologists, who have maintained that *their* services are cost-effective, that in order to control escalating health care costs, Arizona has enacted a gatekeeper system that, in essence, grants physician control over all aspects of health care, including eliminating direct access to psychological services (Young, 1984). This federally funded and waivered system of fourteen contracts includes only minimal emergency mental health services. Where AHCCCS has contracted with an HMO, some mental health care may be available. This system, fortunately, is faltering.

These changes in California and Arizona are being closely monitored throughout the insurance industry and by many other states. A contractual or negotiated system of health care will force the development of organized models of care and negotiated rates and, thus, will change many of the current patterns of relations between health care practitioners. Nevertheless, this cloud over solo fee-for-service practice may have a silver lining. If it is ultimately successful in controlling health care costs, it could keep health care in the private sector and put an end to periodic cries for the enactment of a comprehensive national health insurance plan. When one looks closely at the views of the general public and of public officials regarding the health care system, one finds that there is really only limited interest in cost containment proposals that are seen as requiring individuals to substantially modify the ways in which they presently receive care. In fact, only 8 percent of those polled by Blendon and Altman (1984) gave a high priority to the enactment of either "socialized" medicine or a national health service. Similarly, surveys show that rising health care costs are not among the ten most important problems now facing this nation, as listed either by the public or by elected officials. A typical finding was that although 66 percent of those polled felt that doctors are too interested in making money, 72 percent also reported that their own physician was not (Blendon and Altman, 1984). If a satisfactory solution can evolve, there may not be the necessity for the type of systemwide restructuring that some politicians have been advocating.

On a personal basis, contracting for discounted rates will vary in attractiveness by practitioner. It may be worthwhile to guarantee some presence in a particular market. Time filled at a discounted rate may be preferred over empty time by a practitioner or a group. Where a contract is based on a price for a service, with remuneration left internally to the contractee, efficient providers may willingly assume the risk to gain the potential profit.

The day may be fast approaching when the capitalist philosophy will come to the practitioner's doorstep. Government and large-scale private buyers will shop for price, paying as little as possible for the services they buy. Moreover, they may very well unite in their negotiations so that one cannot be played off against the other. Together they can negotiate for significant price advantages and, if desired, modify the very types of services being provided, through the bid process. As private-sector management in particular gains expertise, one must expect that it will look closely at the effectiveness of services. What we are seeing is the beginning stages of the deregulation of the health care industry, a stripping away of regulations, which, under the guise of protecting patients, have in fact shielded providers from economic concerns.

Industrialization of Health Care

During the past several years, Congress has begun to consider the possible impact of true price competition and organized models of delivery. This issue has been raised, for example, during

consideration of various reauthorization proposals for the Federal
Trade Commission (FTC) since the 96th Congress (1978-1979). The
FTC has consistently pointed out that true deregulation with
vigorous enforcement of the antitrust laws could result in
considerable savings to consumers, many of whom are senior
citizens. As an example, the FTC points out that since its "eyeglass
rule" was promulgated in 1978, the consumer price index for
eyeglasses has increased only 4.3 percent, compared with 9.1 percent
for all goods and services and 13 percent for medical care generally
(Pertschuk, 1980). This rule, in essence, eliminated state
prohibitions on advertising by optometrists and opticians and also
required ophthalmologists to provide consumers with copies of
their prescriptions. The American Optometric Association (AOA),
however, has stressed that excessive FTC involvement in the health
care industry could result in the virtual elimination of numerous
"mom and pop" optometry stores across the nation. AOA has
argued that the FTC should be prevented legislatively from
exercising any jurisdiction in the health care arena. Not
surprisingly, both the American Medical Association and the
American Dental Association have joined AOA in this position
(Pertschuk and Correia, 1983). To date, however, Congress has not
decided to significantly restrict the FTC's authority in the health
care area, although this does remain a possibility (Wiggins,
Bennett, Batchelor, and West, 1983). These same issues were also
graphically highlighted in a 1981 national symposium on the
"Changing Dental Care Delivery System" (Rovin and Nash, 1982,
p. 661), where it was stated that "the emergence of alternative
delivery systems is a manifestation of a profoundly changing society
in which the public is demanding better economic performance. . . .
The shibboleth for the coming years will be competition . . . look
at what happened to small businesses after World War II.
Essentially, large retail merchants have all but replaced small
businesses. Now [they] . . . are entering the health care arena [with]
considerably more business acumen than most private practitioners
[and] . . . more capital to invest. . . . The monopoly currently
enjoyed by traditional [solo] practice is going to change
dramatically in the next ten to twenty years." Among the kinds of
emerging practices described at the symposium were department

store clinics emphasizing prime location, shopper volume, and skilled marketing; corporate "in-house" practices; franchise practices, or "turn key" leasing; and extended hospital services— promoting ambulatory care to replace empty beds. To these Bailit (1982), at this same symposium, added insurance-carrier-organized networks of capitated practices.

The June 1983 issue of the APA's *Psychology Today* reported similar prognostications: "The corporations are coming! A medical industrial complex of profit-making companies is already firmly established. Profit-making conglomerates own chains of hospitals, nursing homes, kidney dialysis centers, diagnostic laboratories, pharmacies, medical office buildings, ambulatory surgical centers, and shopping mall emergency centers. In the 1970s these chains grew faster than the computer industry. They will inexorably restructure—and could conceivably take over—medical care in the United States" (Geiger, 1983, p. 85). It would be naive for psychology's practitioners to believe that their practice will not become involved in these fundamental changes. Unfortunately, however, few psychologists have given serious thought to such a future, and almost none have ever considered establishing their own group or corporate practices.

A brief review of the growth of the Hospital Corporation of America (HCA) is quite enlightening. From its inception with one hospital in 1968 to its ownership or management of 364 hospitals both here and abroad by 1982 ("Business This Week . . . ,"1982), HCA makes it apparent that private-sector corporate enterprise can flourish in the health care market. HCA brought to the health care field needed management expertise and an impressive ability to secure hundreds of millions of dollars in investment capital. By concurrently achieving economies of scale, it has handsomely rewarded its investors. It is now the largest owner of private hospitals in the world and, further, owns 18 percent of Beverly Enterprises, considered the giant in the U.S. nursing home industry. It has also established the HCA Psychiatric Company, which owns twenty-five psychiatric hospitals. In 1982 it was rated one of the five best-managed companies by *Dunn's Business Month*. Its annual report that year cited $3 billion in net operating revenues. Health care is clearly big business.

Perhaps the most consistent and vocal opposition to economic market forces influencing the health care system has been the American Medical Association (AMA) and its state medical association counterparts. These organizations have a long history of legislative involvement and are viewed by many as possessing guildlike power, resulting in near monopoly under the laws of most states. The AMA in the past, for example, has fought hard to restrict the role of consumers in establishing health policy, to limit the number of physicians practicing, and to ban doctor advertising. Organized medicine continues to be a major obstacle, especially at the state level, for legislative efforts by the various nonphysician providers—such as psychologists, chiropractors, optometrists, podiatrists, nurse-midwives, and nurse-practitioners—who desire to expand the scope of their state practice acts. The result has been that even today there are all too few alternatives to seeing a physician, and third-party reimbursement is typically not available for services that are traditionally not considered "medically necessary"—for example, well-baby care, holistic health initiatives, or wellness-oriented programs.

Turf Control Versus Open Competition

Since the recommendation of the President's Commission on Mental Health that the practitioners of each of the four traditional mental health disciplines be deemed autonomous under all public and private health insurance plans, the numbers of these professionals have steadily increased. Has this increase led to real competition? Not yet. Instead, the most notable effect to date has been the growing resistance of organized psychiatry to any standards or arrangements that do not expressly provide that the psychiatrist will have ultimate clinical control and responsibility. Psychiatry wants to be considered the "gatekeeper," or the "captain of the ship," for all mental health care.

It has historically been difficult for physicians to control access to ambulatory care provided by nonphysician providers, particularly in the face of state "freedom of choice" legislation. Physicians, however, have closed ranks tightest at the hospital door. Their general approach has been to press for accreditation standards, such as those of the Joint Commission on Accreditation of Hospitals (JCAH), or hospital medical staff bylaws, which can be written and sustained in such a fashion that psychologists and other alternative providers will have no real standing, except as an ancillary service or subordinate staff. In such an environment, no real competition can exist.

Where psychologists are members of the active medical staff of hospitals, a number of patients have selected their services. In such roles and settings psychologists now have a history of effective performance (Rodgers, 1980). Organized psychiatry and psychology must concede that, to a significant extent, all the major mental health professions have overlapping skills. Hence, within the mental health field there exists the potential for considerable substitutability of service. The basic issue, then, would appear not to be the exclusiveness of the scope of one's professional license or concerns about "quality of care" but instead the furtherance of monopoly and the avoidance of competition. Under the guise of "quality of care," the real motive has been economic control of the marketplace. When finally contested, it will involve a "turf" battle of major proportions.

It is therefore worth noting in some detail the extent to which the services of clinical psychologists and psychiatrists are in fact substitutable. Under present state mental health statutes only physicians can prescribe medications or administer electroshock. Further, few psychiatrists have sufficient training or expertise to match clinical psychologists in psychological testing or the behavior therapies, including the clinical applications of biofeedback. A recent review of the mental health inpatient services provided nationwide by psychiatrists under CHAMPUS in 1980 showed that 93.7 percent of all visits were for procedures that can also be performed by psychologists: individual psychotherapy, 86.7 percent; family, couple, or group therapy, 5.1 percent; and psychological testing, 1.9 percent. Each of these procedures falls explicitly within the scope of authorized psychological practice under state licensing laws. In 1980 psychiatrists rendered 82.6 percent of all CHAMPUS inpatient mental health visits, psychologists only 2.6 percent. Of particular interest to those who ultimately must pay the bill is that the average fee, for all the major procedures, was almost universally lower for psychological care.

The CHAMPUS data for outpatient care revealed that the proportion of visits to these two professions was 39.7 percent for psychiatrists and 28 percent for psychologists. In California, which has perhaps the broadest range of state laws recognizing psychological practice, we find the reverse: the proportion of CHAMPUS outpatient services provided by psychologists was 39.7 percent and that by psychiatrists was 28 percent. For inpatient care, however, the California data for the two professions were 5.9 percent and 89.3 percent, respectively. The Hawaii Medicaid data are even clearer. Hawaii is the only state in the nation that has a universal health care act. The numbers of psychologists and psychiatrists practicing in Hawaii were equal in 1980. On an outpatient basis there was a 43/53 percent split in the proportion of patients going to psychologists and to psychiatrists under the state's Blue Shield plan, which provides administrative parity between the two professions. However, under the Medicaid program, which requires medical referral, 31 percent of the beneficiaries saw psychologists while 55 percent saw psychiatrists, 14 percent being served by mental health clinics. On a statewide basis, the Hawaii inpatient mental health data are even more pronounced, with only 1 percent of private patients being seen by psychologists and 72 percent being seen by psychiatrists (Dörken and Cummings, 1981). The power to control a locus of care and the power to be able to determine whether to refer to another profession have a telling effect on patterns of practice.

Despite the general perception that hospitalizations for mental disorders have been on the decline, due mainly, perhaps, to media coverage of problems surrounding deinstitutionalization (Teplin, 1984) and the shrinking census in many state and county mental hospitals, in fact, they are on the rise. There has been a linear increase in the number of mental hospitalizations from 1965 to 1979 (Kiesler, 1982b). This is attributable essentially to the 650 percent increase in mental-health-related admissions to general hospitals without psychiatric units. It is precisely this market (about 1.2 million episodes a year) that will undoubtedly become the focus for the next major "turf struggle" in the mental health arena. The economic consequences are staggering.

Another perspective to be considered is the typical differentiation in coverage between inpatient and outpatient services under the majority of group health insurance plans. Third-party payers generally will cover more visits and require a lower copayment requirement for in-hospital care. Simply stated, the supply of reimbursement money is substantially greater for hospital practice. The stakes involved in maintaining control over access to this market are tremendous. It is clear, however, that costs alone were a major factor in changing the admission policies of state and county mental hospitals. Increasing numbers of elderly patients have been admitted or transferred to intermediate-care nursing facilities, primarily for cost reasons. Costs are driving the delivery of care to an outpatient and less intensive basis. Many hospitals seeing the writing on the wall are opening and expanding outpatient services. Woe to the practitioner without membership on a hospital medical staff! As hospitals and other organizations expand their ambulatory care resources, the office-based practitioner without privileges to practice through a hospital will see his or her practice shrink. The stakes for psychology are very high indeed.

However, the situation under CHAMPUS and also under the various other health insurance programs may be headed for marked change, as far as psychology is concerned. In 1982 the Congress mandated that CHAMPUS must limit inpatient mental health care to no more than sixty days annually, although a waiver was possible for true "medical *or psychological*" necessity. In essence, this removed long-term inpatient care from the basic CHAMPUS mental health benefit structure (and from psychiatrists' incomes). As a direct result, one must expect increasing reliance on the use of outpatient care as a treatment alternative, with corresponding heightened interprofessional competition. The recently published CHAMPUS regulations for the residential treatment center program, which is targeted for children and adolescents, provides for complete clinical and administrative parity between psychologists and their medical colleagues. Admissions, for example, must be on the recommendation of a psychiatrist or other physician *or a clinical psychologist.* The treatment plan must be developed under the direction of a psychiatrist *or clinical psychologist,* and all services must be performed by or under the supervision of a qualified mental health provider. The latter category includes psychiatric nurses and clinical social workers (*Federal Register,* 1984). On another front, in 1983 the District of Columbia enacted far-reaching legislation that mandated (rather than merely authorizing) hospital admission and other clinical staff privileges for qualified psychologists, nurse-midwives, nurse-practitioners, and podiatrists (Tanney, 1983). Such a statutory mandate was a first for psychology anywhere in the nation. As such, it represents a very significant step toward complete professional parity. Finally, as a result of a recent Library of Congress report indicating that psychology is practically the only nonphysician discipline that does not possess at least limited prescription authority, there is now some growing interest within the psychological community to explore this possibility legislatively (Inouye, 1984).

Deregulation: Undoing Private Regulation and Monopoly by Antitrust Action

Before the Supreme Court decision in *Goldfarb* v. *Virginia State Bar,* 421 U.S. 773 (1975), the antitrust laws, which prohibit restraint of trade, were of little concern to health or other professionals (Overcast, Sales, and Pollard, 1982). In 1943 the Supreme Court had held that the AMA and the District of Columbia Medical Society had violated the federal antitrust statute (the Sherman Act) by obstructing the operation of a prepaid medical plan (*American Medical Association* v. *United States,* 130 F.2d 233 (D.C. Cir. 1942), *aff'd* 317 U.S. 519, 1943). Nevertheless, until the early 1970s antitrust attorneys generally believed that the Court and society had intended that there be an implied exemption for the "learned professions" because they were not considered to engage in commerce. Historically, consumers were expected to rely on the "learned professions" to establish their own standards, to ensure quality of care, to police their own practitioners, and, in general, to protect the public good. Economic considerations were not considered a significant factor. Antitrust doctrine, however, stresses almost the exact opposite; that is, competition itself is considered to be in the national interest, and very little, if any, weight is to be given to any purported "benefit" to be achieved by anticompetitive practices.

In the *Goldfarb* case the Supreme Court struck down a mandatory minimum fee schedule imposed by a local bar association. In so doing, the Court stated clearly that the learned professions do engage in commerce and are subject to antitrust scrutiny. The Court did indicate that in certain situations, however, special considerations might be necessary. The implication that professions may enjoy special privilege under the antitrust laws has not been borne out by subsequent decisions, although reference to this possibility continues to be made. Three years later, in *National Society of Professional Engineers* v. *United States,* 435 U.S. 679 (1978), the Supreme Court took another step that questioned the ability of a profession to self-regulate in the public's best interest by striking down a section of the engineering profession's canon of ethics that prohibited members from submitting competitive bids. The Court stated that the sole purpose of judicial analysis in such cases is "to form a judgment about the competitive significance of the restraint . . . not to decide whether a policy favoring competition is in the public interest or the interest of the member of an industry." Making exceptions to the Sherman Act whenever public safety rationales were offered would be "tantamount to a repeal of the statute" (Pollard and Leibenluft, 1981).

Various Supreme Court decisions since the mid-1970s have addressed different aspects of the extent to which the health care industry must be concerned with fundamental antitrust principles. The overall trend is clearly toward requiring those who seek exemptions to bear the burden of proof. As the Court and the entire judicial system become more familiar with the specifics of the health care industry, it will likely become increasingly difficult to justify any exemptions. For example, in *Bates et al.* v. *State Bar of Arizona,* 433 U.S. 350 (1977), the Court held that a state bar association may not prevent the publication of truthful advertisements concerning the availability and terms of routine legal services. This holding was in spite of a number of adverse effects alleged by the legal profession—for example, the adverse impact on professionalism, the inherently misleading nature of attorney advertising, the adverse effect on quality, and the adverse effect on the administration of justice. In *Arizona* v. *Maricopa County Medical Society,* 457 U.S. 332 (1982), the Court held that maximum fee schedules adopted by physician-controlled foundations for medical care, set by the majority vote of participating physicians, were illegal, as they were a form of horizontal price fixing. The adoption of a minimum fee schedule in a subsequent agreement was also struck down as potentially restricting competition. Where the organization, however, is "at risk" and has agreed to deliver all contracted services on the basis of prepaid, or capitated, funding, the establishment of a fixed fee basis for provider remuneration appears to be insulated from antitrust actions. In *Union Labor Life Insurance Company* v. *Pireno,* 458 U.S. 119 (1982), the Court held that a professional association's peer review mechanism to monitor whether treatments and fees are necessary and reasonable was not exempt from antitrust scrutiny. A related decision in *American Society of Mechanical Engineers, Inc.,* v. *Hydrolevel Corp.,* 456 U.S. 556 (1982), held that the setting of standards by one professional group that would have the effect of restricting the marketing of products by another group did constitute an illegal restraint of trade.

Two specific antitrust cases that involve psychology have been the *Virginia Academy of Clinical Psychologists* v. *Blue Shield of Virginia,* 624 F.2d 476 (4th Cir. 1980), *cert. denied,* 450 U.S. 916 (1981), and the companion case *Blue Shield of Virginia* v. *McCready,* 457 U.S. 465 (1982). These cases arose out of Blue Shield's refusal to reimburse clinical psychologists unless their services were supervised by and billed through a physician, even though an appropriately drafted state "freedom of choice" statute had been enacted. In deciding on behalf of psychology, the federal court of appeals expressly noted that "psychologists and psychiatrists do compete" (Bersoff, 1983). The Supreme Court declined to hold contrary. These and other judicial decisions, especially those relating to the potential for antitrust activity in the hospital privileges area, were undoubtedly a significant factor in the decision by the Joint Commission on Accreditation of Hospitals (JCAH) to modify its standards in order to allow flexibility for nonphysician staff membership in hospitals, when state statutes permit (Zaro, Batchelor, Ginsberg, and Pallak, 1982). The continued denial to nonphysician practitioners of membership on medical staffs may be a situation ripe for antitrust action (Dolan, 1980). However, psychologists must not forget that another principle of antitrust law (the Noerr-Pennington Doctrine) provides an exemption for concerted efforts by individuals or organizations such as local medical societies to influence government decision making. Private parties can jointly attempt to attain anticompetitive ends by lobbying the legislature to enact a statute, by petitioning the executive to enforce a law in a certain manner, or by instituting administrative and judicial proceedings (Pollard and Leibenluft, 1981). This means that psychologists must increase their legislative efforts to ensure professional parity under all private, state, and federal health or mental health initiatives. By virtue of tradition, concerted actions in their own interest, and public acceptance, physicians have traditionally held a clear monopoly throughout the health care field. This is, however, changeable.

Cost-Effectiveness

A report by the U.S. Office of Technology Assessment (1980) concluded that "only 10 to 20 percent of all medical procedures have been shown by controlled tests to be beneficial." This conclusion raised a range of profound ethical and public policy concerns. For example, if a clinical service is of no demonstrable benefit, why should it be considered a "billable service"? From a public policy frame of reference, there would appear to be considerable potential for reducing costs by selectively paying for those health care procedures which are of equivalent or acceptable effectiveness and which also are less expensive. Unfortunately, such a perspective has not yet truly been incorporated into the thinking of our nation's health care experts. However, there is considerable evidence that it is steadily evolving (DeLeon, VandenBos, and Cummings, 1983). Less could be more (Sharfstein and Beigel, 1984)!

There is now a substantial basis for believing that psychological services can be cost-effective. A monograph by Jones and Vischi (1979) summarized studies that showed the substantial impact of outpatient mental health care on overall health care costs. It should be pointed out, however, that many of these studies were in organized settings such as HMOs or in industry. In the latter there was a reduction not only of medical costs but also of absenteeism. Kiesler's (1982a, 1984) review of studies of alternatives to mental hospitalization shows that alternative care is consistently more effective and clearly at lower cost. Similarly, psychotherapeutic preparation for surgery has shown "really solid evidence for a beneficial effect on physical health" (Olbrisch, 1979, p. 565). Daily psychotherapy with hospitalized heart-attack patients reduces length of hospital stay and improves the level of recovery (Gruen, 1973; Mumford, Schlesinger, and Glass, 1982). Within the mental health field, short-term therapy is growing in acceptance. Schlesinger and others (1983) have reported that the mean duration of outpatient mental health treatment over five years is only twenty-two visits, the median being six visits. Similarly, Dörken, in Chapter Four, found for CHAMPUS mental health services that, in 1981, 85 percent of beneficiaries were served within twenty-four visits. McGuire and Frisman (1983) have proposed that, in the absence of clear evidence of greater effectiveness for a specific therapy, the better policy guide would be "When one therapy is as effective as another, the lower-cost therapy is preferred" (p. 936). That is, "we may not be certain that behavioral therapy works better than psychodynamic therapy, but we do know that fifty visits cost more than five" (p. 937).

Proponents of the behavior therapies have advocated their effectiveness for a range of well-defined conditions, such as phobias (Miller, forthcoming). Operant conditioning has been remarkably effective in pain control; indeed, it has led to the development of pain clinics. Biofeedback, in particular, has been advocated as effective for the treatment of certain physical conditions, and Aetna, in its federal employee plan, has now recognized it as the "treatment of choice" for Raynaud's disease, phantom-limb pain, and vascular headache. CHAMPUS has announced that it will be initiating a biofeedback demonstration project, as directed by the Congress.

Psychological services are generally less intrusive and less costly than traditional medical procedures. They hold the potential both for reform in health care delivery and for substantial cost reduction, but they are typically still viewed by health policy experts and by third-party payers as "add-ons," not as alternatives. However, there are definite signs of change. The recent announcement by the OTA of its plans to develop a report on the state of the art of treatment in the area of children's mental health and the Senate Appropriations Committee hearings on variations in medical practice, referred to earlier, are indeed steps toward the delineation of specific procedures and the degree of their effectiveness for specific conditions.

Cost-effectiveness considerations have the potential for major reform and cost reduction. Past experience suggests, however, that they are unlikely to be systematically implemented until adopted by individual practitioners, and this may require political confrontation to overcome resistance to perceived external dictates. Nevertheless, as practitioners become more personally "at risk" for the economic consequences of the delivery of their services and more dependent on prepaid rates, the objective evidence of cost-effectiveness will be given considerable weight in shaping practices. The future is rapidly coming upon us.

Reorientation

In a plea to reorient both the training and the practice of clinical psychologists, Fox (1982) notes that we have historically devoted 90 percent of our efforts to serving the needs of only 10-15 percent of the population. He and others have long argued that we must reorient ourselves toward a general practice that would stress offering services to many, rather than continuing an approach that offers services to just a few (Fox, Kovacs, and Graham, 1985; Wright, forthcoming). Whether psychology decides to develop practices in collaboration with family practitioners, pediatricians, internists, or nurse-practitioners or instead to establish practice groups with members specializing in brief techniques, the emphasis in the future must be on delivering affordable services directed toward high-incidence problems that are costly to society and demonstrably responsive to techniques of psychological intervention. The future of psychology is in health care, not mental health care (DeLeon, 1979). Wright, Schaefer, and Solomons (1979) have published an encyclopedia of the treatment of pediatric psychology. It has been only a decade since Marc Lalonde, then minister of national health and welfare for Canada, released his far-reaching report entitled *A New Perspective on the Health of Canadians* (1974). It has been only five years since our government released *Healthy People: The Surgeon General's Report on Health Promotion and Disease Prevention* (U.S. Department of Health, Education, and Welfare, 1979). The behavioral medicine and "wellness" movements are just beginning (DeLeon and VandenBos, 1983). Psychologists must adapt. Psychologists must develop programs that will enable individuals to cope, to reduce stress, and to modify life-styles that place them at risk. Psychology must address the behavioral and psychological aspects of a wide range of health problems. To do so would open doors to a practice that is indeed broad-based—and thus would provide excellent prospects for economic viability.

To make it all work, however, requires an orientation of collaboration and systems participation, rather than preoccupation with individuality. The key to success in the future will be to work with others and to gain public recognition and acceptance. Tulkin (1983) aptly describes this process as developing "credibility." This takes time and effort. It is necessary to establish the required liaisons. Without credibility, no matter how much potential psychology possesses as a science or clinical discipline, its practitioners will never be able to develop health psychology practices. Without credibility, psychology's services simply cannot be marketed.

In Prospect

From many avenues, the prospect is that cost pressure alone and in its various forms—cost/benefit analysis, competition, consumer marketing, price advertising, organizational effectiveness, and so on—will reform, if not transform, our nation's health care system. For psychologists not to heed these pressures or to fail to capitalize on them in order to create their own opportunities will be the road to professional extinction—if not bankruptcy. The choice is ours. The time has come.

References

Bailit, H. "Traditional and Emerging Forms of Dental Practice: Another View." *American Journal of Public Health*, 1982, *72*, 662-664.

Bersoff, D. N. "Hospital Privileges and the Antitrust Laws." *American Psychologist*, 1983, *38*, 1238-1242.

Blendon, R. J., and Altman, D. E. "Special Report: Public Attitudes About Health-Care Costs—a Lesson in National Schizophrenia." *New England Journal of Medicine*, 1984, *311*, 613-616.

"Business This Week: People, A Surgeon Takes Over." *Business Week*, Aug. 30, 1982, p. 32.

Califano, J. A. "Can We Afford One Trillion Dollars for Health Care?" Speech presented to the Economic Club of Detroit, Detroit, 1983.

Casey, T., and Siegel, H. "Compensation and Benefits." *Personnel Journal*, 1982, *61*, 410-411.

DeLeon, P. H. "Psychology and the Carter Administration." *American Psychologist*, 1977, *32*, 750-751.

DeLeon, P. H. "The Legislative Outlook for Psychology: A Health Care Profession." *Academic Psychology Bulletin*, 1979, *1*, 187-192.

DeLeon, P. H. "The Medical Expense Deduction Provision: Public Policy in a Vacuum?" *Professional Psychology*, 1981, *12*, 707-716.

DeLeon, P. H. "The Changing and Creating of Legislation: The Political Process." In B. Sales (ed.), *The Professional Psychologist's Handbook*. New York: Plenum, 1983.

DeLeon, P. H., Forsythe, P., and VandenBos, G. R. "Federal Recognition of Psychology in Rehabilitation Programs." *Rehabilitation Psychology*, forthcoming.

DeLeon, P. H., and VandenBos, G. R. "The New Federal Health Care Frontiers—Cost Containment and 'Wellness.'" *Psychotherapy in Private Practice*, 1983, *1*, 17-32.

DeLeon, P. H., VandenBos, G. R., and Cummings, N. A. "Psychotherapy—Is It Safe, Effective, and Appropriate? The Beginning of an Evolutionary Dialogue." *American Psychologist*, 1983, *38*, 907-911.

DeLeon, P. H., VandenBos, G. R., and Kraut, A. G. "Federal Legislation Recognizing Psychology." *American Psychologist,* 1984, *39,* 933-946.

Dolan, A. "Antitrust Law and Physician Dominance of Other Health Practitioners." *Journal of Health Politics, Policy and Law,* 1980, *4,* 675-690.

Dörken, H., and Cummings, N. A. "Mental Health and Health Care Utilization Under Universal Coverage: Hawaii." Personal Services Contract Report, Mental Health Services Development Branch, National Institute of Mental Health, 1981.

Dörken, H., and Webb, J. T. "Licensed Psychologists on the Increase: 1974-1979." *American Psychologist,* 1981, *36,* 1419-1426.

Federal Register, Sept. 14, 1984, p. 36095.

Fox, R. E. "The Need for a Reorientation of Clinical Psychology." *American Psychologist,* 1982, *37,* 1051-1057.

Fox, R. E., Kovacs, A. L., and Graham, S. R. "Proposals for a Revolution in the Preparation and Regulation of Professional Psychologists." *American Psychologist,* 1985, *40,* 1042-1050.

Fuchs, V. R. "The Battle for Control of Health Care." *Health Affairs,* 1982, *1*(3), 5-13

Geiger, H. J. "Mediplex." *Psychology Today,* June 1983, *17,* 85.

Goldbeck, W. B. "Health Care and the Economy." Testimony before the Joint Economic Committee of Congress, Washington, D.C., 1984.

Gruen, W. "Effects of Brief Psychotherapy During the Hospitalization Period on the Recovery Process in Heart Attacks." *Journal of Counseling and Clinical Psychology,* 1973, *43,* 223-232.

Inouye, D. K. Address before the Hawaii Psychological Association, Honolulu, Nov. 1984.

Jones, K., and Vischi, T. "The Impact of Mental Health, Alcohol and Drug Abuse Treatment on Subsequent Medical Service Utilization." *Medical Care,* 1979, *17*(12), entire issue.

Kiesler, C. A. "Mental Hospitals and Alternative Care: Non-institutionalization as Potential Public Policy for Mental Patients." *American Psychologist,* 1982a, *37,* 349-360.

Kiesler, C. A. "Public and Professional Myths About Mental Hospitalization: An Empirical Measurement of Policy-Related Beliefs." *American Psychologist,* 1982b, *37,* 1323-1339.

Kiesler, C. A. Testimony before Subcommittee on Labor, Health and Human Services, and Education, U.S. Senate Committee on Appropriations, Washington, D.C., 1984.

Lalonde, M. *A New Perspective on the Health of Canadians: A Working Document.* Ottawa: Government of Canada, 1974.

McGuire, T., and Frisman, L. "Reimbursement Policy and Cost-Effective Mental Health Care." *American Psychologist,* 1983, *38,* 935-940.

Markus, G. "Health Benefits: Loss Due to Unemployment." Issue Brief No. IB83050. Washington, D.C.: Library of Congress Congressional Research Service, 1983.

Matarazzo, J. D. "Behavioral Immunogens and Pathogens in Health and Illness." In C. J. Scheier and B. L. Hammonds (eds.), *The Master Lecture Series.* Vol. 3: *Psychology and Health.* Washington, D.C.: American Psychological Association, forthcoming.

May, L. Remarks before Public Policy Forum, Divisions 12 and 38, American Psychological Association, Washington, D.C., July 1982.

Miller, J. J. "Workers, Rolm Gain with Change in Health Benefits." *San Jose Mercury News,* Mar. 13, 1983, pp. 1F and 4F.

Miller, N. E. "The Value of Behavioral Research on Animals." *American Psychologist,* forthcoming.

Mumford, E., Schlesinger, H. J., and Glass, G. V. "The Effects of Psychological Intervention on Recovery from Surgery and Heart Attacks: An Analysis of the Literature." *American Journal of Public Health,* 1982, *72,* 141-151.

Newhouse, J. P. Testimony before Department of Defense Subcommittee, U.S. Senate Committee on Appropriations, Washington, D.C., 1984.

Olbrisch, M. "Psychotherapeutic Interventions in Physical Health: Effectiveness and Economic Efficiency." In C. A. Kiesler, N. A. Cummings, and G. R. VandenBos (eds.), *Psychology and National Health Insurance: A Sourcebook.* Washington, D.C.: American Psychological Association, 1979.

Overcast, T. D., and Sales, B. D. "Psychological and Multi-disciplinary Corporations." *Professional Psychology,* 1981, *12,* 749-760.

Overcast, T. D., Sales, B. D., and Pollard, M. R. "Applying Antitrust Laws to the Professions." *American Psychologist,* 1982, *37,* 517-525.

Pertschuk, M. Letter to U.S. Senator D. K. Inouye. *Congressional Record,* Feb. 6, 1980, pp. S1113-S1114.

Pertschuk, M., and Correia, E. "The AMA Versus Competition." *American Psychologist,* 1983, *38,* 607-610.

Pollard, M. R., and Leibenluft, R. F. *Antitrust and the Health Professions: Policy Planning Issues Paper.* Washington, D.C.: Federal Trade Commission, 1981.

Rodgers, D. A. "The Status of Psychologists in Hospitals: Technicians or Professionals." *Clinical Psychologist,* 1980, *33*(4), 5-7.

Rovin, S., and Nash, J. "Traditional and Emerging Forms of Dental Practice: Cost, Accessibility and Quality Factors." *American Journal of Public Health,* 1982, *72,* 656-662.

Schlesinger, H. J., and others. "Mental Health Treatment and Medical Care Utilization in a Fee-for-Service System: Outpatient Mental Health Treatment Following the Onset of a Chronic Disease." *American Journal of Public Health,* 1983, *73,* 422-429.

Sharfstein, S., and Beigel, A. "Less Is More? Today's Economics and Its Challenge to Psychiatry." *American Journal of Psychiatry,* 1984, *141,* 1403-1408.

Tanney, F. "Hospital Privileges for Psychologists: A Legislative Model." *American Psychologist,* 1983, *38,* 1232-1237.

Teplin, L. A. "Criminalizing Mental Disorders: The Comparative Arrest Rate of the Mentally Ill." *American Psychologist,* 1984, *39,* 794-803.

Trauner, J. *Preferred Provider Organizations: The California Experiment.* Monograph Series, Institute for Health Policy Studies, School of Medicine, University of California, San Francisco, 1983.

Tulkin, S. "Credibility of Health Psychology Practitioners." *Health Psychologist,* 1983, *5,* 4-5.

U.S. Congressional Budget Office. *Containing Medical Care Costs Through Market Forces.* Washington, D.C.: U.S. Government Printing Office, 1982.

U.S. Department of Health, Education, and Welfare. *Healthy People: The Surgeon General's Report on Health Promotion and Disease Prevention.* DHEW Pub. No. (PHS) 79-55071. Washington, D.C.: U.S. Government Printing Office, 1979.

U.S. Office of Technology Assessment. *The Implications of Cost-Effectiveness Analysis of Medical Technology.* Background Paper No. 3: *The Efficacy and Cost Effectiveness of Psychotherapy.* Washington, D.C.: U.S. Government Printing Office, 1980.

U.S. Office of Technology Assessment. *Medical Technology Under Proposals to Increase Competition in Health Care.* Washington, D.C.: U.S. Government Printing Office, 1982.

Wennberg, J. E. "Dealing with Medical Practice Variations: A Proposal for Action." *Health Affairs,* 1984, *3*(2), 6-32.

Wiggins, J. G., Bennett, B. E., Batchelor, W. F., and West, P. R. "Psychologists in Defense of the Federal Trade Commission." *American Psychologist,* 1983, *38,* 602-606.

Winston, D. Remarks before Public Policy Forum, Divisions 12 and 38, American Psychological Association, Washington, D.C., 1982.

Wright, L. "Psychology and Pediatrics: Prospects for Cooperative Efforts to Promote Child Health." *American Psychologist,* forthcoming.

Wright, L., Schaefer, A., and Solomons, G. *Encyclopedia of Pediatric Psychology.* Baltimore, Md.: University Park Press, 1979.

Young, B. *Containing Health Care Costs: The Arizona Experience.* Washington, D.C.: American Legislative Exchange Council, 1984.

Zaro, J. S., Batchelor, W. F., Ginsberg, M. R., and Pallak, M. S. "Psychology and the JCAH: Reflections on a Decade of Struggle." *American Psychologist,* 1982, *37,* 1342-1349.

Herbert Dörken
Bruce E. Bennett

13

How Professional Psychology Can Shape Its Future

Change, whether for better or worse, is always difficult. Today the conditions affecting psychology are in flux, in a continual state of ebb and flow. To remain viable as a health profession, clinical psychologists must be able to sustain themselves in the face of continuing uncertainty.

The essence of a profession is the practitioner's ability to assume responsibility and attempt to address substantive problems even in the face of uncertain knowledge (see Chapter Seven). If all conditions of practice were known, psychology would be a pure science and its practitioners "technologists." Unfortunately, too many practitioners function like technicians and extenders for other professions. This is a by-product of the political situation rather than a reflection of the education, training, or state of knowledge in psychology.

New developments in service delivery and health care financing will bring both opportunity and technological obsolescence. During the seventies, psychotherapy was the preferred mode of practice, and interest in research, testing, and evaluation eroded. But now new markets have opened up for such services as disability evaluation, evaluation of defendants for fitness to stand trial and issues of insanity, competency determination for guardianship, police officer/applicant screening, evaluating cost/benefit-effectiveness of treatment, data collection and management, program design, and evaluation of systems and organizations. In addition, the current information explosion will hasten the technological obsolescence of those without professional skills relevant to changing job markets and public need.

The Changing Face of the Mental Health System

It is the rare instance in which public policy is developed out of scientific knowledge. The political process yields a reality not necessarily congruent with the facts as some scientists or professionals would see them. The changing face of the nation's mental health system is a case in point.

Our professed national policy emphasizes outpatient care, community mental health centers, and deinstitutionalization of the mentally disabled. State mental hospital populations have certainly been reduced dramatically over the past two decades, but this reduction derives more from a transfer process and "dumping" than from discharge. California reduced the number of its state mental hospital beds for the mentally disordered from 37,000 to 5,500. Many of the people thus displaced are now in nursing facilities or local foster care homes—at a lower public per diem cost, particularly for the elderly. Some communities have also experienced an increase in the census of the local jail, owing to increases in public disturbance, public nuisance, and vagrancy charges, as well as the expanding numbers of homeless street people.

But in terms of money spent, it is clear that the actual policy increasingly favors hospitalization and other institutionalization (Kiesler, 1980). Of all mental health dollars today, 70 percent (and increasing) are spent on twenty-four-hour residential facility care (public mental hospitals, general hospitals, private psychiatric hospitals, nursing facilities, and residential treatment programs). The admission of psychiatric patients to general hospitals has shown a linear increase, not a decrease, since 1962. The overall result is more inpatient services rather than fewer.

Today's "law and order" mood has brought about a change in the state mental hospital population in the last five years that is as dramatic in its own way as the change that occurred previously in the hospitals for the developmentally disabled. The person adjudged not guilty by reason of insanity, the mentally disordered sex offender, and the mentally disordered violent offender can be sentenced to the state hospital. Of the occupants of California's 5,500 mental hospital beds, over 3,000 are now penal-code offenders. The state hospital is being "criminalized."

As a result of recent legislation in California, a whole new population of criminal offenders has appeared. For some offenses there is no possibility of parole; for others there is a mandated minimum sentence, which can be substantial; and a number of misdemeanors have been reclassified to felony status. The public outrage about sex offenders and mentally disordered violent offenders has been translated into laws resulting in overcrowded state prisons and involuntary state hospitalization. Further, "unmanageable" patients are typically transferred back to the hospitals from nursing facilities to which they were transferred.

The state hospital penal-code populations in California are being reviewed, and those no longer mentally disordered become candidates for transfer to prison for the balance of their term. Most of these individuals will show a strong preference to remain in the "safety" of the hospital rather than go to prison. The prisons are ill prepared to deal with the mentally disordered in their own population, the more so with overcrowding. In 1982 the California Department of Corrections identified 9,600 of its prisoners statewide as acutely in need of treatment. Legislation introduced in 1985 would mandate the availability of quality treatment for committed offenders with mental disorder and would confer the authority to transfer them from correctional to mental health facilities.

The state hospitals, of course, were neither built nor staffed for such a change in patient population. Indeed, urgency legislation several years ago added twenty-seven security guards to one hospital! Dealing with the reality-oriented antisocial personality and the assaultive psychotic is far different from dealing with the original population of chronic schizophrenics, psychotic depressives, and brain-damaged or senile patients. Public policy initiatives have thus resulted in a "criminalization" of the state hospital.

Toward Health Care: Expanding the Market

Mental health services, now generally in systems separate from general health care, have enjoyed a relatively "protected" status. Mental health care, however, is on the verge of being integrated into comprehensive health services, and separate budgeting will largely evaporate in the process. This will not be because mental health does not have a strong political constituency (which it does not) but because it is becoming evident that psychological intervention has a "marginal utility" in association with other services (Smith and Glass, 1977), much like the catalyst in a chemical reaction, and that these services—by reducing total dollars spent on doctor visits, laboratory charges, and hospitalization—more than offset their costs (Jones and Vischi, 1979).

Mounting evidence points to the fact that stressful life experiences contribute strongly to the development of acute and chronic physical disease, on the one hand (Vaillant, 1979), while significant emotional disturbance can develop as a consequence of physical illness, pain, or compromised physical functioning, on the other hand. It is becoming progressively more apparent that behavioral health (behavioral medicine from the physician's perspective) is a vast new horizon open to professional psychology, the preeminent behavioral science. A growing body of studies indicates that psychological intervention is effective for a wide range of physical disabilities. In addition, among cases of mental disorder, concurrent physical illness is not uncommon (Matarazzo, 1982). Stated practically, Harper, Wiens, and Hammerstad (1981, p. 347) note that "concurrent medical-psychological screening avoids the common, undesirable sequence of events in which physical-mental etiology is first ruled out and then followed by stigmatizing suggestions of emotional distress and psychological treatment." From a holistic perspective, we must adopt treatment strategies that implement the obvious, namely, "that psychological services must comprise one component of general health services in order to deal effectively with the psychological concomitants of physical illness, as well as the all too frequent somatization of emotional problems" (Wiens, 1981, p. 44).

The recognition of mental health services as distinct from general health care has been advantageous for the funding and organization of public mental health services. In terms of private-sector third-party reimbursement, however, either under health insurance or under worker's compensation, the separate status has all too often led to outright exclusion of benefits or to narrower limitations for these "supplemental" rather than "basic" benefits, such as lower annual and/or lifetime dollar limits, fewer doctor visits annually, higher coinsurance/copayment requirements, exclusion of coverage for chronic conditions, and less or no coverage for outpatient, in contrast to hospital, services. However, bringing mental health within general health care permits policy development that recognizes that mental health and psychological services are an integral part of basic health care, not a supplemental service or optional rider. Given the severely restricted coverage for mental disorder under Medicare and the lack of inclusion in almost all national health insurance proposals introduced before Congress (with the exception of the twenty outpatient visits under the HMO law), it seems evident that the integration of mental health into health care will be essential to continued coverage for mental disorders under any future national health plan or scheme for universal coverage.

The recognition that psychology is rapidly developing as a health profession, not simply a mental health specialty, vastly broadens its possible scope of practice and could bring widespread application of many of the innovations introduced by psychology. Biofeedback is coming to be viewed as a treatment of choice for vascular and migraine headaches, Raynaud's disease, and phantom-limb pain and to be seen as effective in other disorders, such as hypertension. Operant techniques have been applied with remarkable success for pain control without the risks or invasiveness of drugs or surgery.

Mumford, Schlesinger, and Glass's (1982) review of the literature notes that in controlled studies of surgical and coronary patients those who were given information and emotional support to help them master their medical crises fared better than patients receiving ordinary care. Moreover, on the average, psychological intervention reduced hospitalization by about two days, evidence that such care is cost-effective. The resolution of depressive dependency problems of patients on renal dialysis and the application of behavior therapy to the control of enuresis, tracheotomy addiction, and other problems in treatment of children (Wright and others, 1979) make clear that the science-based treatment procedures developed by psychology have broad application to a range of health problems.

Moreover, health care is a far broader market than mental health services, since it involves nearly the entire population rather than a small proportion. As aptly stated by Wright (1982, p. 11), "The field of illness or organically related psychopathology is proving to be more vast than what the total continent of psychopathology (neurosis, psychosis, and personality disorder) was originally presumed to be." Wright also notes that a 1978 survey by the American Academy of Pediatrics reported that over three times as many families had sought behavioral and psychological assistance from pediatricians than from psychologists and psychiatrists combined.

Many disorders and much of the early deterioration of health are needless and are due to high-risk behaviors or life-styles that precipitate early morbidity or mortality, such as excessive eating, overuse of alcohol, smoking, and lack of exercise. Research is gradually proving that life-style is critical to health. If there is any profession with expertise in dealing with human behavior and life-style change, it is psychology. Behavioral health is only in its infancy.

Integrating mental health with health care, however, carries the real hazard that the public will perceive health care as primarily medical care with the physician as "gatekeeper," a concept that will be advanced by medical groups to maintain domination of the field, even though the practitioners of a number of health professions are licensed for independent practice. As Dörken and Cummings (forthcoming) have shown, the imposition of a medical referral requirement causes a reduction in visits to psychologists in comparison to programs with open access. Physicians characterize all nonphysicians as "limited licensed practitioners"—that is, their scope of practice, by license, is more limited than that of physicians. It is precisely this philosophy that has been effectively advanced to date to restrict competition from nonphysician health practitioners. With the surge of political interest in deregulation and competition and the procompetition philosophy of the 1980 and 1984 federal administrations, not one of the health plans introduced before Congress would induce competition among the professions, only among various models for organizing medical services. If there is any recognition in Congress that personal behavior—that is, life-style—is *the* major health hazard or that addressing the psychological factors of illness, disease, dying, disability, dismemberment, sensory loss, or accident would materially advance the quality and effectiveness of health care, it has yet to surface as a legislative proposal, although it would be entirely consistent with public health philosophy.

The intrusion of psychology into general health care on a broad basis may also be handicapped by the growing awareness of a physician "glut." In the face of an oversupply of this major health provider group, it can be much harder to establish a public need for broader recognition of psychologists or other nonphysician health professionals. Physicians, in turn, seeking to sustain or establish their own practice, do not welcome competition. Then, too, because each provider generates costs well beyond salary or fees earned, control or limitation of the provider supply by state or federal law or by third parties can be rationalized as a move to curb costs.

The issue for clinical psychologists then may no longer be "psychiatric direction" but medical control. The challenge for parity, if not preeminence, with which psychology as a science-based profession confronts psychiatry is one factor prompting psychiatry to strengthen its medical alliances in its efforts to retain control of mental health services. The trend toward viewing mental health as a component of health care is another factor bringing pressure on psychiatry to "remedicalize."

These developments place in jeopardy the independent status of psychology and the widespread opportunity for positions of leadership now enjoyed by clinical psychologists in community mental health centers and in many aspects of state mental health programs. Apart from independent office-based fee-for-service practice, clinical psychology has not as yet gained the same standing in mental health services in the private sector, particularly in hospital services, although some clear headway has been made (Dörken, Webb, and Zaro, 1982).

The age mix of the population is shifting. The proportion of elderly is now approaching 11 percent and is increasing. The elderly will require specialized services, but very few psychologists are being trained to provide them. With advancing age, physical health problems are more common, and the distinction between physical and mental disability, which can be made more readily among youths and young adults, is more problematic when serving the elderly. Indeed, for psychology to play a major role in health care of the elderly, it will be even more necessary to achieve some functional coordination with medicine.

Although it is true that dentists, podiatrists, and optometrists have established their independence as health professionals and have for years been recognized under the Health Professions Educational Assistance Act (MODVOPP, after the professions included), this independence holds only for office and outpatient practice. Their standing for hospital care is typically limited, particularly at the point of entry, often by a coadmission requirement with a physician if not outright physician admission. This precedent suggests that psychology will have a major struggle to further establish and maintain its independence in the health care field, especially in the hospital sector. It will require major legislation, alliances, and court action to penetrate the hospital/medical monopoly on anything other than a token scale. For example, the accomplishment of the District of Columbia Psychological Association in enacting the first law (1983) to *require* the appointment of clinical psychologists to the medical staffs of all hospitals and with specified privileges illustrates what can be achieved with determined, persistent, well-organized, and well-funded advocacy (see also Chapter Twelve). Over a period of eighteen months, the DCPA invested $60,000 in this effort, plus $20,000 in PAC (political action committee) funds.

Several midlevel professions, at a master's level of training, are emerging as licensed practitioners recognized in the laws of some states—the clinical social worker, the nurse-practitioner, and the marriage, family, and child counselor. However, the limited extent to which they have gained practitioner status for third-party reimbursement under health insurance or government health plans has been on condition of medical referral, with few exceptions. Today, psychiatric nurses and clinical social workers, first recognized directly under the CHAMPUS (P.L. 96-151) on an experimental basis, are established as independent providers.

Psychology, however, while having earlier gained parity within the system, still does not have the power of referral that would qualify the profession being referred to for third-party reimbursement, private or public. This continues as another major structural distinction between medicine and psychology. Thus, psychology's direct-access, independent-practitioner standing is unique, and we can expect pressures to see it eroded.

Legislation furthering the development of HMOs (P.L. 93-222), particularly the fee-for-service physician's practice model, or individual practice association (IPA), is another way to reestablish physician autonomy. The Employee Retirement Income Security Act (P.L. 93-406), by preempting state law for self-funded group health plans, has the same effect.

Psychotherapists Under Competition

Psychologists (and psychiatrists) now in solo practice, largely of psychotherapy, and graduate students (and residents) now planning on such a professional career will, within the decade, find their hopes and practices overtaken by a revolution. Though recognized by statute in only twenty-six states, being licensed in but sixteen (National Association of Social Workers, 1980), clinical social workers substantially outnumber clinical psychologists. Nurse-practitioners are also beginning to emerge as a viable force. If we have found the competition between psychiatrists and psychologists sometimes marked by friction and ill will, it seems likely to pale beside the competition soon to emerge between psychiatric nurse-practitioners and clinical social workers. The nurse-practitioners will have the edge of licensure/registration in all states and a consistent background of training in health facilities. Then, the marriage, family, and child counselors (M.F.C.C.s) are an emerging and expanding camp for a mixture of M.S.W.s and M.A.s with training in psychology, counselor education, human development, and marriage, family, and child counseling. The state colleges and smaller universities across the country continue to graduate terminal M.A.s in psychology who are unlicensable as psychologists in all but four states (Iowa, Missouri, Pennsylvania, and West Virginia). Many will turn to an M.F.C.C.

license where it is available. In effect, "psychotherapists" are proliferating rapidly and will become "a dime a dozen." Note also that many jurisdictions do not regulate the practice of "psychotherapy" and in these areas such "therapists" are already overabundant.

Competition from nondoctoral "psychotherapists" will be intense because their services are less costly. Over the past decade psychologists (and psychiatrists) in public mental health services, particularly outpatient services, have seen their numbers decline as they were replaced by lesser-trained and lower-salaried personnel. Under third-party reimbursement, psychologists in California have seen first clinical social workers, then M.F.C.C.s, and then psychiatric nurses seek direct recognition legislation as independent providers only to be strongly opposed by the insurance industry, Blue Shield, and medicine. The legislation then passed, however, when each profession in turn accepted an amendment to be recognized on medical referral. The established professions can expect the emerging professions to become progressively more assertive and the more so as their numbers continue to rise.

Individual verbal psychotherapy is by far the most common mental health procedure, accounting for over 80 percent of all outpatient mental health visits (Dörken, 1979a). It will be the target for competition from professions whose costs are lower. We can expect to see price advertising and the bid and contract process drive down fees for psychotherapy to a point where, on a broad scale, it may be no longer feasible for psychiatrists or psychologists to invest such a proportion of their time in this procedure. Psychotherapy is essentially too time- and labor-intensive to be really profitable even at today's rates, much less so should the rates become depressed. The extended time frame of traditional psychoanalysis, the general lack of health insurance coverage for an extended series of visits, the rates that analysts must charge to recover sufficient income, and the rising demands for evidence of cost-effectiveness are all forces moving what two decades ago was the treatment procedure of choice to the prospect of extinction. Indeed, the plight of the analyst has even been reported in *Barron's* (McAuliffe, 1982). It is time to be more realistic in providing psychotherapy (Cummings, 1979).

For psychology (and psychiatry) to be competitive with other professions—and profitable—it will have to provide services which are in demand, which can be paid for, which achieve results, and which are unique. These elements of public demand, available financing, proof of effectiveness, and a certain exclusivity will assure a viable market for psychological practice. Exclusivity is particularly important because it is an insulation from or market edge over competition. Psychiatrists can prescribe medications and administer electroshock therapy. Electroshock, however, is increasingly being placed under second-opinion control and barred without patient consent. There is also mounting public backlash to continued and widespread use of drugs. Nonetheless, there is still better assurance of third-party reimbursement. Access to—and control of—hospital services gives an exclusive market edge to psychiatry, one that is quite lucrative, particularly with more comprehensive insurance coverage for inpatient mental health services. Small wonder, then, that psychologists often experience substantial resistance on seeking membership in the organized medical staff of a hospital (Dörken and Webb, 1979; Copeland, 1980)!

Psychology's long-run viability will depend on its exclusivity as a behavioral science. Its competitors in psychotherapy, with the exception of psychiatrists, are essentially without a science base from which to advance technologically. The standardized assessment procedures, objective behavior scaling, the behavior therapies, applications of biofeedback, and program evaluation methods are all major contributions from psychology. They are distinct assets, particularly to the degree that they remain somewhat exclusively within the profession and psychologists are broadly competent in their use.

Defining Professional Psychology

Medicine, the insurance industry, and state legislatures have placed a continuing demand on nonmedical practitioners to strictly define themselves as the price of gaining recognition and acceptance. Their self-definitions typically include training and experience, as well as the nature of services that will be rendered.

The tighter the definition, the fewer the practitioners. The demand on psychology for a uniform definition led to the Model Psychologist Direct Recognition Bill, negotiated with the Health Insurance Association of America (HIAA) in May 1976 and approved by the American Psychological Association that fall. That definition essentially incorporates statutory recognition by the state for practice, a doctoral degree in psychology, and two years of clinical experience in a health care setting. Listing in the *National Register of Health Service Providers in Psychology* can substitute for the latter two criteria. Except for those in the *National Register*, this definition does not include individuals who might look on themselves as "clinical psychologists" even though they are not licensed/certified or their degree is not in psychology, the degree is not at the doctoral level, or they have not had two years of patient care experience in a health facility. Thus, a number of "pseudo psychologists" who have gone directly into private practice on graduation will not meet this definition. It is, however, not restricted to graduates of clinical psychology doctoral programs. The importance of the definition cannot be underestimated.

To decide that we are a health profession carries major implications for training, for interprofessional relations, for practice, for statutory change, and for classification and pay. The Veterans Administration (VA), for example, is the largest employer of doctoral-level psychologists in the country, with about 1,400 on staff in 1981 and increasing. Currently they come under Title 5 within the Civil Service Act. Yet other health professions in the VA, including physicians, nurses, and optometrists, are under Title 38, which was enacted exclusively for health personnel. For several years there has been a lively debate over whether psychology should remain under Title 5 or be transferred to Title 38 (Dörken, 1979b). In 1980 Congress requested that the matter be studied. Amending Title 38 to include psychologists would be an outcome in the direction of health, though admittedly with trade-offs. By 1985 sentiment toward Title 38 had grown, and this resolution may be in the offing. To encourage even higher standards within the profession, in 1984 Congress allowed merit pay recognition for VA psychologists who had achieved diplomate status from a national board, such as the American Board of Professional Psychology.

The rising demand for competency assurance emphasizes specialty requirements, which, in turn, may erode the generic license. It is becoming more obvious that no one practitioner of any broad service profession can be competent in all aspects of that profession, including medicine, a profession that, for political reasons, refuses to face this problem. Specialty certification would be a more moderate step than specialty licensure. "Clinical psychologists" are beginning to be defined in licensing laws (Nebraska, Texas, Indiana, Virginia, Hawaii), mental health codes (Illinois), or health codes (California). Educational psychologists, however, are already separately licensed in some states (for example, California) and have a practice definition that differs from that of psychologists. Although the American Psychological Association continues to advocate generic licensing, the public perception increasingly is that within psychology there are a number of specialties with distinctly different competencies. Consequently, legislatures, when dealing with law pertaining to health care, find it only realistic to limit the recognition of psychologists to "clinical psychologists," broadly defined as those psychologists who provide "clinical" services. A number of key federal laws now cite "clinical psychologists," including the Federal Employee Health Benefits Act (P.L. 93-363), the Federal Employee Compensation Act (P.L. 93-416), the regulations for the Health Maintenance Organization Act (P.L. 93-222), and the Department of Defense appropriation act relative to the Civilian Health and Medical Program of the Uniformed Services (P.L. 94-212). By contrast, the Education for All Handicapped Children Act (P.L. 94-142) has been interpreted by most states as federal program recognition of the school psychologist.

Perhaps ironically, the external demand to define clinical psychology for third-party reimbursement is now beginning to be applied to psychiatry. To the extent that a minimum definition such as "board eligible" or "completion of three years of residency training in psychiatry" and state licensure is adopted, it will substantially restrict the number of physicians who are now self-defined as "psychiatrists" or who limit their practice to psychiatry. For example, under Hawaii Medicaid, mental health procedures are reimbursable only when rendered by licensed psychologists, mental health centers, or psychiatrists, not by general-practice physicians.

It becomes ever more timely for psychology to seek standing under law at the state level so that psychological practice will be broadly recognized. The current move to federal deregulation will increasingly test the strength of state laws. Further, the emphasis on state sovereignty in the current political climate will leave psychologists in many states ill equipped, especially where medicine has a stronghold.

To survive interprofessional challenges, litigation, and claim denials, it is critical that wording of the definition of practice in regulating statutes by consistent with current standards and scope of practice. Practice components must include but not be limited to "diagnosis and treatment of emotional and mental disorder, disability evaluations, or competency determination." Health practice should also include preventive and rehabilitative services and behavioral health care. The behavioral aspects of health are central to the future of psychological practice. Psychotherapy and psychological assessment, the behavior therapies, hypnosis, biofeedback, and life-style change are procedures within the expertise of psychologists and should be made explicit. The determination regarding necessity for services and whether they are to be provided in office, home, or hospital must be the ultimate responsibility of the psychologist practitioner involved in the case.

Evidence is a major element of the forensic process. Evidence is held to be more reliable/correct than assumptions or clinical impressions. Hence, data-based expert opinions derived from standardized psychological tests fit well with the fact demands of court proceedings, whether the question is competency to stand trial, the extent or permanence of disability, individual capability, need of a conservator, or certification for involuntary hospitalization. As statutes change to recognize psychologists in these roles, we can expect a progressive increase in the demand by the courts for psychological "facts" on the case at hand.

As psychologists are increasingly recognized, an awareness will follow that proprietary and nonprofit hospitals cannot employ psychologists on salary and then bill for and retain fees from their services. Because health facilities are not licensed to practice psychology, such procedures would constitute the unlicensed practice of psychology (Attorney General's Opinion, State of California, No. 79-410, June 14, 1979). Pressure is mounting, however, to amend the law so that hospitals can employ physicians and other health professionals on a salaried or contract basis, as is done in health maintenance organizations. With the advent of organized entities for health care delivery, salaried and contract opportunities for health care practitioners may become a reality in the near future.

Exemptions in psychology regulatory statutes have brought about a dual standard of care for those needing mental health services. Professional licensure requirements, necessary for private practice, are often exempted in public services, particularly among state hospitals. As a result, those unable to obtain private treatment may well receive a lower standard of care. Tax-supported public facilities often bill third parties as an additional source of funding. The public policy question is: Should insurance reimbursement be sustaining a public system that is tax-supported? If so, then public services will, to an extent, be in unfair competition with private-sector practice, even more so when the unit cost of public services is higher. To reverse this dual standard, we can look to licensure and the doctoral standard being increasingly required of "professional personnel," not simply to improve the quality of care but as a mechanism for the major professions to maintain programmatic and administrative control.

Direct-recognition, or "freedom of choice," laws and other laws recognizing the practice of psychology have accelerated the licensing of psychologists (Dörken and Webb, 1981). The ratio of licensed psychologists to population is greater in FOC than in non-FOC states (Dörken and Webb, 1980). There has also been a dramatic shift toward full-time practice, increasing from 7 percent of licensed psychologists in 1972 to 23 percent by 1976–1977 (Gottfredson and Dyer, 1979) and 34 percent by 1980 (Dörken and Webb, 1981).

Throughout the 1970s, the number of well-qualified applicants for psychology training programs always exceeded the number of training slots available. By contrast, in 1980, only four of all U.S. residency training programs in psychiatry had all their residency positions filled, despite training stipends that typically were several times larger than those available to doctoral candidates in psychology.

American psychiatry is facing a real-life crisis. Revision of the immigration laws has cut off the supply of foreign medical graduates, many of whom, even though unlicensed (Torrey and Taylor, 1973), staff state mental hospitals. The proportion of U.S. medical school graduates who enter psychiatry declined from 11 to 3 percent between 1970 and 1976, despite continued and major federal funding (Fink and Field, 1978; Tucker, 1978). The production of U.S. psychiatrists today is only about half that of clinical and related specialties in psychology. Such high-cost low-production training, to the extent that it is dependent on public support, is a likely target for federal budget cutters looking to optimal effectiveness, especially when most psychiatrists trained with public monies go directly into private practice, in contrast to only 4.5 percent of psychologists (Schneider, 1981).

In economic terms, psychiatry's decline is perhaps best reflected in net income. From 1970 to 1982, of the specialties considered, when net income was adjusted for inflation, "psychiatrists lost the most buying power, 22.8 percent" (Haug and Seegar, 1983, p. 52). Of course, the average total gross professional income of licensed psychologists, even those in full-time practice, at $51,200 in 1979, though rising, is clearly less than that of psychiatrists. When public mental health service salaries are compared, however, there is usually an even wider gap between the two professions, reflecting in part the generally greater availability of psychologists and the growing shortage of psychiatrists for such positions (Fiester, 1978; Rosenstein and Taube, 1977).

Given the indexes of decline in psychiatry's human resources, psychiatry's continued demands for program control (mental health program direction, hospital staff membership, admission and discharge) and treatment supremacy (diagnosis, treatment plan authorization, psychiatric referral) become increasingly unrealistic and difficult to maintain as a public policy of domination over the mental health field. When services must be provided, alternatives will become acceptable, and the competition that clinical psychology brings to psychiatry will be more broadly recognized. Further, continued recognition of the value of interdisciplinary treatment teams will bring broader statutory acknowledgment of the overlap of functions among various health professions.

The supply of mental health practitioners is one thing, their availability quite another. A distribution balanced with population is essential for easy access to professional services. Today psychology appears to have the advantage over psychiatry in being somewhat less maldistributed.

Interface with Health Organizations

The massive federal support of HMOs, including the federal law mandating that employers make HMOs an available option as a health plan, has resulted in their accelerated development and rapid market gains in parts of the country. By 1979 there were five urban centers in the West where HMOs held greater than an 18 percent market penetration (San Francisco, 32 percent). Indeed, as HMO enrollment increases, the fee-for-service system will shrink, forcing hospitals to compete for patients through health plans instead of physicians (Arstein and Toon, 1981). It follows also that the era of the solo practitioner is drawing to a close (Brett, 1977).

County medical societies and their foundations for medical care are promoting individual practice associations as the fee-for-service competitive answer to closed-panel salaried-staff practice models. Since the physicians practice out of their offices and use local hospitals, little capital is required to form an IPA, which, owing to provider distribution, is also well positioned to rapidly gain local market control. With rare exception, these IPA-type HMOs not only are under medical control but also seldom have opened up membership, participating provider, or shareholder status to psychologists. Psychologists are regularly employed in staff-model HMOs but seldom with an opportunity for advancement into either management or profit sharing. IPAs in states having FOC laws that include health service plans will recognize psychologists for reimbursement, particularly on medical referral, but patients are unlikely to obtain their services unless psychologists are listed in the directory of participating providers. In effect, we are seeing the development of organized models of care that largely bypass psychological practice and, despite state FOC laws, serve to reestablish physicians' monopolies or medical cartels. Blue Shield plans, originally developed by state medical associations as "the doctor's plan for doctors," now hold some 43 percent of the civilian population as members among their seventy plans.

As health insurance becomes even more broadly available and state hospital use less essential, psychiatric units in general hospitals will continue to flourish. There will be demands to create twenty-four-hour residential acute care less costly and more responsive to patients' needs.

As local nonprofit and proprietary hospitals and other health facilities assume an increasing role in twenty-four-hour treatment and care of the mentally disordered, psychologists who intend to provide a full range of services or be in the mainstream of patient care will find it progressively more important to have membership on the organized medical staff and standing to practice at one or more health facilities. Moreover, to be certain that they remain the nucleus of community health care, hospitals are increasing their outpatient services, and some are establishing nearby satellite clinics and are beginning to compete with Blue Cross, the insurance industry, and others for competitive health-plan contracts with employers. Whereas psychologists may not be fully aware of the practice potential within hospitals, the value of membership in the organized medical staff of a hospital is not lost on a physician. For the same reason, the innovation and alternatives—read "competition"—that psychologists could bring to patient care in such facilities may not be welcome beyond consulting privileges on medical referral or as affiliates to the medical staff, providing limited services on medical direction for the physicians' patients. The importance of medical staff membership and clinical privileges is best attested to by the vigor and resources that psychiatry is willing to expend to keep psychologists out. A first step toward overcoming such resistance will be the passage of state laws that recognize clinical psychologists as members of hospital medical staffs. The need to establish a law or change an existing law varies from state to state (O'Keefe, 1978).

The increasing demand for specific standards, facility licensure, accreditation review, and peer review, with authorization contingent on external criteria, will make solo independent practice in health care progressively less feasible. Moreover, the ability to contract on scale will probably become essential. These events will pressure the practitioner into becoming part of some viable system simply for survival. It seems, then, that the solo private practice of psychology outside a system (the "opt-out," or nonparticipating provider) may be a viable alternative only for the older, established practitioner with a direct-pay clientele. Stated otherwise, the demise of the solo clinical practitioner will be hastened by the vertical integration of health professionals into a fairly small number of competing health conglomerates. The sheer numbers of health professionals licensed for independent practice make it obvious that physicians will be in the clear majority. An active clinical practice will then be increasingly dependent on the establishment of mutually constructive interprofessional relationships. Collegial relationships with medicine can be facilitated especially as innovations and techniques introduced by psychology prove to be effective and to be methods of choice.

Even with the discontinuation of the massive federal support of HMOs or the weakening of the Professional Standards Review Organization legislation or the revocation of the Health Planning and Resources Development Act, the thrust of the "big business" methodology appears to be too well underway for collapse or reversal to occur. The concepts underlying these laws will continue to exert pressure toward organized models of health care delivery in much the same way that small businesses (aside from unique crafts) have great difficulty surviving in the face of corporate competition. Rapidly approaching is the widespread promotion (advertising) of health services, another stage in corporate expansion that will be fueled by competition for patients.

As for interprofessional competition, psychologists, as specialists in dealing with human behavior and the *only* profession with systematic preparation in scientific methodology, should have little difficulty holding their own, if not advancing their status— short of being faced with outright exclusionary monopolies, which is also possible. The most serious missing element to better equip psychologists (and other health professionals too) to deal with this specter of future change is professional preparation based on the conception of practice as a business. The almost exclusive focus on the profession's science base and its clinical services, as though the market for practice were neither changing nor appropriate for future clinicians to consider, will prove to be a gross disservice to professionals in training.

Cost Control

The issue of cost control is addressed extensively in Chapter Twelve. However, no discussion of "new directions for clinical practice" is balanced without direct consideration of cost factors. The rapid increases in the cost of health care are draining both personal and public resources. Now moving toward 11 percent of the gross national product in 1984, the national cost of health care is exceeded only by national defense, servicing the national debt, and income security programs. The national cost of about $456 billion in 1985 will force some form of government intrusion. The federal government, after all, now pays over 40 percent of the national health dollar. With the block-grant shifting of federal funds to the states, it may be state rather than federal intrusion, but intrusion nonetheless. To further illustrate the problem, hospital costs are now rising $1 million an hour every day, or $8.76 billion a year. The political choice is: control the costs or increase the taxes.

In the face of such rising costs, procedures that are without evidence of clinical effectiveness will be in danger of elimination. Services that are of doubtful effectiveness should expect only marginal support. Some psychological procedures, such as biofeedback and certain behavior therapies when addressed to selected specific symptoms or disabilities, should flourish on their data base alone. There is a growing awareness, internationally, that psychology must return its costs (Christiansen, 1981). The demand for predictability and outcome effectiveness will lead to a priori requirements for individualized treatment plans based on informed consent and/or for prior authorization by peers. This emphasis on outcome, on prediction, and on program evaluation is a message to psychology that it would be a professional disaster to forsake its research skills.

The cost pressures against extended services will heighten the use of brief and crisis intervention services. Cost pressures will also induce price competition and contracting with providers and provider groups. It is within the realm of possibility that fees will not be set by the hour or some other piecerate basis but en bloc at a specified amount to resolve or assess a particular problem. We are beginning to see psychology groups or corporations, on a capitation basis, providing preventive behavioral health services and limited consultation at life crisis points.

The president of Blue Shield, when interviewed by the American Medical Association News ("Blues President Foresees Negotiated Fee Plan," 1981), made it clear that fee schedules are very likely to return, particularly negotiated fee plans. Alternative methods of payment to providers will shift from UCR to discounted fee schedules, negotiated contracts, per capita payment, and salary arrangements. As public programs, such as Medicare or Medicaid, are capped or are modified with larger deductibles and coinsurance, there will be increased purchase of private supplemental "Medigap" coverage or outright purchase of private plans by states in lieu of their own Medicaid plan. Price controls and competition, however, may make the opportunity to deliver such health services less than fully attractive, particularly for the individual practitioner who becomes the contractee rather than the contractor.

To the extent that cost pressures lead to increased government control or regulation of health care, it will give impetus to providers to develop alternative markets for sources of revenue, such as worker's compensation, forensic or court services, disability evaluation, and employee assistance programs. Psychologists should take special note that few states have laws recognizing them for independent practice in these alternative markets. (For a description of the scope of statutory recognition in California, see Chapter Ten.) Accordingly, the economic underpinnings of the private practice of clinical psychology may shift to less reliance on third-party health-plan reimbursement and more on industrial and legal markets.

Market Forces and the Challenges to Practice

The chain of events leading to our current state of affairs can be summarized through three post–World War II eras. The postwar era of expansion, from 1945 to 1970, saw Hill-Burton funding on a major level for hospital construction, major funding of medical research and medical and allied health training programs, the enactment of Medicare and Medicaid, and the expansion of health insurance benefits. The seventies brought an era of social reform with health planning and certificate-of-need laws, maldistribution, and massive duplication of resources in which specialty services became abundant and most of the population had service accessibility to health care. Economic reform characterizes the eighties, in which both government and industry refuse to support further expansion or the massive inefficiencies that have been built into the health care delivery system. The offshoots include industry coalitions, capitation financing, market-based competition, the development of lower-cost technologies, and the coming "shake-out" of inefficient providers (hospitals and practitioners). Success in this environment will involve competition for the patient at the source of financing (typically through the employer) and possession of sufficient market power to influence the system. To minimize cost, there will be emphasis on improved productivity, use of least expensive treatment mechanisms, and control of services, but with a requirement to maintain acceptable levels of quality. It will not be life as usual back at the practitioner's office.

The health care market is being pushed toward fundamental change that is altering the traditional practitioner/patient relationship. As practitioners plan for the future, they will increasingly have to face:

- A stable population that is aging, with expectations that a greater share of their health care costs will be borne by the government.
- Both government and industry unwilling to continue to bear the growing burden of health care costs.

- Government and industry both willing to change the system to reduce cost and reintroduce price and utilization sensitivity into the system.
- An increasing oversupply of physicians and other health practitioners who will compete in new and aggressive ways for a shrinking patient base.
- The growth of large, well-capitalized health care delivery corporations that will control the financing and delivery of health care and, to an extent, the practitioner.
- Increasing public acceptance of "contract health care" in the form of HMOs, PPOs, and other vehicles that control the flow of patients to and between practitioners.
- A recognition by government and industry that they are beginning to have an impact, which will encourage even more pressure for new measures to control health care costs and eventually, either directly or indirectly, the practitioner.

On this latter note, intervention in practitioner decision making has increased, particularly regarding hospital services, the largest and still growing cost center. With demonstrated cost savings through intervention over physician determination of the use of health resources, we can expect major employers to exercise increased oversight and added criterion requirements to spread. For example, the two years from 1982 to 1984 saw 26 percent rather than 2 percent of firms requiring preadmission utilization review, while 28 percent rather than none were mandating a second surgical opinion. The ultimate cut, of course, would be to pay only for procedures that have been demonstrably effective in the same or similar circumstances.* Of note in this regard is a report by the U.S. Office of Technology Assessment (1978) which found that "only 10 to 20 percent of all medical procedures have been shown by controlled tests to be beneficial."

* J. Trimmer, executive vice-president and chief operating officer, American Biodyne Centers, Inc., provided background material for the development of this section.

Although the U.S. population will continue to grow, the rate of growth will continue to decline. At the same time, the population is aging and increasing its demand for health services. This translates into increased demands on Medicare, which the government will be unable to support without fundamental changes. For its part, industry is shifting more of its health insurance from traditional indemnity programs into HMOs or self-funded programs that look for cost-effective health care. In response, PPOs sponsored by physicians and other practitioners and as joint ventures between hospitals and other corporations are developing rapidly across the nation. The PPO is not without its attractions: the purchaser gets a fee discount, the provider gets patients, the carrier gets controlled costs, the provider's financial risk is minimal, and the PPO can serve a large area. To survive, however, it must have a sufficient enrollment—that is, be successfully marketed.

Illustrative of the joint venture was the announcement in April 1985, between Voluntary Hospitals of America (VHA), the nation's largest not-for-profit multihospital organization, and Aetna Life Insurance Company to market HMOs, "preferred provider arrangements" (PPAs), and other competitively priced health care products. Aetna, the nation's largest private health insurer, now covers 11 million Americans, while VHA's forty-one-state network of locally controlled and owned hospitals accounts for about 15 percent of total U.S. hospital revenues. With VHA's network of health care providers and Aetna's extensive employee benefits marketing experience, this new joint venture was heralded as "the first health care delivery system with a capacity to provide a full range of hospital, insurance, and physician services on a national basis" (VHA/AETNA Venture Creates National HMO Network, 1985). Such a development is what economists call a "market for corporate control."

In the face of this rapidly developing competition and mounting pressures to control health care expenditures, the supply of U.S. physicians continues to expand. As a consequence, since 1975 physicians are having progressively fewer office visits per week—their supply is progressively exceeding demand. Indeed, when adjusted for inflation, physician income has leveled off over the past fifteen years. Nonphysician practitioners are obviously also affected by these trends and are probably even more at risk if they cannot develop alternatives. For one thing, these trends have led to the formation of more and larger group practices in the United States as physicians, sometimes with others, attempt to create a stronger economic entity with which to compete. Even so, they lag well behind the proprietary chains and insurance companies in developing organizations capable of integrated health care financing and delivery.

Our Information Society

The age of electronic communication, information storage, and analysis is about to explode upon psychological practice. We are already familiar with laboratory computer-scored and computer-analyzed tests. We are familiar with computer-scan journal abstract services. We are beginning to appreciate that the formatted information required by third parties as a condition of reimbursement or for billing will force us out of a "cigar box" cash-basis mentality of money management. The day of the minicomputer has arrived, even if many clinicians are not yet aware of it. Properly programmed, the computer will prepare bills and reimbursement claims with greater accuracy and speed than a human can. Given that time is money, practitioners will realize that it does not pay to handle all one's office aspects oneself. The computer will prove a powerful resource in treatment as well. Referral sources can be keyed in for information exchange, and on-time monitoring of patient/therapist interaction according to individualized treatment plans is possible. Patients will be expected to assume more personal responsibility for change. The necessary steps in this process, whether training exercises, role playing, or information acquisition, can be computer-checked. Indeed, we regularly use video replay to monitor and assist in the development of clinical skills during training, and we have been party to the development of teaching machines.

Remote home visiting/therapy will become feasible. The photophone under development will enable direct patient contact and therapy from office to the home and will assist in monitoring patient progress and crisis support and resolution. It will also make available expanded services to the elderly and the physically disabled who now can come to the office only with great difficulty, if at all. Telephone therapy is now available, and there is evidence that it is cost-effective and functional (Bertera and Bertera, 1981). The photophone will add the capacity of observational review and nonverbal communication. All these technological advances will change styles of professional practice. They will also put the therapist more "on line." Such systems will make twenty-four-hour, seven-days-a-week access a true potential. The fact that this is beyond the continued tolerance or capability of any one therapist only underscores that on-call rotation will come to clinical psychologists and that its management will require at least a group practice.

A challenge facing the behavioral sciences is to increase public understanding of psychological constructs and accelerate their applications to everyday life. Enhancing the public's awareness of psychology through personal, relevant experience serves the interests of both the profession and society. In seizing the initiative to establish communication network systems through which to inform and educate people, we are taking steps toward preventing psychological disturbance and promoting mental health—the essential goals of community psychology. The growing wellness movement, which promotes changes in life-style and behavior to reduce risk and improve health potential, lends itself to targeted media intervention and public education broadcasting.*

The current cultural trend is toward an information society. New electronic means of bringing psychology into people's lives are being generated. The developments in communications technologies constitute a major force affecting the cultural and social climate. Naisbett (1980) notes that today 55 percent of American workers are information workers: paid to produce information.

The public relies increasingly on the mass media for news and knowledge. It therefore behooves psychologists not only to tap the potentials of the communications industry for educating the

---

* J. D. Zimmerman, CBS News, New York City, supplied notes on the societal shift to information systems and media communication.

public about behavioral science and behavioral health but to realize that these new occupational markets are now open to psychologists themselves.

Implications of Change for the Practice of Clinical Psychology

To say that health care delivery today is beset by many forces and is in the process of profound change is an understatement. Indeed, this book is an attempt to document some of these forces, the changes underway, and their implications for the future practice of clinical psychology. The purpose of this concluding chapter is to highlight some of the key trends and to outline their implications for clinical psychology.

The health care market differs from other markets: in the health care market, the purchaser is not directly the payer. Health care, therefore, is subject to overutilization (use it or lose it—unlike life, fire, or auto insurance, which one does not wish to use). Nor are most providers market-sensitive. They typically are located (maldistributed) in the attractive sections of large urban settings, obliging consumers to bring their business to them. In addition, providers shun advertising and set fees in accord with income expectations. In effect, they function in a heretofore remarkably uncompetitive environment. But to understand the market changes underway, one must consider several factors: demand factors, supply factors, and economic conditions.

As noted above, clinical psychology increasingly is becoming involved in general health care, which opens up an arena of practice broader by far than its more traditional involvement in mental health services. But even looking back at its roots, we find an increasing *demand* for mental health services. The poor are high users of health care; they are also high users of mental health care. With Medicaid they have had growing access to care. Under Hawaii Medicaid, for example, 9.6 percent of Medicaid eligibles were users of outpatient mental health services in 1983. Then the President's Commission on Mental Health (1978) concluded that 15 percent of the general population is in need of mental health services during any given year. However, a more recent door-to-door household survey begun by the National Institute of Mental Health in 1980 found that about 19 percent of adults suffered from at least one mental disorder during a given six-month period. From 28 to 38 percent of those surveyed reported having had a psychiatric disorder at some point in their lifetime. Kessler (1984), following a suburban cohort for five years, found that 18 percent had actually used mental health services in one or more of those years. Thus, actual use of mental health services is somewhat greater than might have been expected from the earlier literature and is in part probably due to the aging of the population. Need is one thing, demand another. Recent studies indicate that, of those considered to need mental health services, about 20 percent received them. With growing need, improved access, and greater provider supply, the demand for mental health service can be expected to increase.

The *supply* of physicians has increased to about 440,000 in 1985 and is now being described in the popular press as a "physician glut." The growth of licensed psychologists has been quite phenomenal, from about 20,000 in 1974 to over 45,600 by mid-1985, a 128 percent increase in but eleven years. Psychiatrists have shown only a 46 percent growth, to about 38,000, over a comparable period. The supply of social workers more than doubled, and the psychiatric nurse-practitioner has emerged as a practice-oriented mental health profession. Despite this growth among the four mental health professions, household survey data indicate that the nonpsychiatrically trained physician bills for more mental health services than any other single provider group.

As for *economic conditions,* the overriding one is that health care expenditures have tripled in this country every ten years since 1962, with mental disorders now estimated as costing $40.2 billion per year and with 70 percent of this cost attributable to twenty-four-hour residential care. The recession of 1981–1982 highlighted another major problem with our traditional system of employer-based funding of health care—when business and industry failed, health care needs went unmet because the unemployed lost their coverage with their jobs. Thus, many persons, including many who are self-employed and others marginally employed, are outside the health care "system"—gaps that must be addressed under any equitable policy.

Providers, of course, in almost all instances, make the treatment decisions that result in health care expenditures. Moreover, under a fee-for-service model there is an incentive to deliver more service than may be needed, another condition seen by policy makers as indicative of the need for systemic change in order to control costs.

What, then, are the implications for clinical psychology? They are many. The health care system is already in transition, and we shall witness a ten-year "shake-out" with systemic change of major proportions. There will be an array of changes affecting provider organizations, both institutional and professional. There will also be changes in marketing strategies, in insurance and health-plan reimbursement for services, in constraints on treatment, and in competition between and within professions. Opposition to stop the general thrust of these changes will be futile.

Provider Organizations. Hospitals, of course, are the major financial investment and capital asset base of the health industry. Fundamental change cannot occur without change in the role and organization of the hospital. Following years of continued federal Hill-Burton funding for hospital construction, there is now a growing number of empty beds. Moreover, hospitals as independent community-based institutions have been a palace for the practice of medicine. Hospitals catered to "doctors," so doctors would admit their patients. Though always emphasizing service to patients publicly, the symbiotic arrangement generally brought revenue to the hospital and power to physicians, who structured this environment to suit both ends. Competition was largely eliminated, and some services were provided on an inpatient basis that could equally well, or better, have been provided in the office, the home, or an alternative setting. All was well for the players until the financial burden became a weight sufficient to crack the foundation, if not collapse the entire structure. The ranks will thin, and hospitals too expensive to operate, or inefficiently managed, or no longer situated within a sufficient user population, will simply close, fail, or be bought out. Entrepreneurs, the rising health conglomerates, have already seen the potential in the formation of hospital chains under centralized policy, purchasing, marketing and management, raising capital, buying hospitals, and making profits all on a scale not witnessed before in this market.

With the reduction in available beds and consolidation between competing corporations, the diversification of hospital services will be promoted as new lines of business are developed: satellite outpatient services, outpatient surgical and urgency centers, conversion and rental of space as professional offices and the use of "swing beds" for flexibility, and needed specialized services such as skilled nursing units, alcohol detoxification units, even behavioral health centers. There will be active development of alternative health care settings under new forms of licensure and regulation, some freed of the expense and overhead of a hospital, the balance made revenue-intensive. More services will be provided in these less expensive alternative settings. With these developments will come a decrease in funding for hospital-based mental health care except for the most acute and severe conditions.

What we are seeing today is government getting together with big business, often with the support of organized labor and senior citizen groups, in a process that is shifting control of the health care industry from the providers to health care managers, who act on behalf of the purchasers and the owners. The sapiential authority of medicine as its basis of ultimate control is being displaced by business acumen. Indeed, where the nonphysician professional can deliver a service more effectively or at less cost than physicians, such competition will be encouraged.

With this industrialization of health care there will be a continued growth of group and salaried practice. Multidisciplinary professional service corporations will begin to emerge to replace today's predominant cottage industry model of health care. Coequal ownership and control will be possible in these service corporations, avoiding some of the power struggles that have occurred between professional groups.

Reimbursement. Reimbursement will increasingly be based on policies that are less driven by practitioners. Treatment in less expensive facilities will be encouraged, and there will be a continuous move away from cost-based reimbursement toward some type of prospective pricing or rate-setting procedure for all health care. The PPOs will provide for a transition period while the reimbursement system moves to a totally capitated model. Selective contracting and negotiation of special discounts will reflect the price competition induced into the system. Against this background, funding for extensive or long-term psychotherapy is certain to decrease unless there are competing economic costs to the contrary. If anything, the facts today are otherwise.

The entire psychotherapeutic process will be reconceptualized, and the importance of words like *transference, resistance,* and *termination* will be reconsidered. The goals of treatment will be redefined, with greater emphasis on specific symptom alleviation. Such specificity will bring great importance to diagnostic acumen, not in the sense of reliable use of illness nosology but in the sense of valid determination of the patient's operational problem. Identification of patients who can benefit from short-term interventions will be essential to economic viability as the system is pushed toward determining truly cost-effective interventions. In the short run, psychiatry will promote biochemical approaches to the treatment of many mental disorders with the implicit objective of capturing a larger market share, but in time the consumer will revolt from such interventions, which mask, but do not solve, the psychological problem and which carry the hazard, with continued use, of toxicity and neurological impairment.

Constraints on Treatment. With limited resources and heightened competition, casual case management and marginal procedures will no longer be acceptable. Utilization review will be used increasingly, both to assure the appropriateness of services being provided and as a mechanism of cost containment. The more systematic use of such review will oblige providers to reconceptualize the extent and importance of patient confidentiality and privilege. The review systems themselves, of course, will have to become more acceptable to providers, better integrated with practice, and used only to the extent that the cost of the review will be less than the cost of services that might realistically be forgone or where there is a quality-of-care issue.

With the constraints placed on providers, consumers, also, will have less choice—less choice in provider selection, as in a PPO, and less self-determination of the treatment they wish to receive.

Some service decisions will be authorized by phone consultation according to program criteria.

Where short-term interventions prove ineffective, their failure may result in malpractice litigation. New forms of therapy may be challenged as a form of negligence, a challenge that would, of course, put the traditional models on trial as a part of the litigation. Generally, we can expect litigation to increase, not because of increased emphasis on briefer therapies but because mental health services are, in the main, an untested arena for malpractice litigation. Unless legislation is introduced to assure immunity for practitioners who participate in good faith in utilization (or peer) review and unless there is some rational limit placed on civil liability (perhaps a no-fault approach), major costs will be added to health care.

Market Changes. We can expect continued growth of self-funded health care by major corporations, which, since the Employee Retirement Income Security Act (ERISA) in 1974, are no longer subject to state insurance law. The freedom-of-choice laws, which had mandated direct recognition of nonphysician health care practitioners, do not regulate self-funded plans. This development, together with the growth of HMOs, is bringing about a decline in the market share for commercial insurance, developments not beneficial to the fee-for-service practice of psychology.

In an effort to gain (regain) business, providers, like manufacturers, will start to systematically advertise their "products." Specific services will be promoted: stress management, smoking cessation, eating disorder clinics, pain clinics, and so forth. With increased advertising will come a wave of claims, not all of them substantiated. Will the psychology of tomorrow have its "Painless Parker" (of frontier dental infamy)? In addition to advertising services and credentials, price advertising can be expected as therapists with surplus time try to increase their practice by undercutting the market (discounting).

Competition Between Professions. Psychiatry has lobbied to become the gatekeeper of mental health, controlling access to psychologists by referral or by "bill through" provisions. The Supreme Court set aside such arrangements between organized psychiatry and Blue Shield in Virginia. Some prepaid health plans have designated primary-care physicians (family practitioners, obstetricians/gynecologists, and internists) as gatekeepers, excluding the use not only of practitioners of other professions but of other medical specialties except on referral. Widespread adoption of such a gatekeeper approach insofar as medicine is concerned can hardly be viable in the long run, as it would turn medicine against itself. But as a way of dealing with other professions, that is another matter. In late 1984 the House of Delegates of the American Medical Association adopted a $45 dues increase for the major express purpose of opposing the independent practice of any nonmedical health profession. That should generate a "war chest" of about $19.5 million, to say nothing of the AMA's PAC funds and those of state medical associations and county medical societies across the country. Expect the competition to stiffen.

With the increasing numbers of mental health providers, the competition between professions will intensify as their respective associations struggle for "turf" in what can be dubbed the "war of the shrinks." In this struggle a great deal of rhetoric will pass between medicine and the other health professions over issues such as "direction," "supervision," "referral," and "oversight." The objective will not be to clarify relations but, where possible, to assure control. Not only will there be increased competition between the professions, but we shall begin to see overt competition between providers within a profession based on price or service cost (and convenience).

Opposition. Protest by providers against the systemic changes in health care now underway will have little impact. Providers concerned about turf battles are unable to form the coalitions necessary to slow down the process, let alone reverse it. The forces behind these changes exceed the human and capital resources, the votes, and the managerial skills of organized medicine. It will be more constructive for psychologists to seek effective participation and to take positive steps to shape their destiny rather than standing firm and being swept aside by the incoming tide.

Overview

In summary, there are four main messages for the future of clinical psychology:

Professional Preparation. Professional training should reflect the pressures and trends that are seen today. Training psychologists essentially as solo-practice psychotherapists is training for technological obsolescence. Health psychology is rapidly developing as an emergent force in the field of psychology. Psychologists trained for health care will be involved in shaping behavioral health, stress management, and pain control and will be dealing with the psychological aspects of accident, injury, dismemberment, sensory loss, disease, aging, and death as well as emotional and mental disorder. The objective of these services will be to maximize human effectiveness and adaptation by using specific services shown to be effective for specific conditions. In the process, psychologists must come to accept professional responsibility on a twenty-four-hour basis.

Industrialization. The field of health care is undergoing a major revolution: it is being industrialized. With industrialization comes the adoption of broad-based policy, increased centralization, increased emphasis on planning, organization, and marketing; calculated use of communication and data processing; greater vertical integration; emphasis on the procedures that are profitable; expanded use of technical personnel under supervision for routine services; and greater reliance on time-saving electronic equipment that extends professional skills. An exclusive reliance on one-on-one psychotherapy is too time- and labor-intensive for either a psychologist or a psychiatrist to flourish on a long-term basis. The solo independent practice of clinical psychology will prove noncompetitive when faced by organized models of health care.

Legislation. State/provincial psychological associations need urgently to gear up major and continuing legislative programs. The time to effect favorable change and recognition is now, before major contrary parameters are even more firmly locked in statute. The complexities underway require a proactive legislative program not only to acquire standing but also to defend and retain such standing as psychologists have today. As it has been said, "No man's life, liberty, or property is safe while the legislature is in session." If psychologists do not invest the time, money, and effort necessary to develop and sustain an effective legislative program in their own interest, it is certain that no one else will. In addition to specific practice/market issues, state associations must develop a coherent legislative policy and engage in a constructive involvement in the formation and revision of social policy relevant to human welfare. The current political mood to restore and enhance state sovereignty only further underscores the importance of an effective state legislative program. Such a program will prove essential to the survival of our profession. Clinical psychology is, and must be, engaged in a massive effort to expand its horizons.

Diversification. Clinical psychologists must diversify their professional services. Reliance on individual psychotherapy will not be sufficient to assure a viable practice in the future. Rather, it will become essential to search out markets and sources of referral, to contract with existing and newly developing organizations, and, insofar as practical, to develop expertise that is in demand and relatively exclusive. There will also be opportunities to form or participate in the formation of new psychological health enterprises developed to meet a market need. And when a practitioner is faced with saturated markets in an area, he or she has the option of moving to another community where need can more readily be converted to professional opportunity.

No mental health or health professional can afford not to forecast, plan, and prepare for the future. Failing to plan is akin to planning to fail.

References

Arstein, C., and Toon, A. "Hospital-HMO Contracts: An Expanding Market." *CHA Insight,* May 7, 1981, pp. 1-4.

Bertera, E., and Bertera, R. "The Cost Effectiveness of Telephone vs. Clinic Counseling for Hypertensive Patients: A Pilot Study." *American Journal of Public Health,* 1981, *71,* 626-630.

"Blues President Foresees Negotiated Fee Plan." *American Medical News,* Aug. 14, 1981, pp. 3, 9.

Brett, A. "Special Report: America's Doctors: A Profession in Trouble." *U.S. News and World Report,* Oct. 17, 1977, pp. 50-58.

Christiansen, B. (ed.). *Does Psychology Return Its Costs?* Oslo: Norwegian Research Council for the Sciences and Humanities, 1981.

Copeland, B. "Hospital Privileges and Staff Membership for Psychologists." *Professional Psychology*, 1980, *11*, 676–683.

Cummings, N. A. "Prolonged (Ideal) Versus Short-Term (Realistic) Psychotherapy." In C. Kiesler, N. A. Cummings, and G. R. VandenBos (eds.), *Psychology and National Health Insurance: A Sourcebook.* Washington, D.C.: American Psychological Association, 1979.

Dörken, H. "CHAMPUS Ten-State Claim Experience for Mental Disorder: Fiscal Year 1975." In C. Kiesler, N. A. Cummings, and G. R. VandenBos (eds.), *Psychology and National Health Insurance: A Sourcebook.* Washington, D.C.: American Psychological Association, 1979a.

Dörken, H. "Title 38: Fish, Wait or Cut Bait?" *Clinical Psychologist*, 1979b, *32*, 7–8.

Dörken, H., and Cummings, N. A. "The Impact of Medical Referral on Outpatient Psychological Services." *Professional Psychology*, forthcoming.

Dörken, H., and Webb, J. T. "The Hospital Practice of Psychology: An Interstate Comparison." *Professional Psychology*, 1979, *10*, 619–630.

Dörken, H., and Webb, J. T. "1976 Third-Party Reimbursement Experience: An Interstate Comparison by Carrier." *American Psychologist*, 1980, *35*, 355–363.

Dörken, H., and Webb, J. T. "Licensed Psychologists on the Increase: 1974–1979." *American Psychologist*, 1981, *36*, 1419–1426.

Dörken, H., Webb, J. T., and Zaro, J. S. "Hospital Practice of Psychology Resurveyed: 1980." *Professional Psychology*, 1982, *13*, 814–829.

Fiester, A. "JCAH Standards for Accreditation of Community Mental Health Service Programs." *American Psychologist*, 1978, *33*, 1114–1121.

Fink, P., and Field, H. "Residency Training—a Changing Scenario." *Psychiatric Opinion*, 1978, *15*, 13–16.

Gottfredson, G., and Dyer, S. "Health Service Providers in Psychology." In C. Kiesler, N. A. Cummings, and G. R. VandenBos (eds.), *Psychology and National Health Insurance: A Sourcebook*. Washington, D.C.: American Psychological Association, 1979.

Harper, R., Wiens, A., and Hammerstad, J. "Psychologist-Physician Partnership in a Medical Specialty Screening Clinic." *Professional Psychology*, 1981, *12*, 341–348.

Haug, J., and Seegar, R. *Socio-Economic Factbook for Surgery, 1983–84*. Chicago: American College of Surgeons, 1983.

Jones, K., and Vischi, T. "Impact of Alcohol, Drug Abuse, and Mental Health Treatment on Medical Care Utilization: Review of the Research Literature." *Medical Care*, 1979, *17*(12), Supplement.

Kessler, L. "Treated Incidence of Mental Disorder in a Prepaid Group Practice Setting." *American Journal of Public Health*, 1984, *74*, 152–154.

Kiesler, C. "Mental Health as a Field of Inquiry for Psychology." *American Psychologist*, 1980, *35*, 1066–1080.

McAuliffe, K. "Freud with Guilt: These are Financially Depressing Times for Psychiatry." *Barron's*, Feb. 22, 1982, pp. 32–33.

Matarazzo, J. "Behavioral Health and Behavioral Medicine: Frontiers for a New Health Psychology." *American Psychologist*, 1980, *35*, 807–817.

Matarazzo, J. "Behavioral Health's Challenge to Academic, Scientific, and Professional Psychology." *American Psychologist*, 1982, *37*, 1–14.

Mumford, E., Schlesinger, H. J., and Glass, G. V. "The Effects of Psychological Intervention on Recovery from Surgery and Heart Attacks: An Analysis of the Literature." *American Journal of Public Health*, 1982, *72*, 141–151.

Naisbett, J. Excerpt from speech on *The Trend Report*, given in San Antonio, Texas, and reprinted in *Express-News*, July 13, 1980.

National Association of Social Workers. "State Comparisons of Laws Regulating Social Work." Washington, D.C.: National Association of Social Workers, 1980. (Mimeographed.)

O'Keefe, A. M. "State Regulations Which Restrict Hospital Staff Membership to Physicians (and Dentists)." Washington, D.C.: Association for the Advancement of Psychology, 1978. (Mimeographed.)

President's Commission on Mental Health. *Report to the President.* 4 vols. Washington, D.C.: U.S. Government Printing Office, 1978.

Rosenstein, M., and Taube, C. *Staffing Mental Health Facilities, United States, 1976.* National Institute of Mental Health, Series B, No. 14, DHEW Pub. No. (ADM) 76-308. Washington, D.C.: Alcohol, Drug and Mental Health Administration, 1977.

Schneider, S. "Where Have All the Students Gone? Positions of Psychologists Trained in Clinical/Service Programs." *American Psychologist,* 1981, *36,* 1427-1449.

Smith, M., and Glass, G. "Meta-analysis of Psychotherapy Outcome Studies." *American Psychologist,* 1977, *332,* 752-760.

Torrey, F., and Taylor, R. "Cheap Labor from Poor Nations." *American Journal of Psychiatry,* 1973, *130,* 428-433.

Tucker, G. "The Coming Shortage in Psychiatric Manpower." *Psychiatric Opinion,* 1978, *15,* 9-12.

U.S. Office of Technology and Development. *Assessing the Efficacy and Safety of Medical Technologies.* No. 052-003-00593-0. Washington, D.C.: U.S. Government Printing Office, 1978.

Vaillant, G. "Natural History of Male Psychologic Health: Effects of Mental Health on Physical Health." *New England Journal of Medicine,* 1979, *301,* 1249-1254.

"VHA/AETNA Venture Creates National HMO Network." *UFMC Newsletter,* 1985, *5*(2), 11.

Wiens, A. "Estimated Cost Savings for Patients Treated in a Psychological Outpatient Clinic." In B. Christiansen (ed.), *Does Psychology Return Its Cost?* Oslo: Norwegian Research Council for the Sciences and Humanities, 1981.

Wright, L. "Psychopathology Suffering from Atrophy: Major Shift May Be Near." *Ohio Psychologist,* 1980, *26,* 14-16.

Wright, L. "Changing Minds in the Field of Psychopathology." *California State Psychologist,* 1982, *16,* 10-11.

Wright, L., and others. *Encyclopedia of Pediatric Psychology.* Baltimore, Md.: University Park Press, 1979.

Name Index

Subject Index

Oklahoma, and licensed psychologists, 6, 8, 12
Omnibus Budget Reconciliation Act of 1981 (P. L. 97-35), 110
Omnibus Reconciliation Act of 1980 (P.L. 96-499), 105
Oregon: CHAMPUS-CHOICE in, 95-96; and licensed psychologists, 8, 12; standards in, 185
Orphan Drug Act (P.L. 97-414), 108

P

Patients: demographic characteristics of, 23-26; medical care and disability of, 28-32; practitioner interaction with, 208, 220, 226-227; referral of, 26-28
Peer review: in clinical psychology, 96; in group practice plan, 136; and standards, 188-190
Penal Code (California), 252, 261, 262, 263, 265
Pennsylvania: costs in, 323; and licensed psychologists, 3, 9, 12, 13, 46, 358; medical consultants used in, 30; psychological clinics in, 294-297; and third-party reimbursement, 44
Performance Index of Community Living Skills, 229
Physicians: in CHAMPUS, 72-73, 75-76, 80, 85, 88-89, 90-92, 96; and federal purchase of care, 104, 105; as practitioner professionals, 150-151
Practice: components of, 363; fee-for-service type of, 20-43; health facility, legislation on, 265-270; standards of, 174-199
Practice models: analysis of, 283-312; background on, 283-285; brief psychotherapy in, 290-291; community, 291-294; concept of cure in, 289-290; conclusion on, 310; group, 285-287; hospitals as, 307-310; marketing and, 287-288; psychological clinics as, 294-297; psychological health

plan as, 297-300; and targeted intervention, 288-289. *See also* Mental health system
Practioner/patient interaction: basic research on, 208; design of, 220; evaluation of, 226-227
Practitioner professions: and conceptual issues, 160-161; development of, 150-154; harm and benefit balance in, 151-152; knowledge and failure in, 161-167; and mainstream of ignorance, 165-166; model of, 153-154; nature of field of, 157-158; progress in, 163-165; psychology as, 154-161, 167-172; and resource use, 158-160; and science, 166-167
Preferred provider arrangements (PPAs), 373
Preferred provider organizations (PPOs): and costs, 316, 319, 325, 327; future of, 372, 373, 379, 380; and practice models, 284-285, 286, 300, 303
Prepaid Health Care Act (Hawaii), 44
President's Commission on Mental Health, 334, 376, 387
Professional Standards Review Organization, 368
Providers: future for, 378-379; negotiation of costs by, 329-331
Prudential: costs and, 315; reimbursement by, 50, 51, 52, 54, 56, 58
Psychiatric illness, behavioral dimensions of, 168
Psychiatrists: in CHAMPUS, 72-73, 75-76, 77-79, 81, 82, 83, 84, 85, 88-89, 90, 92, 93-95; competition from, 358, 359, 360; defined, 362-363; future of, 364-366; in practice models, 292, 293, 296, 302; psychologists compared with, 124; and substitutability, 335-336
Psychological clinics, as practice models, 294-297